A PATH IN THE
MIGHTY WATERS

A PATH IN THE MIGHTY WATERS

SHIPBOARD LIFE & ATLANTIC CROSSINGS

TO THE NEW WORLD

Stephen R. Berry

Yale

UNIVERSITY PRESS

New Haven and London

Published with assistance from the Annie Burr Lewis Fund and from the foundation established in memory of Philip Hamilton McMillan of the Class of 1894, Yale College.

Yale University Press books may be purchased in quantity for educational, business, or promotional use. For information, please e-mail sales.press@yale.edu (U.S. office) or sales@yaleup.co.uk (U.K. office).

Set in MT Baskerville type by IDS Infotech, Ltd.
Printed in the United States of America.

Library of Congress Cataloging-in-Publication Data
Berry, Stephen Russell, 1970–
A path in the mighty waters : shipboard life and Atlantic crossings to the New World / Stephen R. Berry.
pages cm
Includes bibliographical references and index.
ISBN 978-0-300-20423-0 (hardback)
1. Seafaring life—Atlantic Ocean—History—18th century. 2. Merchant ships—Passenger accommodation—Social aspects. 3. Transatlantic voyages—Social aspects. 4. Ocean travel—Social aspects. 5. Atlantic Ocean Region—Emigration and immigration—History—18th century. I. Title.
G550.B44 2015
910.9163'09033—dc23

2014017670

A catalogue record for this book is available from the British Library.

This paper meets the requirements of
ANSI/NISO Z39.48–1992 (Permanence of Paper).

10 9 8 7 6 5 4 3 2 1

For Dana with love

To him who spread out the earth above the waters,

for his steadfast love endures forever.

Psalm 136:6 (ESV)

CONTENTS

CONTENTS

ACKNOWLEDGMENTS

This book tells the stories of eighteenth-century Atlantic crossings and the human encounters that took place in the wooden vessels that made them. Writing this book has been a journey in itself, and many interactions have influenced it over the course of its voyage. Before embarking on the story of ship travels long past, I find it fitting briefly to recount this book's odyssey and to sketch the debt left in its wake.

As you will discover in the first chapter, it is difficult to identify a particular moment when the transatlantic voyage began. Likewise, it is hard to define precisely when I began this book. The idea germinated in my very first graduate seminar with my advisor Grant Wacker at Duke University. While reading the autobiographies of various nineteenth-century theologians, I noticed that figures such as Charles Hodge behaved differently aboard ship, enjoying a broader range of conversation partners while traveling away from their lifetime of work. After a couple of years quietly musing on similar accounts and what they might mean, I finally verbalized my "crazy dissertation idea" in two settings. First, Betsy Flowers excitedly encouraged the project during our conversations as we commuted to seminars in Chapel Hill. Second, across the table in our booth at

Elmo's Diner, Peter Wood took my small flame of observation and blew life into it, pulling me back into the eighteenth century, where the voyages were longer and the personal encounters more sustained, with a greater range of cultural, ethnic, and religious backgrounds intersecting.

Encouraged that there might be something worth exploring in travelers' accounts, I formally started to research both what eighteenth-century diarists said about their voyages and how modern scholars have thought about travel literature. Providentially, during this time I had coursework and conversations with Tom Tweed, who was then thinking deeply about the intersection of movement and religion in what became his *Crossings and Dwellings: A Theory of Religion*. Out of his seminar came my first, still embryonic, paper on the topic, later presented at the Hawaii International Conference on the Arts and Humanities (a nice trip in itself, though by plane). Thus encouraged that this intellectual journey was worth pursuing, I set out to gather the materials needed for the voyage.

I laid up the intellectual stores for this voyage through sojourns in various museums, archives, and libraries. The Massachusetts Historical Society awarded me the Boston Marine Society Fellowship in 2003. William M. Fowler Jr., Peter Drummey, and their excellent staff oriented me to their collections and provided invaluable assistance in using them to their fullest. In addition to the material aid rendered, Conrad Wright structured interaction with other fellows at a crucial stage of formulation. I especially benefited from repeated conversations with and input from Woody Holton and John Wood Sweet. In 2004, I received a grant from the New England Research Fellowship Consortium allowing me to visit multiple institutions and expand my archival base. I was thankful that I visited the Rhode Island Historical Society before the departure of Rick Stattler, whose knowledge of the collections greatly facilitated my work there. Nancy Milnor and her staff at the Connecticut Historical Society guided me to some of my favorite sources and stories. Christopher Hartmann of the New England Historic Genealogical Society in Boston graciously welcomed me to their gorgeous facility on Newbury Street, where Timothy Salls and other staff members opened their well-organized print and manuscript collections. That summer I made the first of many visits to the G. W. Blunt White Library of the Mystic Seaport Museum, where Paul O'Pecko and his knowledgeable staff aided my first navigations into maritime sources and scholarship. These initial forays into the documentary record were later supplemented with materials from New York, Pennsylvania, and Georgia.

I benefited greatly from my shipmates, a strong intellectual cadre of students at Duke and the University of North Carolina, Chapel Hill. Chris Armstrong, Erin Avots, Elesha Coffman, Brendan Pietsch, Dan Ramirez, Angela Tarango, and Jennifer Trafton heard or read various parts of the work and provided thoughtful comments, suggestions, and encouragement along the way. I still have an infamous email wherein Brendan brilliantly and hilariously lamented the academy's neglect of the religion of pirates. Seth Dowland, Brantley Gasaway, Jen Graber, Sarah Johnson, and Ben Zeller formed a writing group that elevated my prose and pushed me to completion. Although she had already taken up residence in Fort Worth, Betsy Flowers continued our preliminary conversations, and I am grateful for her continued encouragement. All of the above challenged me as a thinker and a writer, and I am deeply grateful for their collegiality and friendship.

The keel of the current book was laid during the defense of my doctoral dissertation, which was less of a trial and more of a conversation that blueprinted this book. A committee of excellent scholars brought different interests and areas of expertise to bear on my work. Wesley Kort, Laurie Maffly-Kipp, David Steinmetz, Grant Wacker, and Peter Wood shaped this book not only through their criticisms and suggestions along the way but also through their modeling of good scholarship. I owe extra thanks to Laurie, who formally responded to a major section of this work that I presented at the American Academy of Religion annual meeting in San Antonio, Texas. Peter Wood got me out onto spars I feared to climb and taught me the ropes of history and writing. My advisor and mentor Grant Wacker gave me direction and propulsion that helped me finish. It took me a long time to implement fully their suggestions and to respond to their critiques, but I credit them for pushing me toward the story-driven structure outlining the chapters ahead. I cannot imagine having better mentors.

I participated in fruitful conversations at the International Seminar on the History of the Atlantic World, a program that Bernard Bailyn established at Harvard University to bring together young scholars working on particular aspects of the Atlantic world. The topic for our seminar was "The Transit of Christianity," and I think I was invited because Dr. Bailyn simply could not believe that two papers had been proposed that considered shipboard religion: Heidi Keller-Lapp's essay on Catholic Ursuline nuns and mine comparing Protestant approaches to the ship. Jon Butler graciously chaired our panel and provided questions and comments whose heft I still carry years later. Two other chairs, Jorge Cañizares-Esguerra and Erik R. Seeman, also provided their ideas and advice, both in the formal seminar and in informal conversations afterward. Among a talented cohort of participants, I owe special thanks to a few particular individuals. Nicholas Beasley and I broached ideas over a bottle of bourbon whiskey during our evening rituals on the porch of the Irving House. Sarah Crabtree, Peter Moore, and Owen Stanwood all shared sources and ideas that have made their way into the pages of this book. I am grateful for the fellowship and dialogue we had in those weeks.

My colleagues in the History Department at Simmons College—Laurie Crumpacker, Sarah Leonard, Zhigang Liu, Steve Ortega, and Laura Prieto—have provided me with a tremendous amount of support. They have nurtured me as a teacher and scholar through their shared wisdom and collegiality. Laura and Sarah, in particular, provided valuable feedback on my scholarship as part of my review process. The Simmons College of Arts and Science provided an opportunity for me to present a synopsis of this book as part of the Colleagues in Conversation series. Three deans—Diane Grossman, Laurie Crumpacker, and Renée White—believed in and supported my work. Other faculty and staff too numerous to mention have also provided friendship and encouragement. While I have resided in Boston I have benefited from participation in the Boston Area American Religious History Group. Peggy Bendroth, Chris Beneke, Maura Jane Farrelly, Cliff Putney, Jon Roberts, Owen Stanwood, Randall Stephens, and many others have provided valuable collegiality and feedback on different aspects of my work. I owe special thanks to Peggy for graciously inviting me to present my research at the Congregational Library and to Randall for connecting me to Yale University Press.

In the summer of 2012, I participated in National Endowment for the Humanities summer institute "The American Maritime People," conducted by the Munson Institute at Mystic Seaport. Glenn Gordinier and Eric Roorda codirected an all-star cast of maritime historians who provided me a long-overdue primer on all things nautical. As the varied seminar participants read this work, I am sure they will find traces of our conversations from that summer. I owe special thanks to my fellow residents of Mallory House—Sarah Crabtree, Sarah Hirsch, Amy Parsons, Jason Smith, Patrick Speelman, and Dan Walden—for their shared conversation, meals, and friendship.

I owe appreciation to the staff of the Yale University Press for their support. As a first-time author, I have been privileged to work with an insightful editor, Jennifer Banks, who has patiently guided me through the publishing process. I am particularly grateful to Eliza Childs for painstakingly editing the manuscript and to Susan Laity for directing the editorial process. I also am indebted to the two anonymous readers who provided valuable feedback on my manuscript.

The Redeemer Presbyterian Church of Concord welcomed my family from the first day of our arrival in Massachusetts, and the congregation has continued to love and support us every day since. I thank you all. In particular, James and Mary Glover directly contributed to the completion of this work, with Mary graciously providing valuable feedback as well as her editing skills. They cannot understand how much my entire family misses them. When we lived in Jackson, Mississippi, Jan and James ("Bebo") Elkin repeatedly demonstrated their love and kindness to my family. Bebo gave me my first taste of oceanic sailing and read various portions of the book along the way, providing a thoughtful perspective from outside the academy.

I cannot express my indebtedness to my many family members for their love and support. One of my sisters, Margaret, and her husband, Andy Wilson, read early drafts of the book and provided their insights and encouragement. My parents, Jean and George Berry, have unhesitatingly encouraged their wayfaring son through his meandering academic career as did my in-laws, Dewey and Joan Thomas. I am saddened that Dr. Thomas passed away before the book was published. He was proud of my work, and I wish I could have shared the finished product with him.

Most of all, I thank my wife, Dana, and our two children, Ann Rees and Stephen, for their love, support, and intellectual stimulation. Dana has always believed in my abilities far more than I have, and without her encouragement, I would have never completed this voyage. I lovingly dedicate the book to her. Ann Rees and Stephen enthusiastically accompanied me on my varied research junkets and inspired me with their joy, wit, and intelligence. I am so glad that I did not have to make this journey alone.

A PATH IN THE
MIGHTY WATERS

INTRODUCTION

CHARTING COURSES

Dripping wet from the raging sea and his own fear, a young Anglican minister felt his way along the dark passageway of the ship in the chill of a winter's eve. As he entered the cramped steerage, he heard the terror-stricken cries of the English passengers mingled with the unwavering voices of the Germans as they raised their psalm from the pages of the *Gesang-buch*. A wave swallowed the ship in the opening moments of their service, tearing sails and tossing men, and he tasted the brine and oakum that poured through the strained planks. The dim sight of these German brethren looking upward in a mixture of awe for their God and wonder at the storm fascinated the would-be missionary, who stood enraptured by their song. When the service concluded, he finally brought himself to speak, inquiring of a nearby companion, "Was you not afraid?" "I thank God, no," the reply echoed between the candlelit decks. The brief exchange invigorated the young cleric. With boldness previously unknown, he then set about encouraging his own congregation with this example of true Christian trust and courage. "This was," he wrote, "the most glorious day which I have hitherto seen."[1]

This anecdote of John Wesley's glorious stormy day on the ship *Simmonds* with the German Moravians often appears in the histories of Christianity and America, cited as an important step in the development of the Methodist movement. A point of contact, a time of a significant change, the episode overshadows the rest of the voyage. The popularity of this story derived from Wesley's own prominence as a central figure of the eighteenth century. Accounts of his life and influence focus on what he did in England or what his followers accomplished in the nascent colonies of Anglo-America. The nearly four months that Wesley spent aboard the *Simmonds* appear to be lost except for this one particular scene. The Atlantic crossing was simply a threshold, an in-between space in an otherwise eventful life. When mentioned, the ship simply provides a means of transport, a brushstroke of historical detail enlivening the great man's portrait. The rest of Wesley's time aboard ship disappears amidst his more tangible accomplishments upon land.[2]

This elision of the oceanic experience from the history of America goes far beyond the story of a single minister. More than 300,000 Europeans crossed the Atlantic and entered British colonies between 1700 and 1775. Nearly another 300,000 Africans forcibly joined their European counterparts' North American entry in the same time span. The historian Bernard Bailyn labeled this "peopling of America" and the accompanying transfer of Western culture across the Atlantic as "one of the greatest events in recorded history. Its magnitudes and consequences are beyond measure." Bailyn deftly noted the complexity and creativity of this oceanic frontier, where diverse groups encountered one another and established new patterns of social organization and distinct cultural formations. Yet, he bemoaned, "We know only in the vaguest way who the hundreds of thousands of individuals who settled in British North America were, where precisely they came from, why they came, and how they lived out their lives." To Bailyn's list of questions could be added how they got there and what they experienced on the way.[3]

Further detailed study of eighteenth-century migration—including Bailyn's own hefty contribution, *Voyagers to the West*—has begun to fill out our demographic understanding of the diverse and multiple movements of people throughout the Atlantic world. The role that the ocean and ships played in these movements of people and culture, however, has not received the full focus that it deserves, often occupying minimal space in stories of migration or in surveys of American religion. Activities performed on solid ground usually take priority over the temporary and fleeting events experienced on the water. The story of the Atlantic world created in Christopher Columbus's wake focuses on the transformation of the ocean from a barrier to a highway. "Oceans connect" has been the watchword of Atlantic historical approaches to the past, which center on the cultural transfers and transformations across bodies of water. Ironically, Atlantic histories can sometimes erase the ocean itself through a narrative structure that squeezes the continents together. The ocean disappears as a site of human history except when its dangers or surprises enliven otherwise terra-centric stories. Historian Jeffrey Bolster has noted the absence of the ocean itself from Atlantic history, particularly a lack of understanding of the marine ecosystem and the human interactions with it. "The salient connections were not only *across* oceans, but *between* people and the sea." While Bolster's point focuses on the missing oceanic environment, it also applies to the way Atlantic history emphasizes the *across* to the neglect of the human presence *on* the ocean.[4]

This book focuses on that temporal moment when people crossed the oceanic threshold between the continents. Why should we give such detailed attention to a transitory period in people's lives? Six overlapping answers to this question present themselves over the course of this book. Together these explanations paint a rich cultural portrait of the ship in order to understand better the role of religion for those aboard, both collectively and individually. First, the ocean offered more than a scenic backdrop to human events. It actively shaped historical experiences through its distinct rhythms. Rather than being a timeless, unchanging space, the ocean has history and shapes history. As one social geographer noted, "History has not been made upon the solid land but upon the trackless sea which is one reason why history is so hard to understand." This complexity derives from the nature of the seas themselves. Far from being featureless, the Atlantic Ocean itself represented an interpretative fiction, a production of human knowledge that connected a host of seas and regions that mariners identified as distinct spaces. The various locales traversed during the Atlantic crossing—the English Channel, the Bay of Biscay, the Tropics, the Gulf Stream, and so on—each differently affected the physical and mental states of those aboard ship. Rather than being a timeless, unitary space, the Atlantic Ocean represented a complex set of changes masked by a seemingly unvarying appearance.[5]

Second, the Atlantic sailing ship served as a significant and distinct site of human encounter. Maritime scholars have long lamented the absence of the ship from the American story. Historians "have taken a narrow view of the sea as a world apart from the land, a place of little consequence to people other than mariners, whose way of life kept them apart from the mainstream American experience of farm, factory, and family." A quote from one recent Atlantic history survey typifies this trend: "But although we focus on the Atlantic as a maritime highway that connected cultures, the real stuff of human interaction took place on land." Although technically true, this statement misses the degree of cultural contact that occurred aboard ship. As the Anglican Wesley's encounter with German Pietists demonstrates, the tight confines of Atlantic sailing vessels made them ideal sites for what anthropologist Mary Louise Pratt has termed "contact zones." This phrase refers "to the space of colonial encounters, the space in which peoples geographically and historically separated come into contact with each other and establish ongoing relations, usually involving conditions of coercion, radical inequality, and intractable conflict." Travel brought together people normally divided by geography, religious affiliation, or social protocol. As a scholar of the nineteenth century observed, "Travelling could remove in minutes the barriers erected over centuries between one class and another." The ship needs to be discovered as a distinct site of human interaction and history.[6]

Third, these interactions took place outside the ordinary routines and frameworks of people's lives. Social structures—such as the daily necessity of labor, ethnic and caste divisions, and the rule of institutional churches—did not exercise their normative power during the Atlantic crossing. The physical confinement aboard ship offered a moment of social freedom during which migrants could potentially reshuffle their cultural priorities within their temporary communities. Aboard ship, people did not normally have to work for their food or shelter, they did not have to live apart from people culturally different from them, they did not have to attend church. As the following chapters show, cultural rules and boundaries did not disappear completely, nor were the possibilities for cultural change limitless. The ship simultaneously reflected terrestrial norms and called into question their assumed power. Nevertheless, the deck of cultural priorities could be, and often was, reshuffled for a time.[7]

Fourth, the cultural history of eighteenth-century Atlantic crossings reveals the central role that religion played in migrants' lives during the passage. Although largely without the established institutional presence of churches and despite the opportunities to jettison religion, passengers did not neglect spiritual duties during the Atlantic voyage. Ships provoked expressions of faith by passengers in the midst of an environment usually thought to be hostile to organized religion. The foul-mouthed, irreverent sailors who crisscrossed the seas evidenced the spiritual degradation of this wilderness. This stereotypical portrait of irreligious sailors has carried over into historical understandings of the ship. The rich literature on Atlantic maritime history typically gives short shrift to religion. A closer examination of the surviving evidence of ship life, especially when passengers are included in that analysis, reveals the central role that religious beliefs played on board Atlantic vessels. Trust in providential care was a rational necessity to crossing the ocean in an age where men could only partially discern their position on the ocean. To arrive in the Americas, transatlantic migrants had to pass through a watery crucible that challenged them mentally and physically. They endured and explained the hardships of their journey through the lens of their various theological traditions. Religious belief persisted, but its practices changed in the absence of formal church structures. The ship made religious maintenance an individual rather than institutional responsibility.[8]

Fifth, the Atlantic crossing demonstrates how religious toleration shifted from Old Worlds to the New. Scholars have long studied the intellectual and legal origins of religious freedom, but its actual practice in people's everyday lives has only been considered more recently. Early modern Europe offered multiple models of pragmatic accommodations to the presence of religious difference, what some have labeled "the ecumenicity of everyday life." The eighteenth-century sea passage did not create pluralism, but it did place multiple worldviews into single communities. The closeness of living arrangements and the precarious state of life aboard ship brought religion to the foreground and illuminated the presence of different belief systems. A close reading of Atlantic travel narratives from the eighteenth century reveals a kaleidoscope of practices and beliefs. For Europeans, people of varying persuasions intermixed on British sailing vessels without the dominance of any single religious tradition. The same processes of cultural interaction and exchange took place aboard ship as in the British colonies where "the meeting of peoples that resulted brought endless negotiations between older traditions and newer realities, among individuals and groups with widely different views." The crossing did not convert passengers to a religious approach based on some least common denominator of belief, nor did it remove intolerance. Religiously motivated conflicts still occurred aboard ships, but the crossing enabled people of different faiths to commune with one another even as it strengthened adherence to their exclusive faith commitments. In short, the ship crossing further anticipated the American approach to denominationalism, involving mutual acceptance and competition, openness and exclusivity.[9]

Finally, the transatlantic crossing furnished a shared experience and metaphor for the ethnically and culturally diverse immigrants of the eighteenth century as they debarked in North America. The ship enabled new societies to form in a new sensory setting as voyagers gained a fresh perspective of the world around them. Life aboard ship furnished a dissociative break from their European affinities and a formative stage in adopting other forms of collective identification. One recent historian of oceanic exploration argues, "The ocean barrier strengthened migrants' original commitment to America and compelled new Americans to look to the future rather than dwelling on the past."[10] Seventeenth-century migrants had emphasized the centrality of the voyage in their autobiographies, particularly those who participated in the "Great Migration" of Puritans to New England. Based on these texts, literary scholar Sacvan Bercovitch claims that "figurally and structurally, the migration to America displaces conversion as the crucial event" and that it initiates the formation of a distinct sense of an American self. Eighteenth-century observers also employed the metaphor "rite of passage" to describe how the crossing symbolically gave birth to the "New World" citizen. The ship served as the spiritual womb that brought forth colonial America.[11]

Protestant beliefs and practices continued to develop during passengers' months at sea and were not transported as fixed entities packed in stasis.

As Ariel sang in Shakespeare's *Tempest*, Atlantic voyagers "suffer a sea-change into something rich and strange" (1.2.401–402). The ocean wrought human culture even as it transmitted it. The ship compressed people's life experiences and squeezed religion to the foreground of human activity. At the same time, the ship largely removed the institutional presence and cultural authority of established churches that necessitated the practice of a singular or particular form of religion. Although suffering physical confinement, passengers encountered the possibilities for spiritual change in a space with blurred ecclesiastical boundaries. Furthermore, the distinct spatial, temporal, and social environment of the ship necessitated that people adapt the practice of their religion to meet the challenges of their new space. Cultural life aboard ship resembled the conditions of frontier places or border zones where the chaos of pure possibility encountered an inner need for stability and continuity, thus producing new permutations of persisting beliefs. Although more subtle and less self-conscious than the tales of dramatic conversion narrated in evangelical autobiographies, the cultural experience of the Atlantic crossing wrought change in the spiritual lives of individuals and the collective practice of the various Protestant traditions that, like conversion, formed a fundamental part of people's self-identity.[12]

Studying a sea voyage offers a particular literary opportunity for the historian to tell a defined story. Every narrative needs its central characters, and the main cast of this book embarked together on a singularly well-documented voyage: the 1735–36 Georgia expedition led by James Oglethorpe. Two merchant ships, the *London Merchant* and *Simmonds*, sailed from London with 227 passengers and accompanied by the British naval vessel HMS *Hawk*. Three English (John Wesley, Benjamin Ingham, and Francis Moore) and three German (Philip Georg Friedrich von Reck, David Nitschmann, and John Andrew Dober) passengers kept journals or published descriptions of these two ships, and still others provided more fragmentary accounts of their crossing, which offer a variety of perspectives on this single voyage. The differences in what and how these different migrants reported on their experience prove instructive and reveal the various mentalities of the individual travelers. The focus of this book, however, remains broader than this single expedition, and comparison with other ships' journeys will help to illustrate and to account for the idiosyncratic aspects of the Georgia expedition. Evidence from other eighteenth-century voyages is used to explain the occurrences aboard the *Simmonds* and *London Merchant*, while the two ships' story provides a template for understanding the typical shipboard experiences of the thousands of vessels under sail on the Atlantic over the course of the eighteenth century.[13]

Following a single voyage also creates an analytical focus on the particular religious movements most visible during the expedition. Rather than catalog the numerous spiritual options possibly encountered on the eighteenth-century British Atlantic, four different groups aboard the *Simmonds* and *London Merchant* represent several types of eighteenth-century Protestantism. Members of the Church of England and the German Lutherans aboard ship exemplified the liturgical spectrum within Protestantism. These High Church traditions affirmed the performance of a set liturgy under the direction of clergy to mediate God's grace to humanity. In the eighteenth century a strong reform impulse within Lutheranism gave rise to Pietism, which was embodied by the Moravians aboard ship. Pietists emphasized an emotional devotion to God expressed through a holy life of accountability within the devout community. Moravians especially emphasized the communitarian aspects of the Christian life. These continental Pietists influenced similar reform movements in English Protestantism, inside both conforming and dissenting churches. These Low Church Protestants stressed the primacy of Scripture over the church, which combined with the emotional tug of Pietism to produce the eighteenth-century evangelical tradition that John Wesley, his brother Charles, and George Whitefield would promote. The fourth tradition was the Quakers, members of the Society of Friends, who relied upon an unmediated, internal experience of divine light. Although smaller in number, the Quakers created an Atlantic-wide community of faith, which gave them a seemingly constant presence aboard ships, including those of the Georgia expedition. Each of these four Protestant traditions emphasized different primary avenues of approaching God: High Church traditions stressed the sacramental and the liturgical; Pietists underscored the emotional and communal; evangelicals elevated the Scriptural and individual; and Quakers emphasized the simple and internal. The experience of the ship passage would force shifts in the practice of all four traditions, and their encounters with one another created fecund conditions for cross-fertilization.[14]

The accounts describing these traditions aboard the *Simmonds* and *London Merchant* form the story arc, but the experiences and phenomena are explained using numerous other accounts drawn from the eighteenth-century British Atlantic. The purpose of this book is to study religious life and its possibilities on the eighteenth-century ship as depicted in the textual residue of those voyages. Hundreds of thousands of Europeans—mainly Irish and German—migrated to North America over the course of the eighteenth century. Thousands of others crisscrossed the North Atlantic more regularly as part of their martial, mercantile, political, or religious callings. The residue of these countless voyages can be pieced together to produce a multifaceted image of shipboard life. Like snow-flakes, no two voyages were exactly the same, but the investigation of multiple voyages reveals broader patterns in human experience of the sea.[15]

Comparing travel accounts reveals that passengers talked about certain social and cultural issues at similar times during the voyage. These commentaries on human interaction can be mapped onto the geography of the ocean. Traditional travel accounts used physical landmarks, such as historic sites or towns, to subdivide their narratives. Each stop on the journey created a natural break in the story, which could then be outlined as a series of stages. Most Atlantic crossings did not involve stopovers and, since they remained out of sight of land, terrestrial landmarks could not partition their voyage accounts. Travelers, nonetheless, demarcated the ocean in their accounts as they recognized different physical characteristics of an apparently featureless surface. Furthermore, paying attention to these geographical stages in people's narratives shows how the North Atlantic actively influenced floating human communities as they passed through each of these zones. Just as in accounts of travel by land, accounts of the ocean voyage can be subdivided into regional stages, each closely associated with different aspects of human life.[16]

An Atlantic crossing possesses the advantage of having a beginning, middle, and end, though these elements were not as distinctly or neatly divided as one might suppose. The chapter divisions build an artifice of structure that helps to understand the voyage, but they are not intended to create an essential, universal model of the Atlantic passage. Not every

Atlantic traveler passed through these stages, and some experienced them in varying degrees or in different orders. For example, the seventh chapter of this book focuses on the Atlantic experience of storms, because the Oglethorpe expedition encountered "a hurricane of wind" as it approached the Georgia coast. Some voyages met with tremendous storms earlier, and others happily reported no tempests at all. Storms were not necessarily step seven in the process of crossing the Atlantic but instead elucidate revealing sets of reactions from people across the timeline of their crossings. An ocean crossing creates a seemingly natural story arc with its clear geographic points of departure and arrival, but even on the same voyage people began and ended their stories differently. The following chapters represent an attempt to give form to the story of the Atlantic crossing so that this book reaches its destination while acknowledging the rich variety of how people told their particular tales.

Eventually, the voyage ended, but the people departing these ships journeyed on. The just-completed voyage offered them a natural opportunity to assess their lives as they began to reestablish them in a new place. Collective remembrance of oceanic experiences revealed the degree to which they had been tested and the extent to which they had changed. Literary scholar Haskell Springer succinctly captured the persistent power of the voyage as described in the surviving narratives. "The ocean crossing is in every age a transforming experience that brings new knowledge and insight, redeems the initiate and transforms secular space into sacred. The burden of telling his tale continues to weigh on the returned voyager, compelling his voice as he remembers the sail, the wave, the dark spars touched with fire." As this telling of the voyage begins, it is important to keep in mind how the experience of the Atlantic crossing lingered in American memory as a defining, community-forming moment. In the enduring words of the great American narrator of things maritime, Herman Melville: "And now, the ship that we had loathed, grew lovely in our eyes, which lingered over every familiar old timber; for the scene of suffering is a scene of joy when the suffering is past; and the silent reminiscence of hardships departed, is sweeter than the presence of delight."[17]

CHAPTER ONE

EMBARKATION

The frustration spilled onto the page even as Francis Moore described the inauguration of a voyage long since completed. As the 220-ton *Simmonds* (variously identified as *Symonds* and *Simonds*) embarked for Georgia in the fall of 1735, Moore witnessed disease, a death, and, most of all, delay. Contrary channel winds erased a week's progress in a single day and kept ships crawling along the coast. Two months after most of the passengers came aboard, the ships still bobbed in Cowes Road, sheltered by the Isle of Wight, just one hundred plus miles from their start point of Gravesend outside London. Moore lamented the mental and physical effects of this extended prologue to their journey. "This Delay was not only very tedious to the People, but very expensive to the Trust; since there were so many hundred Mouths eating, in Idleness, that which should have subsisted them till their Lands were cultivated." The "excessive Price" of replacement "Refreshments" especially grated on Moore, the appointed storekeeper for the Georgia expedition. It did not seem a propitious start to a voyage.[1]

All changed when "the Wind came fair." The speed of their departure contrasted starkly with the stagnating delays of the previous weeks. What a sight the forty-odd sailing ships that had been taking refuge in the harbor presented as they raced for open water. Now the voyage really began. Moore's account acknowledged this germinal moment in an aside to the reader about his method of keeping a sea journal. Rather than mimic ship logbooks marking weather, winds, and direction, Moore promised a more diverting account of the "way our floating Colony were subsisted, and pass'd their time on board." What ribald shipboard diversions did he record first? "We had Prayers twice a Day. The Missionaries expounded the Scriptures, catechised the Children, and administer'd the Sacrament on *Sundays*."[2]

Francis Moore's account demonstrates that the beginning of an eighteenth-century sea voyage left lasting impressions of religious exercises, but it also documents the difficulty of identifying a single starting point for the crossing. The title and subsequent page headings of his travel narrative repeatedly proclaimed the voyage "Begun the 15th of October, 1735," but the text itself starts with inventories of the goods accumulated for the settlers in the weeks prior. As the Trustees' appointed "Keeper of the Stores," Moore began his trip with more extensive preparations than most, but all voyagers had to prepare mentally and physically for life at sea and beyond. Moore had set out for his journey from the Parliament stairs on 14 October, boarding his ship in Gravesend on the following day. Although "at sea," the English coastline remained in close proximity and plain sight (when not obscured by fog) for another eight weeks. Not until 10 December did that fair wind waft him from England's shores. Even then, Moore waited until 12 December to start his "sea journal" with its initial description of religious services. Moore's voyage account raises fundamental questions about the journey. In tracking the history of the eighteenth-century voyage, when did the transatlantic passage begin?

The varied embarking experiences and backgrounds of the passengers aboard the *Simmonds, London Merchant,* and other eighteenth-century ships structured their later interpersonal interactions at sea. The 1735–36 Oglethorpe expedition brought together people from multiple national and religious backgrounds. The agents of the Georgia Trustees had spent months assembling the candidates deemed appropriate for colonial settlement. The Earl of Egmont, John Perceval, recorded the Trustees' international recruitment efforts in his journal. One 1735 entry detailed instructions to procure Highland Scots, persecuted Protestants from Austria and the Palatine, Swiss and Grison servants, and Moravians, as well as the worthy poor of England. Their agents' efforts that year filled the holds of the *Simmonds* and *London Merchant*, as well as the *Prince of Wales*, which departed from Inverness in coordination with the London-based fleet. Each of these distinct groups of passengers began its journey at a different time, sometimes traveling hundreds of miles in order to reach the ships.[3]

Further complicating the picture of identifying a definitive start to the Atlantic voyage, the various groups on ship utilized different calendars. Catholic Europe adopted the calendar reforms of Pope Gregory in 1582, skipping ten days to realign the calendar year with the seasons. Protestant regions in Holland and Germany did not follow these Roman Catholic calendric changes until 1700. Britain remained committed to the older Julian calendar until 1752. In 1735, eleven days separated the two calendars, a difference reflected in the German and English accounts of the expedition. Francis Moore marked the *Simmonds*'s departure from Cowes Road on 10 December, but the calendar read 21 December in David Nitschmann's account. While the Germans turned over to the New Year on 1 January, Moore marked his account as 1735/36 until 25 March. These differences complicated the questions of a voyage's beginnings and illustrated basic problems that emerged from diverse cultures intermingling aboard ships.[4]

Atlantic crossings were not as straightforward as they might initially appear. As noted with Moore, a voyage possessed multiple beginnings even for a single person. The process of embarkation required extensive mental, physical, and spiritual preparations as passengers marshaled the requisite resources to endure a voyage of uncertain length and unanticipated circumstances. Even when shipmasters or promoters like the Georgia Trustees handled material provisioning for migrants, voyagers still needed to brace themselves for the unknown experience of oceanic life. Migrants spent weeks, sometimes even months, gathering themselves in their ports of embarkation. Delays in departure—routine for ships sailing from England's eastern ports—ate into stores intended for consumption at sea and augmented the anxiety of those aboard. As the passenger trade emerged, mechanisms for handling those complications developed.

These preparative processes revealed different material responses and theological emphases to overcome common sets of challenges. The long, indefinite beginning of a journey strained bodies and taxed mental endurance. These uncertainties imbued voyages with an aura of anxiety that brought voyagers' religious beliefs to the forefront in the new environment of the wooden world. The various Protestant groups represented in the expedition undertook different degrees and mechanisms of preparation to steel themselves to embark on their uncertain journeys.

Assembling Human Cargos

Philip Georg Friedrich von Reck's voyage to Georgia began two months prior to Moore's when on 16 August 1735 (N.S.) he received orders from "the Trustees in London to depart with the emigrants and to make haste in order to accompany Mr. Oglethorpe." The relationship between beleaguered German Protestants and the leaders of the Georgia project had begun two years earlier. In 1733, Samuel Urlsperger wrote an impassioned description in London's *Gentleman's Magazine* of the expulsion of Lutherans from the Catholic city of Salzburg. Acting from a sense of pan-Protestant unity, the Georgia Trustees invited the refugees to settle in their nascent colony, offering to cover their transportation and provisioning costs. Although most German exiles preferred to relocate elsewhere in Europe, more than ninety Salzburgers left for Georgia, in two waves, during 1733–34. Philip Georg Friedrich von Reck, the young nephew of England's ambassador to the Diet of Rotterdam, accompanied the initial transport to England and then made his first Atlantic crossing to the Savannah River. He subsequently returned to Germany and resumed recruiting efforts alongside Urlsperger. That only twenty Salzburgers responded to this third call to Georgia illustrated the greater desirability of relocating within Europe and also the presumed risks of North American emigration. Only a fraction of German-speaking migrants—approximately 10 percent—undertook the transatlantic journey.[5]

The added weeks of overland and riverine travel added to the departure difficulties for the German speakers who migrated to English colonies at this time. Before the 1740s, most German migrants to the Americas emigrated in large groups or expeditions like the one organized by the Georgia Trustees. Expedition leaders like von Reck smoothed the bureaucratic and logistical processes required to emigrate, but the process still required considerable expense of time and resources. The twenty Salzburgers destined to sail aboard the *Simmonds* and *London Merchant* began their journey on 28 August when they hastily left Regensburg, Germany. This disappointingly small party under von Reck's leadership reached Augsburg on 30 August, where, along with sixteen other Lutherans exiled from Austria, they started preparations for the real beginning of their Georgia journey. These arrangements involved assembling "both spiritual and worldly goods" necessary "for their long voyage." Von Reck failed to detail what those specific provisions included, but the increasingly regular migration of Germans through the Rhine Valley over the course of the eighteenth century created a knowledge base among migrants of the journey's difficulties.[6]

Precise information of the road ahead formed a key component of the mental preparations necessary for the transatlantic journey. Misinformation increased fear and dissuaded potential migrants. As he recruited among the Highland Scots, the Trustees' agent Hugh Mackay assured would-be voyagers that in Georgia they would not be "yoaked four and four in a Plough and so serve instead of Horses," as some Scottish landlords had represented to them. Accurate knowledge also increased the odds of a successful journey. On the road, a "well-known pastor" intercepted von Reck's group with the intention "to give some good advice and admonition to our emigrants." While von Reck did not note the sage wisdom this pastor passed on to them, a contemporaneous German literary genre circulated travel advice and warnings to potential migrants. Moravians even created their own pamphlet literature to prepare their members for the overseas voyage. These texts coupled practical advice about what to pack with spiritual warnings about the potential stumbling blocks that might be encountered.[7]

Information helped ease some of the material difficulties, but not the emotional turmoil of leaving friends and family. As von Reck's party made the overland journey from Augsburg to a transport waiting in Marktstieft on the River Main, some lamented the difficulties of separation. A German migrant later in the century penned a soliloquy about this initial moment of departure.

> Ah must I thus then leave my native Land
> Yes yes Alas I am resigned to fate
> And this is fates command: rear up the Mast
> Spread out the canvas wide to catch the impase
> Of the fair western breeze that gently blows
> And let our Bark the rolling Waves divide.

The anticipation of their future homes steeled voyagers amidst their current interpersonal losses and difficulties. Even before they entered the ethnically diverse worlds of British ships, migrants navigated a patchwork of principalities with varying political and religious allegiances. As migrants skirted mountain ranges on their way to the River Main, they learned to avoid potential religious conflicts. Friendly Protestant villages welcomed the migrants, greeting them with "great friendship" and "fresh horses," but Catholic-controlled villages, with perceived antipathy to the Protestant refugees, created potential stumbling blocks. After all, the fresh wave of Catholic-Protestant tensions in German principalities stimulated the outflow of these Lutheran Salzburgers. A relieved von Reck noted, however, that they "were greeted with great love [by] even Catholic villages which were under the Bishop of Würzburg. They gave us horse without objections."[8]

Once they were steadily heading down the Rhine valley, von Reck added piecemeal recruits to bolster his shipment of immigrants, exceeding the bounds of his charge to gather persecuted Protestants. Part of his difficulty in recruiting might have been his previous experience overseas, which made him a "Newlander." Over the course of the eighteenth century, Newlanders acquired a reputation for swindling overly trusting migrants. This perception lay behind Leonard Melchior's 1749 injunction, "Have nothing to do with any Newlander." Von Reck accredited himself using his prior Georgia experience, but he might have actually alienated more cautious families with this self-proclaimed expertise. Single males constituted most of these additional migrants, in contrast to the religiously motivated families who had left from Augsburg. The Lutheran minister Johann Martin Boltzius complained about these Rhineland additions upon their arrival in Georgia, regretting von Reck's choice of coarse troublemakers while sympathizing with their disappointment in von Reck's unfulfilled propaganda. "He made too many promises," Boltzius surmised. Although von Reck did not express his motivations for adding these recruits, he probably was conscious of the expenses he had accrued at each toll down the river and the disappointing size of his party. By adding people further downriver, he lowered the overall cost per person for the voyage. These additions diversified the collection of migrants that the English labeled simply as Germans or Palatines, labels that elided cultural and religious differences. An increasingly patchwork assemblage of Germans arrived at Rotterdam on 26 September, where they sought ships to transport them to England.[9]

Waiting to embark from various Dutch ports afforded passengers the opportunity to secure more provisions but exposed them to the predations of unscrupulous merchants peddling supplies at high rates. German schoolteacher Gottlieb Mittelberger lamented, "Because everything is very expensive in Holland the poor people must spend nearly all they own during this period." Both friends and opportunists peppered the migrants with advice about the essential stores needed to cross the ocean. A German emigrant earlier in the century fondly recalled the material aid he received in Rotterdam, particularly a supply of "Bristol water," which "quickened me, as without it I should have been seriously ill." Other suppliers peddled "essential" supplies but with less friendly motives. The port also offered temptations to dissipation. A later German emigrant, John Whitehead, succinctly captured the cost of delay during the six weeks he spent among the "soul sellers," shippers who secured their human cargo by advancing money to secure supplies. The diversions of port waylaid Whitehead's fellow passengers, who "spent the greatest part of that Mony in Dancing which was given them by the Merchant on purpose to lay in a necessary store for so long a Voyage—as Coffee, Tea, Sugar, Rum, Oranges, &c." These migrants not only failed to provision themselves for the voyage, but they also accumulated indebtedness to the shippers who would have to be repaid. Short stays in port cities were to the migrant's advantage as was traveling with a group.[10]

The voyage for continental emigrants to North America began in earnest when they boarded a ship for England, usually in Rotterdam or Amsterdam. Von Reck described his party's departure on 11 September when a "veritable procession" of clergy, town officials, and citizens escorted the migrants to their waiting ship, surrounding them with prayer and song. The hymn choice communicated the uncertainty and need of protection for the long voyage ahead: "Wer unter dem Schutz des Höchsten ist." This musical rendition of Psalm 91 enjoined these sojourners that "he that dwelleth in the secret place of the most High shall abide under the shadow of the Almighty" (KJV). This sentiment, echoed in the accompanying sermon to the passengers and assembled crowd, formally inaugurated the transatlantic passage to Georgia, even though the migrants would not enter the Atlantic Ocean for weeks. A later German passenger Johann Carl Büttner reported a similarly festive departure from Rotterdam where they "received an excellent noonday meal and as much wine as we wanted; perhaps to give us courage." Clearly, German migrants spent their last moments ashore gathering both material and spiritual sustenance needed to withstand the hardships ahead.[11]

The short voyage from Rotterdam to England involved fewer preparations than the transatlantic crossing but still involved considerable risk. Von Reck simply noted that they experienced contrary winds from the west, but other German migrants described the surprising dangers encountered in the North Sea. Whitehead labeled it "the Sea called the Mad Dog." The Moravians in the Georgia expedition boarded an English ship in the Hamburg port of Altona on 9 September but did not arrive in London until 2 October. Similarly, an anonymous German emigrant to Philadelphia in 1728 described repeated delays from a combination of poor weather and human incompetence. Although scheduled to depart on 9 June, they were trapped in Rotterdam until the fifteenth by unfavorable winds. Less than two hours into the voyage, the ship ran aground under full sail, causing severe damage to the rudder. Once repaired, the ship remained mostly anchored over the next week by either contrary wind or "the carelessness of our almost never sober pilot." Finally, on 30 June, "a favorable breeze again rose, which by the grace of God wafted us into the harbor of Plymouth." In contrast, the Salzburgers' journey to Harwich in late September 1735 took less than five days. Crossing from Europe to England was routine but not without dangers. This shorter channel voyage provided an initiation into the wooden world that would structure passengers' lives over the next several months.[12]

Navigation laws required passengers bound for British North America to be transported from British ports in British vessels. This added yet another stage to the trip and opportunity for more costly delays. For religious refugees, Protestant unity greeted the voyagers upon their arrival to London and alleviated some of their difficulties. Von Reck reported that an English charitable society provided "plenty of clothes, money, and other necessities" during their two-week stay in London before boarding the *Simmonds* and *London Merchant.* A particularly sizable gift included a hogshead of Madeira wine that the donor "urged the travellers to drink . . . when they passed the Island of Madeira." The Moravians similarly recorded the generosity of their English hosts, who contributed £115 to cover their London expenses. The Moravian leader of the *Simmonds* Brethren, David Nitschmann, attributed these large expenditures to the high cost of living in London. "This will seem much to you, but when you look over the accounts, and consider the number of people, and how dear everything is, you will understand." Not all German migrants, however, received a warm reception in England or even set foot on British soil. Anchored off Dover, John George Käsebier described a prolonged and uncomfortable confinement aboard a ship as it took on additional provisions and customs officers searched their baggage for commercial goods. Without forward motion to counteract the effects of strong winds, the 170 Germans aboard became "violently seasick." Two children and an unmarried man died. Delays on the English coast could be costly in multiple ways.[13]

Migrants of multiple origins intertwined when passengers finally boarded ships bobbing on the Thames. Journeys that had begun in East Anglia or Yorkshire, Salzburg or Herrnhut, now converged aboard ship. Other Germans joined von Reck's party aboard the Georgia transports departing from London. Twenty-five Moravians under the leadership of David Nitschmann added to the increasingly diverse religious mixture. A reform movement within German Protestantism, Moravians emphasized an inner experience of religion manifested through a holy life. These Pietists viewed the grace bought by the blood of Jesus Christ as emancipation from their own sin as well as a gift that God intended them to share to "all nations." Although only a small percentage of the 110,000 transatlantic German migrants in the eighteenth century belonged to

Moravian communities, their organization and planning set them apart from other groups. Although the English often conflated the various German groups, they recognized among themselves various cultural and religious differences.[14]

The ship combined various nationalities, but it also skewed sex ratios. Men numerically dominated ocean travel. Although a demographic portrait of the entirety of eighteenth-century migrants remains woefully incomplete, historical studies of various particular groups suggest the shape of the whole. In the period 1700–1775, the largest category of European immigrants to enter British North America was indentured servants, and 90 percent of them were male. Bernard Bailyn's detailed investigation of British emigration to America in the years just prior to the Revolution found an overall sex ratio of five to one in favor of males, but that figure varied significantly according to the place of origin. Overall, non-British immigrants from Europe maintained a similar imbalance, although there was significant change over time. Prior to 1750, larger numbers of women and children participated in the exodus from Germany to the British colonies as parts of family units, often traveling in groups with religiously driven motivations. In the second half of the eighteenth century, this out-migration became largely male, younger, and often single. Along with the sailors who ran the ship, these young males produced the core of the temporary communities formed aboard ship, and their desires and beliefs shaped the way they viewed women and religion. Together they created a distinct social space even as their new environment re-created them.[15]

Apportioning Space

The embarkation period of the voyage slowly joined together diverse groups of people into a distinct physical and social space, the ship. As the various European migrants brought their luggage aboard, the spatial challenges of an oceanic voyage came into view. Unlike modern passenger vessels, eighteenth-century ships were not designed with mass human habitation in mind. Shipbuilders constructed vessels as multipurpose transports intended to carry a wide range of cargos. As historian Marianne Wokeck noted, "The same ships they used for transporting tropical woods, tobacco, rice, indigo, and flour eastward were used again to carry German emigrants westward." The physical size of the ship, usually distinguished by the ship's displacement or tonnage, most immediately defined its configuration for passengers. Calculation of tonnage was not an accurate science in the eighteenth century; at least three different measures might exist for a single ship. Generally speaking, the higher the tonnage, the wider and longer the ship. Regardless of the actual tonnage, the interior spaces of ships remained quite similar. Larger ships had more decks and deck space, but not necessarily more headroom. The distance between decks on merchant vessels in the eighteenth century averaged between five and five and a half feet. Construction of bunks and berths further subdivided this space. For example, Pennsylvania legislation in 1765 sought to correct abuses in the passenger trade by mandating a bunk height of two feet nine inches in steerage. This attempt at establishing minimum standards revealed how cramped quarters could be.[16]

Empty of material or human cargo, the space below decks resembled a long, narrow, close-roofed hall with masts, support beams, and companionways breaking through decks. Designed primarily to carry various sorts of physical cargo, sailing ships underwent alterations to make them amenable to human transport. Slave ships perhaps best illustrate the transition of ship space from material to human cargo. On the voyage to Africa, a ship's carpenters remade the vessel to give it the distinct interior aspects that characterized slave ships: impermeable bulkheads to separate men's from women's compartments (with a third compartment for children on some larger ships), and a six-foot-wide, two-and-a-half-foot-high shelf ringing the vessel to store people above and below. In the European immigrant trade, these alterations took place in port with carpenters crafting bunks and creating systems for ventilating the spaces between decks. The specific shape and layout of these accommodations varied according to the type of vessel, growing around the masts and sides while leaving spaces open for necessary vertical and lateral movement.[17]

British vessels used in the African slave trade before 1775 did not differ greatly in type or size from those employed in other forms of transatlantic commerce. In fact, the *London Merchant* under Captain John Thomas carried slaves from Africa to Charleston before the 1735 expedition and would do so again in later years. Slave ships varied widely in size, ranging from sloops as small as 11 tons to three-masted ships with carrying capacities more than 500 tons. At the peak of the trade in the eighteenth century, slave traders favored medium-size ships like the *London Merchant*, in the 150- to 250-ton range, to provide the optimal balance between increased carrying capacity and limited time to fill the hold with its human cargo. In advertisements, ships carrying European emigrants appeared larger than these slave ships—averaging around 300 tons. In reality, ship owners often exaggerated their size in order to produce a more favorable impression on potential passengers. The *Simmonds*, at 220 tons, came in smaller than the average but carried fewer people than the 200-ton *London Merchant*, which Moore described as being of the "same burden" but carrying nearly twice the passengers. The deviations in the standards for measuring a ship's tonnage, coupled with poor record keeping, make it difficult to quantify accurately just how crowded migrant ships were in the eighteenth century. Nevertheless, persons per ton formed the accepted means for judging whether a ship was overcrowded, both then and now. In her examination of the passenger trade, Wokeck found "an average of five passengers filled every four registered tons."[18]

The numbers of passengers and the cargo that each ship carried affected the experience of its physical size. An overcrowded ship could feel small regardless of its tonnage. Bernard Bailyn's detailed examination of the three years preceding the American Revolution discovered that the majority of the 402 vessels listed in the British Register of Emigrants carried small numbers of passengers. Two hundred and twelve ships carried less than 5 percent of Britain's outward-bound population. In contrast, 51 vessels accounted for half of the total load, indicating that the majority of these emigrants traveled in ships carrying large numbers of people. Further accounting revealed regional differences. Scottish emigrants traveled in large groups on ships fitted for the purpose of human cargo. In comparison, departures from southern England and London tended to consist of solitary individuals who found space on board primarily commercial craft. The experience of German migrants to North America mirrored that of the Scots. At midcentury, Philadelphia averaged receiving 20 ships carrying 5,600 Germans a year. Muhlenberg viewed one of these vessels in port. "An English merchant ship also lay not far from us which had two hundred Palatines on board, bound for Philadelphia. I could not ascertain what kind of Germans they were because the English call everybody who comes from Germany and Holland 'Palatines.'" Merchants desired a full hold and did not discriminate as to the origins of the people who would make a voyage profitable. The primary function of eighteenth-century sailing ships was to carry cargo, not passengers, and in these cases, the passengers were cargo.[19]

People who booked passage aboard eighteenth-century ships lodged in one of two dramatically different spaces. Those who could afford it, or who were thought to deserve it—such as clergy—stayed in the captain's suite of rooms at the stern of the vessel called "the cabin." These quarters usually consisted of a ring of small sleeping chambers (termed "staterooms") that opened onto a large center room. On bigger ships, when weather permitted, the great cabin received light and air from windows in the stern, which created a brighter, more pleasant, interior space. These cabin accommodations gave privileged passengers access to the better food of the captain's table and sequestered them from the rest of the passengers and crew. Individual and family sleeping quarters in the cabin gave passengers a degree of privacy with wooden walls and latching doors. Nevertheless, even cabin rooms revealed a ship's inhospitality to human habitation. A later traveler found his ship's cabin "accommodations for Passengers not very good, this ship was built for Profit and not for Pleasure." While cabin accommodations were not always large, clean, or luxurious, some people paid for the privilege of isolating themselves from others aboard ship.[20]

The majority of the people who crossed the Atlantic in the eighteenth century—whether from Africa or Europe—lived closer to the waterline in steerage. Although sometimes broken up into smaller "cabins" by impermanent dividers, for the most part steerage (sometimes called "the hold" by passengers) consisted of a long multifunctional space spanning the width of the vessel in which eating, working, socializing, and sleeping occurred. The length of the space accentuated its limited height, but few passengers experienced steerage when it was not cluttered with bunks, baggage, or people. In contrast to the cabin, privacy was a rare thing in steerage. As one German migrant complained, "There was no apartment for any private business but every thing was performed openly and exposed to the view of all, except some few who had so much modesty in them as to shift themselves or change their clothes in the Night Time." Berths in steerage cost passengers less money and housed more people in closer contact with one another. Gottlieb Mittelberger compared passengers in steerage to barrels of fish. "The people are packed into the big boats as closely as herring, so to speak. The bedstead of one person is hardly two feet across and six feet long." These close quarters resembled those of ships' crews lodged in the ship's forecastle (or fo'c'sle, as commonly termed). If cabins revolved around the elevated social standing of the captain, the crowded steerage created an association of passengers with the common crew.[21]

Place aboard ship indicated power. The physical separation between the cabin above and the steerage below enforced social constructions of caste and labor. Although all shared the same ship, they did not share it equally. Those who consider travel as a category of inquiry "have to grapple with the evident fact that travelers move about under strong cultural, political, and economic compulsions and that certain travelers are materially privileged, others oppressed." Ingham, Delamotte, and the Wesleys stood under no compulsion to travel, but those in steerage during their passage were not so fortunate. The cabin and steerage represented not just two physical spaces but two types of people. Everyone aboard made clear distinctions between "Gentlemen" and "steerage" passengers. Generally speaking, gentleman passengers lodged with officers of the ship in the cabin, and steerage passengers lodged among the crew. Slave ships represented the extreme form of these basic divisions. In this case, a fence or barricade often marked the social boundary—male slaves on one side, women slaves and crew on the other. As historian Greg Dening observed of naval ships, "Space was inseparable from the authority it displayed and the relationships it enclosed."[22]

These two different physical spaces shaped alternate experiences of the Atlantic crossing. John Wesley liked his room for its "privacy, there being a partition" separating him from the rest of the ship.[23] Rebecca Jones's cabin, "through the Captain's kindness, proved a large airy one."[24] The cabin accommodations delivered a greater measure of personal space and might even offer some sense of luxury. Masters equipped cabins with better furnishings, books, food, and drink. The cabin of his ship was so nice that it affronted the Quaker sensibilities of John Woolman with its "sundry sorts of carved work and imagery."[25] Of course, not all cabins were created equal, and some spaces offended the refined sensibilities of their residents. John Francis found his accommodations to be "the most disagreeable of all Confinements." The Portuguese sailors who ran the ship appeared loathsome, "But their Cabin! Oh Heavens! Had I but the pen of a Swift or the Pencil of Hogarth to describe it. The Floor since it was first made, never was washed. The Tables plated with filth and grease of all kinds. The Cloths much worse. The Births overrun with millions of Buggs and Fleas. The Servants with Lice, in short the most filthe immaginable added to the greatest expressive could scarcely picture so compleat a sense of Filth and Nastiness." Others expressed similar sentiments. When Janet Schaw stepped aboard the *Jamaica Packet*, she found her new accommodations dirty and cramped, much like the crew who ran it. Despite complaints about the lack of cleanliness, passengers who could afford cabin lodgings chose to make the passage in those staterooms.[26]

Furnished with better accommodations, cabin passengers still boarded vessels they considered overcrowded. William Downes Cheever complained that the captain of his vessel booked the cabin not "as he promised to 3, but he has I say introduced 8 in number, this small place and not more than seven feet square." He worried about the harmful effects of the arrangement, which "I am afraid will breed some infections and move to where people are not of the cleanest, the French passengers and Dutch Sailors in the hold are 22 more." Charles Wesley lodged a similar complaint against his ship's master during his return voyage to England. "Coming on board our ship, I found the honest captain had let my cabin to another." Suffering from an illness, Charles desired rest, "but now my only bed was a chest, on which I threw myself in my boots, and was not overmuch troubled with sleep till the morning." Janet Schaw's accommodations, "dignified with the title of State Room," was only "five foot wide and six long," a space which she shared with three other women. "Poor Fanny's bed is so very narrow, that she is forced to be tied in, or as the Sea term is lashed in, to prevent her falling over." In these small places, voyagers could not escape the presence of their cabin mates.[27]

Of course, these cabin accommodations seemed luxurious compared to the condition of those in the ship's hold. Treating people as human cargo amplified the effects of overcrowding. As a recent scholar of Irish and German emigration, Marianne Wokeck, noted, "Eighteenth-century travel was almost always stressful and hazardous, but it posed additional risks for emigrants who might spend several months in cramped quarters with many fellow travelers and only marginal provisions." The obvious point of comparison not only for modern scholars but for eighteenth-century voyagers as well was the slave ship. Europeans who traveled in steerage faced similar overcrowded conditions and sailed in the same ships used in the slave trade. Knowledge gained from the forcible shipping of Africans across the Atlantic could be applied to the very different circumstances of the passenger trade. Contrary to prevalent assumptions, slave captains did establish a limit to the number of slaves they would carry in relation to the size of their vessels, although this restraint did not greatly alleviate the human suffering of those in the hold. Crowding made ships more unpleasant, but it did not make them necessarily more deadly. African slave trader John Newton labeled the Middle Passage "the uncomfortable season" in a letter to his wife. "Two hundred people confined in a small vessel, in bad weather, occasion noise, dirt, and trouble enough." The situation below decks on a slave ship especially troubled those residing there. Olaudah Equiano described "the whole a scene of horror almost inconceivable" with the "loathsomeness of the stench" and "the shrieks of the women, and the groans of the dying." The "improvident avarice" of the traders so overcrowded the hold that "each had scarcely room to turn himself."[28]

European passengers also became cargo as the passenger trade emerged, although with stark differences from the trade in Africans. As Wokeck aptly noted, "The outfitting and provisioning of slave ships, becoming more active after 1700, also bore little resemblance to the immigrant trade, because profits for the slave trade were in the resale of slaves, not in the transportation demand of free people, and other uses of slave shipping were limited." Merchants who specialized in the mass transport of emigrants had to overcome public perceptions of dreadful conditions on ships destined for the colonies. Advertisements in the *Belfast News Letter* in the years prior to the American Revolution touted the amenities of ships trying to assemble their human cargos. One notice promised that the 350-ton ship *Henry* was "remarkably high between decks" and that only a "limited no. of pass. will be taken." The owners of the *Jupiter* promised "Good treatment" and later passed on news that the servants on board were "all well." The *Franklin* seemed almost too good to be true, being a "very fine and remarkably speedy vessel; uncommonly lofty in cabin, steerage, and between decks; few will be taken; goods will be carefully shipped." Sometimes merchants made appeals to popular religious beliefs in order to fill their ships' hold. The agent for the *Prosperity* lauded his ship as a "fortunate vessel." The horrible experiences of ship passages that circulated around Europe made such commendations necessary.[29]

Like the sailors they sailed with, passengers in the steerage were subject to the authority of those in the cabin. A ship's officers regulated the lives of indentured servants and convicts, controlling both their diet and their daily activities. William Moraley recorded how "every Morning and Evening the Captain called every one of us to the Cabbin Door, where we received a Thimble full of bad Brandy. We were obliged to turn out every four Hours, with the Sailors, to watch; which was to prevent our falling sick, by herding under Deck." Rules established what was, and was not, permissible in the ship's hold. The settlers bound for the new colony of Georgia in 1735 found their actions and language in steerage policed by their governors.

> Mr. Oglethorpe sent the following instructions for the passengers to Georgia on board the London Merchant: No smoking allowed under the deck; everybody has to deliver his tinderbox, which will be given back upon the arrival in Georgia; it is prohibited to have light under deck except the lantern which the officer on duty can light when nursing the sick; all other lights must be extinguished at 8 o'clock; nobody can swear or take the name of God in vain; nobody is to be rude or insolent; nobody is to quarrel or fight; if anybody goes against these rules, Mr. Von Reck is authorized to arrest those people with the assistance of the captain and deliver them to the Simonds, where they will be punished.

Although not all ships' standing orders contained a moralizing strain, most placed constraints on the behavior of those below decks. The process of embarkation meant coming to terms with the confinement aboard ship, as well as negotiating the power structures in place upon the ocean.[30]

When ship owners herded hundreds of people into the open steerage compartment, conflicts inevitably resulted. To avoid these disagreements, some masters created plans for distributing both space and resources. The Georgia Trustees commissioned von Reck to assign sleeping space aboard the *London Merchant*. Perhaps more organized than most, von Reck drew a map of each deck and created a "berthing plan" (figure 1.1). Using a combination of canvas and wooden compartments, ships carrying passengers commonly subdivided the steerage into separate bunks and rooms assigned to individual groups and families. Makeshift canvas curtains separated each "cabin" from the next. Each berth usually contained wooden bunks stacked one atop the other, although some accounts of steerage mention hammocks. The snugness of each space led passenger Thomas Christie to refer to them as "cradles" during the *Anne*'s 1732 voyage to Georgia. Most berths in von Reck's sketch specified only three persons, but typically steerage compartments contained five sleeping berths, with two above and three below. The sketch depicts space for 117 "persons," but children under twelve were counted as partial freights so they would split bunk space. Whatever privacy these divisions offered was probably enforced only at night when people slept. Usually no one lodged in the middle of the ship beneath the main hatchway—a space normally covered only by gratings or a tarpaulin in bad weather. The drawing displays the favoritism that von Reck demonstrated toward the non-English-speaking immigrants. He assigned the 90 Englishmen to the 70 berths located forward of the main mast and the 59 Salzburgers to the 47 berths around the main hatch and toward the rear of the vessel. The German space received fewer people and housed them in the part of the ship that received the most ventilation and experienced a lesser degree of vertical motion.[31]

In apportioning the ship's space to its human cargo, von Reck's sketch of the *London Merchant* anticipated the more famous and widely circulated abolitionist drawing of the Liverpool slave ship the *Brookes* drawn half a century later (figure 1.2). In pursuit of its abolitionist agenda, the *Brookes* sketch filled the ship space with naked Africans "visualised in a manner which emphasized their total passivity and prioritized their status as helpless victims." Von Reck's sketch emphasized the spatial compartmentalization of the unseen 149 passengers whereas the *Brookes* explicitly

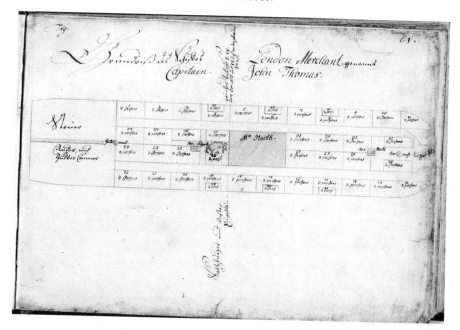

FIGURE 1.1. Berthing plan of the *London Merchant*, c. 1735, in the sketchbook of
Philip Georg Friedrich von Reck, The Royal Library—Copenhagen

attempted to imagine the stowage of 454 bodies, but both sketches tried
to capture the human habitation within naval architecture. Since the
London Merchant subsequently embarked with 381 and 386 slaves from
West Central Africa, a comparison of the sketches provokingly illustrates
two radically different experiences of ship space. Despite the appearance
of dividers in the *London Merchant* sketch, no one in steerage on either ship
could expect any measure of personal space. On both ships people slept
in a ring around the hull, with the remaining space in the middle divided
into two additional rows. The aisle separating the central and exterior
berths appears much more pronounced on the *London Merchant*. Francis
Moore called the gangways running between these makeshift cabins
"streets." In practice, however, the people spilled into the divide, making
it difficult to traverse from one end of the compartment to the other in
either ship.[32]

Despite the similar challenges of stowing people into cargo holds, the
sketches reveal three major differences between the material conditions of
the two ship spaces. First, whereas family units remained together in their

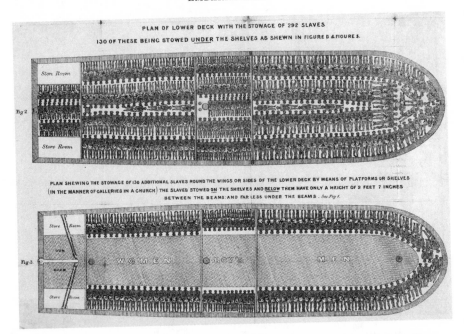

FIGURE I.2. Detail of the lower deck from "The Stowage of the British Slave Ship *Brookes* under the Regulated Slave Trade Act of 1788," Library of Congress

own berths on the *London Merchant*, the *Brookes* divided steerage into separate compartments for men (Section C), boys (Section E), and women (Section G). The lines dividing each section on the sketch indicated wooden barriers about two inches thick. Slavers intended these barriers to prevent interaction between each group. Second, the top part of the *Brookes*'s sketch depicted a wooden shelf that sailors constructed along the side of the ship. Approximately six feet wide, this platform cut the height in half, creating a two-and-a-half-foot tall space above and below. Slave ships used this crude ledge in order to accommodate more Africans in the limited surface area of steerage. The berths of the *London Merchant* similarly limited headroom, but the individual bunks allowed for greater comfort and separation from the surrounding shipmates. Third, although von Reck's sketch did not portray the ship's inhabitants, that of the *Brookes* showed the slaves covering their nakedness. Both groups slept on hard wooden boards, but Europeans padded their berths using material possessions, resources that were denied slaves. Although the *London Merchant* limited the amount of possessions people in steerage could transport, passengers came furnished with their material culture and its benefits.[33]

The sketch of the *Brookes* illuminated the power dynamics of allotting space aboard ship. The slave ship made explicit the disparities in power implicitly present aboard all vessels trafficking in human bodies. With its graphic depiction of human beings laid out in rows and stowed on platforms, the *Brookes* sketch clearly represented people as cargo. Although European travelers' accounts frequently praised the trouble that mariners took to create even Spartan levels of comfort, from a shipper's perspective, stowing people focused largely on considerations of cost. Both slave and passenger ships singled out a privileged group to occupy the more favorable portions of the steerage compartment. Like most slave ships, the *Brookes* lodged women in the stern compartment of steerage. This "privilege" reduced some of the effects of a ship's motion, and it also gave sailors sexual access to enslaved women. This division of the human cargo by sex represented one of the major differences between these two types of vessel and indicated the commodification of the African cargo.[34]

The gender division in berthing aboard the *Simmonds* or *London Merchant* functioned in terms of grouping single men and women separately to prevent sexual immorality. Moore described how the "single men were put by themselves" but did not report a similar division for the single women aboard ship. Most European women traveled in family units, but the smaller numbers of unaccompanied women lived in "exposed" situations aboard ship. Nitschmann reported six women in his party traveling alone on the *Simmonds*. A later Moravian pamphlet warned Sisters to take "especial Regard" in terms of their "Lodging in the Ship" to avoid "Circumstances that would occasion anything unsuitable." A German voyager later witnessed these "circumstances," reporting how wide "the doors of immorality were opened" when the women were indiscriminately berthed amongst the other passengers. The ship space made personal and sexual discretion difficult, particularly for those women who esteemed modesty and chastity.[35]

The close quarters of the ship, with its attendant intermingling of the sexes, particularly challenged distinctive facets of Moravian life. In Europe and America, Moravians divided their communities into choirs according to age, gender, and marital status. When possible, Moravians re-created these gender divisions aboard ship. A nineteenth-century historian described the Moravians' motivation as "a reluctance to expose her members for whose spiritual welfare she was concerned, to the hurtful influences of promiscuous association during the tedious weeks and months of a sea voyage." Rather than allow migrants to undergo the pressures of shipboard religious maintenance alone, these communities encouraged mass movements of people under the care of clergy. For example, on the Moravian-owned *Little Strength*, the choir separations took the shape of the ship divisions. Sisters berthed on the middle deck in specially constructed staterooms, and the Brethren slung their hammocks on the lower deck. The Moravian church even bought its own ship, the *Irene*, to transport emigrants between 1748 and 1759. As they adapted to ship space, Moravians sought not only to prevent sexual temptation but also to carry on traditional, communal forms of life.[36]

Those passengers in steerage frequently competed for physical space and privacy not just with sailors and fellow travelers but also with other more undesirable creatures. Once at sea, Atlantic voyagers had to wage war against traveling pests whose numbers sometimes seemed to reach biblical proportions. Rats, in particular, troubled passengers. Muhlenberg claimed that the rats "were so numerous on the ship that one could count several thousands. They gave me many a sleepless night and came so near me in bed that I had to shoo them away like flies." Although Christopher Sauer had few complaints about his 1724 voyage, he did lament that "all people on shipboard got lice." Other passengers confirmed the uniform distribution of vermin. "My greatest annoyance during the whole voyage were the lice, from which none aboard were free, not even the captain."[37]

The voracious appetite of these vermin sometimes threatened the safety of the ship itself, even at the beginning of voyages. Von Reck described two fist-sized holes in the side of his ship that "had been gnawed by the rats. ... Although these two holes were discovered while still in the Bay of Biscay and closed, God be praised, the ship nevertheless drew a lot of water." In this case, sailors had to tilt the ship to one side in order to repair the damage. The Atlantic crossing became, quite literally, a fight for survival between man and pest. When rats became too numerous or destructive, sailors took action. When the rats robbed Braintree mariner Benjamin Bangs "of 4 or 5 pounds worth in goods," the crew "revenged it in the blood of near 50 of them and recovered some of the goods." Another mariner divulged his ship's plan of attack in the logbook: "We entend to ketch a Tub full of Rats to Nite."[38]

Voyagers also competed for space with the livestock that they brought to furnish fresh food aboard ship. Samuel Kelly described the crowded appearance of his ship: "Our decks were well filled with sheep, goats, pigs and poultry," all brought aboard for the benefit of the twenty passengers. Voyagers had to balance the advantage of keeping livestock in the open air, which exposed the animals to dangers, or keeping them below decks, thus exposing themselves to discomfort. Smaller animals, such as chickens, generally stayed on the deck, but being outside exposed them to waves and weather. Woolman reported "about fourteen [fowl] perished in the storms at sea, by the waves breaking over the quarter-deck." Another traveler described his ship's "sacrifice to the watry god" when a large wave "stove the hen coop to pieces. It washed us about a little on deck, and bore off one of our pigs." Repeated foul weather often necessitated that animals share the space between decks. This meant that the fresh meat, milk, and eggs destined for cabin passengers came at the expense of those dwelling in steerage.[39]

In addition to the residential areas of the ship, other community spaces were also apportioned, often unequally. Different groups sharing the ship divvied out the few common places available for religious gatherings. On the *Simmonds*, Wesley commandeered the main cabin (not without objection) for the English worship service; the Moravians simultaneously gathered between decks, utilizing the spaces around the hatches and ladders. Nominally speaking, Wesley's Church of England assumed primacy of place aboard English ships. Traditionally, the *Book of Common Prayer* provided the ritual basis for social cohesion through shared liturgy. "The entire drama of the faith, an explanation of the meaning of existence, a rule of conduct, and an apprehension of the spiritual were laid out for worshippers in the weekly recitation of confession, creed, collects, responses, psalms, canticles, Old Testament, Gospel, and Epistle lessons." The religious approach of eighteenth-century Anglicanism centered on public performance of the liturgy as a basis of national unity and as a preserver of existing social distinctions. When Church of England clergy were present aboard ship, they sought to reconstitute the performance of their national liturgy in the main cabin.[40]

However, in reality, with the absence of clergy typically reducing actual Anglican presence, the religious use of the cabin represented a process of negotiation rather than a display of intrinsic right. The ship's captain rather than the nation-state controlled access to cabin space. Some masters used their power to forbid shipboard religious services altogether because they interfered with the normal operation of the ship, so clergy, especially dissenting ministers, appreciated when their solicitations reached favorable ears. The itinerant Friend Rebecca Jones noted the divine favor she received in being allowed to conduct Quaker meetings in the cabin. After she requested that the captain allow them to request God's blessing for the voyage, "he readily consented, and appeared willing the steerage passengers might have the privilege of sitting with us, if they chose it." Without Anglican clergy present, other groups challenged for predominance aboard ship. Even when ships contained Anglican clergy, other sects aboard might share the cabin space. During one of his transatlantic crossings, George Whitefield noted the repeated addresses of a Quaker itinerant in "my cabin." The Moravians aboard the *Little Strength* described how they rotated use of the cabin with prayers in German at seven o'clock in the evening followed by Anglican services.[41]

Space above and below decks also needed to be shared. In good weather, people sought the fresh air and bright light of the main deck, but even this outdoor space was regulated. The stern of larger vessels might possess a raised quarterdeck, which was the sole domain of the captain. Even on ships without the physical structure, the captain's permission was required to access the stern portion of the vessel. Beneath steerage was the ship's hold. In this space, the crew carefully stored the ship's supplies and the passengers' baggage. Ships limited the amount of portable property that steerage passengers could bring aboard ship. Pamphlet literature warned potential migrants to ensure that shippers "not send the chests and baggage of the travelers in another ship, but in the same one in which they sail." Those passengers who had baggage stored in the hold did not have immediate access to their belongings.

Because proper stowage in the hold was critical to the ship's sailing abilities and even safety, generally only crewmembers ventured below.[42]

Ships apportioned specific spaces for people, animals, and cargo, but not religion. Ship owners and masters consecrated no section of the ship exclusively for spiritual practices. No chapel existed for private prayer, no altar for public worship. If there was to be room for religion aboard the ship, voyagers had to elbow it out for themselves. When a gentleman passenger aboard the *Simmonds* objected to the cabin being used for daily prayers, the Wesleys searched in vain for a suitable meeting space. "The fore hatchway was the best place we could find there, though indeed it was very dirty and very noisy, and so small it would not hold above half our congregation, and so low none of them could stand upright." A Moravian reported the minister standing on the stairs between decks so those above and below could hear. Atlantic sailing ships packed for their physical needs but did not save room for sacred space. In response, Methodist itinerant Francis Asbury simply exposed himself to the elements. "Though it was very windy, I fixed my back against the mizzenmast, and preached freely on those well-known words, 2 Cor. v., 20." Like other creatures aboard ship, clergy scrambled about trying to find adequate space for their ministries.[43]

Accumulating Provisions

On Atlantic sailing ships, large casks containing food and drink for the journey constituted the main cargo in the hold. In the days before they left port, passengers accumulated additional personal stores to supplement their contracted rations. Physical preparations for the long voyage, particularly the laying up of food and drink, dominated the days before departure. These additional materials would prove crucial once at sea, when passengers discovered the provided ship's stores of food and drink to be of poor quality. Rumbling stomachs painfully verified the inadequacy of much of the pre-voyage planning. As one voyager complained, "My company did not take as much separistic [*sic*] food as I desired or advised them to, because they could not imagine nor could they believe that the voyage would be so long, or that the ship's food would prove so unpalatable." As a result, these German migrants subsisted on a diet of "horrible salted corned meat and pork, peas, barley, groats and codfish" cooked in and washed down with "stinking water." The consequences of poor planning prior to embarking multiplied exponentially as the voyage lengthened. As long as the ship remained in contact with the land, passengers could supplement their ration with fresh victuals bought from shore.[44]

Once the ship finally departed, most food came from a barrel. The shipboard diet consisted mainly of heavily salted meat preserved in casks. Francis Moore outlined the Trustees' stipulated meal plan for the *Simmonds*: "every Week four Beef Days, two Pork Days, and one Fish Day." His description further specified the amounts allotted to each mess, which consisted of five "heads" who shared the ration and sometimes even participated in its preparation (children between the ages of seven and twelve counted as half a head, and children between two and seven received a one-third share). On the beef days each mess expected to share four pounds of salt beef, two and a half pounds of flour, and a half pound of plums or suet, which could be used to make a pie or pudding. The other days consisted either of five pounds of salt pork with two and a half pints of peas or of two and a half pounds of fish with a half pound of butter. Obviously, this regimen lacked variety and nutritional completeness, trading vitamins for sufficient calories. It also contrasted with the normal eighteenth-century European diet, which was heavier in grains and vegetables than meat. Historian Marianne Wokeck succinctly summarized the shipboard diet stating, "Food rations on board were plain but adequate." As the voyage lengthened and shipboard supplies dwindled, contracted rations would necessarily be cut. The nature of the voyage meant that contracted rations would not always be provided.[45]

As the passenger trade became more organized, the various parties involved in supplying ships used their contracts to maximize economic gains, "each striving to make a profit in a market niche that was not regulated and that therefore tolerated—even encouraged—cutting corners, exploitation, and outright fraud." One means of economizing derived from placing poorer-quality provisions aboard ship. Mariner William Almy discovered this practice the hard way, noting in his ship's journal, "Broach'd a barrel of beef, If I have any judgement of horse beef that was horse." In addition to such substitutions, ships bought barrels of hastily or inadequately preserved food. William Cheever reported meat "as black as a shoe" and expressed amazement that anyone could "make a meal of such horrid stuff." At the close of the century the log keeper of the ship *Mercury* "had the Mortification to find instead of two barrels of the best of vineg[ar] only one barrel of stuff which was neither vinegar nor cyder nor water but appeared to be the vineings of cyder barrels thus much for trading to agents." Mariners knew well the possible hazards involved in the largely blind purchase of ship stores.[46]

Provisions intended for steerage passengers were particularly prone to fraud. Linguistic, economic, social, and, above all, spatial barriers shielded ship suppliers from recriminations, even though passengers certainly had complaints. Literate passengers could legally contract for the ship's provisions, which gave them opportunities for redress if the agreed-upon terms were not met. Illiterate, uni-formed, or disempowered passengers did not have such protections. Hearing from the indentured servants aboard her ship, later in the century, Scottish passenger Janet Schaw "had the mortification to find that the whole ship's provision for a voyage cross the Tropick, consisted of a few barrels of what is called neck-beef, or cast beef, a few more of New England pork (on a third voyage cross the Atlantick, and the hot Climates), Oat meal, stinking herrings, and, to own the truth, most excellent Potatoes." Schaw assigned blame for these conditions to the "depraved" owners who abused "fellow creatures in such a manner for a little sordid gain." The small profit margins involved in the transportation of steerage passengers tempted provisioners to cut corners where they could.[47]

In the early part of their journals, passengers commented on the quantity and quality of the shipboard diet. Nicholas Cresswell singled out Friday meals aboard his vessel, which continued Roman Catholic tradition by serving fish. "Before it is boiled, they beat it with Iron hammers against the Anchor Stock to soften it." Although some passengers relished the break from heavily salted meat, the smell of fish permeating the ship sickened Cresswell. The inability to preserve vegetables for the ocean voyage particularly troubled passengers who faced either rotten produce or food that seemed inedible. Gottlieb Mittelberger attributed a host of medical disorders experienced aboard the *Osgood* to "the age and highly-salted state of the food, especially of the meat." His printed account was one of many disseminated among potential migrants informing them of limitations in shipboard food and drink.[48]

Stories circulated about the inadequacy of the shipboard diet, which prompted passengers to bring aboard their own provisions. Leonard Melchior's pamphlet advised emigrants to procure written contracts to ensure shippers would provide high-quality food and only "lightly salted meat." Nevertheless, "the passengers must not only depend on the ship's food but also provide themselves with dried meat, chipped beef, prunes, spices, vinegar, and medicine." More extensive provisions not only reflected personal tastes but also ensured healthfulness over the course of the journey. People knew the debilitating effects of shipboard life and the discomforts of limited food and drink. For example, Moravians warned the Brethren and Sisters about shipboard constipation: "Those that take daily Pains to keep Nature in Order will fare the best." Avoiding such discomforts required bringing one's own food and drink aboard. Those passengers who did not consume their extra resources while waiting to embark amassed them to supplement the ship stores. Estimating the consumptive needs for a voyage of indefinite length was the real difficulty in provisioning ships. Even the most prepared ship owners or passengers could not anticipate lengthy delays in embarkation or during the voyage itself. The difficulties encountered in getting the ship to sea augmented the discomfort and dangers of the coming voyage.[49]

Anxious Delays

Contrary winds frequently extended the duration of shipboard life before the vessel ever departed. Those sailing from London faced the greatest challenge as ships from that port had to make their way to open water in the face of opposing winds. The repeated delays offered voyagers the "melancholy prospect of being detain'd sometime in the Downs." It sometimes took weeks before a ship sailed into open waters. Passengers consumed stores they had laid aside for the voyage and expended mental as well as physical capital during the delay. They found it discouraging "to lie idle so long" and "grew impatient of delay." Cabin passengers might use the interval to say final farewells to friends and family and to perform last-minute errands on shore, but they risked missing the ship's departure. Three Georgia expedition passengers who chose Portsmouth houses over the shipboard accommodations of the *Simmonds* and *London Merchant* hurried to reach the vessels once they departed, but their oared craft could not compete with full sails. Always trying to make the best use of his time, George Whitefield was flitting around London, preaching and visiting, when a boy informed him that "the *Whitaker* [his ship] was fallen down to Gravesend, and ready to sail, if not actually under sail." Whitefield hastily found a ferryman to take him back to the ship only to find that it had not moved. Since they risked losing their passage fare if they left the ship and it departed without them, most voyagers stayed aboard.[50]

The lengthy delay in the Georgia expedition's sailing resulted from a combination of unfavorable winds and the *Simmonds* and *London Merchant* awaiting a companion warship, the HMS *Hawk*. John Wesley noted the missed opportunities for departure: "The wind was fair; but the man-of-war which was to convoy us not being yet ready, obliged us to wait for her." Those aboard the ship did not know that the *Hawk* needed serious repairs, though its captain had recommended to his superiors in early October that the Georgia expedition proceed without him. "By the Account sent me by Mr. Oglethorpe of the readiness of their Ships for Sailing; it will be Impossible for the *Hawk* to proceed with them. I shall therefore follow them (as my Orders direct) to Georgia." As Captain Gascoigne rendered this honest assessment of his ship's lack of readiness, Oglethorpe communicated his preference to wait for the warship. The expedition's leader regarded the *Hawk* to be of "great consequence to our Enterprize." He further emphasized, "Indeed I should be apprehensive that we not having a Kings Sloop." So the ships continued to wait as Gascoigne made alterations to his ship and gathered a crew.[51]

During the weeks waiting, passengers not only consumed supplies intended for the voyage, but they also ate into the limited stores of patience with one another. Nitschmann reported a brawl aboard the *Simmonds* just a few days into their journey. "On deck one man was knocked down by another, striking his head on the deck so as to stun him." Traveling in the Wesleys' wake to Georgia, George Whitefield found himself mediating marriage difficulties as his ship awaited sail. While wind bound in Cowes Road, Wesley's frequent ministrations attracted the ire of his fellow passengers. His diary entry for November 17 noted, "all the people angry at my expounding so often" and "dinner (all people angry)." Mounting frustrations at the delay in sailing found ready outlets in one's shipmates, particularly those who made themselves targets for people's annoyance. Sometimes delays stimulated potential for even more dangerous conflicts. Trapped on the Irish coast by unfavorable winds, steerage passenger Elizabeth Ashbridge discovered a mutiny hatched among the sixty indentured servants aboard her vessel. They designed "to rise & kill the Ship's crew & all the English on board." Concealing her knowledge of Gaelic, Ashbridge informed the captain after overhearing the conspirators' plan, and "so their Treachery was betrayed in good time" before the ship departed the coast. These tensions before the ship had even begun its voyage increased passengers' anxiety about sailing.[52]

The first shipboard experience of death added to the trepidations of the voyage ahead. Precise numbers of deaths aboard immigrant vessels in the eighteenth century remain elusive, and historians have often based their speculation about this mortality on a comparison with the larger and better-studied transatlantic slave trade or with nineteenth-century immigration. Studies of shipboard slave mortality found that the number of deaths peaked at the beginnings and ends of voyages producing a U-shaped curve. "Slaves died at relatively high rates during the first days out from port but succumbed with decreasing frequency during the middle and later weeks of the passage." The conditions experienced before embarkation—lengthy forced marches to the coast, prolonged confinement, and the disease environment of the point of departure—contributed to the high death toll at the beginning of voyages. Statistical studies of mortality rates aboard those eighteenth-century ships ferrying European passengers suggest a lower overall mortality rate than that experienced in the slave trade, but these studies have been unable to break down when in the voyage these deaths occurred. At least some of the factors influencing mortality on slave ships also applied to European vessels, particularly the influence of people's health prior to boarding. This factor helps to understand why deaths often occurred not long after boarding ship.[53]

Qualitative evidence from surviving accounts supports this picture. The first recorded instances of passengers dying often occurred before a ship entered the Atlantic. After the voyage of the *Anne* in 1732–33, Oglethorpe reported to the Trustees that none of the people were lost, except for two young boys, "both of whom were very weakly when I came on board and had indeed been half starved through want before they left London." Francis Moore—whose account later triumphed that "by the Blessing of God, not one Soul died from the time we left the Downs to our Arrival in Georgia"—reported that on 28 October, "died a Child of eight Months old, being Daughter to one of the Colony." This child succumbed to illness after the ship had left London but before it had departed the English coast. Moore apparently erred in fixing the child's sex, because Wesley noted in his diary at "4.30 Buried James Proctor." Concerned with promoting the perception of a healthy voyage, Moore further emphasized, "She was dangerously ill before she came on board." The story of these children's deaths conform to historian Farley Grubb's statistical sample of German immigration, which discovered that "children fared far worse with a passage mortality of over nine percent or almost three times the adult rate."[54]

Just the day before the little boy died, the *Simmonds* removed one of the colony's servants because he "had the Itch." The Trustees desired that the worthy poor settle Georgia and conducted interviews with those migrants traveling on the Trust's account. Once aboard ship, the concept of worth expanded to include health and hygiene. In North America, ports like Charleston and Philadelphia established places to quarantine immigrants to prevent the entry of disease. On the British side, conscientious shipmasters, suspecting that some passengers brought death aboard ship with them, looked for signs of illness on passengers in order to create a healthy ship.[55]

Eighteenth-century voyagers steeled themselves spiritually for the coming uncertainties of the ocean voyage. The prolonged time spent waiting for departure not only facilitated illness but also increased the trepidation of travelers, producing fear and melancholy before the ship ever left land. As he waited to sail, Presbyterian minister Samuel Davies expressed the apprehension of encountering "the Terrors of a Winter-Passage over the tumultuous Ocean. . . . Perhaps I may never set my Foot on Shore more, 'till I land in the eternal World: Solemn Tho't!" The protracted wait caused people to reflect on the uncertainties of life at sea. Individuals' religious beliefs often formulated a ready response to the insecurities of ocean travel. During the waiting period many found time to pray and entreat the protection of providence. "God prosper and bless us and keep us from all Danger and Return to our friends again in Safety," wrote one mariner in his log as his ship awaited departure. Others chose a more stoic approach. Later in the eighteenth century, cabin passenger Nicholas Cresswell expressed his confidence in God. "What will be the consequence is in the hands of the Disposer of all things and the womb of time to bring forth. As I engage in it voluntarily, from honest and generous motives, I am reconciled to my Fate, be it what it will."[56]

The resulting unease from the impending journey frequently prompted voyagers to take stock of their lives physically and spiritually. A last will and testament acknowledged the real prospects of death aboard ship. Pamphlet literature advised that "the occupants of every three or four berths should come to an understanding at sea, first, that in the case of death they will serve as executors or guardians for one another." Not long after his decision to accompany Oglethorpe to Georgia, Benjamin Ingham made his will. Although just twenty-three years old, Ingham had inherited enough property and accumulated sufficient doubts to necessitate putting his affairs in order.[57]

The prospects of the Atlantic crossing stimulated such anxiety that it prompted last-second changes of heart as well as legal preparations. In the same passage of his diary, Ingham described one of his companions: "Mr. Hall, who had made great preparations for the voyage, and had now got all things ready for his departure, having this very morning hired a coach to carry himself and wife down to Gravesend, where the ship lay, at the very hour wherein they should have gone, drew back." Sometimes reports circulating about America dissuaded passengers from pursuing the voyage. A letter from America reporting "that all of the poor people, whom we knew, had suffered such misery on their trip, as hunger, thirst, and scarcity of all help had cost the lives of the majority of them on the ship," deterred a group of German immigrants from continuing to Pennsylvania. The longer the embarkation period lasted, the more opportunity for increasing doubts to dissuade emigrants from continuing their journeys.[58]

Baptisms could also accompany the inauguration of voyages, forming more festive expressions to relieve latent doubts. Both the *Anne* and

Simmonds witnessed baptisms while making their way down the Thames. After describing the festivities accompanying Oglethorpe's entry into the ship, Thomas Christie reported a child's baptism. "The Trustees being informd yt there was a woman aboard lately lain in wth her Child not Chnstnd gave 2 Guins. to make ye Company merry ye day of the Christng." The parents justified the delay because they had been so busy preparing to embark. These ceremonies involved not just the individuals concerned but became festive occasions for the entire ship. John Wesley baptized multiple adults in the voyage's first weeks. For Wesley, the rite was not simply a mere ritual formality but represented a new commitment to the entire liturgy of the church. He reported one family of Quakers who "at their earnest desire, and after frequent and careful instruction, [were] received into the Church by baptism, whereby we gained four more serious and frequent communicants." Baptism's association with death explains the ritual's appearance at the inauguration of voyages. Baptism symbolized the experience of death and resurrection through Christ, which formally marked a person's entry into the Christian Church and access to the means of grace. The ocean voyage offered the very real prospects of death, thus some uninitiated sought a degree of eternal insurance through the ritual.[59]

Even professional seamen recognized the uncertainty of a voyage's onset. Mariners ritualized their response to the unique challenge of the sea with a formulaic call upon the divine at the beginning of voyages. Shipmasters maintained logbooks to provide a systematic account of their voyage and to record their mathematical calculations, which they used to determine the ship's position. At the beginning of each voyage, the log keeper established the points of departure and destination. In order to give an aura of certainty to the future endeavor, masters often provided the positional coordinates for each port along with the anticipated route. Despite these geographical certainties, masters commonly appended the caveat "by God's permission" to their intended destinations. The exact wording of this formula entreating the divine varied from general forces of "fate" and "providence" to more specific expressions of trust in the Christian God. These phrases reflected the degree of ambiguity involved in each passage as well as a desire to avoid tempting fate by presuming success. Uncertainty and the existence of uncontrollable forces tempered

the scientific confidence reflected by geographical observations and mathematical calculations of logbooks.[60]

The inscriptions at the beginning of logbooks sometimes assumed the
outward character of prayer. Typically, mariners uttered brief prayers,
such as John Palmer's request that "God Send her to her Desired Port."
Some log keepers made the prayers in these pre-voyage inscriptions
explicit by the addition of an "Amen," for example, slave ship captain
Nathanael Briggs in his account of "the Good Ship Cald the Cleopatra
Nathl Briggs Master and Bound for the Coast of Africa So God Send the
Ship to her desired port with safety Amen." Others extended the plea for
protection explicitly to include the well-being of the crew: "So God Send
the Good Sloop and all Hir Crue to Hir desired Port in Safety Amen."
Or mariners might appeal only for individual protection, as when Aaron
Bull asserted his trust in "the God that made me I Know will preserve me
from all Evil & Harm for His Mercies Saik." Not all such introductory
prayers focused on the benefits that God's permission granted, but some
turned to praise. John Newton added the ascription of praise "Soli Deo
Gloria" to his log account of a slave voyage. God demonstrated his glory
through the protection of people. Christian mariners used these religious
inscriptions at the beginning of their logbooks to put the divine stamp of
certainty upon a voyage in which nothing seemed certain.[61]

While sailors routinely accustomed themselves to the unpredictable
forces acting upon ships, passengers often reacted with more open
expressions of fear. "The Prospect of Death, or the Dangers of the Sea,
in my present Temper, strikes me with a shuddering Horror," wrote
Presbyterian minister Samuel Davies as he prepared for his Atlantic passage. "Perhaps I may never set my Foot on Shore more, 'till I land in the
eternal World: Solemn Tho't! Father, into thy Hands I commend my
Spirit." Others used the sea voyage as a metaphor for life itself, reckoning
that the present trip would end one journey or the other. "Now, if I am
thus busied, thus anxious and concerned about my going from one
part to another of this terrestrial globe, with what justice will all this care,
anxiety, and concern, be increased, when I must commence my journey
to eternity, and set out for the other world." Bostonian cabin passenger
William Cheever spent a sleepless night before sailing for France during
the American Revolution, his "mind filled with the thoughts of leaving

my home and my dearest connections in life at this most dangerous warlike season, when not only death and the sea perch on one hand, but the Cruill Enemy stands ready on the other." Other voyagers would have shared his wartime worries, since a series of conflicts troubled the Atlantic's waters for most of the eighteenth century. Even though the 1735 Georgia expedition sailed during peacetime, in reality, war with Spain remained a real possibility, especially for migrants settling in colonial marchlands; thus the escort by the HMS *Hawk.* No wonder voyages produced trembling. The ambiguities of ocean travel always involved a measure of risk, and voyagers had to navigate doubt and fear as well as the Atlantic.[62]

Unspoken fears materialized in written prayers at the beginning of journal accounts. The Scottish indentured servant John Harrower penned, "As I am now sailing on the sea; May the great God who made the same and all things out of nothing grant that I and all mankind may meet Christ in mercy." Later in the century, the Rhode Island passenger Henry Marchant prayed for "a blessed Wind" to guide his ship to its destination. Although these petitions do not take the formulaic patterns expressed by mariners, they nevertheless echo that language and sentiment as individuals committed themselves "to the Divine guidance and protection." The businessman Pelatiah Webster began his voyage account with the mariner-like inscription, "May God give a prosperous voiage [*sic*]—Deo Soli Gloria!" Such an inscription reveals the degree to which passengers modeled their narratives on sailors' logbooks.[63]

Prayer and worship provided a spiritual antidote to such fears. In his first journal entry aboard the *Simmonds*, David Nitschmann reported the joy of the Moravians celebrating their evening song service together on ship. His companion John Andrew Dober noted how the moment consecrated their futures with prayer, although his petition focused more on the ends of their idealistic mission than the dangers of conveyance. "We have all given ourselves to the Lord, and pray that the Saviour may comfort our hearts with joy, and that we may attain our object, namely, to call the heathen, to become acquainted with those whom we have not known and who know us not, and to worship the name of the Lord." This worship created confidence in the future through expression of trust in God's will. The first Sunday aboard the *Simmonds* saw multiple worship services in German and

English, the latter of which John Wesley described as drawing "a numerous and as it then seemed serious congregation." These public celebrations entreated divine favor for the voyage ahead and provided a means for passengers to start bonding together to assuage their fears collectively.[64]

When did the eighteenth-century transatlantic voyage begin? The answer to that question is complex because it differed for the various individuals aboard ship. Some voyagers left their native lands several months before their ships actually sailed. These lengthy prologues to the actual crossing stretched resources, often leaving people physically weakened for the next stage of their journey. It taxed people mentally and physically even as it pushed them into the unfamiliar environment of the ship. Passengers found themselves in a very different physical space, one to which they would have to conform. Once begun, the voyage itself proceeded fitfully, with contrary winds or tides slowing progress. Delays in the embarkation period created unease and discomfort for Atlantic migrants. Their present seemed so unfamiliar, their future so uncertain.

Each Protestant group aboard the Georgia expedition had to adjust to the ship space. Members of established liturgical traditions had to deal with an undefined relationship to the ship's space. The ship was not part of a defined parish. Even aboard British ships with clergy, the Atlantic crossing severely disrupted the liturgical context of the Church of England. The ritual aspects of Anglican practice traditionally buttressed the social hierarchy. These rites established order as well as communicated meaning. But in the temporary society formed aboard ship, the community connections lacked clarity. For example, the role of the Anglican priest aboard ship, and the powers associated with that role, remained ambiguous. One of the earliest Society for the Propagation of the Gospel in Foreign Parts (SPG) missionaries, Caleb Heathcote, wrote to the society's secretary urging that naval chaplains be granted more power. An appointment to a ship did not necessarily translate into religious authority. Furthermore, the close quarters pulled back the veil of piety that cloaked Anglican priests with spiritual respect. The leaders of one colonial church protested the appointment of James Honeyman—not because of misdoings in the parish, but "by Reason of Some base actions Laid to his Charge when he was there before Chaplain of a man of warr." The ship placed the Anglican minister in a new and confusing situation. Wesley reflected this confusion when he described his first shipboard service. Although the rites attracted a large crowd, to his surprise, only three communicants partook of the sacrament. The ship was not a parish in any traditional sense of the word, and Wesley's pastoral relationship to the shipboard community remained unclear, as future conflicts would show.[65]

More than any other group, the Moravians recognized the challenge of the ship space and made preparations to accommodate them before they embarked. Rather than allow migrants to undergo the pressures of shipboard religious maintenance alone, or in family units, these communities encouraged mass movements of people under the care of clergy. The Pietist use of small group meetings to form "little churches within the church (*ecclesiolae in ecclesia*)" prepared them for the experience of creating congregations amidst the larger community of the ship. The Moravian desire to consecrate ship space by equating it with the entire ship could go even further. The Brethren bought their own ship, the *Irene*, to transport emigrants between 1748 and 1759. This ship served as a permanent floating congregation that traversed the Atlantic numerous times. When they had full control of a transport ship, the Moravians formally organized *die See Gemeinen*, or sea congregations, with elected leaders appointed as spiritual officers. This institution purposed "to introduce among the passengers on board a complete social and religious organization." Anna Johanna Seidel described her 1761 voyage to America through the lens of this seaborne community. "We made up a complete little congregation on our ship and had our meetings daily and Holy Communion at the prescribed time and spent our days and weeks blessedly." The attempt to make the ocean crossing a redemptive experience characterized these organized mass immigrations. The second attempt at a sea congregation sought to include not just passengers but also officers and crew. The captain of the *Little Strength* was chosen for his piety, and all but three of the other sailors maintained a connection to the seagoing religious community. These later attempts showed how Moravians attempted to equate ship with congregation, but their experience aboard the *Simmonds* demonstrated a comfort with creating a congregation within the ship. More than any other group operating in the

North Atlantic in the eighteenth century, Moravians consecrated ship space.[66]

Part of the Moravian ease at creating community aboard ship came from their ability to transcend the social divide of cabin/steerage that could stand between the clergy and laity. The Quakers demonstrated the difficult decision that this separation could present, especially for traveling Friends. The cabin offered access to the captain's authority and could lead to opportunities to conduct public meetings in the ship's cabin or other approved spaces, yet the space represented a luxury and elitism that offended the egalitarian Quaker theology of simplicity. Traveling Quakers journeyed with the approbation and funding of the larger Society of Friends, and they received funds for their provisions and accommodations. Quaker clergy like John Woolman thus rejected the cabin because of its luxury and added expense. Other traveling Friends, however, chose the cabin for the privacy and protection it afforded, despite the additional cost. Among eighteenth-century European traditions, Quakers alone deployed women as clergy, although with a differing set of expectations for travel. An egalitarian impulse allowed women to travel, but the difficulties of the Atlantic passage necessitated that female Friends choose the ship space that represented socioeconomic inequity. Despite this awkward choice, Quakers like Susanna Morris anticipated the dangers of the crossing with the strong conviction that the Lord had given them a "weighty concern" to travel. "Thus if my dear Lord would help me to strength, I would not disobey him but go in his errands whithersoever whensoever or in whatsoever he was pleased to require at my hands." This strong internal sense of divine calling enabled Quakers to overcome their lingering anxieties about the dangers of ocean travel while also helping them to overcome social scruples about the more luxurious cabin accommodations.[67]

A similar conviction of God's providential calling coupled with the ambiguous authority of the ship space created opportunity for dissenting traditions to claim a public role aboard ship. Like Quakers, evangelicals relied on a committed itinerant clergy who spread the new theological emphasis on both sides of the ocean. George Whitefield served as the most famous and well-traveled of these ministers, crossing the Atlantic thirteen times. Evangelicals recognized that when they embarked upon ship, their range of opportunities would be limited, but in this case, confinement also meant opportunity to evangelize a captive audience. While many Church of England clergy struggled with their precise role amidst the large ship community, and Moravians sought to travel in community, evangelically minded ministers sought to create a spiritual community where none had previously existed. Preaching by nature was portable, as long as ministers could negotiate access to the space. Finding seclusion for private religious contemplation could also prove difficult in the overcrowded conditions of the ship. For example, Whitefield lamented having "no place for retirement," until his ship's captain allowed him the private use of the cabin, "a place very commodious for that purpose." The ship exemplified the mobility and portability of evangelical traditions but still placed considerable discomforts, doubts, and inconveniences in the path of exercising the Christian faith. Adjustments clearly had to be made to fit religion to the sea.[68]

Each of the Protestant traditions faced distinct challenges in starting their transatlantic voyages, but the process of embarkation necessitated the exercise of religion even in the awkward spaces afforded by the ship. When after weeks of exhausting delays, the *Simmonds* and the *London Merchant* finally entered the open Atlantic, it made sense for Francis Moore to start his sea journal with a description of the religious subsistence of "our floating Colony." Their religious beliefs offered a ready means of enduring these uncontrollable difficulties and postponements. As the passengers settled into their ships, they carved out space for prayer and worship to attend to the range of uncertainties attending embarkation. The Atlantic crossing, from its beginning, clearly illustrated the boundaries of humans' control over their circumstances. The oceanic sailing ship represented the most expensive and astounding technological achievement of its time, but its power had confines in this era. Its sailings could not be scheduled with precision. People had to adjust to its limited spaces. Its carefully calculated resources could never anticipate the corrosive effects of time. The ship pulled people from their homes and into an environment that symbolically signaled chaos and death. Entry into the ship postponed the excitement and promise of new lives in new lands, replacing them with an ambiguous set of doubts to which passengers would have to adjust. After fitful deferrals, a sea change had begun.

CHAPTER TWO

SEA LEGS

"Now, at length, it pleased our Heavenly Father to send us a fair wind."
So remarked Benjamin Ingham as the *Simmonds*, the *London Merchant*, and
the HMS *Hawk* raced from the shelter of the Isle of Wight into the open
Atlantic. The moment of departure came so suddenly that the ships left
behind three passengers visiting in Portsmouth, including one man whose
pregnant wife sailed away! At 3:00 p.m., the ships glided past the Needles,
jagged chalk formations rising from the sea on the western end of the
island. The excitement of finally setting sail, combined with the natural
beauty of the slowly receding landmass, produced a sense of exhilaration.
Von Reck painted the moment in his sketchbook, adding a note that the
narrow channel ran deepest closest to the cliffs "on which the waves break
and foam" (figure 2.1). John Wesley tried to paint the scene through words
that credited the divine sculptor for this beautiful panorama. "Those
ragged rocks, with the waves dashing at the foot of them, and the white
side of the island rising perpendicular from the beach, gave a noble idea
of him that spreads out the earth and holds the water in the hollow of his
hand." After weeks of frustrating delays, voyagers overflowed with the
excitement of finally being able to write the words "at sea."[1]

FIGURE 2.1. Sketch of the Needles and Shoals by the Isle of Wight, c. 1735, in the sketchbook of Philip Georg Friedrich von Reck, The Royal Library—Copenhagen

The passengers' delight of the moment passed quickly as the ships exited sheltered waters and headed into the tumult of the North Atlantic. The heaven-sent fair wind that swept them along at seven and a quarter miles an hour also drove the realization that the voyagers had left behind their native element. The fresh breeze now mingled with the foul vomit sloshing through the ship's scuppers. The previously ebullient Ingham lamented, "Most of the passengers were now sick; I was so for about half an hour; Mr. John Wesley scarce at all." The weeks of anxiously awaiting departure suddenly ended, replaced by new sensations and the need to make adjustments to a completely nautical environment.[2]

Sailors and others accustomed to maritime life possessed what contemporaries called "sea legs," "the power of walking steadily on the deck of a ship." In this usage, possessing sea legs denotes that one no longer suffered intestinal or other physical discomforts aboard a moving vessel. Having sea legs also connotes an ability to acculturate to a new situation, visible evidence that one could adapt to life in a different element.

Eighteenth-century Atlantic travelers needed to gain their sea legs in both meanings of the phrase. When John Fontaine wrote three days out of Cork that he was "not very well at sea yet," he described both lingering nausea and his remaining unease with life in a wooden world. As Ingham noted, the process of adjustment differed widely for those on board ship. For some, like John Wesley, life on land appeared to meld seamlessly into life at sea. As his shipmates suffered from the increasingly tumultuous ocean, he quipped in his diary, "sea rough; well!" On the opposite end of the spectrum, Wesley's companion John Delamotte, and others, suffered greatly. They "recovered apace" only after entering a calm sea four days later. Oceanic life could shock body and soul. The range of people's physical reactions to the ship's motion that Ingham and Wesley noted also symbolized the process through which passengers attuned to their new surroundings. An examination of those first days at sea reveals the varying adjustments that voyagers made (or failed to make) to the physical and temporal aspects of ship life and the ways that they used their religious beliefs to adapt to their new cultural surroundings. The potential fears and uncertain futures of the embarkation period gave way to the very present reality of having to reconfigure life on water.[3]

Adjusting to Motion

If passengers embarked on ship with varying degrees of mental unease, they soon found it accompanied by the physical discomfort of seasickness. The constant motion of the ship proved to be a trial that most travelers underwent. Later in the eighteenth century, a French traveler labeled it "the fate shared by almost all people who sail for the first time," even though he reported suffering seasickness on every voyage he took. While often associated with storms, seasickness could occur at any time, even when the ship was moored. For example, although Samuel Davies reported "The Wind [was] not very hard" during his 1753 voyage, he still experienced "little Respite from the intolerable Perturbations of the angry Deep." While passengers' accounts varied widely in their descriptions of seasickness' effects, oceanic nausea remained a constant companion for most voyagers and often the first thing described when at sea.[4]

For some, seasickness remained a physical malady without larger meaning and perhaps even a humorous distraction. As one shipmaster noted in
his logbook: "Passengers rather squeamish. o lord o nothing but Gaging."
In the entertainment-deprived environment of the ocean, the inability of
lubbers to retain their stomach contents created bawdy diversions from
the normal routines of maritime labor. After its effects passed, sailors
could re-create the moment through story, using vivid description to re-
live the amusement at a particular passenger's expense. Some stoically
faced the malady with mute forbearance, and others made a game of it.
Even for travelers, seasickness might provide a passing irritation that disappeared after a short time and could be humorously remembered afterwards. Literally, the distemper could be a laughing matter. Some of the
male passengers during Henry Ingraham's voyage to Charleston tried to
make the best of their situation by wagering to see who would be the last
"to put his head between his knees" (Ingraham won). By making light of
their common difficulty, they were better able to endure it.[5]

Other passengers could not be so sanguine about the disorder. For
many Atlantic travelers the constant rolling of the ocean swells represented far more than a minor inconvenience. A German voyager later in
the century wrote: "I cannot describe how sick you get if you are sick at
sea. Although I experienced it but a little, it greatly weakened the constitution." Constant or recurring motion sickness, even when the ship was
not pitching in a violent storm, left passengers severely weakened and
therefore vulnerable to more serious illness. Aboard the *London Merchant*,
von Reck reflected on the hazards in his journal. "The illness, though not
uncommon, is not always without danger. Some have to stay in bed
for weeks, and some get so sick they vomit blood." Clearly, the ailment
was no laughing matter for some. The Lutheran pastor Henry Melchior
Muhlenberg could find no pharmaceutical or dietary remedy to ease his
suffering during his 1742 voyage to Philadelphia. "My stomach could
retain neither food, drink, nor medicine; everything was expelled *per vomi-
tum*." For heavy sufferers, malnourishment produced bodily weakness and
confined passengers to their bunks below decks, where lying prostrate in
dank, enclosed spaces magnified the disorder's effects.[6]

Later in the century, American statesman John Adams treated the malady as a scientific dilemma during his wartime voyage to Europe. "The *mal*

de mer seems to be merely the effect of agitation. The smoke, and smell of sea-coal, the smell of stagnant, putrid water, the smell of the ship where the sailors lie, or any other offensive smell, will increase the qualminess, but do not occasion it." Increased understanding of the ailment rendered its effects less fearsome. Escaping the anxiety that often accompanied seasickness enabled voyagers to prevent their troubled stomachs from leading to troubled minds.[7]

Since most everyone except the most experienced sailors felt the ill effects of ocean travel, responses to seasickness provide a glimpse into passengers' inner thoughts and the shipboard communities they created. Seasickness could temporarily alter the personalities of those it afflicted. In his 1771 voyage from London, cabin passenger William Palfrey enjoyed passing the time with his cabinmates through cards and backgammon, but the motion caused by a fine wind made his companions "pale and silent, the motion of their intestines has struck them dumb." The suffering of individuals clearly manifested itself and exerted depletory effects on the entire shipboard community.[8]

Religious commitments often determined the nature of individual reactions. For many, viewing the frailty of the body magnified the reality of the soul. Some of those who suffered most interpreted their discomfort as a sign of testing or trial by God. The Quaker itinerant Rebecca Jones found herself "extremely sick" for days and unable to eat, "yet quiet in spirit, looking to the Lord." Access to the divine inner light freed her from undue anxiety even as her stomach remained uneasy. Physical debility provoked religious trust. Passengers like Jones could say, "The sea being very rough, my mind was turned toward the Lord." Later in the century, the Methodist Francis Asbury likewise listed faith as a curative to seasickness. The ocean rocked the ship in a "manner very painful to one that was not accustomed to sailing; but when Jesus is in the ship all is well." Continued seasickness revealed God's gracious designs in testing Christians and through supplying heaven-sent provision. A month after departing England, Henry Melchior Muhlenberg lamented in his journal, "My sickness continued. I had warm wine given to me, but could not retain it." This continued suffering instructed rather than depressed his spirit. "But even though my body was very weak . . . nevertheless my good and faithful Shepherd let me lack nothing in inward refreshment. For as long as Jehovah is my shepherd, I shall lack nothing." A strong belief in divine providence or the personal care of God helped to rationalize the disorder and provided the spiritual sustenance to endure.[9]

Even those who did not suffer physically turned to otherworldly explanations for their escape. John Wesley interpreted his apparent immunity to the disorder as a sign of God's favor. "Hitherto it has pleased God that the sea has not disordered me at all; nor have I been hindered one quarter of an hour either from reading, writing, composing, or any other thing." Quaker itinerant John Woolman believed that it was "through the tender mercies of my Heavenly Father, I have been preserved." Those who suffered very little, like those who suffered a great deal, viewed their situation as a sign of God's providence whether frowning or smiling.[10]

Bouts of seasickness hindered public religious performances. Both Wesley and the Moravian David Nitschmann used the lengthy coastal prologue to sailing as an opportunity to organize communal worship services for their respective communities aboard the *Simmonds*. Seasickness disrupted these proceedings through its affliction of both convener and communicants. Joseph Emerson served as a ship's chaplain during the Louisbourg expedition of 1745, but he reported frequently being unable to perform his expected duties. Those accustomed to, or expecting, public worship services experienced disappointment when seasickness caused the minister or congregation to be indisposed.[11]

Social standing affected the challenge of seasickness for both cabin and steerage passengers. The cabin's location at the stern of the ship meant that the motions of the sea affected it least. Windows allowed for the circulation of fresh air and permitted nauseating odors to dissipate more rapidly than in the windowless void below decks. Access to a greater variety and quality of food and drink increased chances for recovery and decreased the possibilities of longer-term ill effects. As von Reck noted, "It is better to vomit from a full stomach than from an empty one, which may cause a violent hemorrhage." The access granted by his lodging in the cabin allowed the seasick Muhlenberg to ask the "captain for a little warm wine, which is the best remedy, because it draws the stomach together and strengthens it." Less crowded conditions, fresher air, and access to better foodstuffs advantaged the more privileged passengers in cabin accommodations.[12]

People in steerage may have lacked these physical advantages, but proximity to the sailors granted them access to maritime knowledge and experience of the disorder. The various folk cures sailors proffered to passengers might not have been more effective than their medical counterparts, but they certainly did no more harm. In an age predating modern medicine, the scientific cures addressing the effects of seasickness could exercise worse effects than the malady they sought to cure. During his 1724 voyage, John George Käsebier reported that a young German woman who suffered from seasickness died after an English doctor bled her to cure the malady. He "opened such a large hole in her vein that it burst during the second night." For people suffering seasickness and its accompanying dehydration, further loss of blood or fluids could have debilitating, and sometimes deadly, consequences. Although he did not specifically state that the procedure addressed seasickness, David Nitschmann medicinally bled two women soon after the *Simmonds* set sail. This more aggressive medical approach sought to purge the body of the bad humors that caused sickness and to restore a proper balance to the body's fluids. Francis Moore's account of the *Simmonds* praised the ship's surgeon for his skillful use of both bleeding and pharmaceuticals, observing that "Carduus Vomits gave the Sick great Relief: If that did not do, Bleeding and some Powders which the Doctor gave, (which were chiefly either Compositions of Salt of Wormwood or testaceous Powders) had such Effect, that, by the Blessing of God, not one Soul died from the time we left the Downs to our Arrival in Georgia." Moore attributed the overall health of the voyage to the aggressive interventions of the ship's surgeon purging the body through both emetics and incisions.[13]

Part of the difficulty adjusting to ship life stemmed from the unpredictability of the ocean. Conditions could change swiftly and with surprising ferocity. Sudden fluctuations in the weather humbled the naturalist William Bartram, causing him to draw lessons about human egocentrism. Fine breezes and bright sunshine seemed to portend a "quick and pleasant voyage . . . but, alas! how vain and uncertain are human expectations! how quickly is the flattering scene changed! The powerful winds, now rushing forth from their secret abodes, suddenly spread terror and devastation; and the wide ocean, which, a few moments past, was gentle and placid, is now thrown into disorder, and heaped into mountains, whose white curling crests seem to sweep the skies!" Voyagers repeatedly found that the sea's initial warm embrace quickly transformed into the deadly grasp of mountainous waves. Unsurprisingly, Moravians derived spiritual instruction from the sea's harsh reception. The ocean quickly reminded them that "from the earth God had made them, and on the earth He had work for them to do."[14]

If the weeks spent embarking from the English coastline gave passengers the sense that they had adjusted to life aboard ship, the first week on the open ocean showed that initial impression to be a false one. The swells of the North Atlantic added a level of difficulty to even the most routine activities. Although Janet Schaw's ship, the *Jamaica Packet*, experienced "little wind" after departing Scotland in 1774, she complained that "we are jaulted to death by the motion of the ship" to the extent that one risked chipping a tooth while trying to sip tea. The captain and mate assured her of the relative ease of the current voyage, especially when compared to earlier sailings, when they had faced storms so violent that the hogs had "their brains knocked out against the sides of the ship." Schaw inscribed her rhetorical response in her journal, quipping, "How happy are we, who are only in danger of losing teeth and breaking limbs." A German voyager later in the century noted the seagoing challenge of a more base human function. When a sudden ferocious storm smashed the deckside "private chambers" constructed for the passengers, they had to resort to the more primitive and immodest sailors' toilets labeled "the heads." "Each one, when one wished to relieve oneself, must hold to the ship's rope with one hand, while with the other, hold one's clothes over one's head and let oneself be splashed by the brine whenever the waves ran high enough." Attending to bodily needs proved difficult particularly to those who sought to maintain an appearance of modesty and decorum.[15]

The ship made simple, everyday functions particularly difficult for women. Space was at a premium, and multiple women often shared a small room with their children, clothes, luggage, and bedding. Because ship space necessitated functionality, not privacy, the desire to maintain modesty made bodily functions and getting dressed problematic. Moravians advised Sisters to be especially careful in choosing lodging aboard ship, "not so much with regard to Conveniency as Circumstances that would occasion anything unsuitable." Living in a space designed for and occupied largely by males created new challenges for women. Again Janet Schaw bemoaned, "The toilet engages much more of my time at Sea than ever it did at land; we sit in bed till we dress, and get into it, when ever we begin to undress." Seasickness increased the confinement of some women and deepened their dependence upon men. Rebecca Jones reported the physical debilitation that kept her in bed "till near noon; was much tried with sea sickness, so that I was not able to move from my chair but with assistance, which Captain Sutton, John Collett the mate, and our men in the cabin were all very willing to render."[16]

The usual route for North American–bound ships from Britain did not make acculturation easier. Rather than sailing due west and straight to North America, ships departing England normally sailed south into the Bay of Biscay, a region known for its tumultuous waves and weather. The Georgia expedition of 1735 followed this southerly route, and Wesley attributed the discomfort of his shipmates to their being in the bay. The bay's fearsome reputation often preceded the experience of it, particularly among mariners. A "Seaman's Song," inscribed in Timothy Boardman's journal from later in the century, used the Bay of Biscay as the terror-inducing refrain.

> The Next we Lost our foremast, which was a Dreadfull Stroke
> and in our Larbour Quarter, a Great hole there was Broke
> and then the Seas come Roleing in, our Gun Room it Did flow
> Thus we Rold and we told, in the Bay of Biscay, O
>
> It was Dark and Stormy Weather, Sad and Gloomy Night
> Our Captain on the Quarter Deck, that Day was killd Outrite
> the Rings that on his fingers were, in Pieces burst Also
> Thus we were in Dispare, in the Bay of Biscay, O

Moravians sailing from London to Philadelphia in 1742 could testify to this shanty's truth. When their ship encountered a typical Biscay storm, survival required the labor of those passengers not incapacitated by motion sickness to help with the ship's ropes. The extension of the continental shelf into the bay created shallows, which augmented the effects of even relatively mild oceanic swells. The evangelist George Whitefield noted the results of this wave magnification, commenting in his journal, "Being now in the Bay of Biscay, the ship rocked very much, though there was a great calm." Most passengers aboard English ships thus received their Atlantic initiation in a region notorious for its tumultuous conditions.[17]

The Bay of Biscay also offered the dangers of a lee shore. "Lee" denoted something located on the downwind side of the ship. The force of the wind drove the ship toward objects on its leeward side. Since wooden sailing ships could not sail directly into the wind, only at angles to it, they needed "sea room" to maneuver away from potential danger. Ships that could not ascertain an accurate position because of foul weather might find themselves driven toward the coastline and without room to navigate. Charlotte Browne, an Englishwoman who voyaged to Virginia aboard a British troop transport in 1754, described a flurry of activity at first light. "At 6 in the Morning all Hands call'd on Deck and we were much surpriz'd with the Sight of Land on the Coast of Portugal wore the Ship and got clear." This close call with a lee shore demonstrated the continuing physical and mental unease of passengers while yet in proximity to Europe.[18]

Over time, people adjusted and left the Bay of Biscay in their wake. The sea swell that initially caused so much discomfort increasingly became a diverting matter. As described by one voyager: "The Palatines had their fun with it. When our ship would sometimes roll or pitch, they said: 'The lion has fetched another mouthful of water.'" Levity signaled a degree of comfort and acclimation to oceanic life, but the transformation was never complete. "When the most skillful thinks he is standing on one side of the ship, lo and behold, he finds himself on his behind on the other side of the ship." At sea, the ground always shifted beneath one's feet.[19]

Most passengers found their footholds and learned to steady themselves for the other challenges that life at sea presented. In a letter home two Scottish travelers described how the passengers, after a fortnight aboard their ship, "acquired what the sailors called a sea-brain, and became very stout and healthy. Slowly their experience of the voyage changed on multiple levels. The post-seasickness shift in the quality of life manifested itself tangibly to German voyager Johan Carl Büttner. "After we had recovered, food began to taste all the better, we were merry; we sang and whistled." Music and mirth signaled the return of intestinal fortitude and marked a decided change in the quality of life. When personal queasiness faded, passengers took advantage of the opportunity to socialize. Janet Schaw noted the aural dimensions of her company's recovery, emphasizing the dreamlike qualities that the voyage now took. "The weather is now so soft, that my brother and Miss Rutherfurd are able to amuse themselves with their musick. His German flute is particularly agreeable, and one would think, by the number of fishes that are crouding round us, that he were the Orpheus of the water. If some of the sea-green nymphs would raise their heads and join their Voices, it would be a pretty concert."[20]

Adjusting to Nautical Time

Gaining one's sea legs involved more than adjusting to the rhythms of the ocean's movements; it also meant adapting to the cadences of shipboard time. Time passed differently at sea than on land. Gaining one's sea legs meant adjusting to variations in the organization of a day in an environment with limited options for both labor and leisure. Voyagers often experienced this stark divide during their first night. John Wesley's various accounts emphasized the temporal disjunctions experienced at sea. When the *Simmonds* seized a nighttime opportunity to slip out of the shelter of the Downs and make westing toward the Cowes Road, the "great noise" of the sailors' labors roused Wesley from his sleep, with his manuscript diary stating abruptly, "afraid to die!" His published journal account tamed the momentary terror by turning it into theological reflection. "Upon inquiry I found there was no danger, but the bare apprehension of it gave me a lively conviction what manner of men ought those to be who are every moment on the brink of eternity." The normal, intense efforts required to put a sailing ship into motion during the middle of the night struck Wesley as alarmingly unnatural and untimely.[21]

Other eighteenth-century voyagers shared Wesley's initial temporal discomfort. After Janet Schaw's first night aboard ship, she pondered the possibility that sleep would elude her for the entirety of the passage. She described the tumult resulting from the call "All hands on deck" being issued in the middle of the night. "My Brother descended from his Cot, the boys sprung out of bed, all hands were on Deck, hurry, bustle, noise, and confusion raged thro' our wooden kingdom, yet it was surprizing how soon everything was reduced to order." Like Wesley, her fears of eternal wakefulness proved to be unfounded, and she soon found sleep to be "obliging." Wesley's and Schaw's sudden introduction to the round-the-clock labor of sailors proved to be just the beginning of their adjustments to nautical time.[22]

Wesley's and Schaw's struggles over the shipboard shaping of time reveal that the temporal rhythms of nautical life required intentional cultural adjustments. What seemed so unnatural to passengers was the sailors' normal, though uncomfortable, mode of existence. Oceanic life enmeshed maritime laborers within a different mode of organizing time. The demands of eighteenth-century sailing vessels necessitated a labor force twenty-four hours a day, seven days a week. Although labor patterns in Europe at this time underwent a shift from agrarian to industrial models, for the most part work was performed in daylight hours. Traditionally, African and European cultures associated time with its function. These agrarian communities set apart certain periods for activities like work or worship, which marked the passage of time. The biblical injunction "To every thing there is a season, and a time to every purpose under the heaven" (Eccles. 3:1, KJV) still governed most Europeans' lives. A new cultural attitude toward time, however, emerged alongside new means of manufacturing goods. In this system, the clock, rather than nature, controlled life. The advancing industrial approach made every moment of every day available for any activity, particularly work. All time was useful. No particular time was holy. Aboard ship, the oceanic environment required mariners to keep continuous watches and work in shifts day and night. The unpredictable variability of the Atlantic demanded vigilance and near instantaneous action. In this way, the temporal rhythms of a mariner's natural oceanic world required more modern intervals of labor, which the factory would later epitomize.[23]

The regular changing of the watch, not the rotation of the earth or specific seasonal functions, established the basic pattern of life aboard ships. The ship's "watch" constituted the most basic unit of nautical time and resulted from the shipboard demand for constant labor. The officers divided the crew into two parties called "watches"—usually denoted starboard and larboard—that took turns running the ship. A thirty-minute hourglass established the basic unit of time. The ringing of a bell marked the glass's completion. Every four hours—at eight bells—the watches switched, ensuring that the ship would be capably manned at all times. The nighttime watches, shorter two-hour periods called "dog watches," proved to be the most difficult. One seaman noted the exertion required when they "in a hurrey mustered out Between Sleping and Waking." Because the Quaker itinerant John Woolman lodged among the ship's crew during his 1772 voyage, he was able to note the difficulties involved in such an arrangement. "A ship at sea commonly sails all night, and the seamen take their watches four hours at a time. Rising to work in the night, it is not commonly pleasant in any case, but in dark rainy nights it is very disagreeable." Even those more socially distant from the sailors could not escape the noisy tumult after the ringing of the bell that set the entire crew into motion. The change of watch interrupted many a traveler's first attempt at sleep. After his first night aboard a London-bound ship, Presbyterian minister Samuel Davies noted, "The Novelty of my Situation and the Noise on Deck hindered my sleeping, so that I am heavy and indisposed." Passengers eventually adjusted to these temporal rhythms and, in the words of evangelist George Whitefield, "began to be more reconciled to a ship life."[24]

Mariners also measured their days differently, as conveyed by the ship's logbook. Instead of days, masters often began log entries "This 24 hours . . ." (figure 2.2). Ship days began and ended not at midnight or at sunset but at noon, with the master's calculation of the ship's position. Speed also factored into the shipboard marking of time as mariners carefully recorded the distance sailed. Columns in the log designated the direction of both the ship and the wind. These climatic elements bore close association with the experience of time. Gales blowing from the wrong quarter seemed to make time stop. "Mity Sorraie times you May depend," lamented James Rhodes as the prospect of a lengthy voyage loomed over the schooner *Nancy*. Two days later little had changed. "Wind as you see Mity Sorry[.] You May depend Mister it makes me groe olde fast." Speed and distance tracked the passage of time at sea as much as manmade timepieces. Impediments to the ship's spatial progress had temporal effects. Aboard the *Simmonds*, David Nitschmann recognized

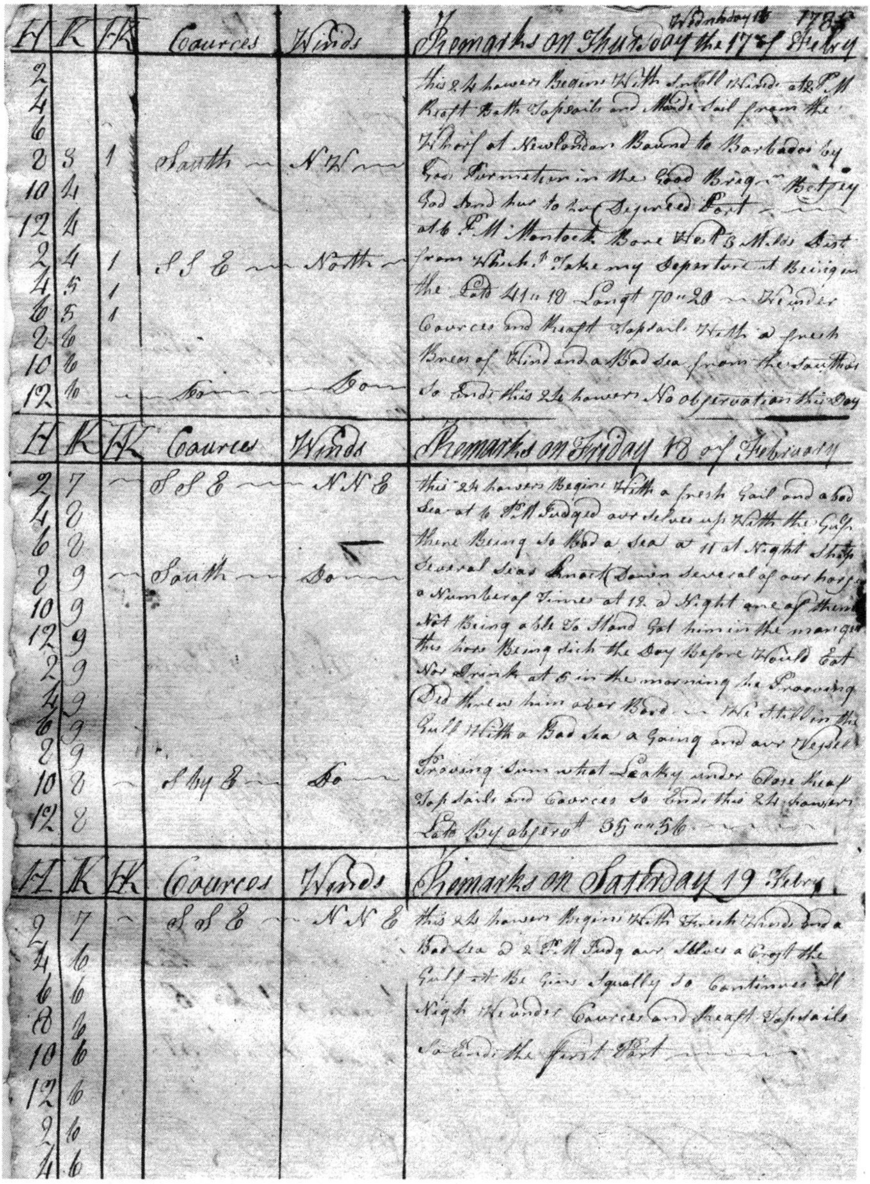

Wednesday 16 1785

FIGURE 2.2. Page from the logbook of the *Betsey*, c. 1785, from the John Palmer Papers, Coll. 53, Manuscripts Collection, G. W. Blunt White Library, Mystic Seaport Museum

that delays in sailing ate away the time available to pursue his calling. "I prayed for a good wind, since we do not wish to lie in one place and be of no use." The turning of the glass, striking the bell, changing the watch, observing each twenty-four hours, and calculating the distance sailed all marked out the passage of time aboard ship.[25]

Journal accounts sometimes reflected the desire of cabin passengers to adapt to nautical ways on board ship. Thomas Perkins marked his first shipboard entry, "First part of the day, or rather the 24 hours (for this memorandum is kept in nautical days)." Diaries and journals also illustrate how even single individuals measured time differently on land and sea. For example, Robert Treat Paine—who achieved fame as the prosecuting attorney in the Boston Massacre trial and as a Massachusetts signer of the Declaration of Independence—spent almost five years at sea as a mate and commander of sailing vessels. Paine marked the passage of time differently in his "sea journal" than in the diary he kept onshore. The most notable variation stemmed from the treatment of Sunday. On land, his notation of when and where he attended religious service created a weekly rhythm centered on this market day of the soul, but on ship, the Christian Sabbath disappeared. An undifferentiated succession of days marked by location, miles sailed, wind direction, and a host of other daily routines replaced a calendar revolving around sacred days.[26]

Life at sea produced unusual time patterns, especially in regard to sacred time. The different approach to Sunday narrated in ships' logs and journals often reflected the lack of a formal religious observance among seamen. The time did not become sacred because no religious activity set the day apart. As the Presbyterian minister Samuel Davies bemoaned, "Indeed there is Nothing that has the Appearance of a Sabbath among Sailors." European nations often required that ships of a certain size carry a chaplain to conduct religious services, but the majority of vessels did not meet the threshold, and ship owners frequently skirted the law. A chaplain seemed to them just another mouth to feed and a presence that did not contribute to the functioning of the ship. Some voyagers concluded that obligatory religious services actually caused more harm than good. A passenger aboard a French vessel at the end of the eighteenth century thought that the mandatory Roman Catholic prayers muttered by the crew merely "keep up the Farce of Religious Ceremony—I do not see that any good results from it." But mandatory prayers such as these served as the exception on the eighteenth-century Atlantic. The majority of accounts record the absence of public worship rather than its offense.[27]

The lack of religious service on board ship reflected the constraints of the wooden world, not necessarily the antireligious sentiment of the crew. Connecticut sailor Eleazar Elderkin lamented, "I should like very well to attend Church." On Sundays, sailor Simeon Griswold turned his thoughts to "how Hapy the People are that stay at Home at there Ease Numbers there are this Day in Churches spending there time in Hearing the Good Words of ye Gospell." Individual shipmasters, like slave ship captain John Newton, might take it upon themselves to conduct Sunday meetings for their crew, but most appear uncompelled to have done so. Even ships with clergy and obliging officers found themselves disappointed when the weather made such meetings impractical. Ministers often found themselves in positions like that of German pastor Henry Melchior Muhlenberg, who prepared to preach to the English passengers and crew "but was prevented because a strong wind and rain arose, which forced the passengers into their cabin and the crew to their posts." Life at sea made public worship contingent on the weather, the willingness of the ship's master, and the availability of clergy.[28]

Sailors faced the same difficulty in regard to Sunday as did plantation slaves. Forced to work for others most of the week, Sunday became the day on which sailors worked for themselves. Elderkin portrayed the common sailors' Sunday as "all the time they give us to do any thing for ourselves." From the forecastle of his ship *Eliza*, he portrayed his Sunday employments as "overhauling my Cloths—airing them—and making a tarpaulin to cover my hat—must now leave writing and go and wash my Cloaths." When the weather cooperated, sailors controlled their own time on Sundays. Freed from the obligations of the ship's "duty," the hands could be, in the words of one master, "imployd in Reading and sleeping." Even the more religiously inclined mariners enjoyed the resting aspects of the Christian Sabbath in the absence of worship. Nautical labor reserved Sunday for personal occupation and relaxation rather than public worship. Rhode Island mariner George Munro described a typical shipboard Sunday as consisting of "rest All Day there is Nothing Remarkable this Day no Employment So Ends this Lord Day in Peace."[29]

The marine model of organizing time proved discomfiting for voyagers as it stood in stark opposition to the observance of sacred days, particularly the Christian Sabbath. Passengers struggled with maintaining the sacred calendar in an environment that ignored it. Perhaps ministers performed this task best. Liturgically minded pastors, such as Wesley or Muhlenberg, stayed in tune with the rhythms of sacred time, noting not just each Sunday, but where that particular Sunday fell on the liturgical calendar. Members of the Society of Friends recorded time through numbering of the days from the first day to the seventh day, just as they did ashore. Those whose professional calling centered on sacred calendars tried to re-create familiar patterns of religious observance on board ship, but the onus for organizing such meetings fell upon the individual person. Every ship did not have clergy, and every member of the clergy did not feel compelled to conduct public worship. Anglican layman Nicholas Cresswell expressed excitement that his ship had a clergyman aboard and thus he would benefit from regular religious observance. To his dismay, the clergyman chose to spend the day in other activities, once reading a text on scurvy.[30]

Lay passengers without an active clergy aboard ship tried to remember the Sabbath day even when it lacked formal observance. Cresswell punctuated his record of Sundays with the refrain, "No prayers to-day." Some lay passengers—particularly those from liturgical traditions—took matters into their own hands and conducted public service. For Anglicans, this form of public worship often consisted of reading from the *Book of Common Prayer* or an appropriate sermon. Even with ministers aboard, some laity stepped in to lead public religious service. The German schoolteacher Gottlieb Mittelberger assumed all the duties of a minister. "I held daily prayer meetings with them on deck, and, since we had no ordained clergyman on board, was forced to administer baptism to five children. I also held services, including a sermon, every Sunday, and when the dead were buried at sea, commended them and our souls to the mercy of God." Others observed sacred time as individuals. The account of African Ayuba ben Solomon, commonly referred to as Job, recorded his shipboard observance of Islamic devotional practices during his remarkable return from slavery. "He was very constant in his Devotions; which he never omitted, on any Pretence, notwithstanding we had

66

exceeding bad Weather all the time we were at Sea." Other voyagers similarly practiced their faith in isolation. When afflicted with seasickness, Rebecca Jones "spent the latter part of this day alone in our state room, my heart being turned towards the Lord." The more religiously inclined voyagers took greater responsibility for their spiritual maintenance in the absence of clergy and supportive communities.[31]

The neglect of sacred time proved irritating to religiously minded voyagers, and some feared the long-term effects of nautical life. The general apathy of sailors toward Sabbath observance on board ship could be contagious. On a Sunday toward the end of his voyage to Boston, William Palfrey noted, "My Shipmates pay little regard to the day as they are now upon deck shooting Gulls." Sailors' antipathy toward the observance of sacred time created particular frustration when in Catholic ports. Salem mariner Nathaniel Bowditch lamented the time lost in Lisbon since "about 120 days in the year are set apart for the worship of their saints on these days." Such statements reflect how mariners internalized the modern emphasis on efficient use of time. The physical demands of nautical labor superseded the temporal observance of the sacred as voyagers discovered during the voyage's first weeks. Gaining one's sea legs possibly meant adjusting to a lack of religious observances.[32]

Adjusting to Confinement

The spatial and physical deprivations of life on a ship at sea added to the environmental and chronological adjustments that the Atlantic forced passengers to make. Seasickness, waves, weather, and the need to keep the decks clear constrained people to remain in their berths below decks. Although people might have been on ship for several weeks before the actual voyage began, being under full sail made them experience their space in new ways.

Even passengers not in chains frequently described their experience of the ship's space in terms of imprisonment. Part of the sense of confinement resulted from the physical space itself. Presbyterian minister Samuel Davies described his feeling of entrapment. "I never appeared to myself so helpless in all my Life; confined to a little Vessel, in the midst of mountainous Seas, at a dreadful Distance from Land; and no possible

Prospect of escaping Death, if any Accident should befall the Ship."
Passengers accustomed to open spaces and freedom of movement felt the
walls of the ship closing in on them once at sea. A Massachusetts sailor
described the ship as "a kind of hell or a prison," a characterization that
anticipated Samuel Johnson's famous comparison of the two modes of
confinement. "A ship is worse than a gaol," he wrote. "There is, in a
gaol, better air, better company, better conveniency of every kind; and a
ship has the additional disadvantage of being in danger." One passenger
claimed that the effects of confinement struck women particularly.
"Ladies who are used to an easy life, how hard does it not appear to them
to be confined in a close cabin."[33]

The experience of shipboard imprisonment described by eighteenth-
century European passengers paled in comparison to the actual forced
transportation of African slaves. The men and women aboard transatlantic slave ships endured greater physical discomfort than seasickness, and
additional physical horrors and metaphysical barriers complicated their
adaptation to nautical life. Seamen openly discussed distressing slave
ship conditions as they circulated through other trades in the Atlantic
labor system. The tales the sailors told "respecting the voyages to Africa,
and the manner of bringing the deeply oppressed slaves" troubled the
sleep of Quaker passenger John Woolman and steeled his growing anti-
slavery sentiments. Before his ship departed for America, English passenger Nicholas Cresswell sought advice from an old friend who served as
steward aboard a Guinea ship that had just docked. He found his friend
"so disguised with dirt and sickness I did not know him; indeed I never
saw such a Scene of Sickness and Confusion before." The sailors spoke
not only of the appalling physical conditions slaves suffered aboard ship,
but also of their "hearts loaded with grief under the apprehension of
miserable slavery." Samuel Kelly conversed with an "old Guineaman"
who "had given me such an account of the iniquity practised in the slave
trade that I determined never to go into that employ." Seasoned sailors
testified to the deplorable conditions through their attempts to avoid work
in slave ships, and those who experienced this service did not recommend
it to their peers. When slave shipmaster James Fraser testified before a
parliamentary committee that his crew often consisted of landsmen
or "half seamen," he implied that experienced sailors avoided this side of

the service. Despite the efforts of some within the slave trade to paint a rosier picture of shipboard conditions, they could not hide what others saw and smelled.[34]

No wonder then that Africans responded to slave ships with enormous apprehension. People like James Albert Ukawsaw Gronniosaw suffered from the normal motion of the ship, "I was exceedingly seasick at first; but when I became more accustomed to the sea, it wore off," but other aspects of the ship continued the initial distress. The uncertainty of ship-board life heightened what one scholar has termed "a miasma of misun-derstanding and myth." Part of the exacerbated shipboard distress derived from the fear that the Europeans planned to devour them. Thomas King noted the prevalence of the idea among some slaves "that the White People purchase them with intent to take them to their own country, to kill and eat them." The African memoir of Olaudah Equiano described how he fainted because he mentally connected "a large furnace or copper boiling" with "a multitude of black people of every description chained together." When awakened, he asked some bystanders "if we were not to be eaten by those white men with horrible looks, red faces, and long hair." The slavers did not devour Africans in the exact sense that Equiano feared, but the episode demonstrates the initial uncertainty of those who stepped aboard. A ship's surgeon aptly conveyed the gen-eral attitude of slaves as they came aboard, stating, "A gloomy pensive-ness seemed to overcast their countenance." The slave ship provoked an immediate reaction of fear and depression.[35]

These initial impressions did not improve with further acquaintance. Officers saw to it that slaves were stripped of all clothing and shaved of hair to prevent disease. This denuding process stripped them of exterior signs of personal distinction, removed the comforts of material culture, and humiliated individuals. Male slaves suffered the further indignity and discomfort of being fettered at the ankles and often connected to a com-plete stranger. Chains shackled to already shaky sea legs tore into skin and heightened shipboard unease. One leg-scarred survivor described how "we could not move either hand or foot, but with great caution and perfect con-sent." The normal respite from sleep eluded men in these conditions since every move of one's neighbor disturbed one's rest. "When my poor com-rade, in fits of pain, gave compulsive starts and twitches, and sometimes wrenching himself as one possessed with an unclean spirit, he sorely lacerated both himself and me!" Nighttime worsened confinement below decks. Each night the crew descended below decks in order to "stow" their cargo of slaves. In order to maximize the capacity of the hold, mariners took great care, in the words of one, "to make the most of my room, and wedge them in as well as I could." While scholars debate the extent of "tight-packing" and its correlation to shipboard mortality, the slaves themselves certainly felt squeezed for space as they sought the relief of sleep. One slave ship captain testified, "They could—though perhaps they would have found it difficult, all of them, to have lain on their backs at the same time." A nineteenth-century slave, Charles Ball, recounted that the hold of his slave ship "was so full, that no one could lie down; and we were obliged to sit all the time, for the room was not high enough for us to stand." For more than a week after he arrived in Charleston, he was unable to straighten his limbs. These added physical constraints made the process of gaining one's sea legs extremely difficult.[36]

In the presence of such large numbers of people, the conditions of the hold deteriorated in numerous ways. First, the accumulated body and respiratory heat produced by close confinement raised the temperature to stifling levels during the day. One sailor described "the steam coming through the gratings like a furnace from their breath." Another testified that "after being below but a few minutes, had my shirt so wet by perspiration, that I could have wrung it as if it had been steeped in water." Second, the stench of the hold approached mythical proportions. Several open tubs placed throughout the hold served as the only toilet facilities offered to slaves between the decks. The effects of seasickness or other illness worsened an already horrid situation. For days after leaving Cape Verga, the phrase "slaves very sea sick" peppered the logbook of the *Sandown*, which meant that they "cannot eat their Victuals." Later in the voyage the captain, Samuel Gamble, reported an increasingly alarming death toll among both cargo and crew. On the *Alexander*, the ship's surgeon reported "the deck was covered with blood and mucus, and approached nearer to the resemblance of a slaughter house than any thing I can compare it to, the stench and foul air were likewise intolerable." The British naval ship *Racehorse*, stationed off Africa in 1783, made a slave ship raise anchor and move farther down the coast when "the officers, and even crew, complained of the noxious smell continually on the ship." Even those slave captains who downplayed the conditions of the hold admitted their preference for allowing slaves to remain topside as much as possible.[37]

For enslaved Africans, the shipboard experience also involved their mental reaction to the attempt to transform captives into a saleable commodity in the Americas. In the words of one survivor, "the iron entered our souls!" As historian Emma Christopher aptly noted, "To the men and women chained below decks many of the acts of this conversion were simply stark, horrific terror, but they also formed part of the larger panorama that attempted to alter human beings to thing." The ship's very existence on the vast ocean itself represented a major epistemological adjustment for West African cultures. "As for the metaphysical aspect, the very habitat of the ship—the open sea—challenged African cosmographies, for the landless realm of the deep ocean did not figure in the precolonial West African societies as a domain of human (as opposed to divine) activity." The ship necessitated not just material adjustments but an expansion of a person's worldview, forced to incorporate not just the experience of the ship but its very existence. No wonder that a significant minority of the enslaved cargo resisted acculturation.[38]

Surviving accounts often identified suicide as an initial response to slave ship life. More than just an expression of despair, suicide furnished a means of asserting spiritual power and control of one's body. Some West and West Central African cultures retained taboos against suicide, but not all of them regarded it as a negative act. Warriors facing capture who chose to end their lives rather than suffer under the hands of their enemies often received praise rather than condemnation. Combining defiance with belief in a world with blurred boundaries between the natural and supernatural, suicide represented a final assertion of control over one's destiny. Enslaved Africans willingly chose a type of martyrdom based on the certainty of their religious convictions instead of suffering a degrading, unknown future. Slaves who saw death as inevitable sought to choose the moment and method of their demise. John Newton described the suicide of a dying man who cast himself overboard not long after coming aboard ship. Although the sailors managed to recover his body, "he dyed immediately between his weakness and the salt water he had swallowed, tho I imagine he would have lived but a little while being quite worn out." Already near death in the eyes of Newton, this man summoned the courage to face death on his terms. Africans often chose death over adapting to life on the slave ship.[39]

Slave captains later testifying before Parliament about the happiness of slaves aboard their vessels negated their own testimony by subsequently describing the material preventatives they took to stop intentional drowning. Sailors fastened shackled pairs of male slaves to a large chain fixed to the deck, rendering them a literal part of the ship. Nettings extended from the sides of vessels to impede those intent upon drowning, and a constant watchfulness prevailed among the crew. These numerous precautions might prevent slaves from casting themselves overboard, but they could not prevent men and women from losing the will to live. Olaudah Equiano described both his desire for death and the physical barriers that prevented it. "Could I have got over the nettings, I would have jumped over the side, but I could not; and, besides, the crew used to watch us very closely who were not chained down to the decks, lest we should leap into the water." This desire for death commonly manifested itself in people's visages. Europeans described a type of severe depression, which they labeled "fixed melancholy," that often resulted in death. For example, in his log, John Newton lamented the loss of "a fine woman slave, No. 11, having been ailing some time, but never thought her in danger till within these 2 days; she was taken with a lethargick disorder, which they seldom recover from." This disorder that Newton described resulted from mental as well as physical causes. One ship's surgeon trying to determine the origin of the malady accepted the slaves' interpretation. "I have heard them say in their language, that they wished to die." Equiano's account offered a personal glimpse into the thought processes undergirding refusals of food and medicine. After experiencing the initial shock of life below decks, he wrote, "I became so sick and low that I was not able to eat, nor had I the least desire to taste anything. I now wished for the last friend, Death, to relieve me."[40]

A severe melancholy or depression often accompanied this refusal to eat, but starvation could represent something more than a passive acceptance of death. Despondency led many slaves to refuse sustenance, literally willing themselves to die. Some slaves chose to starve themselves rather than fatten the wallets of their captors. Eyewitnesses occasionally described an attitude better termed "fixed determination" than fixed melancholy. Isaac Wilson recalled a male slave who refused to take any sustenance whatsoever. He resisted both enchanting enticements and brutal beatings, keeping his teeth shut so tightly that his captors could not intrude by means of a speculum oris or of a knife. Near the end his resolution appeared to wane, and he requested water. But this refreshment only renewed his determination, and he died. Rather than submit to the will of his captors, this young man conducted a hunger strike that defied the slavers' assertion of total power. He did not resign himself to his fate but acted out of his convictions and chose death.[41]

Last words and surviving shipmates provided a glimpse into the stimuli behind suicide. The most prominent explanation offered was the belief that death would initiate a return to the lost homeland. Suicide reduced the cargo of the *Hannibal* by twelve souls, slaves who acted from "their belief that when they die they return home to their own country and friends again." One sailor asked survivors why a woman aboard his ship starved herself to death despite repeated beatings intended to compel her to eat. "I was told by some of the women Slaves that she spoke to some of them the night before she died, and said, 'She was going to her friends.'" Ecroyde Claxton claimed slaves cast themselves overboard "thinking that they should get back to their own countrys." He also described how the captain mutilated the corpse of one suicide victim, publicly beheading the body to send a message to the surviving slaves. If "they were determined to go back to their own country, they should go back without their heads." Whereas the captain's grisly counteraction did not accurately reflect African conceptions of dismemberment, it did demonstrate an understanding of the religious motivations underlying suicide. Rather than view their shipmates' actions with disdain, surviving slaves continued to hope that death had secured their companions' release from the grip of slavers. The belief that death initiated a return to Africa would endure in North American plantation communities. This connection to homeland also explained why suicides often occurred in the early stages of a voyage, while still close to land.[42]

The willingness to die rather than submit to enslavement also inspired outward acts of violence while the African shoreline still loomed on the horizon. Examination of the known shipboard insurrections revealed that "most slave-ship rebellions occurred while ships were at the African coast or just after the vessel left for the simple reason that slave vessels spent more time at the coast than sailing the Middle Passage." Three-fourths of the documented revolts rook place during the coasting phase or during the voyage's first week. For slave ships, rebellion formed a noticeable part of the ship's embarkation and acculturation processes. The Fante slave Quobna Ottobah Cugoano described the planned rebellion aboard his ship, one that combined the motives of rebellion and suicide. "Death was more preferable than life, and a plan was concerted amongst us, that we might burn and blow up the ship, and to perish all together in the flames." Cugoano was not alone in his desire. One mariner noted "that many of them [the slaves] are unable to bear the Loss of Liberty, and try every Means to regain it." Although Cugoano did not specifically mention a religious motivation, the revolt on his ship revolved around an oath—a ritual common in many African societies. The men in the slave hold bound themselves to achieve their violent purpose using solemn practices that would have been familiar to them.[43]

From the fetters on men's feet to the armed sentries, an expectation of trouble clung to the slave ship. One group of scholars recently estimated that one out of every ten voyages saw a slave revolt. Shipboard insurrections remained a constant and troubling threat. Newton confessed that it was this tension—not moral scruples—that drove him from the trade. During one voyage the mariners were "continually alarmed with their almost desperate attempts to make insurrections upon us . . . when most quiet they were always watching for opportunity." The effrontery of the slave ship itself, rather than any specific acts of violence, sparked shipboard insurrections. One ship's carpenter asked the male slaves aboard his ship why they tried to seize the ship. "The reasons that were given me were, 'What business had we to make Slaves of them, and carry them away from their own country? That they had wives and children, and wanted to be with them.'" Separation from home, the loss of family, and the desire for liberty motivated the uprisings that sailors feared and slaves anticipated.[44]

Standard practices of transatlantic slave ships often ironically enabled shipboard rebellions. Slave ship masters congratulated their own humanity for allowing women and children to remain unfettered aboard ship, yet this practice often facilitated insurrection. Newton "providentially" discovered a plot aboard his ship, which was facilitated by the relative freedom of the African boys. With the aid of thumbscrews, Newton secured the confession of four boys who smuggled "knives, stone, shot, etc., and a cold chissel" to the men in the hold. Cugoano's revolt also relied heavily on the participation of those dwelling outside the men's cabin, for it was "the women and the boys which were to burn the ship." Recent studies add statistical weight to these anecdotes about the participation of women and children in shipboard rebellions. European assumptions about gender granted women greater access to information and objects useful in facilitating revolts.[45]

Since the number and participation of women in rebellions displayed regional variation, certain cultural influences might have facilitated these uprisings. Parliamentary investigations often asked witnesses about African practices of witchcraft and how the prosecution of witches led to the enslavement of them and their families. The crimes involved appeared hazy and capricious to Europeans, who found African sorcery to be enigmatic. One witness confessed, "I conceive it to be a sort of secret religious business, which they keep entirely to themselves." Women appear to have been more likely to be condemned to slavery for these crimes. Some women assumed a familiar leadership position when they came aboard slave ships because of their position as sacred specialists. The prominent role of women in attempted slave revolts reflected their greater freedom of movement as well as an assertion of traditional spiritual functions.[46]

Sometimes Africans overtly turned to religious practices to secure their physical release. When asked to speculate what motives lay behind shipboard slave insurrections, London merchant Thomas King identified religion as a major cause. Downplaying the responsibility of the physical conditions created by Europeans, King testified, "There are particular Nations who have religious Priests among them, that induce them to make those attempts." Newton's crew flew into a panic when they believed their ship's water casks had been poisoned. A combination of relief and spiritual superiority followed when they discovered that the slaves "only conveyed some of their country fetishes, as they call them, or talismans into one of them, which they had the credulity to suppose must inevitably kill all who drank of it." What Newton dismissed as "credulity" represented a display of traditional West African religious practice. Newton responded to their spiritual assault by turning to his own sacred power, praying to God that "they make no worse attempts than to charm us to death." Although Newton wrote off the religious means utilized in this attempted insurrection, he took heed that "it shews their intentions are not wanting." An event such as the attempted revolt aboard Newton's ship exhibited both a constant desire to escape the confines of the slave ship and a continued trust in the power of African beliefs and practices. Slaves waged a religious war against their captors, turning to traditional spiritual practices to win their freedom.[47]

The prevalence of suicide and rebellion in surviving descriptions set the slave ships apart from those narratives of the eighteenth-century passenger trade. The withdrawal of ships from the rapidly receding African coastline represented a loss of families, ancestral homelands, and spiritually endowed landscapes. While seasickness taxed their bodies, the ship and its purposes could strain enslaved Africans' understandings of the world and thus produce active resistance. Indentured servants or convicts occasionally plotted to seize ships, but few chose suicide over the voyage. Although bodies might be poorly equipped physically for a voyage's hardships and minds might retain serious anxieties about its dangers, Europeans' knowledge of their destinations forestalled the more radical kinds of resistance. The voyage produced anxiety for all but desperation for only a few.[48]

Although not all went through it equally, everyone experienced a period of adjustment to the wooden world. Seasickness did not distinguish between those who could afford a cabin room and those who berthed in steerage. Some passengers could afford better food and drink, and thus might recover more quickly, but all had to make mental adaptations to constant movement. The lucky voyagers who did not suffer from seasickness still had to come to terms with the distinct rhythms of nautical time and adjust to their new physical space. Life in the wooden world differed from the urban and pastoral spaces of Europe. Even as passengers adapted to, and sometimes enjoyed, sea life, they remained conscious of their abnormal circumstances. The enterprise seemed unnatural. "The sea was not their proper element." Religious belief offered a means to survive a voyage that many characterized as a trial.[49]

Each of the Protestant groups aboard the *Simmonds* struggled to synchronize their religious activities with the distinct rhythms of the ship, particularly wrestling with how to implement sacred performances aboard ship. Wesley's accounts noted how the missionaries struggled to secure time and space for prayers, but the accounts of other ships' Anglican ministers reflected a more hands-off approach to shipboard religious life. Ebenezer Miller's terse account of his voyage from Boston to London in 1726 to receive Episcopal ordination made no mention of liturgical observances aboard ship. Only when he reached London did he mention in his journal the spiritual activities of reading prayers, preaching, and receiving sacraments each Sunday. His narrative attached the liturgy to specific sacred sites, thus public prayers seemed incongruous with the mobile secularity of the ship. Anglican ministers struggled to create context for their shipboard ministrations, which seemed out of place in the wooden world. In response to this challenge, organizations such as the Society for the Propagation of the Gospel tried to create formal church structure aboard ship by having clergy appointed to the position of chaplain. This mechanism both helped to remove awkwardness from the performance of clerical duties aboard ship and created a formal mechanism to defray the costs of the voyage that North Americen clergymen had to make. During his voyage to Boston, newly ordained Anglican clergyman George Keith attempted to minister to everyone aboard ship. "To my observation and knowledge, the seamen, as well as the officers, joined devoutly with us in our daily prayers according to the Church of England, and, so did the other gentlemen that were passengers with us." Keith used his advantaged position, for only Anglican ministers could serve as official chaplains on British ships. Although these chaplains ministered on just a fraction of transatlantic voyages, their presence indicated an attempt to establish an official Anglican clerical presence to adapt the ministrations of the church to life at sea.[50]

Traveling in community, in a sense, allowed Moravians to ignore that they were aboard ship, or at least to employ their collective voice to combat its noisy distractions. Despite storms, the work of the ship, or other oceanic intrusions, the Moravians strove to sacralize time aboard ship in ways that captured outside observers' attention, particularly through the fervency of their hymnody, which could transcend language barriers.

After the voyages ended, the music continued to ring in the ears of English passengers like Francis Moore, who reported, "Particularly the Germans, sung psalms and served God in their own way." Benjamin Ingham claimed that the only time "you could know they were in the ship, was when they were harmoniously singing the praises of the Great Creator, which they constantly do in public twice a day." The Moravian leader David Nitschmann acknowledged the battle to redeem shipboard hours in his journal. "To me the time is precious, and passes too swiftly. It is as though we were in the midst of wild beasts, which are bound and cannot harm us."[51] Moravians relied upon each other to steady themselves amidst the hostile elements of the sea.

While Moravians approached the challenges of the Atlantic crossing through community ritual, Quakers fortified themselves to encounter the ship alone. Itinerants often sought to travel with one another, but solitary peace of mind was as important as the company of others. The contemplative nature of Quaker practice encouraged quiet reflection. During his 1772 voyage back to Ireland, Samuel Neale described how he "Sat alone, and was desirous that a heart might be given and continued, to remember the kind dealings of a gracious God, who wonderfully sustained me in this journey." Rebecca Jones similarly treasured the solitary times she found aboard ship. "Spent the latter part of this day alone in our state room, my heart being turned towards the Lord, and my confidence renewed in his sufficiency and strength, for the fully supplying of our various needs." Itinerant John Woolman praised God for both public meetings and the times he could be alone. "My mind, through the merciful help of the Lord, hath been preserved in a good degree watchful and quiet, for which I have great cause to be thankful." Friends sought quietude amidst the potential cacophony of ship life.[52]

Evangelicals depicted the period of adjustment to shipboard life as a contest of worldviews, particularly in regard to the observance and use of time. The ship served as a battleground in which secular concerns threatened to shunt religion aside, especially on the Lord's Day. To wage this war against the corroding effects of time aboard ship, evangelicals deployed the internal and external weapons of private devotions and public proclamation. For example, Presbyterian Samuel Davies took solace in the time for private meditation afforded by seasickness but lamented when the troublesome ocean would not allow him to address the crew. "May I live to God, while tossing upon it! May the sickness of the Sea, which I expect, be sanctified to me! and may our Conversation and Preaching be useful to the Company!" Although evangelicals frequently described the voyage in terms of confinement, they sought to make ship life redemptive. Davies lamented the time wasted during "this inactive Season" and hoped that he was at least "laying up proper Furniture for active Life upon Shore!" Yet, as Davies' own diary recorded, the ship provided a good amount of time for the traditional Protestant tools of spiritual growth: prayer, Bible reading, and preaching. Because itinerant evangelicals often sought to create spiritual communities through preaching, rather than ministering to the needs of a clearly defined constituency, they readily accommodated their public exercises to the times and spaces that the ship afforded while continuing to resent the ship's intrusion upon the sacred calendar.[53]

These varied disruptions occasioned by crossing the Atlantic created an opportunity to form new relationships, whether for this world or for realms beyond. People on sailing ships found themselves dwelling in smaller spaces occupied by more inhabitants—human and otherwise— than in their former homes. The new patterns of time and the abbreviated social spaces aboard ship stimulated close interactions. Confinement aboard ship produced a variety of interactions with people of different cultural and social backgrounds. The cramped, vermin-infested quarters shadowed those social interactions, but the ship facilitated sustained interchanges. As voyagers gained their sea legs, they used them to encounter their shipmates.

CHAPTER THREE

SHIPMATES

The confrontation did not bode well for the voyage ahead. On 27 October, a "gentleman passenger" aboard the *Simmonds* approached James Oglethorpe to complain about the twice-daily ritual of holding public prayer in the ship's cabin. The man who lodged the complaint, a Mr. Johnson, was the son of a former governor of South Carolina, and his social status conferred on him a cabin berth adjacent to the large open suite in the vessel's stern. The crowd that gathered in the great cabin to read from the *Book of Common Prayer* proved a "great inconvenience to him" by exiling him from his rightful place. He "strongly opposed our having prayers in the great cabin. . . . He said he could not bear to stay in the room when so many people were in it; and that he could not stay out of it while they were there, for fear of catching cold." After a lengthy disputation, which John Wesley characterized as "angry," Oglethorpe proposed a compromise. Morning prayers could take place in the cabin while Mr. Johnson slept, and the young ministers from Oxford would find somewhere else to host evening prayer. Now it was Wesley's compatriot Benjamin Ingham's turn to be perturbed: "We were forced to submit to the inconvenience of having them between decks in the afternoons." Apparently, Mr. Johnson remained unsatisfied, having only "half carried his point," for the following week he raised the issue of prayers again, this time with the captain. Two opposing parties occupying one ship guaranteed that someone would be "inconvenienced."[1]

This particular confrontation did not, in fact, foreshadow conflicts to come. A month later Ingham rejoiced "that We now again had prayers in the great cabin, the gentleman afore-mentioned having yesterday left the ship." Mr. Johnson disembarked from the ship in Portsmouth, "more and more impatient of the contrary winds," and returned to London. In Wesley's view the privilege of again having prayers was just "one of the many blessings consequent on his leaving us." Others felt differently. Francis Moore lamented the loss and saw the gentleman's departure in another light. "Mr. Johnson, Son to the late Governor of South Carolina, was taken ill here of a Fever, which prevented his going [on] the Voyage. This was a great Disappointment." Did he leave the ship because of illness or impatience? Or did ship confinement and the long delay in sailing incubate the nameless malady? Whatever the actual reason, Ingham interpreted the removal as a divine favor, suggesting that God delayed the voyage for so long purposefully to remove Mr. Johnson. "Blessed be God! who delivered us from him, for he very much opposed us. I did think, and I told it my friends, that, we could not sail while he was in the ship." From Ingham's perspective, the preemptive providential removal heralded a more peaceful voyage, but Moore grieved the loss of a gentleman whose leadership might have prevented future difficulties.[2]

Conflict was not inevitable though. "Mr. Johnson kind!" wrote a surprised Wesley in his diary a few days after the initial confrontation, noting the possibility of friendliness in addition to hostility. The dispute over conducting prayers in the cabin, nevertheless, exposed the potential for dispute among the diverse ethnicities, religious beliefs, and social castes aboard ship. The 227 passengers aboard the *Simmonds* and *London Merchant* epitomized the diversity that might exist aboard British sailing vessels in the eighteenth century. If one counts the Scottish highlanders aboard the *Prince of Wales*—which sailed to Georgia from Inverness in coordination with the Oglethorpe expedition—the resulting picture mirrors the overall flow of Europeans to North America. Germans and Scotch-Irish constituted the bulk of the emigrants, with a comparatively smaller number of

English. Often, as in cases of the *Simmonds* and *London Merchant*, individual vessels combined elements of this diverse migrant flow. The maritime workers aboard these ships contributed even more diversity. Historian Marcus Rediker succinctly describes the intermixture of British crews who seemingly "came from almost everywhere: from every corner of England, America, the Caribbean; from Holland, France, Spain, all of Europe; from Africa and even parts of Asia. Regional, national, and ethnic identities abounded in the ships of the world." Transatlantic ships carried motley crews as well as variegated human cargos.[3]

The heterogeneous quality in the human composition aboard ships was especially evident in terms of religion. Atlantic travel narratives from the eighteenth century reveal a kaleidoscope of practices and beliefs from multiple continents. Europeans of varying backgrounds intermixed on British sailing vessels without the establishment of any single religious tradition. Anglicans (traditional and evangelical), Moravian Pietists, Salzburg Lutherans, and Quakers all traveled on the *Simmonds* and its consort the *London Merchant*, not to mention the wide-ranging spiritual loyalties of the crew. Englishmen increasingly expected that the spiritual comforts of their church would accompany them across the globe, and in this vein, Wesley and Ingham conducted frequent services in the Church of England tradition aboard the *Simmonds*. Yet, as the opening conflict with Mr. Johnson showed, the presence of these services in transit was negotiated, not established. The ship was not parish. The numerous faithful adherents of other Protestant traditions from across Europe ensured that only a fraction of those aboard ship would participate in Wesley's prayer meetings.[4]

Francis Moore's account of the *Simmonds*'s voyage recognized that the practices of the established Church of England did not sail alone. Although the Church of England ministers preached, prayed, catechized, and administered the sacraments on ship, "Mr. Oglethorpe shew'd no Discountenance to any for being of different Persuasions in Religion. The Dissenters, of which there were many on board, particularly the Germans, sung Psalms and served God in their own way." Moore's adulation credited Governor Oglethorpe with maintaining the peaceful coexistence of competing religious sects, but further study reveals that faiths commonly intermingled on eighteenth-century voyages. The process

Moore attributed to Oglethorpe's singular skill, in reality, repeated itself on voyages large and small. Embarking on a transatlantic voyage often meant sharing close quarters with other religious faiths.[5]

The process of acclimating to the close quarters of the ship extended the full duration of the voyage, but passengers often assessed their ship-mates near the beginning of their written accounts. These descriptions filled the narrative void occasioned by delays in sailing, as was the case in the *Simmonds*'s dispute over cabin usage. In the absence of the exhilara-tion of setting sail, voyagers wrote about the other people who occupied the ship. This descriptive process continued after departure as the trials of going to sea forced interactions that could be avoided while the ship remained in contact with the shore. Once on the Atlantic, there was no more escaping the Mr. Johnsons of the wooden world. For better or worse, people remained stuck with one another aboard ship. Once at sea, they were irrevocably shipmates, but did they constitute a community?

Historian Stephanie Smallwood has argued that in comparison to European passenger vessels, the slave ships forcibly transporting Africans did not constitute cohesive communities but instead "brought strangers together in anomalous intimacy." Her phrase "anomalous intimacy" sa-gaciously captures the essence of the slave ship. "Anomalous" captures the abnormality of grouping together various African peoples whose lan-guages and cultures might differ from one another as much as from the Europeans who carried them. Slave ships did not carry communities but rather motley assemblages of people who lived in extremely close, per-sonal contact with one another. Over the length of the Middle Passage, their intimacy might produce relationships, and even a community of sorts, but the subsequent disaggregation of these human commodities through the internal slave trade could destroy the connections. The possi-ble products of this anomalous intimacy, however, survived in the fictive kinship relationship between "shipmates." Runaway slave advertisements from colonial South Carolina testified to the tight bonds formed aboard ship. Masters often assumed that slaves who escaped at the same time would remain together because they "both came here in one ship." The evidence of enduring relationships formed on ship has led some scholars to argue that "the bond between shipmates . . . became a major principle of social organization in widely scattered parts of Afro-America." Anomalous intimacy could indeed produce shipmates.[6]

Although not to the same degree, European emigrants also found themselves in close contact with strangers whose languages or customs differed from their own. Obviously, these (largely) free migrants faced a vastly different set of mental and material circumstances aboard ship than the enslaved Africans. Nevertheless, eighteenth-century British vessels carried a diverse set of passengers to North America. Except in cases where entire communities, such as the Moravians, emigrated en masse, Atlantic sailing ships brought together people of different cultures, religions, and social standing. Even when less than anomalous, intimacy remained. People crowded together aboard ships creating an unusual forced sociability even for people familiar with a lack of privacy.[7]

The first weeks aboard ship—especially once at sea when escape was impossible—manifested the multiple kinds of difference that existed between shipmates: between sailors and passengers, between men and women, between cabin and steerage passengers, and between multiple ethnic and religious groups. The ship brought together diverse elements from across the Atlantic basin that geography, politics, or belief normally kept separated. Studying the human effects of the evolution of the ship, "foremost among all man's tyrannous appliances," social geographer Sidney Reeve noted, "The elements of a society do not consist of persons but of *relationships between* persons." The environment of the ship facilitated interpersonal connections between the diverse societal elements on board. Sometimes these shipboard interactions fostered conflict, but they also promoted mutual understanding and begrudging acceptance. Atlantic voyagers divided the same physical space of the ship into a complex mosaic of social, cultural, religious, and sexual difference. Examining the connections made across these divides demonstrates the transition from strangers to shipmates during the voyage.[8]

The ship required a reorganization of practice to enact spiritual order on the chaotic sea. Large numbers of ministers and laity from each of the traditions traversed the ocean in the eighteenth century, leaving journals and diaries in their wake. In all of these cases, Atlantic travel proved to be necessary to the health of the movement as well as catalyst for change. Part of the change resulted from the incubation of multiple religious traditions aboard ship. Recent scholarship on religious toleration and pluralism has shown that competing Protestant and Catholic traditions could and did coexist in a number of forms across Europe, sometimes even sharing the same church building. Shipboard life, however, made the realities of religious difference starker as it collapsed living, work, and worship spaces into a single vessel.[9]

Navigating Social Differences

The physical spaces of the ship structured people's interpersonal interactions. For example, differences in social standing complicated the dispute between the ministers and Mr. Johnson over the great cabin. He resided adjacent to that space, while they lodged in the forecastle on the opposite end of the ship. The actual physical distance amounted to a few dozen feet, but the social divide between cabin and steerage remained significant. Ingham communicated his cognizance of status difference by constantly referring to Johnson as the "gentleman passenger." He used this phrase not just as a personal descriptor of Johnson but also as signifier of broader social distinctions. An episode a few days after Johnson's initial complaint further emphasized Ingham's consciousness of his social inferiority. Desiring to catechize the children, Ingham gathered his young pupils together on the quarterdeck one afternoon, but he did not teach them "because some gentlemen were there who laughed at me for it, I was ashamed to proceed." Although Ingham did not record the specific content of their mockery, his narrative suggested that he desisted because of "fear of man." In this case, the close quarters of the ships exposed Ingham to the scorn of his social betters, which dissuaded his pursuit of religious duty.[10]

Travel narratives often reflected the social divisions between cabin and steerage passengers, but they also revealed the possibility of connections across those boundaries. Aboard the *Jamaica Packet*, Janet Schaw thought her extended family in the cabin were the only passengers aboard. She was mistaken. One morning after departing Scotland, she awoke and found "the deck covered with people of all ages, from three weeks old to three score, men, women, children and sucking infants." The ship owner had crowded the hold of the ship with indentured servants from the

Scottish isles, with orders to keep them locked below decks until the ship put out to sea. They did not make a good first impression upon Schaw. "They looked like a Cargo of Dean Swift's Yahoos newly caught," she said, using language often employed to describe the herd-like numbers and activities of breeding livestock. Just as Jonathan Swift's Gulliver subsequently preferred the company of horses to people, so Schaw resolved "no more to encounter these wretched human beings."[11]

She soon found that on a small ship avoiding them would be impossible. A friendship blossomed with a young mother and her family. The encounter changed Schaw. "Where are now the Cargo of Yahoos?" she would ponder. "They are transformed into a Company of most respectable sufferers, whom it is both my duty and inclination to comfort." On shore, Schaw might have skirted past people whose filthy appearance offended her sensibilities, but on ship she could not avoid them despite her resolution to do so. The same steerage passengers who once repulsed Schaw now caused her to exult, "I have made many friendships since these last two days, and was not a little vain, on my coming on deck this morning, to hear the children with infantine joy, call to each other: 'O there come the Ladies.'" The foreign Yahoos transformed into familiar shipmates.[12]

The ship gave cabin passengers a firsthand look at the life of those economically beneath them. Sometimes the repulsion occasioned by the first impression remained throughout the voyage, but other times the human spectacle created sympathy. The Huguenot John Fontaine, traveling in steerage, described his friendship with a cabin passenger named Monsieur Isne. "His behaviour was so civil & noble that he easily won my esteem & not entirely against my will I felt compelled to be more courteous with him than with the others, although I supposed them to be of the same station." When the other cabin passengers above him disturbed the repose of his ill wife and daughter, Fontaine appealed to Isne for help. "I often requested him to complain to the captain. He not only complied, but strove to prevent them, as much as he could." Even when sympathy could not be followed with action, the plight of those confined below decks did not always go unnoticed. While waiting in Portsmouth for favorable winds, Anna Maria Falconbridge witnessed a ship full of convicts being transported to Botany Bay. The sight produced the following reflection: "The destiny of such numbers of my fellow creatures has made what I expect to encounter, set lighter upon my mind than it ever did before; nay, nothing could have operated a reconciliation so effectually: for as the human heart is more susceptible of distress conveyed by the eye, than when represented by language however ingenously pictured with misery, so the sight of those unfortunate beings, and the thoughts of what they are to endure, have worked more forcibly on my feelings, than all the accounts I ever read or heard of wretchedness before." Associations formed between individuals of different social standing proved temporary, but the impressions might last a lifetime.[13]

Life aboard ship enabled relationships that transcended class boundaries through the sharing of space. Religious meetings often enabled steerage passengers to enter the more privileged places aboard ship. The cabin crowd that so disturbed Mr. Johnson consisted of people drawn from the lower ranks and who invaded his social sphere. Quaker itinerant Rebecca Jones entreated her captain to open the main cabin for meetings, and he "appeared willing the steerage passengers might have the privilege of sitting with us, if they chose it." Later in her journal she described a crowded meeting in the cabin, which included "the Captain, cabin passengers, most of the steerage passengers, and as many of the seamen as could be spared from working the ship." Moravians similarly recorded shipboard religious meetings that brought Germans and English together with part of the crew in the cabin for evening prayers. George Whitefield used one religious meeting in the cabin to preach the supremacy of Christian truth over class standing, stating "that great men should not be angry if ministers should reprove them out of love." Religious meetings on ships gathered people of various standings into a single space and provided opportunity to critique some aspects of the social divide.[14]

The professional position of ministers not only conferred the ability to traverse the social divide between decks but also gave them reasons to visit these spaces. The Lutheran pastor Henry Melchior Muhlenberg frequently described visiting a family of Salzburgers and others below decks. "I . . . examined several of the steerage passengers as to whether they had understood and retained anything from the Sunday sermon. They declared that they had understood it all." Ingham and Wesley purposed "to visit, each of us, a part of the ship, and daily to provide the sick people with water-gruel, and such other things as were necessary for them." They sought Oglethorpe's approbation before this venture, but their clerical status and interests provided the real permission. Ministers had access to the cabin, using their religious position to curry favor of those in charge. Ship's officers in turn buttressed their own standing by cultivating friendship with clergy. As a testimony to Oglethorpe's lack of pretension, Moore lauded that "not only the Gentlemen his Friends eat at his Table, but he invited, thro' the whole Passage, the Missionaries and the Captain of the Ship, who together made twelve in Number." The captain of the *Two Brothers* invited August Spangenberg to dine in the cabin during their voyage to Georgia earlier in 1735, but the Moravian leader declined because "their light jesting was distasteful to him." Nevertheless, his position as a minister gave him a degree of mobility that other steerage passengers did not possess.[15]

Whereas those in steerage needed permission to enter the ship's cabin, cabin passengers ranged about the ship more freely, often touring and reporting on the conditions of those beneath them. A combination of surveillance and benevolence accompanied cabin passengers during their visits to steerage. As leader of the expedition, Oglethorpe maintained constant vigilance over the conditions below decks. Ingham lavished praise on the expedition leader's "fatherly care and tender compassion," which Oglethorpe displayed through inspecting "several times about the ship to comfort and encourage the people." His physical ability to enter the space demonstrated his position in the social hierarchy, and his frequent gifts to the people communicated the qualities of his leadership. Von Reck assumed a similar role aboard the *London Merchant*, having been deputized to investigate rule breakers and "to arrest those people with the assistance of the captain and deliver them to the *Simmonds*, where they will be punished." This unidirectional mobility demonstrated the hierarchical gulf between cabin and steerage passengers.[16]

Yet another cultural divide existed aboard ship, this one between the passengers and the crew. Clergy found this social division harder to bridge. The notion of the irreligious seaman had a long pedigree in Western culture, and this popular conception persisted throughout the eighteenth century. Such portrayals of the sailor built on biblical imagery of the sea and its defining characteristics. "The sea or the great waters, that is, are the symbol for the primordial undifferentiated flux, the substance which became created nature only by having form imposed upon or wedded to it." The Western scriptural tradition equated the ocean with chaos and unpredictability. The Bible used the image of the ocean to characterize people whose faith was unstable, as in James 1:6: "He that wavereth is like a wave of the sea driven with the wind and tossed" (KJV). The sea provided an analogy for the wicked whose turbulent lives filled their souls with flotsam and jetsam. Not surprisingly, the wildness and intractability of the ocean symbolically stained the men who worked upon it. Shakespeare, for example, humorously employed the prevalent picture of irreligious sailors in the *Tempest*. The sailors' turn to prayers rather than labor, shouting, "All lost! to prayers, to prayers! all lost!" authoritatively signaled the ship's doom. The seventeenth-century Puritan divine John Flavel buttressed his description of sailors by appealing to the ancient authority of Plato, who depicted sea life as "the Schoolmaster of all Vice and Dishonesty." Daniel Defoe characterized the seafaring life in *Robinson Crusoe* as the occupation "most destitute of the fear of God." Some observers universalized this label and applied it to non-Western cultures. For example, one traveler found that seagoing peoples in Africa appeared "roguish, while those in the country are innocent."[17]

People perceived sailors to be different, and few spectators then or since have been inclined to think seamen religious. The conception of the sailor as "irreligious" continues to color historical understandings. As historian Marcus Rediker summarized, "Seamen believed in omens and apparitions, but they did not believe many of the teachings of the Church of England, or any other church for that matter." Life at sea was an ongoing struggle of man against nature or of man against man, and these struggles rendered God irrelevant at best. For some, the attempt to describe maritime religion appears pointless, if not futile. However, the nearly unanimous conception of sailors as irreligious sometimes downplayed contrary evidence, to the point of excising religion from texts. The early twentieth-century editor of mariner Samuel Kelly's journal expunged the "disease" of "psalm-singing" and moralizing from the diary, acting on the conviction that these traits had little to do with life at sea. For Kelly, however, those things had everything to do with the sea.

Other accounts of seamen frequently cast their tales as religious narratives, although often rehearsed in light of subsequent conversions. An alternative reading of the sources leads to a more complex characterization of seamen's spirituality.[18]

The irreligious verdict had as much to do with class perceptions as religion. Eighteenth-century travel narratives did not uniformly depict seamen as unspiritual, but the accounts varied according to the social and religious location of the observer. Sailors stood out among the working classes. A sailor's dress, bodily ornamentation (tattoos or jewelry), and distinct speech marked his particular occupation. Simon Newman's investigation of Philadelphia's poor identified sailors as "the lower sort's single largest occupational group and also its most easily recognizable." People noticed sailors, and that identification often communicated social inferiority. Historian Jesse Lemisch summarized the rough edges of the popular perception of sailors. "In his dress he is, in the words of a superior, 'very nasty and negligent,' his black stockings ragged, his long, baggy trousers tarred to make them waterproof." One group of landsmen identified the maritime trades with poverty claiming, "They took the Sea to be fit only for those who could not get Bread by Land." A pious Scottish surgeon who enlisted in the navy to settle his debts dramatically characterized sailors in a letter to a clergyman. "I believe the demoniacs in the gospel were never more under the devil's power than many of these men are, whether we look to their lives or their language." Sailors' speech and culture offended refined sensibilities, especially when people encountered them aboard ship.[19]

Most passengers traveled on vessels whose crews joined specific ships because of the availability or compensation of the employment, but not all sailors could exercise choice. The sailors serving aboard the privately owned *Simmonds* and *London Merchant* knew that any able-bodied seaman could be impressed into the British navy. In fact, part of the delay in sailing came from waiting for the escort ship HMS *Hawk* to recruit seventy sailors. Necessity forced Captain Gascoigne to resort to impressment to reach the ship's full complement. He reported to his superiors, "the Impress-Warrants being called in . . . it would be impossible to have her so, by any other means." The scourge of impressment was the great fear of sailors who valued their liberty. When passengers recorded their interactions with sailors, they often encountered men driven aboard ships by necessity or press gang.[20]

Clerical descriptions most strongly reflected the long-standing stereotype of mariners as irreligious. Methodist itinerant Francis Asbury described the sailors on his ship as "insensible creatures" who behaved decently enough but neglected the means of salvation he offered to them. The Lutheran Henry Melchior Muhlenberg similarly found his moral instruction to be wasted on mariners, for "they shook it off as a dog shakes off the rain." Although he continued to evangelize seamen for the entirety of his three-month passage, the voyage did not raise his opinion of them: "To be among such people is a foretaste of hell." The aggressive nature of these ministers' probing into the spiritual lives of sailors put seamen on the defensive. The manner in which ministers treated mariners provoked vehement responses that further fueled clerical suspicions about sea life. Ministers attacked the ungodly activities they suspected of sailors; in turn, the prickly reaction of sailors fulfilled those irreligious expectations.[21]

This use of religious and class conceptions to lock sailors at the bottom of the shipboard social hierarchy carried over to captains and mates, whose close connections to their vessels also polluted them in the eyes of passengers. Transatlantic cabin passengers expected ship officers to behave with an extraordinary degree of magnanimity and generosity. When they failed to act according to these standards, they received harsh characterizations in voyage accounts. A later Georgian immigrant, Elizabeth Bland, wrote to Oglethorpe that "after a ten Weeks disagreable [*sic*] Voyage in a very bad Ship and rude Commander wanting every thing in this Life we arrived at Charles Town." Bland complained, "The barbarous Company and Capt. that was in the Cabbin took all occasions to pick Quarrels with us." Her language emphasized how she placed the captain on the same social plane as the ship's crew—lacking in requisite hospitality and civility. Janet Schaw similarly recounted that when "the Nasty Captain coming down to take a dram from his gin case, set all our stomachs topsy turvy by the smell," his mere appearance ruined an evening's pleasant diversions. Despite the social difference between a ship's officers and crew, the popular characterizations of sailors also stigmatized captains and mates.[22]

Much of the stereotype of sailors derived from their own actions. In a sermon directed to seamen, the Puritan divine Flavel cataloged their

chief sins as "Drunkenness, Swearing, Uncleanness, Forgetfulness of
Mercies, Violation of Promises, and Atheistical Contempt of Death."
Eighteenth-century observers frequently drew attention to these elements
in sailors' lives as proof of their religious insufficiency. Ship's surgeon
James Meikle affirmed Flavel's catalog of iniquity in his journal description of entering the ship on 7 July 1758. "This day, when I took a serious
survey of the wickedness practised around me, when I saw all fear of
God cast off, heard them on the morning of the Lord's day swearing,
and singing obscene songs, and observed the ship's boats bringing
lewd women aboard, no respect being paid to the holy Sabbath which
God has set for a sign between the Christian world and himself, yea the
very shame of sin being gone, I was filled with vexation, grief, and, might
I say, holy indignation, till my breast ached, and I was pained at my
very heart." Such taxonomies of sins reappeared in the accounts of other
voyagers and often started, as Meikle did, with a condemnation of
swearing.[23]

Swearing seemed such an inextricable part of a sailor's life that it
confounded concerned passengers. Samuel Davies discovered sailors "so
habituated to Blasphemy, that Oaths and Imprecations flow spontaneous
from them: and I am in Pain and Perplexity what Measures I shall take
for their Reformation." Whitefield wondered whether seamen could "pull
their ropes without swearing." He carried with him a sermon against
swearing and adapted it specifically for sailors when given an opportunity.
The association of foul language with maritime occupations is so strong
that even today we use the idiom "swear like a sailor."[24]

Why did sailors curse? Some scholars have noted that attitudes toward
swearing revealed class-based assumptions. One of the few occasions in
which the normally upright Eleazar Elderkin cursed in his diary reflected
class tension. After the crew caught a dolphin, the officers ate it for dinner, "but Damn the bit did the people get any." By reliance upon an
expletive, Elderkin identified with his messmates over the ship's masters.
"Such language expressed clear opposition to the 'polite,' mainly bour-
geois elements of society." Observers reported incidents of incessant
swearing more often in harbor than at sea. Swearing thus formed a large
portion of the first impressions that sailors presented. A sailor's language

transgressed most at those instances of greatest contact with the outside world, especially when landsmen interfered with their labor. Shakespeare caught this attitude in the *Tempest* when the boatswain transgressed social boundaries. Rather than obey the requests of Antonio, the Duke of Milan, he responded by giving his own orders to the prince. "You mar our labour: keep your cabins: you do assist the storm." In this sense, sailors used swearing to counter the unwanted interference of people who presumed to be their social and religious superiors.[25]

Sailors swore at sea among themselves as well. Here, the impulse toward profanity reflected gender more than class. The desire for peer acceptance and to prove one's masculinity accounted for this predilection to foul language. Mariner Simeon Crowell penned a poem that connected swearing with the need to project a certain masculine image.

> When first the sailor comes on Board
> He dams all hands at every word
> He thinks to make himself a man
> At every word he gives a dam

The desire to be accounted manly inspired much of the bravado that cursing represented, whether directed toward one's betters or one's peers. Weariness with shipboard labor also factored into word choice. Expletives provided an immediate and clear release from the tension of troubling circumstances. The African seaman Olaudah Equiano recalled one occasion when "being weary with the duty of the day, and tired at the pump (for we made a good deal of water), I began to express my impatience, and uttered with an oath, 'Damn the vessel's bottom out.'" Later, on the cusp of conversion, when encouraged to enumerate his sins, Equiano confessed, "that I sometimes swore on board ship." Swearing seemed natural aboard ship among one's male peers. While class and crisis partially account for shipboard foul language, the desire to demonstrate one's masculinity pushed much of the bluster.[26]

Some tried to make light of this predilection to cursing. Many sailors saw themselves as rowdy romantics whose manners and appearance might be weather-beaten but whose hearts remained unscathed. Mariner Henry Gardiner waxed poetic about his life at sea.

The sailor whose life is boist'rous, and whose
Manner's rough, inures to toil his weather
Beaten frame; oft enjoys a sensibility
Of heart, a sympathy of soul, that would
Not blush the fairer sex to own; or mar
The joys the good philanthropist may feel

The brusque nature of a sailor stemmed from environmental causes that gnarled his body. The vices of seamen perplexed outside observers because sailors so frequently mixed them with virtues, an apparent inconsistency that Samuel Davies encapsulated in verse, "Such daring Rebels, who in one vile Breath / Blend Prayers and Curses." The very same "offensive" seamen could display profound attention to religious matters.[27]

Those who took the time to look past the rough outward appearance of sailors found the best qualities of humanity to be abundant rather than absent. As the Anglican clergyman aboard Nicholas Cresswell's ship passed Sunday perusing a text on scurvy, the sailors consecrated the day reading the *Book of Common Prayer*. "I find these men not such an unprincipalled [*sic*] set of beings as they are represented to be," Cresswell noted. "It is true they swear most horridly in general, but when they pray, which I believe is very seldom, they do it heartily." Janet Schaw attributed the pleasing tone of her shipboard community to "the benevolence, sincerity and warm hearts we generally meet with in Sailors." Quaker itinerant Rebecca Jones seconded that opinion, admiring "the quiet, civil, and sober conduct of the whole crew, among whom scarcely an indecent or unsavory word was heard." Perhaps these observers had a thicker skin than their male clerical counterparts, or perhaps their presence drew out more decorous behaviors. But they, and others, recognized that the prevailing notions of unlimited depravity did not always portray seamen justly.[28]

Although socialization occurred across these social divisions—between passengers and sailors, cabin and steerage—travelers established boundaries nonetheless. Schaw forged friendships with steerage passengers, but she does not indicate that she ever shared a meal with them or invited them to her cabin space, and she provided no firsthand descriptions of steerage. The Lutheran pastor Henry Melchior Muhlenberg clearly loved the Salzburg immigrants who traveled in steerage of his ship and recorded spending much time with them. Nevertheless, even when his frustration with the bawdy talk and behavior of the gentlemen in the cabin reached its pinnacle, Muhlenberg continued to reside in that social sphere. Those who crossed the boundary between steerage and cabin exercised a clear choice—and they had the power to make that choice in the first place. When the Quaker itinerant John Woolman chose his ship for a passage to London, the ostentation and luxury of the main cabin offended his Quaker sensibilities. He chose a simple existence in steerage, conversing with sailors. Nevertheless, he dined and socialized in the main cabin, an option not available to his fellow steerage passengers or the ship's crew. The majority of those who made the Atlantic passage simply had no choice of where they would lay their heads.[29]

The spatial distinctions of the residential quarters clearly structured the societal configuration aboard ship. A feeling of captivity resulted from dissatisfaction with one's fellow detainees. Interpersonal difficulties often emerged during the embarkation stage of the journey, but proximity to shore offered occasions for non-ship human intercourse. The sea trapped people with their fellow passengers for better or worse. Samuel Davies succinctly expressed the social constriction of the ship. "The Ships Company, to which I am confined, are a Parcel of the most profligate, audacious Sinners, that I have ever been among." The physical space of the ship affected perception of the voyage, but so did the people in that space. A successful ocean crossing involved navigating these societal differences.[30]

Navigating Gender Differences

When women boarded Atlantic sailing ships, they discovered a physical and social space that had been engineered for men. Even on the *Simmonds* and *London Merchant*, whose carefully selected families ensured a healthier shipboard sex ratio, women experienced an added set of difficulties in this confined space. To live aboard ship was to live in close quarters with a male majority that had formulated distinct notions of gender. Sailors singled out shipboard women as scapegoats or sexual partners. Nor did ministers fit easily into the nautical world; some recorded sailors treating them as pariahs who brought ill winds. Narratives linguistically linked women and clergy as opponents of the sailors' way of life. Often it was the mariners' displays of masculinity that made women uncomfortable and clergy nervous.

Unbridled masculinity formed a portion of what set sailors apart as a social group. Furthermore, men constituted the majority of ship's passengers on Atlantic crossings; the wooden kingdom was a masculine domain. Not only did men outnumber women, they created an environment that reflected particular notions of masculinity. The treatment of women illustrated that men perceived the ship as their sphere. Even if women passengers received good treatment from the crews and male voyagers, their narratives clearly demonstrate that they had entered a male space.

Life aboard ship increased the travails that accompanied women's reproductive role. In addition to the normal difficulties of the Atlantic crossing, some women faced the added challenge of pregnancy and childbirth. Francis Moore emphasized the health of the Georgia expedition through touting the reproductive labor of some of the women: "Instead of lessening our Number we increased, for on the Passage there were four Children born." Anticipating future need, the men who had been left behind in Portsmouth had gone ashore to seek a midwife for the voyage. The wife of one of them gave birth to a young son aboard the *London Merchant* in January. The physical motions of the ship added to the struggles of pregnancy. The ministers aboard the *Simmonds* believed that Mrs. Welch, a woman "big with child, in a high fever, attended with a violent cough," to be near death in the voyage's first week. They relocated Mrs. Welch to Oglethorpe's cabin where, Wesley reported, "she earnestly desired to receive the Holy Communion, and from the moment of her communicating she began to recover, and is now in good hopes of a safe delivery." The healing properties of the sacrament notwithstanding, Mrs. Welch's physical removal from steerage to the cabin sped her recovery and she delivered aboard ship in the days after their arrival on the Georgia coast.[31]

Such births often occurred below decks in crowded steerage compartment. After describing the horrid conditions of the Scots immigrants confined in the hold of her ship, Schaw singled out the misery faced by a mother-to-be. "In this wretched situation, a poor young woman, who had been married only a few months, was so terrified, that she miscarried." George Whitefield also encountered a shipboard miscarriage aboard the *Whitaker* and administered to the woman "an exhortation applicable to her circumstances." Samuel Kelly described a nighttime birth aboard a troopship. Going "below amongst the troops soon after, I found the place completely illuminated to the great annoyance of the poor woman, as they were also very noisy." Sometimes neither mother nor child survived, as one German schoolteacher recounted. "On board our ship, on a day on which we had a great storm, a woman about to give birth and unable to deliver under the circumstances, was pushed through one of the port-holes into the sea because her corpse was far back in the stern and could not be brought forward to the deck."[32]

The close quarters and lack of privacy also produced uncomfortable situations for non-pregnant women in steerage. Traveling in the cabin with her fellow Friends, Quaker itinerant Rebecca Jones discovered the shocking "exposure" of a single woman who shared steerage with twenty-two male passengers and crew members. Jones described her as "a sober girl, and in a tried situation" and sought to protect her by "advising her that when she cannot becomingly and consistently converse with them, she had better remain quite silent if she cannot withdraw." Jones instructed her protégé to create a barrier of silence to make up for the lack of physical barriers in steerage. The openness of the space below deck appeared to lend itself to verbal and physical sexual assault. Other Quakers worried about the exposure of female Friends aboard ship. Thomas Chalkley wrote to encourage two unmarried women about to undertake the voyage, reminding them of the God-given strength of endurance and rewards for faithfulness. "And dear maidens, as your cross is great, you being two innocent young women, in giving up your names to cross the sea, which I know is a great trial, the seamen, too, generally being rude, dissolute people; so your crown will be great also."[33]

What the Quakers feared for traveling young women, two German emigrants, John Whitehead and Johann Büttner, witnessed during their 1773 voyage to Pennsylvania. In their journals both wrote of sexual promiscuity in steerage, which Whitehead euphemistically described as "the operation of bringing forth the Innocent Produce of mutual Embraces (which ought to be performed with all manner of decency and secrecy imaginable)." Although a sexual division between the sleeping quarters had been intended, "for the greatest part they promiscuously lay thro' one another: Male, Female, the Youth and aged." Büttner labeled the situation "a deplorable custom" and assigned intention to the distribution of sleeping berths. "Men and women did not sleep in separate cabins; the sixty girls were distributed among the three hundred men in their quarters." This intermixture produced open sexual activity because "there was no apartment for any private business but every thing was performed openly and exposed to the view of all." The familiarity and lack of privacy in steerage threatened to destroy a woman's character. Büttner's experience of the voyage led him to "advise unmarried women who have not the means to take quarters in the Captain's cabin, not even to enter a ship. Their innocence is much more in danger than on land."[34]

During Schaw's voyage, the ship's cooper repeatedly entered the bed of a woman in steerage. When she protested, he claimed it to be an "accident, for as their beds lay along side of each other."[35] In the dark and open spaces of steerage, women often found themselves fending off unwanted sexual forays. Elizabeth Hughes sought justice for her treatment aboard ship. Although a servant, Hughes lodged with the family she served, sleeping on the floor of the great cabin. One night she found herself awakened by the sexual advances of Archibald Ramidge, the ship's captain. When she informed her employers in the morning, they laughed off the attack. Later in the voyage, she aroused the displeasure of her mistress and master, who released her from their service and turned her over to the captain. He fastened her to the deck, "thrust an iron spike into her privy parts for not complying with his wishes . . . and then bade the crew to view her." After raping her, he confined her below decks with the crew who sexually assaulted her until the end of the voyage. No wonder Rebecca Jones and Johann Büttner feared for women "exposed" in steerage.[36]

Not all shipboard liaisons involved violence, but even romances revealed the drawbacks that women faced aboard ship. Schaw joked that Cupid's arrows found "as good sport shooting our sea gulls as your land pigeons." Her Scottish waiting woman, Mary Miller, had "got a scratch, tho' she was a very prude at land." There were two or three handsome sailors aboard the *Jamaica Packet*, "one of whom I suspect, she has Cast the eye of affection." The attention and compliments paid by a ship's officer tempered the brusque nature of the servant woman. "It is wonderful how this gentle passion has sweetened her temper, and we think ourselves much obliged to David, for so he is called, for her good humour." However, "Scandal, that sad amphibious monster" devoured the chubby deity of love. Mary discovered "he had another fair one on Board, to whom he paid more attention than to her." He even took the bottle of wine Miller had given him and used it to woo this other woman. Her initial impression of her good-looking Davy changed, "But now I think he is not handsome a bit, for handsome is, that handsome does." Davy benefited from the greater freedom he had aboard ship both as a male and as a member of the crew. He used the social barrier between the cabin and steerage passengers to mask his amorous activities in each sphere. The ship placed women such as Miller at a disadvantage.[37]

Sailors often did not know how to handle the presence of women aboard ship because they had become so accustomed to their absence. Male crews sometimes viewed women aboard ship to be "Jonahs," on whom could be placed the responsibility for seagoing misfortunes. During her voyage to Virginia, nurse Charlotte Browne described the treatment an officer's wife received at the hands of the crew. "A Great Squall on Deck of Wind and Rain the Reason of it was as the men say; because Mrs. Barbut heav'd out so soon being up before 11." Even dreaming of women foreboded an ill turn. Perhaps sailors humorously placed blame in these cases, but, good-natured or not, such accusations could carry severe consequences. A Catholic priest coming to Maryland in the prior century reported an instance in which sailors charged a woman aboard with witchcraft, murdered her, and threw her body overboard in an attempt to settle the raging seas. Eighteenth-century sailing vessels were anything but gender-neutral sites.[38]

Clergy also faced accusations of being shipboard Jonahs whose presence stilled winds and slowed vessels. The itinerant George Whitefield suspected that his shipmates believed "that our ship was looked upon with an evil eye, upon my account and that I was the Jonah in the fleet." The Lutheran pastor Henry Melchior Muhlenberg also identified with the alienation of Jonah, finding his shipboard isolation reminiscent of the prophet. "I had somewhat the same thoughts as did the Prophet Jonah, in so far as Jonah was a man. . . . They kept hushing one another in their conversation not to speak so loudly that the preacher would hear, but that only made my misery worse." Similarly singled out, clergy and women sometimes joined forces in enduring the physical and social threats of the Atlantic passage. Ministers appreciated the presence and support of women in their shipboard congregations. When sailors failed to respond to a minister's appeals, clergy gleaned encouragement from the attentive participation of women. John Wesley peppered his shipboard diary with daily religious conversations he had with women. After catechizing the women aboard his ship one Friday afternoon, Whitefield concluded he "had still greater reason to bless God for bringing me to sea." Clergy sought to resist the corrupting influences of life aboard ship and relied on women as their allies in this battle.[39]

As ministers proselytized on the ocean, many of their success stories involved female converts. Muhlenberg saw his shipboard ministry rewarded when an Englishwoman in the cabin "proved for a long time to be different from what she had been in the beginning. She showed a reverence for God's Word and disapproval of idle gossip, separated herself as far as possible from ill-behaved company, and even spoke out in rebuke when she heard anything against God." John Wesley's journal followed the spiritual meandering of a "gay young woman" named Mrs. Hawkins who afterwards paid particular attention to his religious reading. "She was always attentive and often much amazed." Women seemed to respond to clergy's ocean-going ministrations more than other shipboard unbelievers.[40]

Where possible, women turned to each other. When faced with the difficulties posed by the masculine ship space, women depended on same-sex communities of their own. The presence of a friend or another woman on board made the oceanic passage more bearable. For captain's wife Mary Parker, female companionship improved otherwise disagreeable circumstances. "With my companion Mrs. King, and the society of the ship, I seldom, if ever, found any thing unpleasant, except the pitching of the ship." The Quaker itinerant Rebecca Jones revealed her inner light to men and women alike, but she especially treasured the times when just the women aboard ship met together. One First Day afternoon they settled again and "a word of counsel and encouragement was given me, for my dear female fellow passengers, which had an affecting tendency." Later, she testified to God's "goodness and the sufficiency of His mighty power" for providing her with "suitable companions" during her travels. Cabin passenger Louisa Wells witnessed the divine presence in the society of women as she suffered through a night of seasickness and sleeplessness. "Good God! Without Thy powerful aid, could I ever have been able to encounter and overcome so much trouble and distress? but that hand which lays the burthen also gives strength to support it." Amidst the difficulties that arose in a male-dominated, oceanic environment, women took refuge in relationships with one other, providing mutual encouragement and physical support.[41]

Sailing without companions added to the hardship of the voyage. Some women described the isolation that resulted from being the sole woman aboard. Even though Catherine Green Hickling sailed with her brother, she still "was disappointed a few hours before I sailed in not having a woman who had engaged to accompany me, so that I am the only female on board." She later described the "melancholy day" when she set sail without fraternal company. She suffered that first day back at sea not from motion of the ship but from the emotions swelling up inside her. "I am not sea sick, but heart-sick." On Louisa Wells's next voyage, she feared that she would gain "very little pleasure or improvement in the conversation of my fellow travellers, nor was I disappointed. I wanted Miss Thorney." Quakers recognized the comfort brought by same-sex traveling companions. Quaker meetings often approved a woman's call to itinerate overseas when the leading of the Spirit identified another female volunteer to accompany her. This policy sought to remove the isolation and discomfort women felt when they came aboard ships.[42]

Navigating Cultural Differences

Atlantic vessels mixed classes and skewed sex ratios, and they also produced an environment that encouraged cultural encounter and exchange. The tight confines of Atlantic sailing vessels made them ideal sites for what Mary Louise Pratt has termed "contact zones." This phrase refers "to the space of colonial encounters, the space in which peoples geographically and historically separated come into contact with each other and establish ongoing relations, usually involving conditions of coercion, radical inequality, and intractable conflict." Travel brought together people normally divided by geography, religious affiliation, or social protocol, although with some barriers and discrepancies in power intact. The ship served as a marketplace of cultural exchange.[43]

Aboard the *Simmonds* and *London Merchant*, the main cross-cultural encounter took place between Germans and the English. The effects of this exchange upon the young John Wesley and the future shape of Methodism have been much debated, but it is clear that the Anglican minister spent considerable shipboard time and energy engaging the Germans. At first he grieved over the lack of English language among the Moravians aboard, expressing the wish that the shipmates would "be not only of one tongue but of one mind and one heart." His opinion of the strangers improved with contact, and he began learning German while aboard ship. On the Moravians' part, David Nitschmann noted his first encounter with the "two English clergymen, who asked concerning our ordination and our faith." The Germans used the time on ship to learn English, which facilitated the discussion of "many points of doctrine." The two sides purposefully employed the time to engage and potentially convince the other.[44]

Vessels sailing in the British North Atlantic afforded spaces that encouraged such cultural and religious interaction. Von Reck enumerated the various national backgrounds aboard ship, including English, German, French, and Irish. These national cultures could be further subdivided by their religious commitments. In addition to the famous encounter with the Moravians, John Wesley's journal noted the shipboard presence of Quakers, Roman Catholics, and Lutherans, along with those who engaged in "raillery" against Christianity. Given the growing use of black seamen in British merchant fleets, the young minister may have conversed with his first non-European. He recorded such an encounter on his return passage to England, when he spent time explaining "some passages of the Bible to the young Negro. The next morning another Negro who was on board desired to be a hearer too." Whether or not he encountered an African worldview on the voyage to America, Wesley certainly confronted Native American belief at the voyage's end. When the ship came within sight of the Georgia coast, Creek leader Tomochichi came on board. Wesley donned his religious regalia for the formal reception, and he sought opportunity for private conversation through an interpreter. The ship made such meetings possible but did not remove the difficulties that attended cross-cultural contact. Besides barriers of communication, Wesley had to overcome the walls of his own assumptions. In this case, Tomochichi possessed far more cross-cultural experience than the young Oxford minister, having sailed to England in 1734. His ocean voyage as an honored cabin passenger had created a very different set of possibilities for shipboard encounters from what most people experienced.[45]

Neither Wesley nor Tomochichi were alone in their experience of shipboard diversity. Numerous voyagers' journals recorded varying cultures intersecting aboard ship. The chronicler of the Moravians' sea congregations described "the pleasing exhibition" of the topside conversations between individuals of fourteen nationalities. This diverse group did not constitute a floating "Babel, but a band of Brothers, brought together by the call of the Lord, and animated as one, by His spirit." While unusual for its range of shipboard diversity, this voyage illustrated the type of intersections that took place.[46]

Other encounters with cultural diversity occurred on a more individual basis and with varying degrees of harmony resulting. George Whitefield engaged with a Quaker itinerant during one voyage, even allowing "(at his desire) the use of my cabin in the afternoon" to conduct a religious meeting, where the traveling Friend "spoke chiefly concerning the false pretenses and education of those who run before they are called of God into the ministry of the Church of England. Woe be unto those who give the adversaries cause thus to speak reproachfully of us." In this case, the shipboard meeting of two religious leaders contributed to spiritual Babel rather than a band of brothers. Adversarial or not, the relationship still produced shipmates, for despite the contrary message, Whitefield allowed the Quaker itinerant continuing use of the cabin. Neither man backed down from his convictions, but both learned to share the ship despite differences in their religious beliefs.[47]

Moravian passengers did more than just accommodate themselves to the peculiarities of their shipmates; they actively sought to convert them, often with disappointing results. Aboard the *Two Brothers* in 1735, the Moravians attempted to address the perceived spiritual and physical needs of the forty Swiss émigrés, but their religious instruction "met with utter indifference." Later that year, David Nitschmann aboard the *Simmonds* similarly "spoke with the Wittenberg carpenter concerning his soul." The results of that shipboard evangelization remained unspoken, but it was one of many attempts at religious persuasion aboard the *Simmonds*. Dober reported how Moravian services drew Wesley close to their community. "He likes us. We wish we could converse freely with him, so that we could more carefully explain the way of God to him." Although Wesley and Ingham did not immediately convert, as the Moravians might have desired, the seeds planted during these initial encounters might sprout later. Some have argued that there was a distinct Moravian influence on John Wesley's Methodist movement, and Benjamin Ingham later did join the Brethren and became one of their principal purveyors in England.[48]

While religious distinctions did not disappear, or cease to be important, the ship put divergent beliefs in close quarters and facilitated types of exchange across normal cultural boundaries. Ship space facilitated interpersonal religious engagement. Lutheran pastor Henry Muhlenberg devoted a lengthy passage of his journal to the theological views he exchanged with a Spanish Roman Catholic cook (aboard a British vessel). Muhlenberg overheard the cook's repeated prayers to Mary and used the occasion to assert "that the invocation of Mary and all the saints was in vain, absurd, and sinful." The cook's response demonstrated that "he understood it well," but the Spanish sailor proceeded to instruct the Lutheran minister "that they also make a triple cross, one for the Father, one for the Son, and one for holy Mary, and that that was the best means of unifying the Holy Trinity." Their discourse continued until evening when it ended with a handshake between the two men. Despite the cook's promises to follow Muhlenberg's advice, neither man succeeded in converting the other, but the lengthy conversation they had illustrates the possibilities of the ship space.[49]

Muhlenberg's encounter with the Spanish cook underlines the fact that sailors provided a primary source of cultural and religious variety. Historians have rightly described North Atlantic ship crews as "motley." One woman demonstrated the multiethnic nature of ships' crews when her town received "last night 30 or 40 poor souls of all nations—Turks, Greeks, Spaniards & Frenchmen, arrived here from a Shipwreck." The needs of maritime labor often required ships to replace sailors while in foreign ports. Mariner William Richardson found his fellow crewmen aboard the *Prince of Kaunitz* to derive from diverse backgrounds, much to his chagrin. "Such a crew as I never would wish to sail with again, they being a mixture of English, Scotch, Genoese, Italians, French, Flemings, and Prussians." Richardson's account shows that though not always producing a happy combination, the forecastle often contained a mixture of humanity. The nature of a crew's composition varied as greatly as the ports that encircled the Atlantic Ocean.[50]

Living in a confined space alongside people of other cultures could increase tolerance and acceptance of diversity. On her around-the-world voyage, Mary Ann Parker expressed the hope that soon people from other cultures would no longer be considered "mere savages." She quoted the poet William Cowper, "Skins may differ, but affection Dwells in white and black the same." Abstract concepts, such as race, assumed a different dynamic when attached to a human face. Janet Schaw penned similar expressions of shipboard sympathy regarding "Ovid, our owner's poor Devil of a Negro man on Board, who was to be laid in Irons, 'till we were fairly out at Sea." While her interest did not lead to intervention, the encounter brought the harshness of Ovid's everyday experience to her immediate attention. Others took action. As New England mariner Thomas Nicolson passed by the island of Guadalupe, he rescued a mulatto man trying to escape the island on a log. "Humanity oblig'd me to allow him to remain on board." The slave ship provided the dominant model for black-white interaction on the ocean, but the Atlantic world offered a range of other options.[51]

Black sailors and Creole travelers appeared regularly in travel narratives and their presence provided deeper interaction between African and European cultures. Olaudah Equiano's narrative portrayed one such relationship that developed between him and a young white Virginia sailor named Richard Baker. Equiano found Baker to be "an agreeable companion, and a faithful friend; who, at the age of fifteen, discovered a mind superior to prejudice; and who was not ashamed to notice, to associate with, and to be the friend and instructor of one who was ignorant, a stranger of a different complexion, and a slave!" The relationship proved to be mutually beneficial. Baker furthered the African's education in nautical life, the

English language, and the Christian religion. Equiano helped the youth from a slave society "discover" other interracial options besides prejudice. Shipboard relationships set Equiano's course toward literacy and the Christian faith. Ship space also allowed Equiano to recover some of his lost adolescence. Although still enslaved, Equiano roamed freely with the other ship's boys: "our time was spent in play."[52]

Equiano's facility at establishing shipboard friendships had roots in his experience of the Middle Passage's anomalous intimacy. He had roughly experienced the shock of isolation as a lone individual coming aboard ship, and this introduction to the maritime world colored his descriptions of later shipboard relationships. He fainted from despair after being tossed aboard the slave ship and only found relief when *amongst the poor chained men, I found some of my own nation, which in a small degree gave ease to my mind.* Gaining familiarity with someone with whom he could share information and express his fears helped convince Equiano that his "situation was not so desperate." Lacking this ability to communicate with others produced a crippling isolation. During his voyage as surgeon on the *Young Hero*, Ecroyde Claxton noted that all the slaves aboard understood each other except for one who spoke a language unknown to the others. The inability to communicate with one's fellow sufferers "made his condition truly lamentable, and made him always look very much dejected." An elderly Omar Ibn Said refused to recount his Middle Passage experience in depth, but he did relate his coming "in company of only two who could speak the same language." This brief phrase reveals the sense of isolation created by an inability to communicate and also the comfort brought by having some intelligible shipmates. As scholars have noted, these linkages helped maintain survival. "New slaves who were shipped with countrymen or friends probably survived the horrors of the middle passage and the New World seasoning better than those who faced these trials alone." Inability to communicate isolated slaves, but a common tongue established the basis of a new community.[53]

Studies of the Middle Passage have long emphasized the compositional diversity of slave ships. Captains openly proclaimed their desire to prevent rebellion by ethnically mixing their cargos to hinder communication and cooperation. William Snelgrave warned a first-time slave ship captain that he had too "many Negroes of one Town and Language," which proved prescient when a subsequent shipboard revolt took the captain's life. Yet recently historians have recognized that slave ship captains had to balance this wish to create linguistic divisions with the need to assemble a human cargo as quickly and in as few ports as possible. This desire to quickly fill ships' holds meant that the diverse people aboard would be drawn from a limited geographic range, ensuring the presence of a critical mass of culture and language for some aboard ship. Descriptions emphasizing the diverse backgrounds of those aboard ship thus also revealed the process by which connections could be formed. For example, sailor William Butterworth reported a woman who initially could not find someone she could understand among the "fourteen different tribes of nations" aboard ship. "At length, some of her own nation addressed her; and she listened with delight to a tongue as that spoken by her friends and relations, now a long way off and perhaps severed from her for ever." Despite attempts to create a waterborne Babel, slave ships inevitably carried people of shared ethnic and linguistic backgrounds. Slaves continued to bear the outward and inward marks of their originating cultures, which allowed individuals like Equiano to readily identify with "countrymen" and create the support system necessary for survival.[54]

Slave ships sometimes might have produced the cacophony of tongues desired as a security measure, but even then, slaves possessed the ability to communicate with others aboard the slave ship. Historian Marcus Rediker has ably argued for the wide intelligibility for those intermixed between decks. West and West Central Africa contained diverse populations, but these peoples had a pre–slave trade history of trade and interaction. Equiano recounted his surprise that all the nations he passed through on his long journey to the coast "resembled our own in their manners, customs and language." In many cases, shared language, not unintelligibility, characterized the experience aboard slave ships. Others noted the ease with which West Africans learned new languages. When asked to characterize the intelligence of West Africans, botanist Anthony Pantaleo How noted that they "were quick in learning languages." Stripped of possessions and outward signs of distinction, the Africans in the hold re-created semblances of their societies based on shared language.[55]

This pressure to collect a full cargo quickly also meant that a fortunate few experienced the companionship of family members during the

Middle Passage. Kinship ties enabled relatives to comfort one another and provided demonstrations of familial love that could not pass unnoticed. The mariners aboard slave ships demonstrated an awareness of these family connections among their African cargo. Dr. Thomas Trotter particularly remembered the presence of "husbands and wives, and many other relations of different degrees of kindred." His sense of decency compelled him to help nurture and maintain these bonds across the tightly maintained gender divide. Brothers and sisters or husbands and wives requested permission to eat with one another or visit above decks. When such interaction was not possible, Trotter acted as a go-between and "often carried the child from the mother to the father, who always received it with much affection."[56]

Siblings also desired to remain together in order to calm one another's fears and strengthen their resolve. When Alexander Falconbridge passed over a man for selection aboard his ship, he "observed a tear to steal down his cheek, which he endeavoured to conceal." When the doctor inquired why he cried, "he said, he was going to be parted from his brother; this induced me to take him." The cruel traffic in persons that usually dismembered families could occasionally provide touching shipboard displays of human emotion. Equiano recounted the tears of several brothers on his ship who survived the voyage together, only to be sold to different owners in Barbados. Ripped from their homes, slaves sought to maintain their last shred of family connections. On at least one occasion, sailors facilitated a reunion between a brother and sister. "The similarity of whose countenance and colour we supposed them to be relations, which we afterwards found to be true." The slave ships that so often broke the ties of kinship strengthened the bonds between remaining family members through a shared experience of suffering.[57]

Even those less favorably disposed to slave families reluctantly testified to their existence aboard ship. Robert Norris hesitated to allow interaction between the sexes, stating, "When a Man and Wife are on Board they are permitted to speak to each other but seldom." Here Captain Norris acknowledged the existence of married families aboard his ship while justifying the separation of spouses. Communication between the sexes could foster rebellion aboard ship, but mariners restricted interaction between enslaved families to alleviate other anxieties. Familial affections demonstrated the fundamental humanity of their cargo that crew members did not wish to witness and which hindered the commodification of the Africans. Some involved in the trade testified to their conviction that enslaved Africans "seem to have very little affection" nor "any such fine feelings." By denying communication between family members, slavers could assuage any lingering guilt by denying their "cargo" suffered from human affections. But the readily apparent connections between family members witnessed aboard slave ships undercut these assertions. After she had survived aboard the brig *Ruby* for three months as it collected its cargo off the coast of Bimbe, the woman slave Eve greeted her eight-year-old sister. The older sibling helped to soothe the fears of the younger, and together they found strength to endure the Middle Passage. Isaac Wilson described the tender ministration a dying man received from his sister. Every morning she immediately asked the doctor about her brother's condition and then "attended him with the greatest care imaginable." He perished, but his sister survived the passage to South America. The ties of kinship enabled survival and maintained the basic building blocks of identity.[58]

The destructive forces of the Middle Passage cannot be overstated, but neither can the capacity of Africans to assert corporate and individual identity. Cruelty occasioned creativity. Degraded and humiliated by their circumstances, individuals overcame differences to concentrate on the common need, survival. The slave ship could forge a fictive kinship between those aboard ship, with "shipmate" likened to fraternal relationships. Shared suffering created a special bond among shipmates. As one pair of anthropologists noted, "The bond between shipmates . . . became a major principle of social organization in widely scattered parts of Afro-America." Runaway slave advertisements from colonial South Carolina testified to these shipboard connections. Masters often assumed that slaves who escaped at the same time would remain together because they "both came here in one ship." Writing about the British West Indies in 1793, Brian Edwards reported, "The term shipmate is understood among them as signifying a relationship of the most endearing nature; perhaps as recalling the time when the sufferers were cut off together from their common country and kindred, and awakening reciprocal sympathy, from the remembrance of mutual affection."[59]

The distinctive aspect of slave ships was not so much the shipboard ethnic and cultural diversity (which was intentionally present) but people's ability to overcome potential isolation, maintain connections of language, and create new and sometimes lasting associations with one another. The anomalous intimacy of the slave ship meant that these connections remained tenuous. As historian Stephanie Smallwood noted, we cannot infer that shared language represented a common community, "as if people who could talk to each other can be assumed to have wanted to talk to each other." Nevertheless, communication aboard ship did furnish a means by which slaves could forge the tools of resistance and survival that would aid them in their attempts to re-create life on the American shores.[60]

Grievances as well as agreements could be nurtured through shared language, and cultural conflict characterized life aboard slave ships. Samuel Gamble reported a fight in the hold of his slave ship that led to the amputation of a slave's finger from an infected bite wound. Shipboard proximity enflamed longstanding national feuds. James Bowen witnessed the fights that broke out when "men of different Nations" were "linked together in Irons." One slave captain described how his ship attempted to avert ethnic conflicts. "We prevent that as far as we can by chaining those together who speak the same language." This mariner's testimony illustrated the dangerous side of the ship's anomalous intimacies. Although an outside identification might link shipmates together under a racial or religious label, other identities took precedence and proved more salient.[61]

Living in a confined space could produce cross-cultural conflict whatever the vessel. During his voyage to France, William Cheever had to intervene repeatedly between his French messmates and the Dutch captain. By the time they entered their port of call, he did not have a high opinion of either. Master Elijah Durfy described the conflict aboard his ship, which began with "a few words difference with the Portuguese" and ended with "some blows." The Quaker itinerant Elizabeth Ashbridge successfully thwarted a mutiny of Irish indentured servants aboard her ship because she could speak the language and overheard their plotting. The poor conditions in steerage combined with ethnic and religious difference to stimulate this attempted rebellion. The same divisions contributed to the swiftness and severity of its suppression. In the forecastle, the black seaman James Albert Ukawsaw Gronniosaw reported meeting "with many enemies, and much persecution, among the sailors." Black sailors may have been in the same physical locale as their white counterparts, but that did not always translate into smooth relations or alleviate prejudice.[62]

Shipboard conflicts assumed a sharper edge when religion was involved, as the conflict between the Methodists and Mr. Johnson over the cabin space showed. Latent tensions erupted into open clashes when those with competing perspectives shared the same space. Von Reck encountered a Quaker itinerant aboard the *London Merchant*. At first, he reacted positively to this middle-aged man, but the initial impression did not last long. "At the beginning this man acted very serious and expressed extreme distaste for the wicked life of the ship's crew; but all the while he did not notice the beam in his own eye. He bragged that he had never had a button on his hat or a pleat in his coat, and that he had never committed a deliberate sin. But he used filthy and shameful language and, in spite of his age, was as lascivious a man as I have ever seen." The close quarters of the ship allowed those with differing religious perspectives to interact with one another, sometimes for the first time, leaving lasting impressions.[63]

The Atlantic passage created a middle ground—a wooden island surrounded by water—that fostered, simultaneously, conflict and exchange. One scholar's summary of the nineteenth-century voyage could be applied to that of the eighteenth: "Cooped up on migrant ships for long periods of time, bored (if they were lucky) and increasingly at odds with one another, they fought over access to different parts of the ship, over religious observations and with the crew." Community aboard ships had to be created, and those formulations resulted in distinct, but not unique, class, gender, and cultural spaces. In many ways, the demographics of the ship mirrored the heterogeneous populace found in eighteenth-century taverns, during community festivals, or on election days, but the Atlantic passage reproduced these exceptional communities over a much longer period. Social assumptions shaped life on the ocean, and ships, although small, maintained certain facets of social boundaries even when making those boundaries somewhat porous. Yet these floating spaces mingled multitudes of religious beliefs outside the boundaries of any single institution. It was the nature of travel for "Contraries [to] coincide for the duration of a journey." Even as the physical space of the ship confined diverse people together, it fostered an individualistic approach toward life. Mutual consent rather than community enforcement governed physical and spiritual life.[64]

The different Protestant groups each faced obstacles and developed mechanisms that characterized their particular responses to social and religious difference. The eighteenth-century Anglican emphasis on increasing religious conformity in the colonies found the ship space challenging because of its unclear demarcation of spiritual authority. Nevertheless, missionary-minded clergy attempted to bring the shipboard community into a common practice of the faith. For example, Wesley was keenly aware of the paucity of communing Englishmen aboard the *Simmonds* and rejoiced when he baptized four former Quakers into his shipboard flock. He saw these additions as the fruit of his daily explanations of the doctrines in the *Book of Common Prayer*. Longstanding tensions with nonconformists colored the Anglican shipboard response toward people from dissenting traditions whom staunch apologists for the Church of England rhetorically painted as dangerous enthusiasts and rivals for power. Travel could bring these prevailing assumptions into question through the firsthand experience of differences.[65]

At the same time, the ship gave Anglicans a glimpse into non-British religious traditions, and accounts revealed that they viewed these practitioners with more sympathy and less direct competition. Ships demonstrated that the pan-Protestant ethos that predominated in the British Empire after the Glorious Revolution placed religious groups from different national or linguistic backgrounds into a category separate from the English-speaking dissenters. The various German Protestants, the French Huguenots, and even the nonconforming Scottish and Irish could be viewed not as religious threats to the standing political order but as fellow soldiers in the fight against the threat of Roman Catholic hegemony. At the same time that Protestant groups could expansively identify with Protestants worldwide, liturgical traditions remained committed to their particular tenets. The experience of a more inclusive shipboard community fostered maintenance of exclusive practices of the Protestant faith.[66]

Like Anglicans, evangelicals employed labels, such as "Anabaptist" and "Quaker," to readily identify the people whom they encountered for their audiences, but these accounts also showed the possibility for a deeper rapprochement between individual persons. For example, Whitefield's travels led to an encounter with an "Anabaptist teacher" whom the itinerant evaluated to be a "spiritual man." Although unsatisfied with the man's ecclesiology, he could rejoice in their agreement on the necessity of being born again. The group label remained but so did a desire to engage with individuals on a personal level. Shipboard evangelism necessitated sustained interaction with shipmates who wore different labels. These encounters gave evangelically minded traditions a more detailed understanding of opposing belief systems even as they sought to eliminate those beliefs. The desire to evangelize provoked sustained engagement and more detailed descriptions of opposing beliefs.[67]

Quakers engaged others aboard ship often without applying specific appellations. Rather than assess others through baseline conformity to a particular set of beliefs or rituals, Quakers emphasized how the divine light within each person undercut manmade distinctions and divisions. The Quakers' lack of a centralized liturgy and emphasis on openness fit the ambiguous nature of life aboard ship. Although they utilized group meetings, their message and goals offered a more individualized application. Quakers took advantage of a more diverse religious space. They could compete with other shipboard religious options by organizing their own meetings with the stamp of the captain's authority. Women itinerants found attentive and receptive audiences aboard ship, allowing them to exercise their gifts on neutral ground. Quaker itinerants desired to create a community of the spirit aboard ship, but their lack of a central message disappointed those who sought concrete direction. They ministered within the ship but did not attempt to order and unify its religious life.

Moravian shipboard identity derived from a clear demarcation of the boundaries between religious insiders and outsiders. The formation of *die See Gemeinen* (sea congregations) and the purchase of vessels to transport their groups en masse testified to the desire to isolate the community from outsiders. Much of the advice literature for Pietist travelers emphasized the means to maintain peace with outsiders. When the sailors got too busy or too boisterous, one pamphlet advised Moravians "to step aside" and to avoid bringing "the Sailor's Anger upon them." Furthermore, the Brethren warned voyagers to avoid placing themselves in situations that would expose them to ridicule. Physical demeanor was an important concomitant to spiritual testimony. The emphasis of the pamphlet, though, lies not on spiritual engagement but on maintaining outward friendliness. "If they give the Cook a Glass of Brandy now and then they will keep him so friendly that there will always be Room for their Tea-kettle on the Stove." Despite being proponents of an aggressive international missionary campaign across the Atlantic world, during the voyage Moravians emphasized maintaining the purity and safety of their community. Harmony with outsiders overrode shipboard evangelism.[68]

Together, voyagers from each of these Protestant traditions built their shared wooden kingdom and the divisions within it. They lacked major cultural pieces, however. The ship reduced the visible displays of property and wealth that largely defined social class. The physical distance between those of higher and lower standing was shortened even if the social divides remained. Women did not cross the Atlantic with the same frequency nor in the same numbers as men, and thus the ship took on a distinct masculine shape. Amidst the diversity of cultural backgrounds, English religious traditions found themselves to be one option among many. Wesley gathered attentive spectators but often few communicants. The ambiguity of the ship's space made it difficult to form a unified community, but passengers of varied backgrounds became shipmates. The ship facilitated encounters across multiple social divides, and as the voyage progressed those relationships held the potential to produce new understandings of each other as well as of the world. The ship steered religious faiths in different directions. The ocean served as the logistic lifeline, but it altered these approaches even as it transmitted them.[69]

CHAPTER FOUR

UNBROKEN HORIZONS

On 1 January 1736, the Germans aboard the *Simmonds* and *London Merchant* who followed the New Style Gregorian calendar observed the New Year. For the English, who still followed the Old Style Julian calendar, the date remained 21 December, marking James Oglethorpe's thirty-ninth birthday. Although for the English the year was still 1735 and not yet Christmas, everyone aboard ship reveled that day. Benjamin Ingham's diary summarized the day's festivities and the accompanying sea change in people's lives. "This being Mr. Oglethorpe's birthday, he gave a sheep and wine to the people, which, with the smoothness of the sea, and the serenity of the sky, so enlivened them, that, they perfectly recovered from their sea sickness." The Germans joined in feting Oglethorpe, presenting him with verses composed for the occasion. As the ship slid through placid seas under clear blue skies, the people aboard ship feasted on food, wine, and song.[1]

The various narrations describing the enjoyments of this inconsistently enumerated date emphasize the celebration of not just a new year or the expedition leader's birth but a definite turning point in the Atlantic voyage. The diarists sensed that something was different. Francis Moore emphasized the climatic change. Although it was "about Christmas it was as hot as in

June." Aboard the *London Merchant*, von Reck noted that "nothing particular happened except for sailing," but he immediately followed with a vivid description of the whales and sharks following the ship. For the Moravian John Andrew Dober, "It was a beautiful day, warm and calm." Benjamin Ingham echoed his sentiments, proclaiming it "an exceedingly calm and pleasant day. The sky appeared to me more beautiful than ever I had observed it in England." Even John Wesley's terse manuscript diary labeled the day's providences as "Well; lively." The language of these accounts demonstrates a change in the voyagers. With their sea legs under them, gliding into tropical climes, and somewhat familiar with the ways of their shipmates, they opened their eyes in new ways to the world surrounding them.[2]

Those crossing the Atlantic encountered not just new physical and social spaces, but a different natural order. Voyagers entered a new natural world on the way to the New World. They discovered beauty in an unbroken horizon, sublimity in clear azure skies, and zoographical abundance welling up from the deep. Even amidst the horrors of the slave ship, Africans like Olaudah Equiano found themselves enraptured by the beauty of the oceanic setting and amazed by the world of wonders around them. Once the initial wave of nausea passed and ships entered the predictable breezes and pleasing climes of the tropical trade winds, people turned their senses to the mysterious environment surrounding them. In a seemingly barren landscape, they discovered numinous wealth and variety. Travelers crossing the Atlantic encountered an inspiring natural world that broadened their conceptions of the universe's order while simultaneously increasing their belief in humanity's capabilities. This new perspective on nature instilled admiration of its beauty, instilled terror by its power, fostered solitude by its immensity, and created awe through its wonders. At the same time the natural Atlantic pointed voyagers to seek answers for its mysteries in other sources. In this way, the oceanic environment engendered increased reliance on both God and man.[3]

Beauties of the Deep

The stark oceanic landscape accentuated its beauties. The monotonous regimen of the ship's diet and activities might temporarily divert voyagers' attentions from aesthetic pleasures, but inescapable scenes of splendor surrounded them. The sometimes spectacular, but often ordinary, beauties of the ocean provided rich meditative sustenance that contrasted with their previously known lives. The nineteenth-century journal of Bostonian James Savage nicely encapsulated the uniqueness of the ocean's beauties. "On land, where there is an endless variety of beautiful objects to be illuminated with different degrees of lustre, the sensation is very different." Virginia Presbyterian Samuel Davies used the word "variegated" to contrast the beauties of land with those of the sea. Davies expressed appreciation for the visual stimuli of the ocean, but he found those scenes to lack the variety that made life on land so enjoyable. Wonders appeared at sea in fewer numbers but often on a grander scale. Simplicity created an excellent stage for sublimity. As Ingham noted aboard the *Simmonds*, "The clouds are finely variegated with numbers of pretty colours." Seaborne communities discovered natural beauty in the sky and sea and in the creatures dwelling therein.[4]

When at sea, Atlantic voyagers beheld two expanses of blue separated by an endless horizon. Bostonian Catherine Hickling described both the attraction and ennui occasioned by this oceanic vista. "The motion of the Vessel prevents me from writing, so I will go up on deck, and look at vacancy, for I am surrounded by nothing, the sky above, the water beneath, and God every where." In the absence of lofty church spires, thick forests, and undulating hills, those on ship beheld the unbroken sky. "Beautiful" sounded the repeated refrain upon viewing this sight.[5]

The rising and setting of the sun at sea especially created awe in those who beheld the spectacle, especially those who had never sailed the ocean before. In the pages of his journal, cabin passenger Henry Ingraham sketched a sunset scene, which he also painted in words (figure 4.1). "The Setting Sun this Evening was beautiful & I was so lucky as to persuade Miss Hall to stay upon Deck to view the same in all its Splendour. It threw its rays all around, Shew its drunken face & sunk as it were in the bottomless Deep." In addition to the benefit of sensory pleasure, such vistas raised some voyagers' thoughts to the divine. George Whitefield exulted at sunset "in the works of the Lord, and the beauty of the great deep." During a previous Georgia voyage, a Lutheran pastor exclaimed, "The setting sun presented such a magnificent view on the water and in the sky that one could only admire but not describe it. We reflected that

FIGURE 4.1. Pen sketch of sunset, 1802, Henry Ingraham's Journal, Courtesy of the Massachusetts Historical Society

if the creation is this beautiful, how beautiful must be its Creator!" The ships' physical space may have seemed confining, but it also expanded the experience of the natural world and its pleasures.[6]

Atlantic voyagers found natural beauty even in the terrifying storms of the Atlantic. Ingraham found beauty not only in the oceanic sunset but also in the tempest: "Believe me it is a scene sublime to the Eye as well as horrible to the thoughts." During one storm later in the eighteenth century, the newspaperman Benjamin Franklin Bache ascended onto deck with a friend "for the purpose of contemplating the beauty of this spectacle." Beholding the terrifying display of nature's power only for a moment, he then dealt with its effects, returning below decks "to bale out the water; which had come into the chambers in great quantity, and to tie down the sick who were turned upside down." Some felt a rush of excitement from the wild ride occasioned by storms. As Bache noted on the day after the storm, "For my part I was very well satisfied with having enjoyed so fine a spectacle and with having escaped the danger without accident." Storms mixed the terrifying and the beautiful, and the Atlantic passage brought voyagers into contact with both.[7]

Oceanic creatures aroused the voyagers' appreciation and curiosity. Von Reck's description of the grampuses (probably a reference to killer whales) and sharks that swam in the *London Merchant*'s wake revealed the intersection between personal observation and sea lore. "The grampus is a sort of whale, their power concentrated in their tails, with which they are said to be able to destroy a ship!" The sleek power of this sea creature clearly attracted von Reck and caused him to seek further information about it, probably from the presumed authority on all things oceanic, sailors. The mariners seem to have fed von Reck's appetite for information, but they embellished the facts by emphasizing the mammal's ability to destroy ships. Von Reck's description of sharks further demonstrated the seamen's practice of playing on the passengers' fears and credulity. He recognized them as "dangerous beasts" with "gluttonous appetites," and he added a further detail about the shark's ability "to cut off a leg in one or two bites." Since this particular expedition did not witness any deaths by sharks, the predator's rapacity and the ease with which it severed limbs must have come from mariners' yarns rather than observation. Von Reck's account indicated the overall fascination of voyagers with sea creatures, and it also explained the sometimes hyperbolic elements of their descriptions.[8]

Dolphins attracted great curiosity from those aboard ship who admired the beauty of their appearance and power. "We have caught a very handsome dolphin. I had never seen one, and one may imagine how its beautiful colours have struck one," reported one traveler. Another described the dolphin as "the beautifullest fish that ever I saw long & slender with a forked tail of a beautiful variegated green mix'd with blue spots." Whitefield "delighted with seeing the porpoises roll about the great deep." He derived religious instruction from their beauty stating, "O Lord, the sea is full of Thy riches! marvellous are Thy works, and that my soul knoweth right well. O that I may live to praise Thee for them!" For travelers, dolphins represented the unexpected delights of the sea voyage.[9]

These pleasing reflections on the beauty of the creature often arose from more mundane needs—sailors and passengers caught dolphins to eat them. The beauties of oceanic life that passengers described often served as prologue to a freshly killed rather than heavily salted meal. A German on his way to Philadelphia in 1728 connected the beauty of the dolphin with its dietary value. "We caught some exceedingly beautiful large fish, which the English call Dolphins, and were delicious to eat, the broth tasting as good as if from a chicken." One sailor noted how they "live like heroes to day you may depend" as they dined on a fare of "porpoise & Daulphin." After some lean weeks at sea another logbook recorded that they "caught another dolphin & we begin to grow fat Since we began to catch dolphin." The death of the dolphin removed traces of its former beauty, "its blue colour faded, it then became green, then becoming dead it became yellowish." Man's ability to hunt the dolphin brought an end to the aesthetic experience. The impulse that created the encounter with the dolphin's beauty led to its destruction. The exotic fish and fowl encountered during the voyage inspired thoughts of sublimity but also of subsistence.[10]

The beauty of these undersea mammals often raised voyagers' thoughts. When a dolphin appeared on the deck of his ship Muhlenberg found occasion for both aesthetic description and heavenly praise. "The glory of the Creator was beautifully evident in the fish. It had the most beautiful gold and silver colors, and when we had it in a water-tub on the ship it changed its colors as many as ten times in a minute." Whitefield drew a similar "lesson of instruction" from the death of a dolphin aboard his ship. The creature "was most beautiful when drawn out of the water, but its colour soon changed. Just so is man; he flourishes for a little while, but when once death cometh how quickly is his beauty gone!" The ocean offered real, but fleeting, beauties. Such a realization put thoughts of eternity into the minds of voyagers. As one passenger noted, "The influence of climate is surely powerful in raising ideas, if not in modifying principles." The voyage seemed especially beneficial when viewed through a spiritual lens. More than just pleasing sensations, the time spent on Atlantic sailing vessels caused many travelers to reflect on life.[11]

The beauty of the ocean could make the dangers of the Atlantic passage worthwhile. "Such an agreeable temperature of air & such delightful moon-shiny Nights, as we experience just now, would tempt almost any one to traverse the Ocean." The attractions of the sea vistas sometimes tempted travelers to take unwarranted risks above decks. The Moravian Augustus Spangenberg blamed a bout of illness on his overexposure to the night air while gazing at the brilliant heavenly display of the tropical latitudes. Sea life also afforded a form of entertainment. John George Käsebier limned an amusing scene of a mad scramble resulting from an exhausted bird alighting on deck. "The Palatines chased it over the ship for a long time." At moments the sea offered pleasures that made up for its dangers and discomforts.[12]

Terrors of the Deep

The natural environment not only occasioned reflections on its beauty but also struck terror through its power. Sharks lay beneath the shimmering waters, and storms lurked over the edge of the horizon. Mariners appreciated the beauties of the sea but knew how quickly things could turn ugly. In the middle of his logbook, one ship's master found an Isaac Watts hymn applicable to life at sea.

> Each pleasure Hath its Poison too
> & Every Sweet a Snare
> the Brightest things Below ye Sky
> Give But a flattering Light
> We should Respect Some Danger Nigh

The sea had its pleasures and poisons, and passengers experienced both in a voyage's first weeks. Crossing the Atlantic required a negotiation of nature's powerful and unpredictable forces both physically and mentally. The natural forces that could make an Atlantic passage terrifying drove voyagers to seek a higher power in whom they could trust.[13]

Mariners understood nature's danger best, although not everyone recognized their knowledge. After one particularly violent storm in the Bay of Biscay, John Wesley thought the sailors to be insensible, for they "denied we had been in any danger." But sailors measured the power of storms on a different scale, judging them on the strength of the true hazard posed rather than on appearance. Contrary to Wesley's opinion, sailors understood the ocean's power and risked everything in order to control those forces. On board his slave ship, John Newton reflected on the force unleashed by the power of the Atlantic storm. "The force of the sea when enraged by the wind, is inconceivable by those who have not seen it, and unimaginable by those who have seen the most of it." The sailors knew the power of Atlantic tempests, but they also understood how to respond to those forces safely. Sometimes they found it appropriate to fly before the wind, sometimes to scud under bare poles, and sometimes to cut masts to stay afloat. By experience, mariners parsed the degrees of nature's dangerous forces and chose the appropriate reactions.[14]

Water represented the most visible and pervasive danger to wooden vessels. Even in periods of calm, the ocean found ways to infiltrate the ship. As one maritime historian succinctly noted, "Because of the way they are built and the stress they undergo, all wooden ships leak to some extent—some more than others." The passengers aboard the *London Merchant* experienced the permeability of their vessel not long after entering the Atlantic. Von Reck recorded the troubling discovery that "the ship had taken lots of water." While some crew members worked pumps to remove the rising water, others searched below decks for its source, finally locating what von Reck termed "a big hole in the stern," which they covered with several boards and "a layer of lead." Unfortunately, the water continued to encroach. As they passed the Bay of Biscay, they discovered a second hole below the waterline on the port side, which, according to von Reck, "had been gnawed by the rats." This perforation required more drastic measures. "The ship had to be tilted to one side, so the men could reach the hole from the outside, and it was closed with a wedge, which was tarred and sealed with lead." Moments like these illustrated to passengers that a relatively thin and vulnerable layer of wood served as the barrier between life and death.[15]

In some vessels this battle against invading water lasted for the entire passage. Even after the holes had been located and patched, "at least six men were at the pumps day and night" until the *London Merchant* reached Georgia. Sailors often complained about the added labor that leaky vessels required. During Charles Wesley's return voyage to England, he noted that the sailors lamented "being forced to pump without ceasing." Since the working of bilge pumps required unskilled labor, ship captains often requested—or necessity required—passengers to assist. One mariner's journal noted how "the passengers fatigue at the pump daily." Catherine Hickling reported observing the pumps which were "going night and day, I often stand at the Pump with Capn Scott in his watch, he says I am an admirable sailor." A leaky vessel changed the nature of the voyage with the rhythm of the pumps, blistered hands, and aching muscles, reminding voyagers of their fight against the element surrounding them. No wonder then that von Reck concluded his description of patching the ship's leaks with the refrain "God be praised."[16]

The ocean's combination of raw power with mysterious symbiosis increased the awe of those crossing the Atlantic. The power of nature assumed animal form as well, most often in the figure of the shark. Like von Reck, voyagers frequently commented on the size and fierceness of the predator. Many Atlantic travelers viewed nature, too, as ready to swallow them whole. Shipmaster Isaac Gorham noted in his logbook catching "a very Long Shark 12 feet Long." Another ship's log noted the killing of a mother "shark 10½ feet long in her there was 83 young sharks." Sometimes the sharks seemed to be of mythical proportions. The cannibalistic practices of sharks formed an impression on the American statesman John Adams. After catching one shark, the sailors aboard his ship "threw overboard his head and entrails, all of which the other, who was playing after the ship, snatched at with infinite greediness, and swallowed down." Another aspect of the shark, its self-control, amazed von Reck. "No matter how hungry they are, they never eat the pilot fish!" that accompanied them. This discriminating palate fostered the idea that the shark nursed a special appetite for human flesh, that the shark represented nature's desire to consume man.[17]

Sometimes man and beast struggled for supremacy in the oceanic food chain. It would seem that food carried on board ship would be safe from oceanic predators. The Georgia Trustees stipulated that on beef days, each 5 passengers shared 4 pounds of meat, with children receiving smaller shares, thus the 227 people aboard the two ships expected to consume 700 pounds of beef per week. To soften the tough meat preserved in casks of salt, ship's cooks suspended it in a net beneath the bowsprit where it would catch spray but not be constantly submerged. Although neither the *Simmonds* nor the *London Merchant* specifically mentioned any difficulties from this process of preparing meat, other logbooks record the feeding frenzy this practice aroused in sharks. One particularly ravenous shark "took from the cooks net about 16 beef" before the ship's crew could harpoon him. "After we got him on bord, opened him took the beef and cook[ed it] for dinner." Another crew similarly recovered their beef from inside the shark and further "took Eighteen young ones of her by way of Retaliation." Other crews were not so lucky. The mate of the *Elizabeth* lamented in his log that his ship "Lost our Beef by a Shark." Sharks and sailors thus often battled for the same dinner.[18]

Sailors killed sharks not for food, like dolphins, but for sport and spite. Sailors hated sharks, which represented the ocean's fiendish appetite for death. John Singleton Copley's famous eighteenth-century painting *Watson and the Shark* represented a shark attack in the waters off Cuba and visually captured the sailors' perspective. The shark symbolized an attitude of kill or be killed. The lingering presence of these predators lurking in the depths shaped maritime rituals such as burial at sea. French and Spanish Roman Catholic mariners usually transported the deceased in the hold of the ship so that they could be interred in consecrated ground, but the British navy created customs for burial at sea. Sailors prepared the bodies of their deceased crewmates by sewing them into their hammocks, placing shot or other weights at the feet of the corpse to assure its more rapid descent to Davy Jones's Locker. Not only did they not want the body haunting the ship, sailors did not want to witness their shipmate being devoured. During his 1721 voyage to the West African coast, surgeon John Atkins witnessed firsthand the "voracity" of sharks. "I have seen them frequently seize a Corpse, as soon as it was committed to the Sea; tearing and devouring that, and the Hammock that shrouded it, without suffering it once to sink, tho' a great Weight of Ballast in it." Sharks represented what sailors feared, and by attacking them they sought to stave off that fear.[19]

Dolphins and fish but were killed for sustenance, but sailors harpooned sharks out of abhorrence. Although possible to "Sauce Sum of him" for consumption, most reported that they "Let him Gow after killing him." People feared the cannibalistic taint of consuming the man-eater. Unsurprisingly, the exception to this scruple against eating sharks came when sailors served them to enslaved Africans to conserve supplies. "They are good victuals, if well dress'd, tho' some won't eat them, because they feed upon men; ye Negroes fed very heartily upon them, which made us salt up several of them to save ye Ship's provisions." The conscientious Africans who refused to eat sharks demonstrated another way in which they associated cannibalism with slave ships. The African Equiano's fear that perhaps the European sailors really did prefer human flesh was reaffirmed when he witnessed them catching and killing a shark, only to throw its carcass overboard. "This renewed my consternation; and I did not know what to think of these white people; I very much feared they would kill and eat me."[20]

Most passengers recoiled at consuming sharks, even though these fish haunted ships' wakes. Although none appeared to act with the deliberation of Herman Melville's infamous white whale, sharks certainly learned that ships occasioned meals. Sharks so often accompanied Atlantic sailing vessels that Thomas Nicolson could joke, "Even the sharks despise our company by turning up the nose & leaving us as soon as they see how badly our vessel sails." Sharks lurked in ships' wakes. Presbyterian minister Archibald Simpson spotted "a shark about eight foot long came up to the stern, & went often around us." Although the sailors deployed a hook baited with a "large piece of beef" to induce the shark to come closer, he kept his distance with his retinue of pilot fish. Whitefield marveled that "in the midst of our meal we were entertained with a most agreeable sight. It was a shark about the length of a man, which followed our ship." The lurking presence of the shark afforded diversion, but it represented a lingering threat to the wooden world. A dead calm and roasting sun spurred Benjamin Franklin to exercise his aquatic prowess, "and should have done so, had not the appearance of a Shark, that mortal enemy to swimmers, deterred me; he seemed to be about five foot long, moves round the ship at some distance." A later poem called the "Mariner's Creed" used such lingering ominous shadows for religious instruction. "Knowest thou not that death is near, / When gleams the shark in the white wake's yeast."[21]

Sharks especially trailed transatlantic vessels coming from Africa. Slave ship captains frequently recorded sharks taking advantage of the human tragedy left in their wake. Off the African coast, Thomas Phillips described the "prodigious number kept about the ships in this place, and I have been told will follow her hence to Barbadoes, for the dead negroes that are thrown over-board in the passage." Sharks stalked slave vessels as a type of natural grim reaper awaiting a timely feast. Sailor William Richardson described the near-instantaneous death of two female slaves who tried to escape over the side of the slave ship. "The boat alongside was instantly sent after them, but before the poor creatures had got a few yards from the ship the sharks had torn them in pieces, and not a fragment of them to be seen except the water tinged with their blood." Similar scenes accompanied slave ships' arrival in American ports. One observer in Kingston, Jamaica, complained, "The many Guineamen lately arrived here have introduced such a number of overgrown sharks ... that bathing in the river is become extremely dangerous." Sharks learned that the human refuse of slave ships occasioned a steady diet.[22]

The association of sharks with the African slave trade became pervasive in the eighteenth century. John Wesley himself recognized the relationship between predator and the predatory trade in his 1774 *Thoughts upon Slavery*, which described a dead slave "flung into the sea, to be devoured by the sharks." It seemed natural to connect the most terrifying of sea creatures with the deadly trade in human beings. A gripping abolitionist satire from 1792 imagined the sharks themselves addressing Parliament to demand the continuance of the slave trade, which provided the petitioners "with large quantities of their most favourite food—human flesh. That Your petitioners are sustained, not only by the carcases of those who have fallen by distempers, but are frequently gratified with rich repasts from the bodies of living negroes who voluntarily plunge into the abodes of your petitioners, preferring instant destruction by their jaws, to the imaginary horrors of a lingering slavery." More than just occasioning natural terror, these literary sharks furnished a moral compass for the British nation. The "demon fish" reminded sinful humans of the heavenly course of action.[23]

Sharks also represented the mortality that held sway over a powerless humanity. No wonder narratives sometimes contrasted the oceanic predator with the heavenly protector. When a storm cast the black sailor John Marrant overboard three times, he found a renewed impetus for the Christian life in a shark's jaws "of an enormous size, that could easily have taken me into his mouth at once, passed and rubbed against my side." Marrant "then cried more earnestly to the Lord than I had done for some time; and he who heard Jonah's prayer, did not shut out mine, for I was thrown aboard again; these were the means the Lord used to revive me." When he first encountered a grampus, Olaudah Equiano "believed them to be the rulers of the sea." "They looked to me extremely terrible, and made their appearance just at dusk, and were so near as to blow the water on the ship's deck." These creatures seemed so powerful that some voyagers assigned to them attributes of deity. Equiano wondered why such creatures of obvious strength and might did not arouse the awe of his European counterparts, who mocked his fears, "which appeared ludicrous enough in my crying and trembling."[24]

The power of the ocean with its uncontrollable forces raised questions of divine sovereignty. As wondrous and powerful as these creatures were, sight of them stimulated thoughts of one who was even more powerful, one who could "break the heads of the sea monsters in the waters." The minister Samuel Davies ruminated on "the majestic Appearance of this vast Collection of Waters," which to him suggested the "Majesty—and Power of God, the Author—and his uncontroulable Government who rules so outragious an Element as he pleases." The power of nature raised thoughts to a heavenly creator who possessed even greater might. Massachusetts mariner Samuel Russell included in his navigation note-book a hymn depicting the power of God and decorated with signs of the sea.

> The earth Jehovahs is
> With all the store of it
> The habitable world is his
> And they thereon that sit
> For its foundation
> he on the Seas haith laid
> And it the water floods upon
> most solidly hath staid

The ocean's most terrifying apparitions directed people to God for comfort and assurance. When nature threatened destruction, those on ships turned to the divine for deliverance. Encroaching water and sharks represented those elements of the sea that people feared. Some voyagers overcame those apprehensions and relied increasingly on man's ability to direct oceanic forces for useful ends and make meals of leviathans. Others recognized the limits to man's control of the seas and thus turned to God, who overruled Atlantic tempests. In these conceptions the words of Psalm 89:9 rang true: "Thou dost rule the swelling of the sea; when its waves rise, thou dost still them" (KJV). When the powers of nature threatened to overwhelm them, voyagers could always turn to one who had the power to command the waters, "Peace. Be Still."[25]

The Immensity of the Deep

The ocean aroused thoughts of God even when calm because it appeared bigger than anything passengers had ever seen. Its immensity presented a stark contrast with life on land. The Boston lawyer Josiah Quincy Jr. juxtaposed the limitations of life on land with the open horizon of the sea. "Instead of stable earth, the fleeting waters: the little hall of right and wrong is changed for the wide-expanding immeasurable ocean." Voyagers expressed cognizance of how life changed when they entered what they termed "the vast Atlantic," the "wide expanse," and the "spacious Ocean." Possibilities seemed as endless as the sea once travelers escaped the difficulties of life ashore. As the loyalist Louisa Wells noted during her voyage to London, "Never did any of us experience joy, so truly, as when we found ourselves in the wide Ocean." The expanse of the ocean seemed a natural place to lose oneself from the cares of the world, but this same Atlantic communicated one's finitude amidst a seemingly infinite sea.[26]

The intimate confines of the ship's social space contrasted strongly with the natural space through which it sailed. Despite the beauty and possibility of the surrounding azure seas, ocean travel constantly reminded voyagers of their isolation. Except for the irregular and informal convoys during wartime, ships usually sailed alone. Although the wooden hull of the ship pushed people on board together, the ocean pulled them from others. Catherine Hickling noted that she "was surrounded by nothing." The unchanging seascape reminded voyagers of their solitude and drained their spirits. Despite the joy that Louisa Wells felt in escaping Charleston, she found that "the wide expanse of Sky and Water soon tires." John Adams echoed her sentiment, sighing, "We see nothing but sky, clouds, and sea, and then sea, clouds, and sky." The ocean did not offer much in the way of company.[27]

Sometimes the Atlantic deeps seemed to bury all signs of life. As the mariner William Almy noted during one voyage, "Not so much as any fish or fowl to be seen Or any living creature." The emptiness conveyed the stark reality of distance from home. One passenger noted the unexpected appearance of a land bird, "which come and Lit on our Quarters it all most Tird to Death." A solitary bird chancing upon a solitary boat conveyed a feeling of isolation in the vast Atlantic. The lack of variety presented by the passing seas fatigued even those passengers excited by the prospect of the voyage. "The novelty of a ship ploughing the trackless ocean, in a few days became quite familiar to me; there was such a sameness in every thing (for some birds were all we saw the whole way) that I found the voyage tiresome." Initial feelings of awe at the ocean's immensity sometimes gave way to a sense of isolation and weariness. Passengers' refrains mirrored that of von Reck: "Nothing particular happened except for sailing."[28]

If the absence of other humans on the surface of the water produced melancholy, the abundance of animal life was a source of amazement. Although birds were frequently associated with nearness to land, Presbyterian minister Samuel Davies found there was "a great Plenty of Birds to be seen all over this Ocean." Numerous travel accounts echoed those words, "a great plenty," in regard to Atlantic fish, fowl, and mammals. One entry in a mariner's logbook captured this abundance of animal life. "Saw A Grate Maney Sunfish in the Wart[er] Saw devil fish Caught Sharkes and Herrinkogs Saw dolphin and Barrecooders and Olerbecores and the Warter Very thick and Black Saw Small Birds and Gulls and So forth." On a North Atlantic whaling voyage, Massachusetts sailor Benjamin Bangs described being "among ye fish as thick as bees and as wild." The profusion of creatures surrounding ships reminded some that they were the intruders in this watery world. Another mariner, Daniel Coit, described meeting "a School of Porpoises, which seamed to consist of many thousands, they followed the Vessel some miles and seem'd to regard it as some thing unusual." Janet Schaw depicted sea creatures attending a German's shipboard flute recital, "and one would think, by the number of fishes that are crouding round us, that he were the Orpheus of the water." Ships seemed strange to creatures even as the ocean's natural wealth amazed those aboard ships.[29]

The immensity of the ocean along with its endless watery landscape offered the greatest challenge to premodern sailors. How does one mark a ship's position in the absence of earthly landmarks? Mariners found the answer in the heavens. Seaman William Spavens began the geographical portion of his autobiography with a description not of ports or notable landmarks, but with the solar system. For the mariner, the stars did not just appear beautiful. They fixed one's place on the earth. Navigators used a quadrant to locate a ship's position on the Atlantic. The quadrant measured the altitude and angle of celestial objects above the horizon and was used to find the ship's latitude, the parallel distance from the equator. The process amazed educated voyagers who sought to describe it in their journals and sometimes to try it themselves. Once passengers moved freely around the wooden world, the daily ritual of fixing the ship's position attracted their attention from both pragmatic (interest in knowing how much longer the voyage would take) and metaphysical (reflection on humanity's place in the cosmos) perspectives.[30]

Calculating a ship's latitude required a modicum of education to perform the necessary mathematical calculations and was a skill that set officers apart from common sailors. Would-be shipmasters often studied navigation with an experienced captain, and the skill enabled some to move up in the world. The attempts to prevent others from learning navigation demonstrated the social mobility this knowledge conveyed. Olaudah Equiano reported studying navigation on board ship, but his instruction ceased when "some of our passengers, and others, seeing this, found much fault with him for it, saying, it was a very dangerous thing to let a negro know navigation." Mastering the immensity of the Atlantic required a degree of scientific achievement, but it also revealed the limits of human knowledge. As his ship exited the Bay of Biscay during his 1714 voyage to Virginia, the Huguenot passenger John Fontaine took the time to record in detail the method of calculating a ship's noontime position with the use of a quadrant. Although his account gave the sense of mathematical certainty, he prefaced his description by noting the vagueness of their ship's position. "We had no right observation, but we reckon ourselves to be in the Lat. of $44°33'$, but not very certain for it was cloudy and no shade." Cloudy skies, rolling seas, mistaken instruments, or poor calculations doomed ships to uncertainty about their position. Eighteenth-century mariners negotiated the immensity of the Atlantic but never fully mastered it.[31]

Even in the early stages of a voyage, the wideness of the Atlantic and its mysteries produced reflection on the finitude of humanity and the power of its creator. In a poem he penned on the inside cover of his journal Isaac Lee connected the ocean's immensity with the worship of God.

He formed
the Deeps unknown
& gave the Seas thear bound
the watery world are all his oxen
& all the solid ground

Come worship at his throne
& bow before the Lord
ye are his works and all his own
He formed us by his word

The ocean's immensity proved impressive in itself, but it also gave rise to thoughts of a greater presence who set the Atlantic within its bounds.[32]

A horizon unbroken by the structures of God or man astonished travelers by its beauty but disturbed them by its immensity. The ocean appeared so enormous, and ships seemed so small. Atlantic travelers had little trouble assenting to the words of Psalm 104:25 "So is this great and wide sea, wherein are things creeping innumerable, both small and great beasts" (KJV). Even as the ocean reminded those on ships of their solitude, it teemed with animal life beyond belief. Although the ocean's magnitude appeared untamable, man's ability to navigate its waters demonstrated both the achievements and the limitations of scientific endeavors. Sailors could successively track a ship's course across a landscape devoid of earthly landmarks, but only when conditions allowed. Sometimes the ocean's enormity necessitated a belief in an even greater presence, one that safely guided a ship across its depths.

The Wonders of the Deep

The ocean produced not only admiration and awe but also wonder. Atlantic voyagers found themselves entering a mysterious world that enthralled them with marvels that often surpassed human comprehension. They expected to see fantastic things while at sea and longed to be past the barriers that prevented them from enjoying the natural world's mysteries. Samuel Davies expressed the desire of many a passenger who hoped his seasickness would soon pass because "it would be particularly pleasing to me to survey the Wonders of the Majestic Ocean." The ocean crossing set the stage for an encounter with the divine. George Whitefield found himself "very thankful that God called me abroad to see and admire His wonders in the deep." The word "wonders" not only expressed astonishment at amazing sights previously unseen but also labeled objects and events that had a supernatural quality. These wonders could include both the ordinary providences embedded within nature and the special interventions that served as more direct indicators of the divine will.[33]

Eighteenth-century voyagers encountered wonders ordinary and extraordinary. Ships conveyed men and women through a natural world unlike anything they had ever experienced. Each creature they encountered seemed more fantastic and seemed more otherworldly than the next. While passengers frequently described dolphins as beautiful and sharks as terrifying, they thought of flying fish as wondrous. Flying fish could appear anywhere, but voyagers most frequently encountered them as they entered tropical and subtropical waters. These fantastical creatures could temporarily transport thoughts to a world of wonders even amid the horrors of the slave ship. Olaudah Equiano described his amazement the first time he encountered flying fish. "During our passage I first saw flying fishes, which surprised me very much: they used frequently to fly across the ship, and many of them fell on the deck." An animal that combined elements of fish and fowl hearkened to the bizarre hermaphroditical creatures found in fanciful travelers' tales. John Fontaine provided a description in his journal, which emphasized the mixture of elements in this single organism. "We see some flying fish, which are about 6 inches long, and have leather wings like unto a bat, and fly when pursued sometimes hundred yards and will dip themselves in the water and take their flight again, but can fly no longer than their wings or fins are wet." Von Reck sketched a picture of these and other fanciful aquatic creatures (figure 4.2). The wonders of the ocean produced memories that would last a lifetime.[34]

Oceanic wonders often stimulated reflection on nature. Flying fish amazed seafarers who connected their capabilities with the fishes' desire for survival. Zuriel Waterman penned a poem after the "very pretty appearance" of some flying fish flashing above the water.

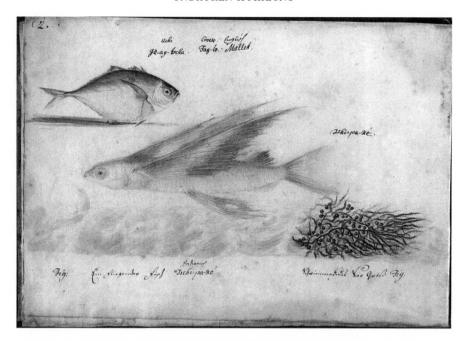

FIGURE 4.2. Sketch of a mullet, flying fish, and floating sea grass, c. 1735, in the sketchbook of Philip Georg Friedrich von Reck, The Royal Library—
Copenhagen

> The flying fish now ships o'er the sea
> Pursu'd by Dolphin with speed does flee
> But sometimes as he rises in the air
> The Birds they see him & attack him there
> Danger now attacks him on ev'ry side
> The fear of both at once his cares divide

The wondrous creatures of the ocean provided living illustrations of nature's dangers and adaptations.[35]

The ocean also aroused admiration of humanity's ability to navigate its wonders. Samuel Davies noted that "to form and rule such an Ocean is a Work becoming a God," but piloting ships through oceanic tempests displayed man's power as well. "It is most amazing how we can possibly live upon so turbulent an Element." Quincy expressed a similar sentiment about "the ingenuity, the adventurous spirit, the vast enterprizes of man" when "a little skiff, scarce a speck in this wide expanse, flew threw the waves and plyed this angry flood; braved the threatening dangers—this world of night and chaos." Man's ability to navigate the seas confirmed his own wondrous position in the universe. Even enslaved Africans could appreciate the presence of human ingenuity amid the ocean's marvels. The young, inquisitive Olaudah Equiano caught the sailors' attention as he eagerly watched the daily use of the quadrant. "They at last took notice of my surprise; and one of them willing to increase it, as well as to gratify my curiosity, made me one day look through it. The clouds appeared to me to be land, which disappeared as they passed along. This heightened my wonder: and I was now more per-suaded than ever that I was in another world, and that everything about me was magic."[36]

The sky at sea also displayed wonders that often passed unnoticed on land. The absence of a physical landscape, which marked one's daily progress, often drew the eye upward. Equiano found the clouds of this sky to be magical replacements in the absence of terra firma. The appear-ance of the sky stimulated thoughts of the divine heavens. Mariner Isaiah Pratt, aboard the brig *Peggy*, found heavenly teaching in the surrounding expanse. "The Spacious firmament on high with all the Blue ethearial Sky & Spangled heaven A Shining Frame theire graet oreginall proclaim the unwearied Sun from Day to day Doth his Creators power Display And published to Every land the work off an Allmig[hty]."[37]

Even in preindustrial Europe, before the widespread effects of fossil fuels and artificial lights obscured the nighttime luminaries, the sky daz-zled those at sea more than those on land. "This night saw plenty of Stars which To us is strange." The vast host of stars splashed against the deep backdrop of space made a spectacular impact. "Tis surely more soothing to behold ten thousand luminaries, than to see one proudly superior to the few, that dare to shine at the same moment with her, and causing all the rest of the same family to 'hide their diminished heads.'" The sky bedecked with innumerable stars proved suitable raiment for the divine when viewed by those in the wooden world. Whitefield soaked in such scenes from the deck of the *Whitaker* and turned clear nights into occasions for praise. "The evening was exceedingly calm, the sky clear, and all things conspired to praise that glorious and lofty One Who inhabits eternity, who stretcheth forth the heavens like a curtain, and holdeth the waters in the hollow of His hand."[38]

The appearance of the nocturnal sky in all its wonder caused some to reflect on its even more glorious creator. Ingham waxed poetic:

> What, though, in solemn silence, all
> Move round this dark, terrestrial ball;
> What, though nor real voice nor sound
> Amidst their radiant orbs is found;
> In reason's ear they all rejoice,
> And utter forth a glorious voice,
> For ever singing as they shine,
> "The Hand that made us is divine."

The oceanic environment furnished spiritual consequences that would accompany travelers long after the voyage ended. "The various Phenomena of the Ocean have suggested to me such Hints as might be well improved by a spiritual Meditant," Samuel Davies reflected. Nevertheless, he marveled at "those who traverse this Region of Wonders, who see so many Dangers and Deliverances, are generally tho'tless, vicious and impenitent." If humanity missed the glories of God at sea, the problem did not lie in the clarity of the display, but in the eye of the beholder. The sky at sea combined the senses of beauty, power, immensity, and wonder, and created an experience that many could only describe as divine.[39]

Sometimes the nighttime sky at sea displayed "remarkable" signs and wonders, as when mariner Benjamin Bangs noted in his journal the appearance of a "blazing star in ye West." Sailors often read these un- usual phenomena as signs of future events, particularly the weather. The Huguenot James Fontaine noted one such wonder, "At the rising of the moon a star rose close after and followed the moon, which the sailors said was a great sign of a tempest and upon the like occasions that it com- monly happens." John Wesley experienced the storm-borne phenomenon of what some mariners called St. Elmo's fire. "Toward the end of it we had an appearance on each of our masts which the ancients called Castor and Pollux, the modern Romanists *corpus sanctum*. It was a small ball of white fire, like a star." Sailors interpreted this phenomenon to be a good omen, even though it appeared in the middle of the storms, because it often signaled the end of a tempest. Mariners connected these natural phenomena with supernatural forces. Seaman Samuel Kelly noted, "Sailors in general, call these lights 'corps sants,' which I imagine is a term used by Popish seamen, and the meaning is that they suppose it to be the spirit or corpse of a saint."[40]

Certain wonders defied explanation altogether and amazed even the most experienced mariner. The ocean did not give up its secrets easily. One woman noted the deceptive power of the oceanic environment with the appearance of plants and animals hundreds of miles from land. "Well might poor Columbus be deceived and conjecture himself not far from Land!" Another logbook noted the appearance of a "very remarkable thing" just after sunset that changed color and direction several times. "The first appearance of it was like the shooting of a Star w[ith] a long continued Stream of fire from it this continued in a streight line & of a fiery colour the space of one minute then chang'd to a purple its form then alter'd to that of a Snake w. a tale at ye upper end having a motion like a pendat at a Vessels masthead then chang'd to a light blue & alter'd its form nearly resembling a W this continued in sight 15 minutes & keeps its places w[ith]out moveing in ye air." The log keeper offered no explanation but did attempt a sketch of its movements, illustrating that some wonders of the Atlantic could be described but not understood.[41]

Other celestial signs found a ready-made interpretation in the pages of the Christian Bible. Shipmaster Nathaniel Bowditch recorded in his logbook the evening appearance of a "very bright lunar rainbow" at the end of a day filled with "brisk breezes, variable weather, squally, rain, clear." The appearance of rainbows caused some to reflect on the purpose of such wonders. "Today God permitted us to see a rainbow at sea for the first time and we made use of it to strengthen our faith." The rainbow served both as a wondrous natural phenomenon and as reminder of God's covenant promise with Noah.[42]

Although scholars describe the eighteenth century as the great age of man's enlightened reason, sea journals reveal that there was still plenty of room for the wondrous, especially on the oceans. Logbooks normally focused on the measurable phenomena of the oceanic travel, but even they reserved space for recording the remarkable. The unique creatures and the starry hosts testified to the limits of humanity's understanding of the universe. Herman Melville's nineteenth-century sea writings linked this theme of the ocean's unfathomable mysteries with the inscrutability of God. For eighteenth-century Christians, these wonders pointed to a God who used the natural order to reveal the divine glory. The words of Psalm 107:23–24 resonated in their ears and hearts: "Those who go down to the sea in ships, who do business on great waters; they have seen the works of the Lord, and his wonders in the deep." The ocean certainly had its wonders, and while these spectacles remained navigable and observable, they often defied explanation. These marvels simply remained wondrous indicators that the boundaries between this world and the next were not so broad.[43]

When the passengers of the *Simmonds* and *London Merchant* entered the Atlantic Ocean, they discovered a natural world that delighted their senses and provoked their thoughts. Bostonian Josiah Quincy Jr. later well expressed this feeling: "While thus surprized and gratified, I rejoiced to think of my undertaking; and was pleased with the hopes being wiser and better." While voyagers found beauty in the sea and its creatures, they missed the variety provided by the earthly landscape and manmade skylines. When voyagers sailed out of sight of land, they experienced the ocean's immensity. In its vastness, the sea offered rich prospects to those given the chance to view its splendor. Sharks and storms threatened voyagers with destruction and symbolized the violence of the oceanic order, yet humanity could marshal control of those forces. The ocean's beauty also contained power. Yet as isolating as this experience was, the ocean still proved navigable to man and still seemed small compared to God. Each of the four Protestant traditions traveling on the *Simmonds* and *London Merchant* derived instruction from the natural world surrounding their ships, but that knowledge filtered through distinct aspects of each tradition. The experience of the ocean's natural environment produced awe of God and man and left voyagers hungry for understanding and guidance.[44]

Even a short voyage communicated a new experience of the natural world. When the naturalist William Bartram sailed from Philadelphia to Charleston in 1773, oceanic beauties enraptured him. "Nothing can be more sublime than the view of the encircling horizon, after the turbulent winds have taken their flight, and the lately agitated bosom of the deep has again become calm and pacific; the gentle moon rising in dignity from the east, attended by millions of glittering orbs; the luminous appearance of the seas at night, when all the waters seem transmuted into liquid silver; the prodigious bands of porpoises foreboding tempest, that appear to cover the ocean; the mighty whale, sovereign of the watery realms, who cleaves the seas in his course." Ever the keen observer of his physical surroundings, Bartram grasped how different a perspective the oceangoing vessel offered: one seemingly empty but beautiful nonetheless. Although the view appeared unvaryingly empty around the points of the compass dial, nature filled the void with ever-changing celestial and natatorial scenes.[45]

CHAPTER FIVE

CROSSING LINES

Almost three weeks after racing out of Cowes Road into the Bay of Biscay, the *Simmonds* and *London Merchant* glided across an invisible boundary line—the Tropic of Cancer—that marked a major turning point in the voyage. They had been experiencing pleasant weather and warm temperatures for over a week (in areas that still draw tourists and cruise ships), but on 30 December 1735 (O.S.), they formally entered tropical waters. The word "tropic" itself derived from the classical Greek word *tropos*, which means turning. The Tropic of Cancer marks the most northerly position of the sun, occurring on the summer solstice, after which it turns south toward the equator. Crossing of this line also meant a physical change in the ships' direction. As von Reck recorded in his journal: "On the 10th in the morning at 10, we passed the Tropic of Cancer. Having to this point steered Southwest by South, we now changed our course to Southwest by West." North Africa was the closest mainland to their east, but the ships now sailed more west than south, having picked up the trade winds, which Benjamin Ingham described as blowing "much the same way all the year round. The air is balmy, soft, and sweet." This arc of wind along with the North Equatorial Current carried the ships through tropical waters for ten days until they again traversed the Tropic of Cancer as they now headed northwest. Just these physical changes in the surrounding environs showed that crossing the line represented a pivotal transition during the Atlantic passage.[1]

The ships' physical location also spurred sailors to celebrate a key rite of passage for their trade—the sailor's baptism. Seasoned mariners roughly initiated sailors who had never previously crossed the tropical line (a ritual repeated at other significant oceanic boundaries, for example, the equator) through shaving and ducking the neophytes, the swearing of oaths, and drunken celebration. On this day, the ship transformed into theater and the social hierarchy inverted, as the seasoned male sailors performed the roles of Neptune (and sometimes Neptune's female attendants). The ship's captain and officers receded into the role of audience as these mythological powers came aboard to demand payment and obeisance from the green hands. The assorted accounts of passengers who observed the ritual showed the multiple levels of meaning accorded to these mid-sea actions. Some witnesses recoiled at the bawdy aspects of the ceremony, which might include cross-dressing and heavy sexual undertones. Others feared the ceremony as a disruptive challenge to the normal power structures of the ship, as common sailors made demands on their social betters, including passengers. Still others dismissed the rite as merely a charade for sailors to get drunk and avoid work. Sailors themselves viewed it as one of their traditional rights to maintain their own cultural brotherhood and experiential authority.

Aboard the *Simmonds*, Oglethorpe forbade the rite's performance despite the fact that "the sailors wished to adhere to their custom of initiating those who crossed the Tropic of Cancer for the first time." The Moravian John Andrew Dober did not provide a specific reason for the prohibition, but Oglethorpe's ban displayed unease with the ritual and its possible effects. Perhaps he remembered the disorder created aboard the *Anne* in 1732 when to prevent the ducking of passengers, he had to promise "the Ships Crew to give it 'em in money when he came ashoar." It represented an interruption of the ship's normal routine and hierarchy, a turn he did not wish to take. His boycott seemed to have been ship specific, because on the *London Merchant*, von Reck observed the sailors' "strange habit: all who have not passed the Tropic of Cancer have to be ducked in the water!"

Unlike most observers, von Reck noted the portability of the ceremony and its long, widespread history. "They use the ceremonies at the equator, at the tropics, at the polar circle, at the Newfoundland Banks, at the Strait of Gibraltar, in between Denmark and Sweden and at the Dardanelles." While Oglethorpe denied the ceremony as an unwanted intrusion upon the order of the ship, von Reck viewed it as a strange, but prevalent, practice of seamen everywhere. Despite the sometimes painful hazing that first timers experienced, sailors regarded "ducking" as a "good time."[2]

Noting the ambiguities within this ritual's practice and the various meanings assigned to it is central to its historical usefulness. Sailors celebrated the crossing of the line as an Atlantic holiday that turned the world upside down for a day. Passing over the tropical line and the ceremony that celebrated this crossing symbolized the larger cultural blurring that took place aboard ship. Ship space condensed social distinctions and also brought distinct absences of mainland culture to the forefront. Some of these changes elicited commentary from travelers, but others seemed to pass unnoticed. The ritual of sailors' baptism illustrated both open social disruption and deeper cultural currents of change. The ship undertook cultural shifts alongside its physical tacks in direction.

In particular, the crossing-the-line ceremony highlighted the gendered ambiguities of ship space and the absence of religious institutions. The ship skewed the natural sex ratios of land, creating a cultural space that emphasized women largely by their absence. Certain aspects of the ceremony, which themselves transgressed social norms, reflected the realities of shipboard sexual demographics. The labeling of the ceremony as a "baptism" along with other religious aspects of its performance highlighted the absence of religious authority aboard ship. Even though the *Simmonds* and *London Merchant* traveled with larger numbers of women and ministers than normal voyages, their presence brought forward the difficulties both clergy and females faced in an environment normally governed by mariners accustomed to acting in their absence.

At least three elements demonstrate the gendered nature of eighteenth-century sailing vessels as connected to the absence of institutional religious authority. First, the ceremony itself intermingled religious and gendered elements into its practice. It symbolized realities present throughout the entire voyage but which received verbalization at this particular moment. Second, necessity meant that shipboard men assumed duties often performed by women ashore. Basic human needs required males to perform labor that society considered feminine. In response, sailors assumed a hypermasculine persona that often troubled religious authorities like Wesley. Mariners celebrated those male qualities—boasting, jesting, fighting, and drinking—that so offended their clerical observers. Shipboard ambiguity encouraged male aggression that countered the expected decorum instilled and practiced in churches. Finally, shipboard journals, letters, and poems reveal otherwise hidden male desires for absent women. Sailors lamented the absence of heterosexual companionship even as they enjoyed homosocial conviviality. These longings sometimes stimulated religious thoughts and increased reliance on the divine power that could maintain mutual safety and fidelity despite separation. The various turns of the tropical waters brought these aspects of ship life to the foreground, especially in the rite of initiating sailors. Examining the crossing ceremony closely opens the door for seeing the deeper effects that shipboard gender and religious dynamics subtly worked on voyagers.

Reading the Rites

Crossing the Tropic of Cancer and entering the Trades brought material changes to the working lives of sailors. Von Reck succinctly summarized the qualitative change in their existence. "When the sailors come into the trade wind, they set all sails and topsails and rarely have to change them but just let them stay up day and night. Then the sailors can sleep calmly, take their meals quietly and have time to spin their yarns, &c." In the Bay of Biscay, the frequent storms and the threat of a lee shore (land that is downwind of the ship) necessitated a high degree of vigilance on the part of sailors and more frequent changes in sail configuration. Parts of the North Atlantic made heavy labor demands upon sailors, often in frightful conditions. In the tropics, labor did not cease, but its pace and quality changed. Sailors possessed more sea room both physically and culturally. It is no coincidence that the tropics formed the background to the "deep play" of the crossing ceremony.[3]

By the eighteenth century, the crossing ceremony was a ubiquitous element of ship life, practiced on European vessels regardless of the ship's nationality. Sailors' baptism pervaded both the formal documentation of ships' voyages and the informal accounts of individuals. Normally, the keepers of ships' logs did not comment much on the daily lives and activities of sailors. Strictly defined, logbooks recorded the measurable particulars of a ship's direction, rate of progress (measured by the use of an apparatus called a "log," hence the name logbook), and position, if discernable. During the voyage, the logbook tracked a vessel's course across a featureless landscape allowing the ship's master to determine the time and heading needed to reach port safely. Logbooks allotted some space for describing a day's remarkable occurrences, and the rite of initiating sailors entered into this space.[4]

Even the tersest eighteenth-century logbook entries sketched out the main features of the ritual. Connecticut mariner John Palmer noted in the 13 February 1777 log entry of the *Revenge* that "this Day We Crosed Tropick Line and We had full imploy of Shaving the hands and Swearing them." Usually Palmer briefly mentioned the crew's various shipboard labors—for example, "under all sail imploid it Setting up Wriging etc.,"— but when they crossed the line their "imploy" consisted of initiating "the raw lads." Palmer's account highlighted two major aspects of the initiation ceremony, shaving and swearing. The Reverend Thomas Prince documenting his voyage earlier in the eighteenth century prioritized two other aspects: drinking and ducking. "By our ob[servation] yesterday noon we f[oun]d ourselves past ye Tropick of Cancer. In 4 H afternoon accordingly a list of 12 or 14 was brought in yt hadn't cut it, one of w[hi]c[h] refusing to Produce his Bottle for ye general Entertainment was by ye Prevalence of Marine customs, duck'd [thri]ce from ye M[ai]n Y[ar]d arm." The shaving, swearing, and ducking of first-time sailors served as the common experience shared by all of the crew, regardless of their diverse social backgrounds. It bound sailors to a world ritually set apart from the passengers they carried.[5]

These brief logbook descriptions do not capture the harshness or specific content of these rites. Other sailors' narratives provided a fuller picture of what each of these descriptors meant. Sailing before the mast as a common seaman, Connecticut mariner Eleazar Elderkin described in detail his first crossing of the equinoctial line. After he worked in the rigging and cleared the decks in the morning, the afternoon watch began with the uninitiated secluded in the forecastle while the seasoned sailors completed the preparations to greet Neptune's arrival. Around 1:00 p.m., "we were hail'd with a trumpet and ask'd if any of Neptune's Children were there we answered yes." One by one, Neptune called each green hand on deck where they were immediately "blindfolded and kiss'd by Neptune." Neptune then placed Elderkin's hand on the pump and made him swear to the following oaths.

that I would never leave that pump till she sucked

that I would never go up the lee Shrouds when I could get up the Weather ones

that I would never kiss the Maid when I could have the Mistress

that I never would let a fresh hand pass without serving him as bad, as myself was

The sailors then strapped Elderkin to a chair where he "was Daub'd all over my face with tar, slush and hog Dung—they shav'd with an old rusty knife." Neptune placed a speaking trumpet in his mouth and commanded him to hail the line, but as Elderkin spoke "a Bucket of water was poured into it which almost strangled me—had then five or six more hove in my face." Finally Neptune led Elderkin to a mock baptismal font where he was sprinkled and cleared. Evidently no worse for the rough treatment, the young sailor concluded his account asserting, "We had a fine Afternoon and a good deal of Diversion for the whole Ships Company."[6]

The particulars of the initiation might vary. Sometimes a more elaborate cast of characters might appear, including sailors dressed as female sea nymphs or Neptune's wife, Amphitrite. Other oaths—such as, "Never to drink water while you can get grog [or] Never to eat brown bread while you can get white"—might be added to the basic stipulations. Rusty barrel hoops might serve for razors and "fowl's and hog's excrements, tar and grease, mixed together for a lather." The celebration afterward varied in the flow of alcohol and ribaldry, "but the scene generally ends with a bucket of grog from the captain, when songs, toasts and jokes circulate till the bell rings for eight, then the watch is set." For sailors this ritual served as an essential part of community formation and the transmission of certain cultural forms from one generation of sailors to the next. Samuel

Robinson referred to the ceremony as being "brothered," a term that captures the ritual's role in building shipboard male camaraderie. Despite the variations within the rite, its chief purposes for sailors combined practical commitments upholding the well-being of the crew with enjoinders to aspire to a higher quality of life. The rough treatment created a sense of belonging to the group and strengthened the solidarity of a group typically drawn from motley backgrounds. Finally, the moment occasioned a holiday of sorts, giving sailors a welcome break from the grind of their round-the-clock working lives and an excuse to consume alcohol in excess.[7]

Passengers fixated on this final purpose. In their estimation, the sailors simply desired to get drunk and be abusive. Janet Schaw gave a detailed description of the visit of "Tropicus . . . preformed by an old rough dog of a Tar, who needs very little alteration to become a callaban in mind and body, but his wife is played by a very handsome fellow, who is completely transformed." The amusing spectacle took on more sinister overtones as the shaving commenced. "The sharp notches soon brought blood, and the poor devil starting from the pain, tumbled into the boat amongst the water, and thinking it the sea, roared with terror." Even more disturbing, Tropicus threatened to perform the ritual upon all passengers who did not pay five shillings each. "Tho' many of the Emigrants appear sensible, yet all Highlanders and Islanders are so superstitious, that they may be easily imposed on, in such a thing as this." Panic ensued and violence threatened as Highlander men prepared to defend their families. Schaw and her brother vigorously protested to the captain, who replied that "it was the custom, and only intended as a little drink money to the sailors." Once an acceptable sum was collected "they returned three cheers . . . and serenaded us with the favorite song":

> O grog is the liquor of life
> The delight of each free British tar

Voyagers linked the ceremony with alcohol consumption, finding the sailors' references to the customs of the sea shallow excuses to demand liquor from them.[8]

The drunken inversion of authority and the relaxed frivolity that line crossings occasioned were not quite universally experienced aboard Atlantic vessels. Ships actively carrying slaves from Africa do not seem to have performed the rite. Presumably all the European sailors underwent initiation as they crossed the Tropic of Cancer on the voyage to the African coast. Captain John Newton described his Liverpool slave ship's initiating eight new men in "compliance with the customary form observed in crossing the tropicks." Similarly, Samuel Robinson described his boyhood experience of the ritual on the way to Africa, emphasizing how the playfulness of the rite could "serve to smooth down the harsh points in a sailor's life, otherwise it would be intolerable." European sailors having been initiated on the way to Africa had no need to experience the rite again. Significant numbers of those initiated European sailors, however, succumbed to disease and died on the African coast, necessitating that they be replaced by whatever maritime labor could be found. Emma Christopher's study of slave ship sailors discovered a significant multiracial presence among the crew. While sharing the labor of the ship, those replacement mariners do not seem to have undergone initiation into the shipboard brotherhood, at least not during the Middle Passage. The potential powder keg of a rebellious enslaved cargo did not lend itself to the levity and power inversion that the initiation rite represented.[9]

On European ships, however, the ritual was so common that Moravians felt compelled to warn their Brethren and Sisters about the practice. "In a certain Climate the Seamen have a Custom to dip those that pass them the first Time, at which they commit some disorderly things." The Moravians advised that the discomforts of this ceremony could be avoided through payment in the form of brandy. The ritual's "disorder" came from inverting multiple aspects of daily life, including males dressing as females, open expression of thoughts possibly mutinous in other contexts, and the consumption of much larger quantities of food and drink than the normal ration.[10]

Modern scholars have compared the crossing rituals to charivaris or other folk festivals that maintained bottom-up cultures apart from the strictures of church or government.[11] Eighteenth-century observers drew the same comparisons between these popular traditions of land and sea. Like so many other passengers, the Lutheran pastor Muhlenberg critiqued the useless frivolity of the ceremony. To him, the crew merely "wanted to play." He also saw the rite as a kind of folk robbery, in which these lower-class sailors extorted funds from their social betters. It was not the alcohol, however, that Muhlenberg found so offensive. "They were not to think, however, that I begrudged the poor fellows, who had many a hard and laborious hour, a necessary refreshment." Instead, Muhlenberg objected to the "heathenish" aspects of the rites that crossed established social boundaries. Muhlenberg lamented: "These old customs are hard to abolish on water and land. How difficult it is on land to wean the peasants away from the kermis and Whitsun ales! It is just the same with the old customs at sea. They are ancient privileges and they will stick to them come life or death." The use of the word "ales" as a synonym for festival emphasized the importance of drinking at these popular events, but they also served as a means of addressing a community's needs. During these "ancient" folk celebrations, as Judith Bennett notes, "ordinary people— many of whom faced hard poverty during at least some portions of their lives—looked not only to the 'better sort' for relief, but also to each other." While it seemed as if the crossing ceremony merely provided an opportunity for sailors to have a good time, sailors created a community-building exercise that invited total participation.[12]

Although passengers recorded both the ritual and ribald aspects of the ceremony in their narratives, they focused heavily on the consumption of alcohol. By concentrating on the role of alcohol, passengers exaggerated the avarice of seamen and contributed to the popular association of sailors with heavy drink. As the crossing ceremony demonstrated, shipboard revelry often resulted from intoxicating spirits. For many, drinking was synonymous with sailing. As Shakespeare had Stephano demonstrate in *The Tempest*, sailors often celebrated the pleasures of alcohol in song. One sailor tucked the following ode linking drink and camaraderie into the pages of his logbook.

Come here is a Little Charming Liquor See how brave how Clear it Looks
It Would make a Cripple for to Caper and the Lawyear burn his Books
It would make a madman Run Distracted & a Dumb man Set & Sing
It would make a Coward Draw his draper heres a health to george our king
if there is any Blockheade around us Refuses will my health to Pleage
Do wish him quite confounded under him old Roten hege
and the French pox over take him on his nose it may appear
and his wife a Cuckold make him to sume Jovel Cavellier . . .

o here a health unto you gentlemen on you now I Let it fall
You may have a Little of this Liquor if I Dont Chance to Drink it all

Sailors alleviated the hardships of ship life and enlivened otherwise unre-
markable circumstances when "all got boozed."[13]

Sailors resorted to alcohol for a variety of reasons, but mariner Samuel
Kelly nicely summarized the general impulse when he noted that they
"drunk pretty freely, I imagine to drown their troubles and exhilarate
their spirits." Seamen also used the ritual of drinking to tie the bonds of
fellowship. As one mariner noted after a pleasant day, there was "plenty
of Punch and friends enough while it Lasted." Whether imbibing formal
toasts to wives and sweethearts on Saturday night or their daily ration of
beer at mess time, sailors aboard ship seldom drank alone. Drink formed
the basis for male sociability. While his captain tarried on shore, Noah
Robinson and his mates made themselves "verry happy in the Cabbin
Drinking Punch and Smoking Segarrs." Sailors used alcohol in a ritual of
remembrance for the friends and relations they left behind. Liquor could
also anesthetize sailors to the harsh environment in which they sailed.
Inured to the harsh sea elements, sailors sought comfort in a "can of
flip." Alcohol brought forth mirth out of misery, such as when it "Sprang
up a very heavy Squall of Reign and Wind and Being our Watch on
Deck We had a fine Wetting frollick."[14]

The crossing ceremony exemplified how sailors used strong liquor as a
respite from their harsh existence. Alcohol and ship life went hand in
hand and inspired Whitefield to compose a sermon on drunkenness,
which he readily and repeatedly tested before shipboard audiences. While
decrying the dangers of drink for common seamen, observers frequently
took greater umbrage at drunken officers. The behavior of the captain
during his return voyage shocked Charles Wesley, for it appeared to be
"nothing but punch, and drams, and drunkenness without end." Even
sailors complained of commanders whose penchant for strong liquor
interfered with the running of the ship. During the Seven Years' War, the
sloop *Roby* chased down a straggler from a British convoy and found the
captain "in his glory he was so Drunk he Could hardly stand." Such
behavior on the part of the captain cast a ship into grave danger, but it
also diminished the social distance meant to separate captain from crew.

Common seamen usually managed the ship capably when drunkenness disabled officers, but their social position made such control unseemly in the eyes of observers. Most passengers thought that the better classes ought to run the ship and thus expected officers to behave better.[15]

Contrary to popular opinion of them, common sailors generally knew their limits and the dangers to which drink exposed them. Although reputed for their uninhibited revelries on shore, merchant seamen accustomed themselves to moderate rations on board ship, recognizing that the limited supply of alcohol would have to last the entire voyage. When the crew on passenger Adam Cunningham's voyage discovered someone stealing wine, "the principal rogue was hanged up at the main yard's arm and then plunged into the sea for 3 or 4 times successively." The sailors dealt out this punishment primarily because they had almost expended their supply of liquor and the water alternative was "very loathesome to drink." Alcohol was necessary to the voyage. It furnished the grounds of male sociability, served as a means of social control, and constituted the primary means of potable hydration during the months-long voyages. Observers lamented the inebriation of sailors, and officers sometimes punished it. But as historian Greg Dening put it, the necessary role of liquor made "drunkenness an ambivalent crime."[16]

Others did not think such frivolous activities so innocent, and many critiques focused on the dangers of drunkenness. Quaker itinerant John Woolman reasoned "the poor creatures" apply "to strong drink to supply the want of other convenience." The addition of drink to the nature of the sailors' duties made for a dangerous combination, both for them personally and for all on the ship. Mariners literally stood one step away from death, and alcohol did not make them surefooted. "Tripp fell over board and was drowned one Night, I suppose in a state of intoxication," noted one mariner in his diary. Drunkenness meant that mariners might be "verry inattentive to duty." Mates controlled the fate of everyone aboard ship, and a drunken decision could leave the ship dismasted, run aground, or worse. Drunkenness also contributed to shipboard conflict, removing the inhibitions that restrained brewing disputes. Drinking encouraged frivolity and camaraderie in shipboard societies, making the time pass amiably, but it also aroused fear and conflict that created barriers to community formation. When the crew of the brig *Betsey* became inebriated, they "Got A Fiting with Clubs & A hammer And Bruse themselves Varry Bad."[17]

The crossing ritual allowed the performing of activities that society would perceive in other contexts as major transgressions of social norms. As Schaw noted and as Oglethorpe feared, the ceremony disrupted the ship's order, giving temporary primacy to cultural experience over legally defined authority. The ceremony allowed sailors an accepted means of voicing demands for higher-quality rations and fair treatment. Their afternoon of drunkenness countered the daytime productivity expected of laborers and gave sailors accustomed to seemingly ceaseless labor a non-calendric holiday. The ceremony transformed each of these potential offenses into farcical transgressions forbidden as realities but allowed as symbols. These turnings of social norms through ritual rendered them less offensive but not less meaningful. The rites and vows expressed the difficulties and deprivations inherent in seamen's daily lives. It was these practices that Oglethorpe prevented and von Reck witnessed as the ship entered tropical latitudes.

Gender Confusion

The crossing ceremony visually illustrated the effects of the gender imbalance aboard ship. For some observers, dressing as sea nymphs and greeting other sailors with kisses strayed dangerously close to homosexuality. Mariners not only crossed geographical boundaries, such as the Tropic of Cancer, but necessity required that they break down society's sexually based divisions of labor. The oddness of the single-sex environment appeared most evident to cultural outsiders. As the young African Olaudah Equiano surveyed whites for the first time on the deck of the slave ship, he had lots of questions. One of the first revolved around gender. "Where were their women? had they any like themselves? I was told they had: 'And why,' said I, 'do we not see them?' they answered, because they were left behind."[18] Equiano was not the only one who suffered confusion. Ships muddied the waters of gender, leaving sailors to navigate the tricky shoals of life without women. Their separation from women created many ironies for maritime men. Operating in a same-sex community, sailors had to do "women's work." At the same time, seamen projected an appearance of hypermasculinity through storytelling, drinking, and fighting. They verbally celebrated their masculinity most during those tasks that seemed least manly.

Men performed all the necessary shipboard tasks, but certain labors— such as cooking, cleaning, and mending—still connoted gender. These responsibilities bore a stigma of inferiority, but aboard ship, men, rather than women, suffered this ignominy. In compensation for their labors, cooks received less pay and more grief. In his description of the crossing the line ceremony, the Massachusetts lad Samuel Curson singled out the ship's cook "who was last initiated, much questioned, berated, and then soundly ducked." Connecticut mariner Solomon Scovell reported the flogging of the cook Coffee Jack for an unnamed offense aboard the brig *Digby*. On his voyage, Benjamin Franklin reported "our steward was brought to the geers and whipped, for making an extravagant use of flour in the puddings." Sometimes such punishments issued forth from the authority of the officers, but other times common seamen inflicted the penalties for perceived offenses. When the cook aboard William Palfrey's vessel delayed dinner to an unreasonable time, "the Men determin'd to Cob him as they call it" with a thick piece of oak. Such judgments showed that sailors considered cooks to be beneath them, not because of outward markings like sex but because of the gendered nature of their work. In the masculine shipboard hierarchy those who bore the least risks and responsibility received the most opprobrium.[19]

The ships did more, however, than simply designate certain men to perform the labor normally done by women. Shipboard communities depended on the breaking down of gendered conceptions of work. Sailors' tales lauded the dangerous jobs of reefing and furling sails in rapidly deteriorating conditions, but the chores of cleaning and mending more accurately characterized daily shipboard labor. The "sundry tasks" that shipmasters described in their logs often revolved around labor typically associated with women. Sometimes masters assigned to Sunday "those things that are Necasary to be done such as Washing, mending, and &c." Other ships' logs depict cleaning and twisting yarn as part of everyday life. Mariner Elijah Durfy expressly linked the weaving work of sailors aboard the ship *Rebecca* with the tropical line. "All hands Imployed makeing Sinet this day Crossed the Line or tropic of Cancer." Sailors wove an odd number of rope scraps together into sinnet, flat woven, often decorative cord-age used for chafing gear. Eighteenth-century sailors made sinnet for practical purposes aboard ship but added their own ornamental touches, which displayed their creativity.[20]

Most sailors became practiced in the art of needlework, a skill neces-sary for mending the ship's sails as well as their own clothes. Samuel Kelly described being "kept much at work both in the tops and on deck, in mending and shifting cloths in the sails." Another sailor poetically lamented the drudgery of such tasks.

> With handing & mending, our work is never
> ending, for any thing I See, untill the day we die

Mariner and future Massachusetts attorney general Robert Treat Paine logged a day "full of Scenes of Sorrow & Dejection," in which the crew carefully mended the mainsail only to see it shredded by a violent wind. Shipboard labor often required the manly, weather-hewn hands of sailors to perform delicate work in addition to more brash duties. All forms of labor were not equally desirable to sailors, but men had to perform all the shipboard chores.[21]

This underlying sense of labor confusion fed sailors' open attempts to demonstrate their manliness. Although mariners often found these sundry jobs monotonous, when performed by groups these tasks furnished occa-sions for male socializing and community building. As von Reck noted aboard the *London Merchant*, in the tropical latitudes sailors "have time to spin their yarns." This phrase referred to both the manual weaving work done by mariners and the verbal spinning of tales aboard ship. As the crew members gathered on deck, they verbally "spun yarns" of manly exploits while they physically wove hemp scraps into rope or mats. Storytelling and song proved effective means to assert masculinity while engaged in such seemingly emasculating tasks as mending or sewing. Elderkin summarized an uneventful week by noting, "All hands are Employ'd every day in work-ing up old junk into Mats for the Ship &c." These leisurely labors enabled sailors to craft a manly reputation through conversation and song.[22]

Seaborne minstrels frequently emphasized the trait of heroism. One nautical poet called his shipmates to heed his tale, which centered on that most valued quality:

> Come all you Joval Seaman, with Courage Stout & bold
> that Value more your Honour, than Mysers do their Gold

Manly courage required doing one's duty in spite of horrifying conditions, and music encouraged sailors to fulfill their oaths. Their songs illustrated the qualities that sailors sought to inculcate, but they also allowed experienced sailors openly to demonstrate their manliness in calmer waters. Joseph Pinkham's log of the ship *Falcon* lauded the bravery of whalers.

> Come all ye jovial mariners who plou' the seagoing main
> Who go to sea in merchant ships and safe return again
> Pray listen to my story which I must now relate
> Concerning us bold whaling men and our most dismal fate.

The celebration of whalers represented an assertion of prowess and authority. All sailors experienced risk, but some dared more than others.[23]

Sailors' songs celebrated martial as well as nautical courage. The *Simmonds* and *London Merchant* sailed during a time of European peace, but their companion warship signaled the possibility of conflict and the need for readiness against Britain's traditional foes. Versifying the experience of battle provided another means for mariners to demonstrate heroism to their peers. Their "hearts of steel" set sailors apart from other men, as William Spavens sang:

> How little do the land-men know
> Of what we sailors feel,
> When seas do mount and winds do blow!
> But we have hearts of steel.
> No danger can affright us,
> No enemy shall flout,
> We'll make our cannons right us,
> So toss the can about.

The numerous imperial wars of the eighteenth century tinged the Atlantic with blood of sailors. Seafaring men encouraged in one another the resolve to shed more. Amidst the Seven Years' War, a Rhode Island mariner prodded his shipmates to bravery against the French:

> Again should proud Rebellon Glow
> Or bould in Versions spread its wings
> Then armed Revengefuld Revengefuld in your forces
> To save your Cuntry & your King
> All Couragous Couragous generous wise
> The antigallicans shall rise

Sailors who had served in naval vessels recounted their heroic deeds in the face of battle in order to augment their standing in the forecastle and also to encourage such traits in new seamen. Even when the repeated eighteenth-century wars between Britain and France and Spain were cold, chanteys allowed rehearsal of those virtues that constituted the British tar's "heart of oak."[24]

In addition to being the subject matter of songs and poems, shipboard storytelling in itself demonstrated male competitiveness. Sailors sought to outdo each other with tales of bravery, sexual exploits, or just plain humor. The ritual of Saturday night toasting often transitioned into tales of manly conquest of women. The men aboard a colonial privateer spent the evening "talking about there wifes and Sweetherts which held till twelve aclock PM and in drinking Toasts and Singing Songs and telling the bigest Storeys that we could muster as for the rest that we did talk about I shall not minuate it down." Sailors competed not just through claiming greater conquests but tried to outdo one another with their ability to tell such tales. This weaving of good tales furnished another means for male sailors to entertain each other aboard ship while outdoing each other in manly arts.[25]

Humor proved to be entertaining as well as competitive. Simeon Crowell entertained his messmates with stories he drew from the Apocrypha. "And finding this seemed to pleas them it raised my vanity and increased the pride of my heart." One shipboard songwriter amused his watch with a song about a drunken Church of England cleric.

> Give Ear to a Comical story I'll tell
> tis of an old Doctor you know Very Well
> who tho Grave as a Saint Got as Drunk as all Hell
> it was one Sunday as all Have a greed
> for ye Doctor he held it a part of his Creed

that ye Beter ye Day ye Better ye Deed
He sat & he Drank & he tosted old Crissey
But he Her suspected he Er should prove tipsey
& When he had gotten Drunk as ten Bears
He put on his surplice & staggerd Downstears
tho not able to speak he Resolvd to Read prayers
to ye Desk then he Came & Bowed low on Each Side
ye will Rise & will go to my father he Cryd
But stumbled & provid that he Dambably lied
to ye psalms then he got but would you know how
He spewed on King David & Likely I trow
for he was as Drunk as was David old sow
to ye Collects he got them with great Hesitation
While ye Company were all in Grand Expectation
Instead of a prayer Came an Ejaculation
& Now in Respect ye Gown & ye Band
How Bravely must flurish ye Church & ye Land
Supported on pillars Not able to Stand
    tol de Rol lol Daidle Didle De

This ditty entertained through mocking a minister's inability to hold his liquor and perform his duty, a feat often attempted by sailors. Verse again connected sailors closely to alcohol as a means of displaying manliness.[26]

Mariners verbally admired the ability to handle strong liquor, thus drinking provided another display of masculinity. Alcohol often served as the axis of male sociability aboard ship. One sailor of the era claimed, "Liquor is the very cement that keeps the mariner's body and soul together." Drinking was tied to the hardships of nautical life as well as being enmeshed with other masculine virtues. One shipboard poet focused on the purpose of liquor.

If there is Pleasure on the Seas it is when the Wind and Weather is faire
with a bowl of Punch here is to you Jack Thanks Tom Lets Drink &
    dround all cares
hardships there is fool well you know and where we Done Not flinch
    @ all
Dark dismal Night and Lofty Seas Contreary wind Rain haile and squall

Drinking both encouraged joviality when there was little work to be done and steeled men's resolve when labor threatened life. Bostonian William Downes Cheever described the aftermath of a sailor falling overboard and drowning. "When soon the wine was ready, the poor young man was forgot even by his poor ship mates." Alcohol cloaked their emotions and helped them avoid potentially paralyzing fear.[27]

Alcohol also instigated more violent displays of masculinity. In his diary, cabin passenger Nicholas Cresswell made the connection between liquor and aggression. "I believe every man aboard (the Captn., Passengers, and first Mate excepted) are drunk, swearing and fighting like madmen." Sailors frequently proved their mettle through both organized fights and spontaneous brawling. Mariner Samuel Kelly listed boxing matches as part of his larger initiation into the world of British naval ships. "In my watch I was stationed in the tops and was trained to the exercise of small arms, as a marine, and to frequent boxing bouts with the other boys." Olaudah Equiano similarly described participating in such sport "for the diversion of those gentlemen" who rewarded the combatants with cash prizes. Shipboard fights also arose spontaneously. Muhlenberg grieved over a drunken brawl that disturbed the nighttime peace of the steerage compartment and injured one of its occupants. "The drunken sailors continued their violent fisticuffs, and the one tailor, who was a mild, quiet man, tried to separate them and was stabbed in the breast with a knife."[28]

When preaching to sailors, ministers often addressed the sins issuing forth from the same-sex community. In a widely circulated tract for seamen, the Puritan divine John Flavel cataloged their chief sins as "Drunkenness, Swearing, Uncleanness, Forgetfulness of Mercies, Violation of Promises, and Atheistical Contempt of Death." Ministers throughout the eighteenth century encouraged seamen to leave behind swearing, drunkenness, and fighting—those things that demonstrated their manliness. Clergy saw sailors demonstrating a model of masculinity that competed with that of Christianity. Woolman used the experience of young men aboard ship as a model of how not to live. "The present state of the seafaring life in general appears so opposite to that of a pious education, so full of corruption and extreme alienation from God, so full of the most dangerous examples to young people." The seafaring life exposed sailors to vice, but it also allowed them to shirk those Christian responsibilities expected of male heads of household. Sailors accustomed themselves to life and labor in a same-sex environment that ministers viewed to be sinful, yet their songs and alcohol-laced performances revealed deeper desires for things absent in the wooden world.[29]

Male Desires

The sailors who shared the forecastle with Eleazar Elderkin doodled on the cover of his journal a debate over whose sweetheart surpassed the others. One lauded Miss Mary Cushman as the "Chief Ornament of Her Sex." Another fancied "Miss Catherine Forrester of Lively witt— Distinguish'd Beauty—Large Fortune—and an Honour to the Female World." The journal's owner, however, felt "none can come in Competition with Miss M Bissell for every thing that is virtuous & Sensible." Shipboard verse was similarly competitive, extolling the qualities of each sailor's woman over all others. Sailors noted the absence of the women from their shipboard lives, and alcohol greased the expression of their internal longings. Drunken revelries also facilitated expression of bawdier imaginations about women. Surviving documents from mariners indicate that, though distant in body, women never strayed far from men's thoughts. Shipboard celebrations like crossing the line helped to give voice to these inward longings through poetry and public performance.[30]

Logbooks recorded the wanderings of the heart in addition to charting the course of the ship. On a scrap page in Robert Treat Paine's logbooks he doodled pictures of unnamed women and whales (figure 5.1). Some logs simply repeated the names of loved ones like a mantra. Connecticut mariner Aaron Bull repeatedly scrawled "Abigail Bull" on the tattered covers of the logbook. Another sailor, Owen Arnold, similarly peppered his wife's name throughout the log of the *Nancy*. These daydreamed scribbles sometimes gave way to more in-depth expressions of longing. In June 1755, Arnold noted how life back in Rhode Island seeped into his unconsciousness. "Last Night and this Morning I dreamed Very Much A Bout home I thought I was talking With My Wife A Bout Avaith Making the Bedsts." Sometimes sailors chose to express these yearnings through correspondence. In a letter to an unnamed woman, Benjamin Davis confessed how he suffered from oceanic separation, "My heart is wounded with greafe when I thinke of you."[31]

These private longings received public expression through the ritual of weekly toasts in honor of those left behind. On his voyage to Virginia in 1774, Nicholas Cresswell described the practice: "This evening drank our Sweethearts in a large Can of Grog. It is a custom at Sea on Saturday nights." A Massachusetts mariner logged his convivial encouragement toasting, "Boys make a Can of flip hear is Love to wives an Sweat harts." Although sailors' reputation for profligacy caused some to discount the authenticity of the ritual, seamen raised a glass to the women they desired. Massachusetts passenger William Palfrey thought the ritual to be "only matter of form" to his companions, but he recorded how, nevertheless, they faithfully "spent the Evening as usual. In Remembrance of wives & sweethearts." Other occasions for celebration supplemented this weekly remembrance.[32]

Sailors expressed their desires for women through these rituals, but these longings fostered community among men. The sailors aboard the *Rebecca* in 1744 roasted one of their companions for his successful courtship of a Nantucket woman.

> And up he goes in a great heat
> And with a female chanced to meet
> And after giving compliment
> He let her know his whole intent

The good-natured ribbing ended with a gift of shoes for the shipmate and would-be bridegroom. As in the crossing the line ceremony, humor and teasing about the courtship of females helped to create cohesion among men. The sailors aboard the British warship the *Prompte* derived ongoing amusement from a parcel of letters they discovered in a piece of misplaced luggage. "They were read over, which caused great diversion, as they were copies of love-letters and full of sweet words, as 'my darling,' 'my angel,' and wishing he had wings like a dove to fly to his dearest love." The amusement did not end even after a shabby purser claimed his bag, for the "words 'my angel' and 'O my darling' were quizzing words long kept up in the *Prompte* afterwards."[33]

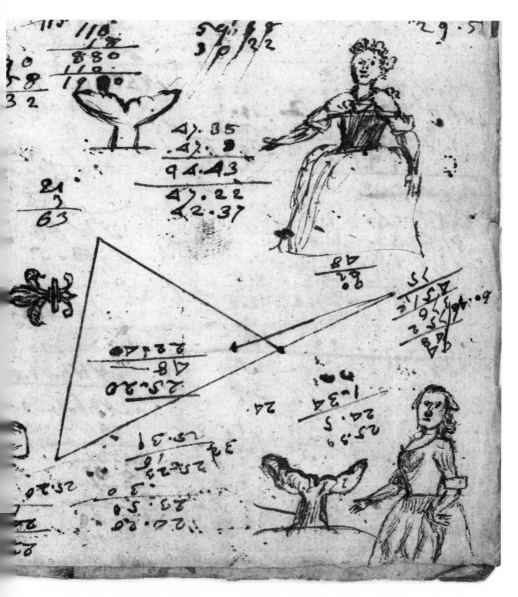

FIGURE 5.1. Doodles of women and mathematical calculations on the cover of the logbook of the sloop *Seaflower*, c. 1754, Robert Treat Paine Papers, Courtesy of the Massachusetts Historical Society

Passengers enacted similar scenes of remembrance in the midst of the Atlantic. Married passengers who sailed alone saw the physical ties to spouses broken by distance. As with sailors, uncertainty accompanied the loss of contact. As the winds pushed the ship farther from home, anxieties buffeted spouses on both ship and shore. After the weekly ritual of remembrance, John Adams encapsulated the mutuality of doubt. "This is Saturday night; a fortnight yesterday since I took leave of my family. What scenes have I beheld since! What anxiety have my friends on shore suffered on my account, during the north-east storm which they must have had at land!" Although crossing the Tropic of Cancer did not yet equal the halfway point of the voyage, it represented a point of no return where the separation from loved ones sunk in. As the turmoil of seasickness and early storms gave way to the more pleasant tropics, people possessed more time to reflect on the distance from one's homeland.[34]

While passengers reflected on the anxiety of oceanic separation, mariners more openly discussed the physical effects of distance from women. What the sailors often missed was sex. Seaman Samuel Lord explicitly expressed his sexual yearnings with an acrostic that spelled out a sexual slang term, hoping the woman in question would "the first Letters of my Lines fullfill." The reputation of sailors' licentiousness preceded them, and sometimes logbooks gave a glimpse of their libidos. One sailor turned in at night hoping "God grant my head may lay as well as some of the Lasses Arses." Shipmaster Thomas Nicolson desired for the sea to return him to the arms of his "Charming Molly" for then he could obtain "the Least of her favours." William Almy made a poetical connection between bodily desires and heartfelt sentiments. "Lust thro some certain Straines well & refind to Gentle Love and Charms all womankind." Romantic aspirations made for a better poetical subject matter, but sexual desire underlay much of the seamen's yearning for women.[35]

The entrance of females into the confines of this male community could create a sexually charged atmosphere. The Anglican pastor Charles Woodmason noted the presence of some "Ladies of Pleasure" on board his Charleston-bound ship in 1762. They may have been actual prostitutes given that the British transported convicts to America, but Woodmason might have simply labeled them such after they "behav'd indecently" with the captain and others. Women bore the brunt of the blame in these encounters, despite the participation of sexually charged sailors. A French Protestant sailing to Virginia with a group of London prostitutes at the end of the previous century admitted that the "fairer sex" provided a source of temptation to him, until he viewed their conduct aboard ship. "I saw those wenches behave so shockingly with the sailors and others, in addition to the distress caused by their songs & dances, that it awakened within me so intense a hatred of such persons that I shall never overcome it." The close quarters of the ship made sexual activities difficult to conceal and gave public expression to women's sexual interests, often to the dismay of observers. Shipboard sex was public.[36]

Sailors' sexuality and aggressive masculinity combined to create a volatile mix in the transatlantic slave trade. Slave ships stowed their cargo of men and women in separate areas of steerage, usually divided by a third compartment for boys, companionways to access the hold, or thick bulwarks. Barriers above and below decks prevented unobserved interaction between male and female slaves, which often formed a key component of successful shipboard rebellions. But no such physical obstacles barred sailors' access to enslaved women. Located in the stern of the vessel, the women's compartment stood in close proximity to the ship's officers and crew. Slave captains generally did not shackle female slaves and granted them liberty of movement on the quarterdeck, especially once the ship sailed out of the sight of the coast. Ironically this freedom from restraint, which should have alleviated bodily suffering, exposed them to sexual assault. The gender compartmentalization of the slave ship rendered African women accessible to European sailors while denying them the protection of African men.[37]

In this setting where violent intimidation formed an integral part of maintaining control, mariners had access and opportunity to coerce sexual relationships with the enslaved women. When the parliamentary committee investigating the slave trade asked one captain what prevented rape aboard his ship, he could only reply, "Orders are generally issued for that Purpose by the Commanding Officer." For the women aboard ship, these verbal barriers did not provide much of a defense. Fear of a "sharp reproval" did not provide much of a deterrence to rape. The pious John

Newton instructed his sailors in Christian doctrine twice each Sunday, but even he could not prevent sexual assault. His log recorded that "William Cooney seduced a woman slave down into the room and lay with her brutelike in view of the whole quarterdeck, for which I put him in irons." Newton feared that this pregnant rape victim might miscarry. Rape aboard ship exemplified the dreadful conditions that African women endured aboard ship.[38]

The presumed sexual availability of African women might have offered a rare inducement for some sailors to participate in a trade that seamen typically avoided. Slave ship surgeon Alexander Falconbridge claimed, "On board some ships, the common sailors are allowed to have intercourse with such of the black women whose consent they can procure." How sailors achieved this consent—whether through exercise of force, proffering of material rewards, or as the result of a calculated choice on the part of the women—Falconbridge did not say. On those ships that did try to prevent sexual assault, sailors employed more furtive means to get what they wanted. The log of the Rhode Island slave ship *Mary* reported the discovery that "this morning found our women Slave Apartments had been attempted to have been opened by some of the Ships crew, the locks being spoiled and sundered." In the description of his Middle Passage, Ottobah Cugoano reported it "common for the dirty filthy sailors to take the African women and lie upon their bodies." Sex in this instance divided the interests of the enslaved cargo when one of these women betrayed a plotted shipboard insurrection by disclosing it to the mate. Other women used sexual relationships to facilitate slave revolts. Their greater ability to move about the ship allowed them to gather the tools and information necessary for a planned revolt to succeed. The sailors' desire for sex and pursuit of these women enabled these female slaves to use sexual relationships to their own purpose.[39]

The foremast hands were not the only ones in search of shipboard sex. Captains and mates often identified "favorites" from among the female cargo for their "own use." While Falconbridge labeled the common sailors' sexual exploits as consensual, he emphasized the unnatural power exercised by their shipboard superiors. "The officers are permitted to indulge their passions among them at pleasure, and sometimes are guilty of such brutal excesses, as disgrace human nature." In similar language, sailor James Stanfield felt compelled to mention "one instance more of brutality . . . as practised by the captain on an unfortunate female slave, of the age of eight or nine, but that I am obliged to withhold it." His concern for the delicacy of the reader prevented him from specifically describing what occurred "though the act is too atrocious and bloody to be passed over in silence." Abolitionists marshaled these and similar episodes of shipboard rapes and sexual assaults to critique the slave trade, but other forms of evidence testify to the practice. While these testimonies cannot be quantified, Historian Michael Gomez astutely notes, "It mattered not that the violation was with great or little frequency, or that the number of women so violated was large or small." That any such instances occurred testify to the sexual desires and power of mariners aboard ship.[40]

The consistent presence of women and increased opportunities for shipboard sex distinguished slave ships from other Atlantic vessels. Whereas ministers expressed moral concerns about the unnatural, extended separation of sailors from marital relationships aboard other Atlantic vessels, in the slave trade, clergy feared an unbridled sexuality unleashed upon the bodies of African women. In his abolitionist tract *Thoughts upon the African Slave Trade*, written long after the conclusion of his maritime career, John Newton exposed how the slave trade endangered British seamen as well as decrying evil inflicted upon Africans. While some captains "maintained a proper discipline and regularity in their vessels," on other ships, "the licence allowed, in this particular, was almost unlimited." This "lewdness, too frequently, terminates in death," he argued. Without specifically detailing cases of rape, Newton salaciously sketched how the inherent environment of the slave ship demeaned African women and uncivilized European men. "When the women and girls are taken on board a ship, naked, trembling, terrified, perhaps almost exhausted with cold, fatigue, and hunger, they are often exposed to the wanton rudeness of white savages." The Reverend William Leigh similarly "decried how African women were "subject to the wanton lust and unrestrained licentiousness of the crew," but he was equally concerned with the threat to British seamen. "The diseases which are contracted by the sailors from this promiscuous intercourse are such as help to lessen their numbers considerably." Participation in the Atlantic trades threatened sailors' spiritual health by removing the marital outlet for sexual activity, but clergy feared the African slave trade more because of sex without boundaries.[41]

The hypersexuality that mariners exhibited on slave ships testifies to the way that they sought shipboard outlets for their sexual urges. Given the absence of women and the presence of sexual imagery in both the crossing ceremony and in sailors' songs, modern scholars ponder the degree to which sailors engaged in homosexual relationships. Atlantic travelers lamented the absence of women, but they did not directly report witnessing instances of homosexuality. Nevertheless, the suspicions and stories circulated. Historian Daniel Vickers used a religious address of Cotton Mather from Boston to describe life among the "Sea-faring tribe." Mather "was pretty certain that 'Serious Piety' was not high on the list. Instead, he complained, sailors were much more interested in drinking, 'Wicked Speeches,' 'Filthy Songs,' gaming, superstition, sodomy, and masturbation." Existing literature prepared passengers to suspect homosexuality even when they did not witness it.[42]

If not homosexual, sailors certainly fostered emotionally intimate same-sex relationships. The development of male camaraderie assumed greater importance aboard ship than on shore in the maintenance of religious beliefs and also as a matter of human survival. The sailor Robert Dunn expressed the desire for companionship in his log through the following truism, "Remember well and bear in mind a trusty friend is hard to find but when that you have found him just and true Never chainge him for a Hue." Friendship was especially vital for black seamen operating in the context of Atlantic slavery. Although a freeman and sailor, James Albert Ukawsaw Gronniosaw found himself in an exposed condition, subject to racial identification as a slave in the numerous ports he visited. He confessed that his vulnerable condition "alarmed me greatly" for "I had no friend in the world to go to." In these instances, he had to developed supportive bonds with other men aboard ship. Similarly, Olaudah Equiano highly valued an older messmate who instructed him in the ways of the ship and the Bible. "In short, he was like a father to me; and some even used to call me after his name; they also styled me the black Christian." Male friendship brought comfort and spiritual reinforcement, making the difficulties of heterosexual separations bearable.[43]

The wives of mariners similarly suffered from the absence of their emotional and sexual partners. An anonymous Massachusetts mariner reported an incident of "Cucholdom" involving Rust, a fellow sailor, and a man named Dike. "This Dike wd accompany Mr Rusts wife wn he was att Sea." When Rust returned unexpectedly, he found the two in bed. The mariner attempted reconciliation with his wife, but "She refuses, Goes, and cohabits with Dike." The case represented the deepest fears of attached sailors—sexual infidelity.[44]

Mariners spoke openly of the sexual desires of women. Because sailors believed the women they left behind experienced the same sexual urges, they often penned mutual encouragements to faithfulness and chastity.

> But if you'd Single Tarry
> Till I Croast ore the main
> theire None But you I'll Marry
> When that I Return A Gain

Thomas Nicolson entreated his second wife to remain "constant as the sun" and hoped that "our affections never rove." Another sailor confidently asserted at the beginning of his log that he had nothing to fear by absenting himself from his sweetheart.

> Sence my Molly She is true As She is fair
> My greaf I will fling unto the wind
> It is O Pleasing Return to My Care
> Since My true Love is Constant and kind

Sailors wrote poems both to assert their love for those distant and to comfort themselves for creating that distance. Sometimes it is unclear to whom sailors directed these encouragements to fidelity—to themselves or to women. On the cover of a diary of the ship *Ceres*, a sailor penned:

> Oh Beauty! smiling Cherub of the sky
> Tis thine to warm the Heart & Catch the eye
> Alike a Canker's Rose thy bloom decays
> And all thy glow is but a borrow'd blaze
> If sacred Virtue does not round thee stand
> And spotless Honor guide thee by the hand

Sailors' poetry demonstrated that they worried about the ability of each partner to remain faithful.[45]

Sometimes separation produced infidelity, and disappointment in women became the subject of poetical musings. Like Stephano's drunken song in *The Tempest*, shipboard poems often came at the expense of women.[46] One sailor composed several acrostic poems in the pages of the sloop *Ruby*'s logbook equating a woman named Eunice Rhodes with an "Everlasting Plague unto the Male Race." He warned others:

> *E*nthrawld n'er be by this Damned Evil
> *U*nequall'd felt, an offspring of the Devil
> *N*or let the Coquet see, that you can be
> *I*n love with such a Devilish Slut as she
> *C*ontent yourselves & Blieve I tell you truth
> *E* . . . ce was made to impose upon our youth

The poem expressed the author's feelings of hurt but also exacted a measure of revenge through publicly damning her in shipboard performance. Another shipboard poet depicted his jilting in the context of world history.

> What Jangling and jars since the World first began
> Have subsisted alas! between Woman & Man

Sailors realistically appraised the troubles connected with long-term relationships and entertained one another with negative depictions of women.[47]

Life in a same-sex community could produce a wariness of women in mariners. Distance created uncertainty and potential for pain. Samuel Kelly retold the story of his second mate who eloped with a shoe peddler. "A few days after this one of our crew saw the wife hawking about her husband's old Greenland boots for sale." Some seagoing poets emphasized the treachery of women. One cursed "the girl that has broken my heart" and claimed that if he had it back "never would give it to women again." Martin Page attributed his troubles as a seaman to "Woman Wine and a Codfish." Another hearkened to the Creation account in Genesis 2 and concluded that God fashioned women "out of a Long and crooked bone." When sailors reflected on the absence of women in their wooden world, they did not always interpret the distance as unhealthy.[48]

The appeal to Genesis reveals how sailors closely linked God and women in their thought processes. Samuel Russell penned a poem imagining what he would prefer if God gave him "The Choice." He opted for "some obliging modest Fem" in order to complete his life, "for theres that sweetness in a Female mind." Belief in another world fashioned a means for separated lovers to remain faithful in this one. Thomas Nicolson entreated his wife to give unto "our Uniter praise with songs divine." Sailors sought to ensure the steadfastness of their loves by encouraging them to trust in God.

> oh beautifull princess then embrace
> and nourish in your arms
> allmighty Love and you'll be blest
> with all its frutfull Charmes

One sailor built on scriptural analogies and used the romantic relationships between man and woman to characterize his desire for God. "Be thou my husband Lord and head," he pleaded, "as in a marriage covenant." As some mariners tried to navigate the difficulties of maintaining long-distance relationships, they turned to the Bible for guidance.[49]

Seaborne men utilized religious beliefs to encourage fidelity in their wives and sweethearts and also to comfort themselves in the absence of women. Only God could protect the loved ones they left behind. This conviction arose in seaman Owen Arnold the morning after "I Dreamed Very Much A Bout home But I hope all is Well With the Blessing of God." The combination of separation and insecurity often produced expressions of trust in divine providence. When downhearted, Bostonian William Palfrey called "to mind the dear pledges to whom I am going— God grant I may find them in health at my return." Doubts about those left behind encouraged assertions of theological certainty.[50]

Those voyagers most convinced of divine truth often expressed anxiety more openly. Not surprisingly, traveling ministers called upon the God who had sent them forth across the ocean to protect the loved ones they left behind. Quaker itinerant John Woolman's thoughts turned to his family one Sunday after meeting.

In the afternoon I felt a tender sympathy of soul with my poor wife and family left behind, in which state my heart was enlarged in desires that they may walk in that humble obedience wherein the everlasting Father may be their guide and support through all their difficulties in this world.

Fellow Quaker Thomas Scattergood prayed that God would assume the role he had abdicated by taking ship. "O that the Lord my God may be pleased to be a husband to my dear wife." Unable to provide physical or spiritual support to their distant spouses, ministers hoped that God would repay their sacrificial travels with blessings. Presbyterian Samuel Davies "had sundry Intervals of tender Tho'ts about my dear Family. O that my painfull Absence from them may be of Service to the Public! This would be more than a sufficient Compensation." Davies's and Woolman's pensiveness about their family's situations did not indicate doubt in God's providence but acknowledged the inscrutability of the future. The seaborne separation from family offered a trial whose ultimate lesson remained ambiguous.[51]

Appeals to the divine notwithstanding, the potential problems presented by the masculine nature of nautical space aroused notice. It struck Jacques-Pierre Brissot de Warville as "unnatural." "At sea he lives alone, separated from his wife and children. The result is that he ceases to feel for his wife that tenderness which is kept alive by domestic life; he cannot bring up his children; he cannot be cherished by them. All alone, what can a woman do? Left alone for months at a time, is it surprising if she falls into debauchery? If she stays faithful, she is unhappy, for she is always devoured by anxiety. Life at sea is a lottery; you can win and lose a great deal at it." The difficulties of life at sea seemed insurmountable. Sailors appeared to lack stability and the family support necessary for physical and spiritual health.[52]

Most troubled onlookers concentrated on what sailors lost—their wives, their families, their churches, even their lives—but mariners focused on the positive aspects of sea life. What sailors often enjoyed most was the company of other men. Rather than dwell on the connections that had been broken, they worked to create a new society—one that transcended normal boundaries of race, ethnicity, or national identity. The underlying basis for this new community was manhood. Life in this same-sex community gave rise to its own sets of challenges and ambiguities.[53]

The crossing of the line marked multiple turning points in the voyage, but it also symbolized how the voyage itself initiated people into a different society. The various aspects of the ritual reflected how shipboard society adjusted to cultural absences. Life aboard same-sex sailing ships increased sailors' estimation of women while decreasing their dependence on the traditional sexual division of labor. Men cooked, cleaned, and sewed for themselves. Similarly, men had to maintain their own devotional practices without the aid of wives and clergy. The absence of family and church placed the responsibility for religious maintenance on the males aboard ship. The ship raised the question of whom clergy really trusted with the maintenance of things sacred. Individual devotional exercises necessarily replaced family devotions, but ministers did not trust the ability of single men to provide spiritually for themselves. The crossing ceremony illustrated the creative and flexible adjustments that sailors were willing to make to traditional religious practices.

Surviving songs and correspondence indicate that women influenced shipboard life even when not present. The sentimental importance of women grew as men aboard ships did without their physical presence. Similarly, some storm-tossed sailors sentimentalized religion and created a nostalgic picture of comfortable worshipers performing their weekly exercises. Yet even as mariners elevated the importance of institutional communions of believers, they localized these practices to places on shore, diminishing the importance of group worship aboard ship. Sailing vessels afforded sites of male sociability to seamen, not public religious displays. A combination of factory and inn, the ship provided for public labor and leisure, but it made religion a matter of individual conscience.

The elements from which American culture would be forged passed through this unconventionally masculine furnace. The Atlantic passage participated in the gender formulations that would characterize religious life on the American shore. The ship stimulated an association of women with religion. Historian of American religion Ann Braude has aptly noted the high proportion of women in the pews of North American churches throughout its history. On board eighteenth-century ships, however, women were almost always in the minority and churches practically nonexistent. This demographic divide partially explains why people stereotyped those employed in the nautical trades as irreligious.

They lacked the women and clergy associated with a healthy spiritual existence.[54]

Although the crossing of the tropical line did not mark the halfway point of the voyage, it demarcated the stage where people looked more forward than backward. Ministers such as John Wesley continued their attempt to transform ship into church, but now they began more active preparations for their imagined tasks on the North American continent. For example, Benjamin Ingham began "to write out the English Dictionary, in order to learn the Indian tongue" while coasting through the tropical zone. The ministers aboard the *Simmonds* also sought out time with Oglethorpe, "from whom we learnt many particulars concerning the Indians."[55] People looked forward, but they still had thousands of miles left to sail and weeks to pass aboard the ship. They had made a dramatic turn in the voyage but not the climactic one.

CHAPTER SIX

TEDIUM

John Wesley's journal provided no description of the events from 1 January until 11 January 1735/36 (O.S.). In his account he did not detail every day spent aboard the ship, so it was not unusual for a few days to pass without comment. These ten days, however, represented the longest period that Wesley failed to describe any daily occurrences during the voyage. The published version extended the silence, providing no commentary from Christmas until 15 January. Spatially, this gap embodied the time that the *Simmonds* sailed with the trade winds, covering more than one thousand nautical miles of ocean. From the perspective of these documents, nothing really happened in those tropical waters.

Wesley was not the only one on the Georgia expedition whose narration had holes. After initially praising the sweetness of those climes as the ships crossed the tropical line, Benjamin Ingham also went silent, providing just one brief entry between 29 December and 12 January. Aboard the *London Merchant*, von Reck also remained relatively taciturn about this period, filling the paragraph after the crossing ceremony with a vibrant description of flying fish. His Moravian counterpart John Andrew Dober summarized this missing period with the phrase "We are still in the Trade winds, and sail swiftly and steadily." The favorable wind increased, the sun rose highest, the air felt warmest, but time stopped.[1]

Only time did not stop, and things did happen, despite this narrative lacuna. People continued to work, eat, converse, fight, and pray, as documented by John Wesley's manuscript diary, which fleshed out each hour with staccato descriptions of how the Oxford Methodist spent his time. Why the interruption in the narrative? Later in the eighteenth century, Bostonian Catherine Green Hickling provided an answer to this question, explaining how her initial excitement of embarkation diminished into weariness. "The monotony of a Sailors life, furnishes but little to write about, calling the Watch, turning the Glass, and listening to the song of the man at Helm, is my chief amusement." The drudgery of the sailors' life mirrored her own limited prospects for entertainment. "I read and work, play backgammon, and walk the deck with my brother, 'eat and drink and sleep, good friends what then, why then I eat and drink and sleep again,' so my time passes." Hickling's account emphasized the way time decelerated. If each day mirrored the next, empty of variation, then time did stop in a narrative sense. Even Native Americans who traversed the Atlantic to conduct diplomacy in England summarized their passage by declaring, "We have undertaken a long and tedious Voyage."[2]

The ennui of passing time clearly weighed on passengers. The gap in the accounts of the *Simmonds* and *London Merchant* represented the period in the Atlantic crossing when the novelty of ship travel dissipated. The beginning of the voyage combined anxious uncertainties with new experiences, and the voyage ended with the dangers of landfall and anticipation of new vistas. The middle of the passage seemed to empty shipboard time of major variations, making one moment seemingly indistinguishable from the next. Multiple factors explain this change in perception. One reason is geographical. The warmth and winds of the trades had climatic effects on voyagers which disguised a ship's more rapid progress. The absence of regular work furnished a second reason for the sensation of stasis. Once passengers steadied their sea legs, they found little room to use them and were unaccustomed to the extensive leisure time that the ship afforded them. As Wesley's daily diary showed, in the absence of work, each day was filled mainly with conversation with one's shipmates or through reading. The ship placed limitations on the range of both.

Over time, shipboard companions seemed tiresome, furnishing the final component of this oceanic time drag. The imperceptible progress of the ship, the physical absence of regular labor, and the lack of variety in both companions and circumstances conspired to prolong even the speediest of Atlantic crossings. The result was tedium. Religion often flowed into this temporal vacuum, giving meaning to the lives of some and offering a form of entertainment for others to pass the time. As passengers battled with tedium, religion afforded them a key weapon in the struggle.[3]

Avoiding Doldrums

The ennui of the ship passage often set in just as the ship entered the North Atlantic trade winds. The word "trade" means "course, way, or path," and its English root conveyed the idea of tracking the footprints of an animal. Obviously, the ships plying the North Atlantic left no physical traces on the ocean's surface that subsequent ships might follow. Each particular ship's path dissipated with its wake, leaving behind only a flotsam trail that the ocean soon swallowed. Mariners called this pathway across the Atlantic "the trades" not for the physical traces they could follow but because of the body of meteorological knowledge that allowed them to sail where others had before them. These hydrographical phenomena created a somewhat predictable course for sailing ships that relied on favorable wind and current conditions to reach their destinations. Ships did follow certain pathways.[4]

A much less hospitable region for ships lay just south of this predictable band of winds and currents. Sailors labeled this region of light and fickle winds around the equator "the doldrums" conveying the dullness and depression that resulted from the ship making little headway. Usually only ships bound for the southern Atlantic encountered these dead calms, but occasionally American-bound ships essentially came to a stop as their sails slackened. Mariner John Ellery sailing from Ireland in 1760 described a morning of "small winds & very Variable so that we could keep no Regular Course." By the afternoon, sky and sea seemed to cease activity altogether. "Middle & Latter part Intirely calm the Sea as smooth as Oyl." The cessation of forward movement combined with the lack of a breeze to augment the effects of the equatorial sun. A South Seas sailor later in the century described the cumulative results of five days of light and variable winds. "The Heat was very excessive, this day, one of the Men was very much overcome by it a cooking." When a ship stopped its forward motion in the midst of the dead calm, its atmosphere changed. Frustrations mounted as those aboard endured poor conditions without purposeful progress. To avoid these conditions transatlantic voyages attempted to stay firmly in the pathway of the trades.[5]

The exact latitude of the trades varied from year to year, and even season to season, which created competing bodies of experiential knowledge between shipmasters. Misjudgment might lead to an unnecessarily lengthy or uncomfortable voyage. As the *Simmonds* and *London Merchant* recrossed the Tropic of Cancer (Dober dated it 20 January N.S., but von Reck placed it on 24 N.S.), the captains of the two ships disagreed over the proper heading to take. Von Reck did not specify either man's proposed course of action but asserted with the benefit of hindsight that they chose the wrong path. "Though the opinion of our captain later turned out to be the right one, he had to obey his colleague this time." Each man argued based on his past experience of the trades, but the Atlantic's variability could render such judgments moot. Sometimes the trade winds drifted toward the equator, while in other seasons they might be encountered in surprisingly northerly latitudes. Despite these variations, once found, the prevailing winds blew from predictable quarters, and most important for wooden square-rigged vessels, this wind blew steadily in the same direction as the ship's heading. As long as no sudden storms appeared with possibly damaging wind gusts, ships could spread their maximum amount of sails. The North Equatorial Current also cooperated for a time to push the ship westward. These geographical elements meant that a ship often reached its greatest speeds during this time period.[6]

Ironically, passengers' senses might not have perceived the faster pace. Running downwind (i.e., the wind blowing mainly from the stern) reduced the sensation of the wind's force to persons on deck because they did not feel the wind blowing across the ship's deck at an opposing angle. No visible landmarks existed to communicate a visual sense of speed. Everything moved in the same direction at seemingly the same pace. Seasoned sailors judged the ship's pace based on how the bow cut through the ocean or from the water's sound as it raced along the ship's sides. The steady stern winds that sailors sought did not always produce in passengers an accompanying sensation of speed. Although the ship ran with the wind, passengers might have sensed that their pace slowed to a crawl. This physical effect shaped passengers' mental perceptions of the voyage, which seemed increasingly uninteresting.

The real measure of the ship's speed came from the casting of the log, which in the classical measure recorded the distance of line run off a spool in thirty seconds. Ascertaining the ship's speed every two hours allowed mariners to calculate the distance they sailed from their last observed position. In the absence of an accurate measure for longitude, sailors used this measure of speed over time to chart their position, a process known as "dead reckoning." The logbook of a ship meted out each day's time spatially through a record of miles sailed. A log blocked out the day in two-hour increments; the ship's speed and the estimate of the miles sailed offered the key points of data. By joining together hour of the day with the ship's position, sailors created yet another measurement of time, through the number of miles sailed. Only passengers who had access to these daily calculations could perceive their true speed.[7]

With no geographic markers in sight, a ship's rate of progress seemed abstract to passengers. The emigrant John George Käsebier tried to conquer boredom by imagining this maritime connection between time and space. After calculating the differences between German and English conceptions of the mile, Käsebier tried to reverse the sailors' reckoning of distance by measuring space through time. When he asserted that "from coast to coast there are eleven hundred German hours," his statement did not total the time he actually spent on the ship but his imagining of the Atlantic's width measured at two and a half miles per hour. While not accurate, the calculation emphasized the perception of the hundreds of hours spent aboard ship, hours that passed one at a time. The major question arising by the middle of the voyage: How were those hours to be passed?[8]

Shipboard Labor

The on-and-off twenty-four-hour workday of sailors stood in stark contrast to the life of the unemployed passengers. Without the normal patterns of labor to govern their lives, voyagers struggled to pass the time during the months-long voyages that some aptly labeled the "Inactive Season." With fewer requirements on one's time, passengers like John Wesley and his companions proactively addressed the temporal challenges of the ship. These Methodists aboard the *Simmonds* drew up resolutions at the beginning of the voyage to hold each other accountable for their time usage. "We now began to be more in earnest. We resolved to rise early, and to spend our time regularly and carefully." The contents of Wesley's private diary, which he had been keeping since 1725, revealed that he took this resolution seriously throughout the voyage. In fact, with its accounting of every waking hour in this "exacter" form, Wesley kept perhaps the most detailed accounting of shipboard activities of anyone in the eighteenth century. Although he was not the typical voyager, Wesley illustrated in his diary the common challenges voyagers faced in filling their days.[9]

A close reading of a day's diary entry (Tuesday, 6 January) from the unreported period in Wesley's journal reveals the range of activities available aboard ship. He awoke early, arising at four in the morning and dressing for the day by half past. Most of the time before seven o'clock, he spent in prayer (both ejaculatory prayer and using the *Book of Common Prayer*), reading the Bible, and singing. Around seven, other people aboard ship began to stir. Before breakfast he engaged in "religious talk with Hodgkinson," a fellow passenger who "seemed convinced" of an unnamed subject. After breakfast, he continued his study of German, which he had begun in October to communicate with the Moravians and Salzburgers aboard ship. His formal study of the language melded into spending time in conversation with some German passengers. He and Ingham engaged in religious talk until their dinner at one o'clock. After dinner, he instructed the ship's children in the catechism, which he followed with more religious conversation with his fellow passengers Reed and Mrs. Hawkins. At four in the afternoon he read aloud the prayer service and expounded for an audience of unknown size. After the service, he recorded spending most of his time in religious and necessary talk with Oglethorpe, the Germans, a "serious and open" Mrs. Hawkins (three separate times), and "Charles, etc." He spent the final half hour "with Heddon," until he retired to sleep at half past eleven.[10]

If we take the apportioning of time in Wesley's diary literally, religious devotions (five hours), reading/language study (three hours), public worship/instruction (two hours), and conversation with fellow passengers (nine and a half hours) filled the waking hours of this day. As the editor of his diary noted, this seemingly thorough, blocking out of the entire day masked countless other moments of life. Nevertheless, the entry reveals that most of the day from breakfast until bedtime consisted of interaction with other people. Since his calling was as a minister, Wesley undoubtedly counted most of that time as his labor. He taught, he counseled, he studied, he prayed, but almost always in the presence of others. His work took place in a relational environment.

A Moravian accounting of a day at sea similarly emphasized the connectivity of shipboard life. They rose at six o'clock, worshipped at seven, and breakfasted at eight. Some of the Brethren spent the morning learning English, and the others found some sort of "useful occupation" to stave off the potential harm of idleness. After dinner at noon, the Sisters took their turn to learn English. In the late afternoon, these Moravians gathered into their separate class meetings, divided by gender, for mutual spiritual instruction and devotion. After supper at six o'clock, these Moravians conducted two public prayer meetings. They conducted the first in German on "the middle and lower decks," while the "Liturgus takes his stand near, or on, the stairs which connect the two decks, thus becoming audible and in part visible to both." The day concluded with "English evening prayer in the cabin, which holds from thirty to forty persons" led by the ship's captain and attended by "part of the crew." Like Wesley, these Moravians were exceptional. Rather than migrate as individual units, they purposely traveled together as a *See Gemeine,* a sea congregation. Nevertheless, their accounting of the day mirrored those activities and challenges that Wesley's diary communicated. These Germans worked and ate, studied and prayed, but they did so as a community to tackle intentionally the room the ship created for leisure.[11]

The deliberate Christian zeal of the Oxford Methodists and German Moravians set them apart from other types of eighteenth-century voyagers, but all transatlantic migrants in some form addressed the question of what to do amidst an absence of regular labor. They worked, but often from necessity or as a form of leisure rather than pursuing a particular calling. Passengers performed a variety of tasks on ship; most had to prepare their own meals, mend their own clothes, and even lend the sailors a hand in times of difficulty. But in comparison to life on land, they had plenty of time. The time passed for voyagers not through labor patterns but primarily through social relationships, the biological necessities of life, and whatever means of entertainment they might devise.

Some work did result from meeting the necessities of everyday life. Preparation of meals furnished continuing labor aboard ship. Cooking could be challenging amid the limited facilities and rations of the ship. People shared resources and access to the ship's stove. Ships organized passengers into messes to make the distribution of food easier. Within those divisions, the labor was not always shared equally. Over a month into Charlotte Browne's voyage, she reported, "Mrs. Barbut up and making a sea Pye being the first she ever made." Her companion's continued seasickness irked Browne and seemed like an excuse to shirk her duty. "Mrs. Barbut up but not able to work." Throughout Browne's voyage she criticized her fellow passenger's work ethic and ability. "Mrs. Barbut 4 Hours making a Cake bak'd it 6 in a rusty Pudding Pan it eat like a Pancake." Shipboard cooking was not without risk. Käsebier described the death of a woman "who had fallen into the ship's hold with an iron kettle of soup." Handling hot and heavy pots aboard a moving vessel proved anything but routine.[12]

Male passengers also participated in meal preparation. The Moravians aboard the English vessel *Little Strength* in 1743 chose "a man of excellent education" to be their head cook, with three other male Brethren serving as his assistants. This appointment was not without gendered considerations; they assumed that women would be unable to handle the mental challenges of shipboard cooking. Brother Reuz was appointed "because of all persons he was less likely to loose [*sic*] the equilibrium of his mind through the many distraction attending that business." Serving as cook aboard a ship involved not just physical balance but political savvy to negotiate the demands and complaints of various people aboard.[13]

In addition to meals, passengers worked hard at keeping the ship clean. The damp, wooden, overcrowded quarters of the ship created a miasmic environment, which Europeans believed to cause serious disease. The Georgia Trustees, especially, sought to ensure the health of their venture and gave instructions for cleaning the ship. "Whenever the Weather would permit, the Ship was clean'd between Decks, and wash'd with

Vinegar, which kept the Place very sweet and healthy." Having dozens of sometimes sick people sharing close, poorly ventilated quarters, often with animals, made cleanliness a challenge. The heat of the tropical regions increased the perspirations (with the accompanying odors) of the human cargo. On the *London Merchant*, von Reck noted the effort needed to make the ship livable in the trades. "As it was very hot in this area, vinegar was given to everyone twice in order to wash the cabins and the ship's insides to improve the smell." Passengers worked to improve their shipboard environment through attempts to remove the human filth and bad air it occasioned.[14]

Passengers worked at finding ways to work. Other forms of shipboard labor for passengers derived from intention rather than necessity. For example, aboard the *Simmonds*, Oglethorpe doled out work to keep people occupied. Moore reported how "the Men were exercised with small Arms. There were also Thread, Worsted, and Knitting-needles given to the Women, who employ'd their leisure time in making Stockings and Caps for their Family, or in mending their Cloaths and Linnen." This passage closely associated these forms of shipboard labor with the leisure time created by the absence of passengers' everyday calling. They needed to keep busy. Female passengers similarly reported sewing and mending of clothes as a routine means of passing the time.[15]

Moore's account gendered the division of labor—men shot, women sewed—but some male passengers emulated the example of seamen whose labor, especially in the tropical zones, broke down such divisions. Charlotte Browne critiqued her fellow female passenger through a description of her husband's labor. "Mr. Barbut up and a mending of Stockings, his Wife fast Asleep."[16]

Sometimes labor became a matter of life and death. Times of crisis required passengers to lend the overwhelmed sailors a hand at the ship's pumps or lines. One captain commended a group of Moravians for hauling lines after a sudden sea squall violently struck the ship. During a 1742 voyage to Philadelphia, a diarist described "one occasion, when a sudden squall struck the ship, and the sails and the tackling became entangled, those colonists who could stand on deck, rendered valuable service, by assisting the sailors at the ropes." Normally, the phrase "all hands on deck" called the off-watch sailors from the fo'c'sle to assist in major endeavors on deck. During emergencies aboard passenger ships, the refrain also summoned able-bodied male passengers as noted during Scotswoman Janet Schaw's voyage. "All hands, (a fearful sound) were now called; not only the Crew, but every man who could assist in this dreadful emergency."[17]

Some viewed work, any work, as a necessity for a healthy physical or spiritual life. Sea captains often kept their crews busy "doing nothing" because they believed inactivity debilitated the body. "Capt Page says we must keep Stirring to prevent our having the Scurvy—as exercise is an excellent preventative to scurvy." For passengers, work provided a means to overcome seasickness and lift one's spirits. A British officer sailing to Boston during the American Revolution made his wife "come on deck as much as possible" to keep her spirits up. Once on deck, "she employed herself in working." Work seemed like the obvious cure to both mental and physical shipboard ailments because the absence of regular labor was so noticeable. Benjamin Franklin aptly summarized the prevailing moral wisdom regarding joblessness. "Idleness is the Dead Sea that swallows all Virtues: Be active in Business, that Temptation may miss her Aim: The Bird that sits, is easily shot."[18]

Leisure seemed threatening to some passengers, and labor offered the preventative cure to unredeemed idleness. Like Brethren communities on land, Moravians regulated the use of time and space, in regard to both worship and labor. Moravians expected every believer to pursue their secular calling as an integral part of their spiritual existence. "One does not only work in order to live, but one lives for the sake of one's work," Count Zinzendorf had instructed. In this sense, the Atlantic challenged Moravians by offering them shipboard leisure rather than labor. "Nothing is so hurtful to the mind as complete idleness, on sea even more so than on land." If any semblance of religious normalcy were to be created aboard ship, it would have to involve labor. So whenever possible Moravians continued practice of their trades. For example, once he had recovered from his seasickness, shoemaker Philip Meurer unpacked the tools of his trade aboard the snow *Catherine*. In a matter of weeks, he reshod and repaired the footwear of all fifty-six people aboard. Moravians sought simultaneously to redeem the time in order to pass it enjoyably. As one booklet advised, "If the Brethren and Sisters always employ themselves about something they will have this benefit from it among others, that this can make a Voyage less tedious than it is in itself." For Moravians, work and worship both redeemed time. They responded to the ambiguity of a leisurely life aboard ship using the same organizational principles that structured their lives on land.[19]

Shipboard Leisure

The Oxford Methodists and the Moravians used labor to fill their leisure time. Although their motives for this temporal accounting were largely spiritual, they fostered the emerging modern emphasis on efficiency and order: time should not be wasted. But their primary concern centered on the danger of idleness to their own souls. As Samuel Davies bewailed, "Alas! how unprofitably my Life glides by in this State of Inactivity!" They feared that the ship brought them closer to port but further from God. Evangelicals did not just seek to pass the time on board ship, they desired to make it a sanctifying experience.[20]

The ship limited the range of conversation partners while greatly expanding the potential for talking. Passengers passed the time conversing with each other over meals, during games, and across bunks at night. One historian of the Moravians gave a romantic cast to this stage of the voyage. "Could there have been anything more delightful than to spend the hours of the tropical night on deck, under the canopy of heaven, in unreserved conversation with a knot of intimate friends." Conversation broke the tedium of a largely laborless existence devoid of typical entertainments. Shipboard banter with old companions or new acquaintances could prove quite pleasing to those adjusting to the discomforts of life aboard ship. When the young ladies chaperoned by cabin passenger Henry Ingraham fell ill, he sought to lift their spirits through conversation, enticing them to laugh.[21]

More often travelers found themselves talking to strangers, a potentially disappointing experience. During her voyage to London, American loyalist Louisa Wells strummed her guitar to make " 'the heavy Hours' supportable" because "we had no conversation and I detested cards." The shipboard environment made talking a primary activity, often forcing voyagers into conversation with partners not of their own choosing. The smallness of ships exposed one to other people's conversations. Lutheran pastor Henry Melchior Muhlenberg sought a peaceful retreat to his berth, but "all the passengers were in the cabin on account of the rain and frittered away the time with idle talk, cursing, swearing, and all sorts of sins." Conversation formed an ever-present part of the voyage whether one sought to participate or not.[22]

Language could be a barrier in community formation. The Oxford Methodists studied German and the Moravians tried to learn English, but their conversations still had to cross a linguistic divide. Linguistic isolation depressed a person's spirits and increased fear or distress. The transatlantic slave trade offered an extreme example of this problem aboard migrant ships. During his voyage as surgeon on the slave ship *Young Hero*, Ecroyde Claxton noted that all the slaves aboard understood each other except for one who spoke a language unknown to the others. His inability to communicate with his fellow sufferers "made his condition truly lamentable, and made him always look very much dejected." Differences in language could render even the most pleasant voyage tedious and sometimes dangerous. After a few weeks with his French cabinmates, William Downes Cheever found their conversation "not very pleasant to my ear," so he tried to ignore them "but beg a short passage to France." Conversation could pass the time on board ship or cause it to seem like an eternity.[23]

Sometimes the topic under discussion turned to eternity. In his minute accounting of time usage, John Wesley made the distinction between "necessary talk," which focused on accomplishing a particular end, and "religious talk," which addressed explicitly spiritual ends. Sometimes he would provide a further descriptor to characterize the results of his ministrations. For example, his entries on 8 January 1735/36 noted conversations with Harding ("convinced") and Mrs. Hawkins ("affected"). These brief descriptors revealed Wesley's desire for his conversations to redeem, not just to consume time. Wesley and his fellow ministers sought opportunities to transform ordinary chitchat through giving "the Conversation a religious Turn." The close quarters of the ship made eavesdropping an unavoidable phenomenon, creating further opportunities to provide religious instruction. As he lay in his bed, Muhlenberg heard the nighttime quiet broken by the English passengers near him discussing the devil, each trying to prove himself smarter than the others. The evangelically minded Lutheran pastor could not resist such an opportunity and discoursed with them until "all became silent." More frequently, Muhlenberg found the conversation of his cabinmates less than edifying, and he envied the position of the German emigrants in steerage who were wholly ignorant of the English language. The constant talk on ship provided both opportunities for evangelization and occasions for temptation. Conversation partners could shape the experience of the voyage for better or worse.[24]

The often overcrowded vessels blurred individuals' personal space and fomented conflict. Frequently, diarists expressed disparaging remarks about their shipmates, labeling some individuals as troublemakers. John Adams described a fellow passenger as a man of "unhappy mind" who "must ever have something to complain of, something to peeve and fret about" and consequently "ruined the peace of this ship." A British soldier on his way to America grew "most heartily tired" of a "touchy, passionate, ill-natured, and hard to please" officer's wife, and the ship's company "wished the voyage at an end chiefly on her account." Sometimes personality differences escalated into physical violence. Huguenot nobleman John Fontaine initiated "a dispute with the men" of the ship after a perceived insult that led to blows and death threats. Tempers flared to such a height that "the master locked up my sword and pistols, so I was forced to be easy." The physical confines of the ship cast people into close proximity with one another, augmenting differences in personality and social standing.[25]

These shipboard conflicts heightened an individual's sense of isolation. Young Benjamin Franklin recorded the shipboard court of justice that formed when a passenger was caught cheating at cards. The elaborate mock proceedings provided an entire Friday's worth of entertainment to the cabin passengers, who found the man guilty. The condemned, however, refused to submit to the punishment, which combined public humiliation with two bottles of brandy. As a result, Franklin reported, "Our mess have excommunicated him till he pays his fine, refusing either to play, eat, drink, or converse with him." Less than a week of this "excommunication" brought about repentance on the part of the transgressor. The following Thursday he expressed "himself willing to pay the fine, we have this morning received him into unity again." The incident proved instructive to the ever-observant Franklin. "Man is a sociable being, and it is, for aught I know, one of the worst of punishments to be excluded from Society." Being aboard ship increased the impact of shunning because the excluded had no other society to which he could turn. The human need to have fellowship necessitated that shipboard conflicts be settled quickly and amicably.[26]

As ships sliced through the Atlantic, pushed along by the trade winds, people began to tire of each other's company. The lack of variation in conversation partners increased the ennui. If nothing happened, what did people need to talk about? Travel narratives present this persistent desire for relationship when they recorded the excitement of encountering other vessels at sea. Benjamin Franklin reflected on why a sail on the horizon elevated the mood on ship. "There is really something strangly chearing to the spirits in the meeting of a ship at sea, containing a society of creatures of the same species and in the same circumstances with ourselves, after we had been long separated and excommunicated as it were from the rest of mankind." On 23 January (N.S.), David Nitschmann captured the remarkableness of two ships encountering one another with the simple line, "We saw a ship!" Wonder and excitement stirred in the hearts of voyagers when they saw a tiny white blur on an endless horizon of blue.[27]

The chance encounter with another ship provided a brief respite from the banal existence of one's own vessel as well as opening a channel to the outside world. Ships sailing in the opposite direction proffered an opportunity to send word to family and friends left behind. Later in the voyage as the expedition neared Georgia, they encountered the *Pomeroy* bound from Charleston to London. John Wesley expressed his delight in this pleasing providence. "We were exceeding glad of so happy an opportunity of sending to our friends in England word of our safety." The respective shipmasters exchanged a mixture of shipboard and global news over the tumult of the beating wind and chopping sea. Sometimes vessels would remain in company for several days offering a broader social sphere for stateroom passengers, albeit only briefly. For a moment, their social worlds expanded and gave everyone an opportunity to look upon something else.[28]

Two tiny ships encountering one another amid the vast ocean seemed improbable, but these ships traversed a common pathway. The footsteps of the trades, however, headed in the same direction. Ships could speak to one another only if one sailed significantly faster than the other or if an intentional effort was made to communicate. Janet Schaw expressed the disappointment of others on her ship in not being able to speak with a passing vessel: "As our course was different, we soon parted, and every heart felt a pang at losing sight of a ship we knew nothing of and being separated from people with whom we had no concern. Man is certainly by nature a kindly Social animal." The sight of another ship reminded people of the limitations of their own social spheres.[29]

These fleeting encounters with other ships encapsulated the inner conflicts voyagers felt in regard to the social space of the ship. On one hand, these chance meetings revealed the intense desire for community and the "social animal" within people. Yet, on the other hand, they demonstrated the lack of variation and contentment within a shipboard community. The ship limited people's social sphere and forced them into intimate contact with people not of their choosing. Voyagers made do with the communal building blocks they had on board ship, but their society never seemed complete. They pined for missing pieces of the puzzle, but they assembled working societies by rearranging the elements present. Besides personal conversation, they turned to other means to create larger communities out of the "anomalous intimacy" of the ship.[30]

Much like the chanteys that rang out from sailors as they performed their labors, passengers discovered song to be an amenable means of leisure. William Cheever described a typical morning with his French cabinmates who "this morn ushered in by cards, chequers, single tunes, and whole singing at times." Such activities raised spirits as well as causing the time to pass more agreeably. When the passengers aboard Henry Ingraham's vessel "felt rather low spirited," they proposed "some livily tunes, such as Fisher's Hornpipe, Mummsy Must" and called in others to dance. While many enjoyed this friendly conviviality, others found it offensive. Muhlenberg lambasted the activities of his wild and rude cabinmates who "cursed the whole day, sang all sorts of lewd songs, and stormed about the ship in a manner beyond all bounds." For Muhlenberg, the offense of song and dance came not just from their content but because they seemed too leisurely. He chided one of his cabinmates, asserting that "he had far more important and necessary things to do than dance." Other passengers complained of the noise and filth filtering down from the "sham[e]less creatures [who] kept singing & dancing above my patients." Song could offend or divert depending on one's perspective.[31]

Muhlenberg sought to fight song with song. He recognized the power of music and frequently rejoiced when the Christian family in the ship's hold sang German hymns. In contrast to the licentious influence of his cabinmates' bawdy revelry, the Salzburgers' *Gesang-buch* selections exercised a restraining power over the ship's company. Music could convert as well as corrupt. During one of Whitefield's voyages, sailors believed that their misfortune on the voyage derived from his unceasing religious activities, including singing. "I was the Jonah in the fleet. Our prayers, preaching, and hymns were too frequent." Passengers used singing as an antidote to the mental and physical taxation of the ship. Moravians reported one sister who comforted those confined with seasickness through her soothing songs. Song fought foes within and without. When Wesley resolved "to be more zealous and active, especially from 5 to 10," he referenced the period of his day in which he often sang as part of his devotions. Song could express a wide range of emotions. Janet Schaw noted the sad tones wafting up from indentured Highlanders in steerage. "Some of our fair Shipmates, however, favour us with a melancholy 'Lochaber Nae maer,' or 'heaven preserve my bonnie Scotch laddie,' sounds that vibrate thro' several hearts."[32]

This choral response to loss found its most poignant expression on the numerous African slave ships plying the Atlantic. Seldom are slave ships considered to be sacred sites. However, even amid economic exploitation and social cataclysm, participants lyrically oriented themselves on the seas. The surgeon James Arnold described a scene from his brig that must have brought Psalm 137 to the minds of his parliamentary audience. The words of that ancient biblical lament describing the Babylonians' mocking of their Israelite captives could also apply to conditions aboard transatlantic slave ships. "For there they that carried us away captive required of us a song; and they that wasted us required of us mirth, saying, Sing us one of the songs of Zion." In Arnold's tale, the captain of the *Ruby* forcibly instructed the slaves to sing during their daily exercise. Like some barbaric choir director, he compelled the Africans to intone, " 'Meffe, Meffe, Mackarida,' (that is) 'Good Living or Messing well among White

Men,'" using art to buttress racial hierarchy. But the same slaves turned song against him, utilizing the subversive and spiritual power of music. Arnold also reported the tearful laments rising up from the women's quarters. "Their Songs then contained the History of their Lives, and their Separation from their Friends and Country." The medium that praised whites on deck, now, from the dark hold, castigated them for the pain and suffering they caused. These women used lament as a powerful tool combining political subversion with divine supplication. At least one hearer received the message. "These Songs were very disagreeable to the Captain, who has taken them up, and flogged them in so terrible a Manner for no other Reason than this." These expressions of grief challenged the happy image of the captain's sham performances and reminded the *Ruby*'s master that his power extended only so far. Songs formed a key part of the survival mechanism aboard African slave ships and were a means of drawing community out of anomalous intimacy.[33]

Not all captains displayed pickiness, or even attention, to the content of the slaves' songs. Officers often left the subject matter of song between and above decks to the enslaved Africans. One merchant reported they would "sing to some tune or other in their own way." Another recounted a similar cultural independence when "the Men sing their Country Songs" during the deck-side dances. Their captors might use the stings of a whip to force them to sing, but they could not control the content and meaning of those songs. This indifference toward content allowed Africans to use their distinct languages to mask precise meaning from their captors. The surgeon Ecroyde Claxton recorded the words of one lament sung during the afternoon exercise. They sorrowfully sang "Madda! Madda! Yiera! Yiera! Bemini! Bemini! Madda! Ausera!" which he discovered to mean, "They were all sick, and by and by they should be no more." Amid a brutal forced transportation from Africa, slaves retained memories and hopes of their homelands through song. Music provided a powerful preservative for the orally based cultures on board ship as well as a means of supplicating the divine.[34]

Through the noise of the rigging and shouts of the mates, sailors paused to hear these notes wafting up through the gratings. The mariners who heard them sing during the periods of forced exercise recognized that when the slaves sang of their own accord the tone of their music sounded starkly different. As Henry Ellison took his position for the night watch, he "very often heard them sing mournful tunes when in their rooms." Many ships carried a free African on board as a "linguister" to mediate between crew and cargo. Seaman David Henderson asked such a youth to translate the songs for him. "Their Songs usually contain the History of their Sufferings, and the Wretchedness of their Situation." Alexander Falconbridge displayed the same curiosity. He often approached the linguister "to ask what they were singing about; and he has always told me, they were lamenting the loss of their country and friends." These laments represented verbal prayers. In song, the slaves implored mystical powers to bring back the balance and happiness that had been lost.[35]

Some owners planned for the presence of music aboard slave ships by hiring musicians for this purpose. Mariners carved out precious ship space to accommodate musicians and their instruments because experienced sailors viewed music as essential to the survival of Africans during the Middle Passage. Slave ships posted advertisements seeking "a person that can play on the Bagpipes, for a Guinea ship." Merchants attempted to compel cheerfulness through song, to distract slaves from the misery and fears they suffered. Typically, music fueled cultural clashes: slavers forced African performance according to European musical tastes and instruments, but Africans preferred their own forms of accompaniment. Musical practices furnished one of the few opportunities to transport African material objects. Carolina merchant Robert Norris testified, "They are supplied with the Musical Instruments of their Country" as an encouragement for them "to be chearful." When forced to dance or sing, slaves were accompanied by "one of their Country Drums beating at the same Time." Denied clothes and other personal belongings, some slaves could bring drums, banjos, and other musical instruments that could carry material or spiritual significance.[36]

Beating time for dance furnished the main purpose of these instruments aboard slave ships and, like song, displayed paradoxical intentions. Aboard slave ships, chains and cramped quarters magnified shipboard tedium by reducing people's ability to move. In order to ensure the health of their human cargo and a ready sale, captains forced slaves to exercise on deck in the afternoons when weather permitted, a practice they termed "dancing the slaves." Slave ships thus recognized and built an institutional response to tedium through forced dance. Shipmasters often pointed to these performances as signs of how much Africans enjoyed the voyage, painting a picture of leisurely afternoons gamboling under sunny skies. "Between Twelve and Four, they amuse themselves with Singing, Dancing, or Games of Chance." Other observers found the exalted title of dance to be a misnomer. "After every meal they are made to jump in their irons; but I cannot call it dancing," noted Falconbridge. A similar opinion came from a former officer. "They are made after each meal to jump up and down upon the beating of a drum; this is what I have heard called dancing, but not what I consider as dancing, as it is not to music of their own." Another called attention to the weighty chains that fastened slaves to the deck when he described this dancing to consist of "their jumping, as far as the nature of their confinement will admit of." Those who hesitated or refused to participate in this exercise received incentive in the form of a seaman wielding a cat-o'-nine-tails. An unknown author in 1790 penned a poetic description of the "dance" that captured the brutality and mockery of the practice.

> At the savage Captain's beck,
> Now like brutes they make us prance
> Smack the Cat about the Deck
> And in scorn they bid us dance.

The flashing of whips, the galling of chains, unfamiliar rhythms, and the ridicule of sailors marked the performance of dance aboard slave ships.[37]

These compulsory practices allowed some room for autonomous expression. Some slave ship captains found their cargo participated in these post-meal practices more readily when the slaves assumed greater control over the performance. A practice that could humiliate the naked and encumbered slaves when given some freedom of expression could become a means to subvert the power of the tormentors. Allowing participants to move according to familiar rhythms could lead to a reversal of the dance's intention. In West and Central African societies, dance provided a means of power. It was an action that stomped away affliction and brought healing cohesion through the performers. Because Europeans remained unfamiliar with the meaning and context of the movements involved, slaves could utilize dance to mock the mockers. One recent scholar noted the multivalent meanings associated with these communal activities. "Dance was thus used to solicit intercession, to thwart wrath or punishment that human action might have incurred, to flatter, or to appease." The rubbing of the chains might have inflicted torture, but dance provided a means for slaves through their bodily motions to confront the actions of their tormentors. Dance expressed hidden rebellious thoughts behind a mask of physical motion.[38]

Music and dance bridged the Atlantic cultural divide. Song promoted stability, coherence, and community. In an uncertain situation, comments historian Lawrence Levine, music "served the dual purpose of not only preserving communal values and solidarity but also providing occasions for the individual to transcend, at least symbolically, the inevitable restrictions of his environment and his society by permitting him to express deeply held feelings which ordinarily could not be verbalized." Slaves turned to music aboard slave ships to maintain connections to their cultural past and to seek spiritual power to survive the present and future. Europeans believed music aided the physical survival of the slaves, assisting endurance and ensuring the rudimentary health that would secure a good sale price in the Americas. Their assessment was partially correct. Song allowed slaves to survive by creating a shared ethos through communal performance. Music did not distract enslaved men and women from their sufferings, but it enabled them to focus that pain through song. The lamentations that so captured sailors' attention represented a continued reliance on traditional means of spiritual power. Song's presence alongside the horrendous conditions of slave ships exemplified its ready availability for voyagers of all types. Conversation, dance, and singing thus furnished the most convenient and portable weapons against tedium.[39]

While song seemed like a response available to everyone, other responses were not universally available. In the journals and diaries describing the Atlantic passage, one of the most common shipboard activities was reading. Literate passengers greatly appreciated the portable companionship of books, but not everyone could read or have access to reading materials aboard ship. Literacy was a coveted trait for mariners. Historian Marcus Rediker concluded that three-quarters of merchant seamen might be literate based on the ability to sign their name. Those who could not read begged their companions to teach them. Literary scholar Henry Louis Gates Jr. noted how the "talking book" frequently appeared as a trope in the earliest African slave narratives, exemplified by James Albert Ukawsaw Gronniosaw's narration of his ship master's public reading of prayers. "When first I saw him read, I was never so surprised in my whole life as when I saw the book talk to my master." The book disappointed Gronniosaw when it did not speak to him, but the encounter spurred him toward literacy. Olaudah Equiano similarly mimicked his shipmates by trying to listen to books, until he too learned to read. On subsequent voyages books, especially the Bible, became his most prized possession. Europeans also utilized the time aboard ship to achieve literacy. Charlotte Browne facetiously described her shipmate's acquisition of a new language. "Mr. Cherrington learnt Mrs. Barbut to read and construe Greek in an Hour." Wesley took up the study of German. Moravians acquired English. Others learned to read. The ship became schoolhouse as passengers seized opportunities to gain literacy.[40]

Passengers assessed one another by what they read. Janet Schaw described her surprise when "in the State room we found a number of books. They consisted chiefly of Novels and poetry." The contents of this library conveyed the youthfulness of the captain and mates. When he came aboard the frigate *Boston*, John Adams similarly took stock of the captain's library, concluding that he had "no great erudition." When it came to shipboard libraries, patrons could not be too picky. For example, Schaw and her companions sought to take their minds off a raging storm, so they picked up the nearest book, later laughing that they might have faced eternity "like philosophers not Christians: with a Lord Kaims in our hands in place of a Bible." Rather than the Bible, which she considered more appropriate amid their dire circumstances, Schaw's company diverted themselves with the limited range of books available to them.[41]

Despite the paucity of available books, they still offered a means of escape when conversation proved deficient. When William Palfrey's shipmates took ill and ceased conversing, he passed the day in reading. The Connecticut convert to Anglicanism, Samuel Johnson, carefully maintained "a journal of his voyage to, abode at, and return from England," in which he detailed the books that occupied his days aboard ship. Books offered a means of escape from other duties. The Anglican pastor aboard Nicholas Cresswell's ship read a text on scurvy to avoid leading public prayers. Reading allowed him to use his time in the way he found most diverting or necessary. Even those who could not read frequently requested to have books read to them. When Wesley started to read books aloud in steerage he noted the overwhelmingly positive response. Passengers who desired to kill time sometimes turned to books as a useful occupation so they could say, "I learned something and was not bored." Although not everyone had equal access to books, reading assumed a central place on board ships.[42]

The ship experience accentuated the role of reading in some religious communities. Anglican religious life aboard ship often centered on the private reading of the *Book of Common Prayer*. Its ubiquitous presence granted both familiarity and comfort as an amusing incident aboard Mary Ann Parker's ship demonstrated. After killing a shark, the sailors discovered a *Book of Common Prayer* in its belly. She joked that "it would not have been so astonishing if a *Law-book* had been found instead of a *Prayer-book*,—as the shark was always thought more of the *Lawyer* than the *Parson*." The discovery turned more serious when they realized that book "belonged formerly to a convict, as on one of the leaves was written 'TO DIE,' and underneath 'REPRIEVED.'" An ocean of terrors threatened to devour Anglicans both in body and soul. The public rite in book form served the shipboard needs of personal piety. The *Book of Common Prayer* and Bible both could be found in the inventories of deceased British mariners' possessions. In the absence of clergy, the *Book of Common Prayer* provided the major means of nurturing Anglican piety not through communal performance but through individual devotion.[43]

This reliance on the printed word fostered a more independent and individualized approach to the Episcopal tradition. Even when clergy were aboard, as in Cresswell's case, their ambiguous role left spiritual responsibility in the hands of the laity. When George Whitefield's return voyage to Britain in 1738 took much longer than expected, he mixed encouragement and judgment to provoke a spiritual response from the crew. The ship's surgeon, however, turned to the *Book of Common Prayer* for his comfort. "This morning, the doctor of our ship took up the Common Prayer Book, and observed that he opened upon these words, 'Blessed be the Lord God of Israel, for He hath visited and redeemed His people.' And so, indeed, He has, for about 8 o'clock this morning news was brought that our men saw land." The formula was familiar, the principle was scriptural, but it was an individual interpretation—not a minister's direction—that gave the words their comforting power.[44]

The quiet, introspective piety of Anglican laity allowed others to dismiss their practices as insincere and rote. Sailor Samuel Kelly took note of an old lieutenant aboard his ship who "read much in his Bible and I believe often went through the service in the Liturgy of the establishment but at other times I could perceive he was far from being a pious man." This man faithfully followed the liturgy of his distant community, but strangers judged him according to his actions. Evangelicals especially criticized those who maintained the form of religion while neglecting the substance of one's relationship to Jesus Christ. Such criticisms, however, touched individual inconsistencies, not on the practices themselves. The liturgical context so important to the Church of England was lacking aboard ships. The Atlantic crossing encouraged expressions of Anglican piety to assume a more lay-centered and individualized form.[45]

The ship also encouraged change and creativity of religious expression. As a ship captain, John Newton rewrote the *Book of Common Prayer* to adapt it to sea use because he found it to be "an indifferent rule for such a congregation as mine." The twenty-five men under his command needed a rite more suited to their needs. Therefore, Newton took "the liberty of leaving out or changing, to make the whole to the best of my judgment as suitable as possible." Even when it served as the basis for unifying the shipboard community, the *Book of Common Prayer* lent itself to adaptation and interpretation. Laymen like Newton could mold the rite to suit their personal preferences and individual spiritual desires. The pageantry of church rites carried less power when presented in ambiguous social contexts. Yet the emphasis on a uniform basis of worship also proved to be beneficial. Anglicanism's advantage lay in the portability and adaptability of the *Book of Common Prayer*. A book could go where ministers could not.[46]

Emerging Protestant evangelicals also sought to capitalize on this shipboard reliance on the printed page, utilizing a broader but less unified set of reading materials. Scholars have long noted the vital importance of the printed word to the spread of what later generations termed the

"Great Awakening." The intentional use of the press spread the "New Light" message not only on land but also at sea. Ministers often replaced the "bad books" aboard ship with good ones. George Whitefield left behind books and tracts to continue his ministry. When he came aboard the ship *Lightfoot*, he "dispersed Bibles, Testaments, Soldiers' Monitors amongst the men; exchanged some books for some cards, which I threw overboard." John Newton anticipated the work of nineteenth-century religious aid societies when he suggested "a book of advices and devotions might be composed adapted entirely to the business and occasions of seamen." Evangelicals recognized the need for shipboard diversions and sought to use people's desire for entertainment as a means of spreading their message. Aboard the *Simmonds*, Benjamin Ingham used the evening hours to spread his message. "At seven, I read to as many of the passengers as were willing to hear, and instructed them in Christianity." Evangelical efforts bore fruit in seamen like Eleazar Elderkin, who reported, "I have read some in the Bible when I could steal time."[47]

Evangelicals also used books for individual devotion. The unpredictable oceanic weather perturbed New Light Presbyterian Samuel Davies, but he derived instruction from reading "Mr. Prince's excellent Sermon upon the Agency of God in Droughts and Rains, which suggested to me a Variety of new Tho'ts theological and philosophical." One anonymous sailor recorded his interaction with several religious texts so that he "Spent ye time as proffetably as we Cd. Read Willards Lectures, Byles Sermons, & Watts Hora Lyn." Such reading materials provided glimpses of various Christian traditions, which furnished seamen with a religious education apart from clergy. People treasured and derived comfort from their devotional materials. When suddenly sold and forced to change ships, Olaudah Equiano grieved that the betrayal deprived him of his Bible and favorite book, called *A Guide to the Indians*. He subsequently lamented the difficulty of finding any replacements (except for the Bible) in the Caribbean. Reading offered pleasant opportunities to make ship life passable and blended into community rituals, such as public prayers.[48]

Religious services continued to offer passengers a form of diversion from the tedium of ship life. This shipboard performance involved contradictory impulses. Whereas ministers viewed their services as an attempt to sacralize time, others on board might view sermons and prayers as merely a harmless diversion to pass the time. Even devout Moravians could characterize their love feasts and other religious practices as "forming part of the entertainment."[49]

Some wanting divinity and others seeking diversion, sometimes it was hard to discern motivations for attending religious services. Samuel Davies characterized his shipboard congregation with the words "they seemed attentive," but he harbored his doubts. The Oxford Methodists conducted religious meetings throughout the *Simmonds*'s voyage. Wesley described that his first sermon afloat, while the ship still lay at its moorings off Gravesend, attracted "a numerous and as it then seemed serious congregation." The prospects of a vibrant religious community at the beginning of the voyage thrilled the young cleric. His assessment of his congregation changed, however, when only three of the ship's passengers and crew partook of the Eucharist afterwards. Wesley decided that most of his listeners were not really serious. Each Sunday, Wesley took the pulse of his maritime congregation by tallying communicants and assessing attitudes. For example, on 11 January, he numbered twenty-one communicants partaking of the Lord's Supper and several others affected by his religious message. The waxing and waning of participation continued to vex Wesley, who nevertheless was encouraged by the growth of his seagoing flock.[50]

Other preachers possessed no doubts about their congregation's attitude, especially when members responded with unruliness. The attendees of Charles Woodmason's shipboard services made open sport of his sermons. When he "Read them Lectures of Continence and Temperance," they responded with laughter and ridicule. The following Sunday, he convened service for the ship's company and again they "Behaved ludicrously." By the end of the voyage, he "Refus'd to officiate any more, as they turn'd both the Sermon and Service to Raillery." The Lutheran Muhlenberg faced a similar dilemma. He had an overwhelming compulsion to preach, but he felt hesitant to cast pearls before swine. When one woman approached him about conducting service for the English, he responded by telling "the woman that she should take care because a number of the passengers had a desire for raillery; I therefore could not know whether they were now in earnest with her request." Ministers intended the sermons to convert, but others simply found them to be a means of entertainment, breaking the monotony of life on the rolling

ocean. The shipboard sermon met the needs of the pious and the pro-
fane in an attempt to stave off boredom.[51]

Time did not stop aboard ships, but its rhythms shifted. The trade winds
confused passengers' senses, making them more aware of the stifling heat
and stagnating time aboard ship. Although most North Atlantic vessels did
not get stuck in the doldrums, passengers could well understand what the
region's name connoted. The traveler Rachel Hemming's description
repeated the characteristic refrain of the sea journey. "It is most wearisome. The noise is wearisome, the people are wearisome and life is wearisome. It is too hot to work, and I am getting quite tired of novels, and
there is nothing else on board." Similarly, historian Marcus Rediker captured succinctly the confining presence of the ship upon the activities of
sailors. "Shipboard life constituted a binding chain of linked limits: limited
space, limited freedom, limited movement, limited sensory stimulation,
and limited choices of leisure activities, social interaction, food, and play."
The same confines held for the passengers. Nautical life disrupted the
rhythms of work and worship formulated on land. Labor shifted from a
necessity for life to a remedy for idleness. Religious services moved from
the rational cohesive community of the parish to a more ragtag collection
of individuals who sought entertainment as well as edification.[52]

The foundation of shipboard culture came from conversation and
reading, which for religious groups put as much emphasis on individual
devotions as public worship. The inordinate amount of leisure time for
passengers aboard ships, coupled with the length of voyages, provided
many opportunities for cultural interaction and exchange, both positively
and negatively. The timing was right. At the very moment when the environment interrupted the structuring rhythms of life, leaving voyagers
open to new belief systems, the travelers found time for extended interaction with one another. The nature of these interactions depended largely
on the availability and location of others aboard ship, but on the whole,
voyagers diversified their normal range of conversation partners. The
disruption occasioned by crossing the Atlantic created an opportunity to
form new relationships, whether for this world or for realms beyond.

CHAPTER SEVEN

TEMPESTS

Social and oceanic tempests interrupted the narrative silence in the various journals of the Georgia expedition. The first squall after they recrossed the Tropic took human form on 15 January 1736 (O.S.), arising from a dispute about the ship's declining water supply. John Wesley reported that incensed migrants in steerage formally complained "to Mr. Oglethorpe of the unequal distribution of water among the passengers." John Andrew Dober's account emphasized that the inequality resulted not just from the size of rations but their quality. "As there was little good water left the passengers were given poor water." A few chosen men lodged in the cabin distributed portions to the various messes. As the weeks passed, they reserved the better casks for themselves, serving fetid water to those in steerage. Once notified, Oglethorpe "ordered that all, in the Cabin and outside, should be treated alike, as long as the good water lasted." To ensure fairness, he appointed a new set of men to allocate food and drink. This action incensed cabin passengers, who took umbrage at their demotion from office and the egalitarian distribution of resources. They vented their ire on Wesley. "The old ones and their friends were highly exasperated against us, to whom they imputed the change. But 'the fierceness of man shall turn to thy praise.'" As the voyage dragged on, the dwindling resources of the ship offered fresh occasion for lingering disputes to erupt in stormy conflict. For Wesley, endurance of these conflicts furnished fresh occasions for praise.[1]

Other more threatening tempests soon followed, which seemed to question the benignity of God. Two days after the *Simmonds*'s water dispute, "There was a great storm, the waves went over the ship, and poured into it." This tempest seemed to dissolve the ship's solidity. "It shook the whole frame of the ship, from stem to stern. The water sprung through the sides of the ship, which before were tight, and, also, above the mainyard. Falling down, it covered the decks, broke into the great cabin, and filled Mrs. Welch's bed." In the great cabin, dark water poured through the stern windows, which normally favored the space with light and ventilation. This storm and the fear it occasioned foreshadowed the more turbulent days ahead. Aboard the *London Merchant*, von Reck summarized the period. "From the 28th of January to the 8th of February [N.S.], we had contrary winds West-Northwest and Northwest, fierce gales with thunder, lightning and rain." The ferocity of the storm caused the voyage to cease in terms of human-directed agency, as the ships literally offered themselves to the ocean's control. "All sails had to be furled, the masts put down, the yard arms lowered, the helm made fast, and the ship left to the mercy of God and the roaring and foaming waves." The transatlantic crossing of the *Simmonds* and *London Merchant* climaxed with this experience of a "proper hurricane," which dominated the writings of those aboard.[2]

Shipboard disturbances manifested themselves both in oceanic storms and interpersonal conflicts. Passengers experienced tempest both as a "violent storm of wind" and as a "violent commotion or disturbance" of a more personal sort. Voyage accounts linked the two types of perturbation, often using the same vocabulary. Charlotte Browne employed the term "squall" to describe both the relational and meteorological tumults aboard the troop ship *London*. For example, on 25 January 1755, she described "a great Squall on Deck, with Mr. Lash the Mate and Mr. Black the Clerk of the Hospitall about the tapping of some Beer." One week later, she used the same descriptors for the weather, noting "a Great Squall on Deck of Wind and Rain." Her mind linked these different kinds of deck-side disorder. Sometimes the connection was temporal, since atmospheric troubles occasioned human conflicts. Wesley began his account of the January storm combining frayed nerves with foul weather. "Many people were very impatient at the contrary wind." Adverse meteorological conditions pushed people to their interpersonal limits. During the early Georgia voyage of the *Anne*, Thomas Christie reported both sets of difficulty in a single journal entry. "Squally Wheather wth. Rain. Some of the people falling out altogether, Mr. Oglethorp Ordd. 'em to be friends & gave all Our People a pint of Bumbo Each head to Drink & be friends together." Ships rocked people in multiple ways.[3]

Both meteorological and figurative tempests could erupt suddenly and with frightening ferocity at any time during the voyage, but lengthy descriptions of these squalls became more frequent in passengers' accounts as they drew near American shores. Aboard the *Simmonds*, the young Methodist Benjamin Ingham commented on this phenomenon noting, "Hitherto, we had had a very fine passage; but now, approaching near land, we met with contrary winds, which kept us above a fortnight longer at sea than otherwise we should have been." Similarly, the lengthening duration of the voyage stretched passengers' patience, and competition for diminishing resources pushed people beyond their breaking points. The literal and allegorical tempests equally tested the physical and mental endurance of all aboard ship. These storms also provoked religious expressions, creating climactic moments in both physical and faith journeys across the Atlantic.[4]

Stormy Waters

Geography helps to explain why meteorological storms arose at this latter stage of the transatlantic passage. The *Simmonds* and *London Merchant* followed a clockwise arc of currents across the North Atlantic. Once the ships recrossed the Tropic of Cancer their course was progressively more north than west. Passengers felt the difference and frequently complained of the increasing coldness of air. "We then met with a chilling No. west wind. While rolling in the gulf stream, fell in with a N England schooner bound to No. Carolina. We kept company some time, & saw each other get our decks well swept & washed in salt water." After warm, languid days in the tropics that defied the Europeans' sense of the calendar, the atmosphere reawakened them to the realities of winter in the northern hemisphere. "After Having run before the Trade Wind till we had got Westing sufficient," Francis Moore reported, "we were obliged to stand Northwardly to fetch Georgia . . . so that we had a second Winter, for we found the Weather cold as we came near the Coast of Georgia." The season of the year always shaped the winds and weather of the crossing, but the winter passage especially brought forward the unpredictable variety of the North Atlantic's climate. Lutheran pastor Henry Melchior Muhlenberg found that the sudden climatic change endangered health. "The sudden cold after the preceding extreme heat made a number of our ship's company very sick and weak. The cold and the wet weather gave such a shock to my constitution that I was seized with high fever, lost my strength, had no appetite, and had to lie abed, besides having to vomit several times." The increasing cold created a new set of challenges for passengers while simultaneously reducing their physical and mental capacities to endure such circumstances.[5]

Ironically, as the air around them cooled, the water warmed as the ships crossed the Gulf Stream. This immense, powerful northeasterly current of warm water fueled the North Atlantic current system that brought them west. In 1786, Benjamin Franklin mapped its flow so that American mariners might negate the dilatory effects of the strong current sweeping them north (figure 7.1). Even earlier in the eighteenth century, when its full size and operations remained unknown, passengers noted with fascination this important oceanic phenomenon. During his voyage on the eve of the American Revolution, cabin passenger Nicholas Cresswell felt the change in the water. "A high and short Sea, suppose ourselves to be in the Gulph stream." Quaker itinerant Rebecca Jones similarly expressed her alarm at "the great motion, rolling, and thumping of the waves . . . but our Captain told us we were crossing the gulf stream." While not understanding its true size, von Reck accurately captured the power of the Gulf Stream, describing it as "one of the most remarkable gulfs in the world being very strong, and continues northward until it gets to Virginia." Although their reckoning lacked the deeper scientific understanding of the following era, eighteenth-century voyagers recognized the Gulf Stream from its effects upon their ships.[6]

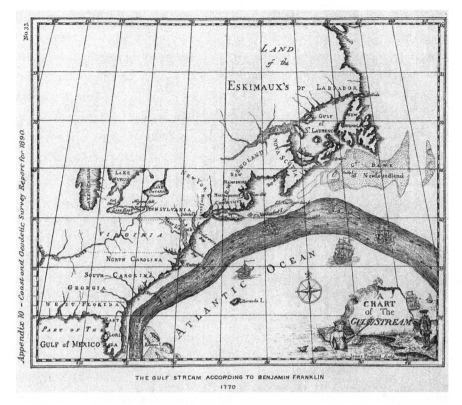

THE GULF STREAM ACCORDING TO BENJAMIN FRANKLIN
1770

FIGURE 7.1. Benjamin Franklin's map of the Gulf Stream, 1770, from John Elliott Pillsbury, *The Gulf Stream: Methods of the Investigation and Results of the Research, Appendix No. 10 from the Annual Report of the Coast and Geodetic Survey for 1890* (Washington, D.C.: Government Printing Office, 1891), 488

In the midst of an ocean seemingly devoid of noticeable landmarks, there were physical markers that indicated one's position. Seaweed served as one signifier of proximity to the Gulf Stream. Passengers frequently noted the presence of what they termed "gulf weed," probably encountering the Sargasso Sea on the western edge of the North Atlantic gyre. This oceanic plant life along with the water temperature and color provided clues to a ship's position. The indicators could be deceptive to the untrained eye. Charleston loyalist Louisa Wells associated the Gulf Stream with its various life forms. "I was much amused when in the Gulph Stream with the Flying-Fish which abound there, and with the

Gulph Weed floating about. Well might poor Columbus be deceived and conjecture himself not far from Land!" The plant life, in particular, captivated von Reck, who noted differences in the sea as they exited the trades and approached the Gulf Stream. "We saw lots of swimming plants here with small berries in the Gulf of Florida, so abundant that the sea looks like a meadow in many places." The sight of such unusual greenery in the midst of a seemingly inhospitable ocean captivated the attention of those longing for land. Among the many unusual plants and animals of Georgia that he sketched, von Reck included a detailed portrait of gulf weed (figure 7.2). These specimens indicated a biotic abundance that passengers associated with land. Some interpreted gulf weed's appearance as a sign that arrival was imminent, when in reality they still needed to traverse some of the most dangerous and difficult waters.[7]

The force of the Gulf Stream posed difficulties for ships trying to navigate the current. Scottish Presbyterian minister Archibald Simpson feared it would sweep his ship beyond its intended destination of Charleston. "We begin now to be sensible of the current of the Gulph stream which carries us fast to the Northward, and we have no Latitude to lose, the Captain now acknowledges this, and keeps the ships head, as much as possible to the southward." If winds did not cooperate, ships found themselves

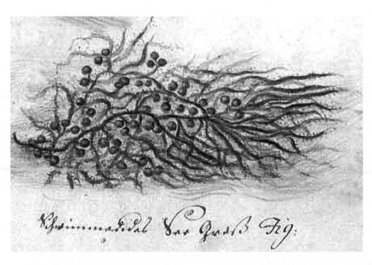

FIGURE 7.2. Detail of floating sea grass, c. 1735, in the sketchbook of Philip Georg Friedrich von Reck, The Royal Library—Copenhagen

having to work hard to reach their destinations. For sailors, exiting the North Equatorial Current and entering the Gulf Stream meant a potentially exponential increase of labor. Over time mariners created a knowledge base of this oceanic space, but as with their understanding of the trade winds, it remained fuzzy and the edges undefined. The masters of the *Simmonds* and *London Merchant* disagreed as to the best route to take and how to interpret the signs the ocean offered. Ultimately, according to von Reck, they chose the wrong route, but the discussion took place because the proper course was not obvious and because they were uncertain about the extent of their western progress.[8]

The Gulf Stream's immense flow, which a later hydrographer described as "a river in the ocean," swept ships rapidly northward, but its warm water also fed the ferocity of the region's tropical storms. This intersection of current and climatic systems funneled hurricanes forming off the coast of Africa toward the coasts of the Caribbean and southeastern North America. Although voyagers did not possess a scientific understanding of what made these oceanic regions so tumultuous, they certainly knew from experience the regionality and seasonality of hurricanes. Simpson critiqued the dilatory sailing of his ship's captain because even the passengers knew the perils of delay in that area. "All aboard think our situation dangerous boating on this coast, in the very middle of the hurricane months, is certainly a very serious matter, to every considerate person." Tension and anxiety rose as passengers approached the North American shore, particularly in those seasons reputed for foul weather. Ships' physical locations influenced the mental states of those aboard ship and intensified their spiritual responses to the experience of oceanic tempests.[9]

Stormy Ships

During his voyage from Virginia to England and back in 1753–55, the Reverend Samuel Davies reflected on the most frightening aspects of the oceanic voyage. "I think there is no Phenomenon in Nature so terrible, as a Storm at Sea, especi[ally] in the Night." Sea squalls emphasized the fragility of the wooden world and the nearness of instantaneous death. The darkness of night added to the confusion and terror of bodies being tossed about and water encroaching from all angles. The sensory experience of oceanic tempests and their accompanying anxieties often rendered travelers wordless. When John Adams tried to convey the experience of a storm at sea, he gave up: "To describe the ocean, the waves, the winds; the ship, her motions, rollings, wringings, and agonies; the sailors, their countenances, language, and behavior, is impossible." Storms muted the descriptive powers of even seasoned mariners such as Captain Henry Gardiner, who described a type of sensory overload. "I would fain depict the appearance of the sky, the noise of the wind, the raging of the sea, and the sensation of the crew, but words would be vain for such a task; one part of it may be seen, and the other felt, but language cannot describe it." When words proved inadequate, von Reck often sketched the oceanic wonders before him. Although no hurricane appeared in his notebook, he did draw a waterspout that dwarfed the ships in the days after a major storm (figure 7.3). The scale of the image emphasized the readiness of the ocean to swallow ships whole.[10]

Voyagers came to a realization that water constituted one of the most potent of nature's powers. By comparison, man-made ships were small and frail. Olaudah Equiano expressed amazement at "one sea, which struck the ship with more force than anything I ever met with of the kind before, laid her under water for some time so that we thought she would have gone down." The waves sometimes rose higher than voyagers thought imaginable. Another sailor described a "sea running so amazing high as to becalm our fore sail." The high swells that could block the

FIGURE 7.3. Sketch of a water spout, c. 1735, in the sketchbook of Philip Georg Friedrich von Reck, The Royal Library—Copenhagen

impulse of the wind tossed ships uncontrollably. "The seas rose in mountains on each side, and we were alternately elevated to the clouds and sunk in the deep. I frequently saw the yards plunged in the waves, and was often sent by force of the motion across my cabin." The frenzy of Atlantic storms threatened to devour ships and those within them. "It is very squally, and the Seas run Mountain-high. It is astonishing we are not swallowed up in this boisterous Deep." Naturalist William Bartram summarized the physical destruction an oceanic tempest left in its wake: "This furious gale continued near two days and nights, and not a little damaged our sails, cabin furniture, and state-rooms, besides retarding our passage." Massachusetts mariner Robert Treat Paine took space in his ship's log to sketch the storm's effects on his sloop (figure 7.4). Those who

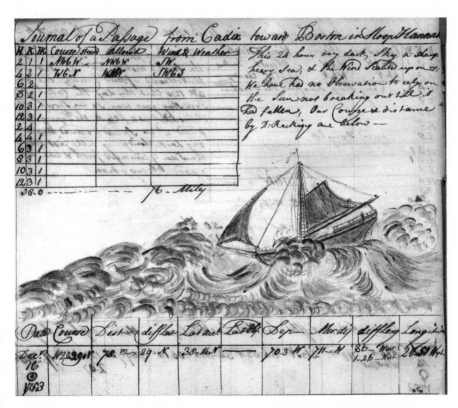

FIGURE 7.4. Sketch of a ship in stormy seas from the logbook of the sloop *Hannah*, 1753, Robert Treat Paine Papers, Courtesy of the Massachusetts Historical Society

witnessed the power of Atlantic storms beheld a spectacle whose impressions lasted a lifetime.[11]

Even those who did not suffer from shipwreck or storm caught glimpses of the ocean's destructive power. One traveler somberly noted the appearance of man-made debris one evening when "we saw three boards, well planed, of ten or twelve feet in length, passing us a quarter of an hour from each other." When storms destroyed the wooden world, they often left little trace. One mariner departing the coast of Rhode Island noted passing by either "a Large Tree with Larger Limb out of water or Else a vesell foundered with her mast Stiking up which I Dont know." Whichever it was, the sight made a somber impression at the beginning of a voyage. The mariner found himself imploring the divine in the "hope I may allways Be Directed And protected By him." The slave ship captain Samuel Gamble inscribed in the log of the *Sandown* a poetic reflection on oceanic evils.

> These seas where Storms, at various seasons blow,
> No reigning Winds, no certain ominous show;
> Surrounding Evils, do we Ponder oer;
> A storm, a Dangerous sea, a leeward Shore.

Those who witnessed oceanic tempests or their aftermath retained serious impressions of the unpredictable forces that could shatter ships.[12]

Storms epitomized a voyage's perils. Travelers in steerage suffered worst, tossed about in the dark beneath closed hatches. Indentured servant John Harrower called his experience of a tempest the "odest shene betwixt decks that ever I heard or seed. . . . There was some sleeping, some spewing, some pishing, some shiting, some farting, some flyrting, some daming, some Blasting their legs and thighs, some their Liver, lungs, lights and eyes. And for to make the shene the odder, some curs'd Father Mother, Sister, and Brother." Storms readily illustrated that ships had not been designed with human transport in mind. Passengers might have accommodated themselves to a ship's hard surfaces and limited comforts, but severe wind and waves removed even the relief of a dry sleep. Steerage passengers already suffering from reduced material circumstances, now wet and cold, found the barest consolations removed. Storms multiplied the voyage's difficulties. As German schoolteacher

Gottlieb Mittelberger noted, "All this misery reaches its climax when in addition to everything else one must also suffer through two to three days and nights of storm, with everyone convinced that the ship is bound to sink." An anonymous poet versified the terror presented by a constant stream of Atlantic storms:

> For full three Months, our wavering Boat,
> Did thro' the surley Ocean float,
> And furious Storms and threat'ning Blasts,
> Both tore our Sails and sprung our Masts.

The effects of storms tormented most those closest to the waterline.[13]

On transatlantic slave ships, chains compounded the misery occasioned by storms. As soon as they left the coast, John Newton noted that the "uncomfortable season is now commencing. Two hundred people confined in a small vessel, in bad weather, occasion noise, dirt, and trouble enough." Those slavers bound for the Caribbean or North America followed the track of hurricanes that formed off West Africa and the prevailing winds and currents swept them to the Americas. This shared route created a close association between Atlantic hurricanes and the African slave trade. In his *Voyage to Guinea, Brasil, and the West Indies*, naval surgeon John Atkins included an entire chapter on hurricanes. He postulated that the fierce storms resulted from "such different Effluvia" arising from the African coast, heated at certain times of the year, and driven into the West Indies. Experiencing a storm that destroyed Port Royal in Jamaica, Atkins concluded, "The Perils of false Brethren was nothing to it." Some slave ship captains rejoiced at the fresh wind and speed such storms provided to their vessels. "No doubt but the Allmighty worker of wonders has provided these hurricanes for a useful end, in rarifying the air, and keeping it in continual circulation."[14]

For the enslaved men and women aboard ship, the storms caused nothing but discomfort. Ship surgeon Alexander Falconbridge described the change in physical conditions between decks during storms. Normally open gratings and canvas funnels forced air below decks, "But whenever the sea is rough and the rain heavy it becomes necessary to shut these and every other conveyance by which the air is admitted. ... The negroes' rooms very soon become intolerably hot. The confined air, rendered noxious by the effluvia exhaled from their bodies and by being repeatedly breathed, soon produces fevers and fluxes which generally carry off great numbers of them." In talking about Atlantic storms, both Atkins and Falconbridge used the word "effluvia," the former to describe their cause and the latter to capture their effects on the human cargo. In addition to creating stifling confinement beneath battened hatches, storms abruptly ended any above-deck respite for slaves. Olaudah Equiano described how rapidly conditions deteriorated between decks during storms. "Many a time we were near suffocation, from the want of fresh air, which we were often without for whole days together. This, and the stench of the necessary tubs, carried off many."[15]

Those in steerage endured the greatest hardships, but no one was immune from the dangers or fear that storms presented. Gales furnished a type of social leveling that transcended passengers' physical location on ship. During storms, Bostonian Josiah Quincy Jr. referred to his cabin as "my hole." During one particularly violent storm the sailors made fast the helm, furled all sails (except one to keep the ship before wind), and retreated below decks to ride out the tempest. Quincy described how the "seas broke over us often; now and then one would strike with enormous force." Nighttime heightened the horrors and made not only sleep but staying in one's berth a seemingly impossible task. "I had no way to keep myself in bed, but by throwing my left arm over the right shoulder and then twisting a cord (fixed to the side of my stateroom) round my wrist. The whole of this night, (after eight o'clock) I believe every soul on board expected to perish." Charles Wesley similarly reported the difficulty of doing anything during a storm. "I rose and lay down by turns, but could remain in no posture long; strove vehemently to pray, but in vain; persisted in striving, yet still without effect." Mental terror accompanied the physical bumps and bruises even for those in the cabin.[16]

In contrast to the fearful confinement between decks, sailors' labors increased in difficulty and danger during oceanic gales. Logbooks provide matter-of-fact accountings of the remarkable work they performed during storms. "The ship makes a Great deal of water & pumps a Great deal of Ballast—In Topsails Blowing very heavy & hail in Great plenty—Up Mainsail & handed him blowing A heavy Gale of wind & dangerous sea." The harsh conditions complicated normal tasks (furling sails) and created additional duties (pumping bilge water choked with ballast). A sailor on the slave ship *Hudibras* suffered the effects of a lightning strike while on deck. "Never had I witnessed such a storm before, and what rendered it more terrific was, the main-top-gallant-mast-head was struck with a force, which made a dreadful crash, and with it were struck the whole ship's company, except Jeremiah Shells." Sailor William Spavens used eight days of gales to reflect on maritime life. "Dreadful indeed are the dangers to which poor seamen are frequently exposed!" The log keeper of the brig *Digby* seconded this assessment: "Came on to Blow and Exstream hard thunder and Lightning and heavy rain all Night Which Put us to Scuding under Bare Poles hard times for Poor Sailors." Even when ships surrendered to storms and protected sailors by removing them from the deck, this action signaled the severity rather than the end of their miseries.[17]

Passengers took note of the additional hardships placed upon sailors during extreme circumstances. Janet Schaw tenderly perceived the physical results of seamen's labor in unimaginable circumstances. "The sailors' hands were torn to pieces by pulling at the wet ropes. Their stock of Jackets were all wet, nor was there a possibility of getting them dried." The need to protect the ship meant that masters sacrificed these men's bodies to the ocean's lashings. Storms could leave visible marks on sailor's bodies, as Nicholas Cresswell noted: "A severe gust of Thunder, Lightning, and the largest Hailstones I ever saw, and the hardest like pieces of Ice cut some of the people's faces till the blood came." Although John Woolman preferred the company and space of seamen to that of cabin passengers, he vacated their quarters out of sympathy to "the poor wet toiling seamen," who needed the additional space. Whatever discomforts passengers experienced, the physical effects of gales at sea fell hardest on those who had to work under horrendous conditions.[18]

The most severe storms necessitated heroic efforts on the part of the crew. Hurricane-force winds caused ships to heel dramatically even with no sails deployed, exposing the leeward side to the encroachment of water and threatening to capsize the ship. Log keeper Richard Dunn reported such circumstances, stating that "during the hardest of the Hurricane our ship lay often down near the M. Hatches & strained her upper works so much that she made a great deal of Water." In these extreme circumstances, the crew might cut down the masts to reduce the amount of spars and rigging catching the wind. Quaker itinerant Susanna Morris described this measure of last resort during her 1746 voyage from London to Philadelphia when her ship was "sorely tried with grievous hurricane of winds." Even after cutting down the masts "the mate said he did not expect that the ship could hold long or words to that purpose, but forever blessed be our great redeemer, for we only lost most of the sails and some other utensils that belonged to the ship, though several of her workmen had a narrow escape for their lives." Morris feared the loss not only of the means of propulsion but lives of the sailors obliged to labor on deck in the storm. Storms forced reflection on the nearness of death, especially for ships' crews.[19]

Storms troubled voyagers' minds and hearts as well as their bodies. Passengers found it terrible to behold storm-driven waves towering taller than ships' masts and to feel winds that easily shredded canvas sails. People's internalized reactions to storms differed, and their descriptions provide a glimpse into the various mentalities present aboard ship. Rhode Island merchant John Francis described the emotions that flashed across voyagers' faces as storms materialized on the horizon. "The Sea running Mountains high threatened us with immediate and unavoidable destruction. Anxiety Hope and Fear were alternately pictured in our Countenances, as different Ideas took their place." At one end of the spectrum, stood appreciation for the raw power—and beauty—in the storm's approach, as expressed by the naturalist William Bartram. "There are few objects out at sea to attract the notice of the traveller, but what are sublime, awful, and majestic: the seas themselves, in a tempest, exhibit a tremendous scene, where the winds assert their power, and, in furious conflict, seem to set the ocean on fire." Others could see only the dark clouds of a foreboding providence signaling the nearness of death.[20]

The terror of storms afflicted even those passengers who experienced good weather during the passage. The repeated horror stories of Atlantic storms braced passengers for the worst, so the absence of storms created an enormous sense of relief. The weather was so mild during German migrant Christopher Sauer's voyage that he could quip, "During the greatest storm we were all, my wife and children, on deck by the fire, and baking cookies. Nor did we hear of any man that was afraid of the sea and the storm." Deck-side preparation of confectionery treats does not fit the normal picture of an Atlantic storm's experience. Anxiety about the voyage had run so rampant that Sauer's wife mocked their former apprehensions of their oceanic surroundings. "I thought people would be afraid if they saw nothing but sky and water." The fear of storms influenced voyagers even when their passage experienced fair weather.[21]

The possibility of a stormy death provoked a religious interpretation and response. Because storms often struck as passengers neared their destinations, they seemed especially diabolic. One Moravian remarked, "It was as if the prince of darkness was spending his last resources to prevent our passage to America." A type of foxhole religion prevailed aboard ship amid these dire circumstances. As in Shakespeare's *Tempest*, when severe danger threatened to overwhelm, eighteenth-century travelers would shout, "All lost! to prayers, to prayers! all lost!" Samuel Davies found the storms drove him to "universal Devotedness to God" who "I find can best support me amid the Dangers of Sea and Land." To express his feelings he turned to verse.

> When the Storm thickens, and the Ocean rolls,
> When Nature trembles to the frighted Poles,
> The pious Mind nor Doubts nor Fears assail,
> Tempests are Zephyrs, or a gentler Gale.

When earthly tempests threatened the wooden world, Atlantic voyagers often found their hope in the life to come.[22]

The voyage also raised uncertainties about the afterlife. Janet Schaw related her family's thought struggles during an Atlantic storm. The tempest raged all night, often wetting Schaw as she huddled in her bed. When the mate called all hands on deck in the middle of the watch, most male passengers, including her brother, lent their aid to the crew. In the morning as they sorted through the wreckage on deck and in their minds, Schaw's ten-year-old nephew, still gripped with uncontrollable fear, continued to wail. The storm at sea had upset the boy's deeply held suspicions about the life to come. Her brother, the boy's uncle, asked him in a scolding voice: "What the duce do you cry for; you are a good boy, if you are drowned, you will go to heaven, which is a much finer place than

Carolina." To which the boy replied, "Yes, Uncle, I know if I had died at land, I would have gone to Heaven, but the thing that vexes me is, if I go to the bottom of this terrible sea, God will never be able to get me up; the fishes will eat me and I am done for ever."[23]

Just as storms provoked theological questions, they sometimes facilitated the answers as well. Although estimates of the event's lasting significance vary, John Wesley's experience of a hurricane off the coast of Georgia is the most famous account of a religious response to an Atlantic storm. The oceanic tempest culminated Wesley's long shipboard encounters with the Moravians. Wesley sought out the Germans as the storm approached bib-lical proportions, having "long before observed the great seriousness of their behavior." As the ship "rocked to and fro with the utmost violence," the English minister sought "an opportunity of trying whether they were delivered from the spirit of fear, as well as from that of pride anger, and revenge." The prior months of engagement primed his encounter with the Moravians' providentially assured courage in the storm. For Wesley, the storm was a chance to test the application of the Moravians' doctrine to see if their belief held up to the force of the wind and waves. The storm provided the theological answer to his question.[24]

The Moravians used storms to assess the mettle of their fellow passen-gers, which they generally found lacking. David Nitschmann described the "great fright among the people who have no God." Although clearly not impressed with the English passengers, he lauded the efforts of Wesley, who "was much aroused, ran to them, and preached repentance." John Andrew Dober's account paraphrased how Wesley explicitly used the storm as a trial of men's faiths. "The preacher Wesley, who is always with us in our song service, cried out against the English, 'Now man can see who has a God and who has none.'" In this tempestuous testing of religion, Dober found the resolve of English women especially deficient as they "screamed and wept" throughout the storm rather than confi-dently submitting to God's providence. The storm gave the Moravians an opportunity to display their faith while facing imminent death and to cri-tique the religious insufficiency of those whose fears overtook them.[25]

Wesley's description of the Moravians' response treats it as exemplary, but religious reactions to storms were actually quite commonplace. Similar events appear in other Atlantic narratives. On the *London*

Merchant, during the same storm that resulted in Wesley's encounter, Commissioner Philip Georg Friedrich von Reck wrote of the reactions of the entirety of passengers and crew. "We were virtually driven together by the storm, weeping and praying."[26] Storms fostered religious expressions and community formation, even if fleeting. Mittelberger stated that during one storm, "All the people on board pray and cry pitifully together." Coming together as a group at such times created a shared sense of fate through worship, allowing people to turn fear into providential trust. Later in the century, Methodist itinerant Francis Asbury could confidently write, "The wind blowing a gale, the ship turned up and down, and from side to side, in a manner very painful to one that was not accustomed to sailing; but when Jesus is in the ship all is well." A suddenly ferocious ocean often facilitated a community consensus as passengers assured one another that all would be well.[27]

Atlantic tempests provoked individual responses as well. In a storm that washed three hogs overboard, Rebecca Jones turned her "mind toward the Lord," meditating on the biblical verse "Let not the water-flood overflow me, neither let the deep swallow me up." Olaudah Equiano stated that he "rejoiced in spirit in the midst of violent Atlantic storms," and George Whitefield claimed he "never was more cheerful in my life." Of course, the authors could express this repose in the presence of imminent death because they lived to tell their tale. In this sense, ocean squalls furnished an extreme form of moral improvement. Samuel Davies reflected, "Every Shock the Ship received from the dashing Waves gave an equal Shock to my Spirit. Guilt made me afraid of sinking in these boisterous Waters." Oceanic gales offered prime opportunities for self-betterment. Many voyagers could have joined with Davies when he expressed the hope that "this providential Deliverance have proper Impressions upon me!" The passing of storms occasioned rejoicing. "The pleasures of a returning sun are not to be conceived but by those who have been in like jeopardies and trials."[28]

Some travelers found in storms metaphors for humanity's inner life. Human passions had long been likened to the unpredictable storms of nature. Atlantic voyagers often drew upon these images. In his memorandum book, mariner Zuriel Waterman included a quotation from a poem:

Our Passions gone & reason in the throne
Amaz'd we see the mischiefs we have done
After a tempest, when the wind are laid
The calm sea wonders at the wrecks it made

Just as the calm afterwards highlighted the explosive power of the storm, so human reason reflected on the harm wreaked by uncontrolled human passions. Samuel Davies drew a similar analogy stating, "The Sea in the Ferment of a Storm gives us an Image—of a Mind agitated with furious Lusts and Passions—and a riotous Mobb." Clergy seized on the violent instability of the sea during a storm as a prime metaphor for human nature.[29]

The critique of sailors' religion partially derived from their different responses to storms. In Puritan divine John Flavel's description of sailors' sins, three related directly to their religious lives: "Forgetfulness of Mercies, Violation of Promises, and Atheistical Contempt of Death." Although he distinguished among them, all three relate to what might be called the religion of the storm. Sailors made oaths in the midst of storms but forgot those pledges when fair weather returned. As seaman "Ramblin' Jack" Cremer noted, the crew "went all to Prayers for our delivery as it began to blow hard." Sailors made supplications and vows during the fury of Atlantic tempests, but when calm returned they frequently did not acknowledge that their requests had been granted and broke those hastily made vows.[30]

To some religious observers, storms further confirmed the irreligious nature of seamen because sailors did not fear the tempests as they should. The wet and trembling passengers took affront that sailors reacted differently to these environmental circumstances. John Wesley could not believe that "so little good would be done by the terror" of the storm and considered the sailors to be "true cowards" for denying that "we had been in any danger." Exceptions to this general rule could catch observers off guard. Wesley's brother Charles expressed a sense of surprise "the first time I have heard a sailor confess it was a storm." Mariners judged the danger of storms differently from passengers and measured the strength and violence of tempests by experience. Whereas passengers like John Fontaine reacted to the "imminent dangers" of gales by drawing moral lessons from them, sailors judged their intensity by the memory of the most experienced "old salt." Dober reported that the "oldest sailors say they have never seen so fierce a storm as the one we had last night." Both the officers and crew of one New Englander's vessel regaled him with stories of storms past and compared them to their current circumstances. Perhaps partly to frighten the uninitiated, they argued that "none had seen so terrible a time." During storms, sailors concentrated on survival rather than on moral instruction.[31]

The criticisms of clerical observers demonstrate how narrowly they conceived the range of acceptable reactions to nature's power. A storm caused Rev. Benjamin Ingham to reflect that a "life of extraordinary holiness" was necessary to face death, and he anticipated that sailors underwent similar thought processes. "I believe, they would then have been glad to have been Christians, how light soever they made of religion before." Clearly, in dealing with storms, sailors engaged in a different type of mental calculus. If sailors reacted to storms by expressions of religious faith, passengers condemned them as disingenuous, for their reaction did not fit the everyday character of their lives. Nevertheless, clerics and other observers repeatedly had trouble in making sense of the matter. If sailors quietly went about their work while surrounded by death, passengers damned them as callous and unaware of their mortal state. Because critics already considered seamen to be irreligious, otherwise admirable qualities—such as bravery—assumed the character of immorality.[32]

The ambiguity of life at sea spurred sailors to seek assurances from various brokers of spiritual power. Sometimes the uncertainties of the voyage stimulated action before a voyage. Seaman Simeon Crowell recorded his trip "to Newport, R.I. where I had my fortune told by a Woman who pretended to know and some things she told me was true but how she came by her knowledge I know not or whether she guessed at what she said." Dreams comforted sailors, reassuring them of their own and their family's safety amid the struggle for life on the ocean. Owen Arnold "Dreamed I Had a Grate fight With a Dead Man for My Right and I Beat him at the Last So I hope the Danger is Past it Was a Bout My dearest frinds and I hope to have My Ends." Seamen like Arnold engaged in a daily struggle with death. Portents of the future comforted them that they would survive. Sailors also sought signs of coming storms in order to prepare for the sea's onslaught. The Huguenot Irishman John Fontaine recorded this vigilance of seamen. "At the rising of the moon a star rose close after and followed the moon which the sailors said was a great sign of a tempest and upon the like occasions that it commonly happens." Mariners read their environment using the wonders around them to raise or stave off fear as needed.[33]

Living on the edge of life and death, sailors believed in contact between the natural and supernatural worlds. Sailors felt themselves surrounded by death. Even the taut psalm-singer Samuel Kelly reported his startled awakening when he felt "a cold hand on my thigh, which did not alarm me a little" since there was only one other person aboard ship at the time. In the midst of tempests, stories circulated of spying the "Flying Dutchman," a fabled ship eternally trying to weather the storm and reach port. Jack Cremer observed "that Sailors in generall have Noshern of fear of Aperishons" and related an anecdote about a swab mistaken for a ghost. Mariners associated various natural phenomena with supernatural visitations from beyond. A British woman drew pictures of a bird called the "Sailors' friend." Their visitations conveyed knowledge of the future, "their appearance portends bad weather. To kill them is unlucky. Each bird is supposed, so legend says, to contain a soul of a dead sailor." Mary Ann Parker provided a similar story of the pintado bird, which "sailors say are the attendants upon storms" and "of course they are not partial to them." Much like later seekers of the millennium, sailors scoured the oceans seeking "signs of the times," although their search had more immediate aims than the coming of God's kingdom. Sailors saw the razor-thin line between life and death and looked for help to postpone the inevitable.[34]

The most common portent discussed aboard ship concerned meteor-like lights that appeared around the masts during storms. The *Simmonds* experienced such a phenomenon toward the end of its storm, captured succinctly by John Wesley in his journal. "Toward the end of it we had an appearance on each of our masts which the ancients called Castor and Pollux, the modern Romanists *corpus sanctum*. It was a small ball of white fire, like a star. The mariners say it seldom appears but either in a storm (and then it is commonly on the decks) or just at the end of one (and then it is usually seen on the masts or sails)." Seaman Samuel Kelly described his encounter with this marvel and attempted a description. "Sailors in general, call these lights 'corps sants,' which I imagine is a term used by Popish seamen, and the meaning is that they suppose it to be the spirit or corpse of a saint." When low-level electricity pervaded the atmosphere, a light would appear at the end of mastheads or yardarms. Mariners provided various interpretations and names for this phenomenon, which was more frequently termed "Saint Elmo's fire." Both Wesley's and Kelly's accounts captured the prevailing idea that this light signified the dead interacting with the living in order to provide a warning of things to come. Like Shakespeare's sprite Ariel displaying "flaming amazement" about the sailors, this glowing visitation struck awe and fear in those who witnessed it. Rather than seek to explain the wonder in terms of scientific description, sailors used supernatural language to account for, and to derive instruction from, the mystery.[35]

Trying to understand and control the unfathomable ocean drove sailors to seek effective supernatural power from a variety of sources. Superstitious practices coexisted alongside orthodox Christian beliefs. Aboard ship traditions blended rather than competed. For example, sailors believed that the name of Jesus Christ had healing powers. One mate instructed a lad to tuck a piece of paper into his hat in order to stave off illness. The note read

> When Jesus saw the Cross he trembled,
> The Jews said unto him why tremblest thou,
> You have neither got an Ague nor a fever.
> Jesus Answered and said unto them
> I have neither got an Ague nor a fever
> But whosoever keepeth my words
> Shall neither have an Ague nor a fever.

Massachusetts mariner Simeon Crowell included in his commonplace book "A Receipt for Curing a Burn" that invoked "the Name of the Father the Son And the holy gost and in three Days you will Be well in the Name of the Lord God." Perhaps worried about the magical aspects of this formula, the evangelically minded sailor added the caveat, "Those Means Cannot help you without A Sted-fast faith & Belief in Christ And the Blessing of Almighty god in whose Hand our Life and Breath is and

Glory be To god in the Highest for his Abundent Mercy." The line between prayerful trust and magical manipulation became blurred aboard ship. As common folk in Europe and Africa had done for centuries, when physical ailments arose on ships, sailors sought power from the senior tars, not from the crude and ineffective medical technology of the eighteenth century. The presence of these traditional beliefs aboard ship demonstrated the continued trust of sailors in powers beyond the natural world that they navigated.[36]

Passing through a North Atlantic storm was a terrifying experience that emphasized human helplessness. Supernatural rituals and spiritual resolves substituted in the absence of physical control over one's circumstances. During the Brethren's first voyage, Moravian leader August Gottlieb Spangenberg penned an oceanic hymn that he sent to David Nitschmann for future voyagers' use. It included the following stanza.

Though our path be set with danger
Nothing shall our spirits shake,
Winds may rage and roar and whistle,
Storms from North and East may break,
Waves may roll and leap and thunder
On a dark and threatening sea,
Thou dost ever watch Thy children,
And their strength and peace wilt be.

Amidst the terrors of oceanic tempests, Moravians clung to the belief that God's sovereign goodness protected them even when their senses might say otherwise. Storms at sea overtook people's thoughts as they overtook ships and drove people to take refuge in God in the absence of other safe harbors.[37]

Stormy Relations

The climatic and oceanographic shifts influenced human interactions aboard ship. The coldness of the air and severity of storms restricted the time spent above deck and constricted passengers to interior spaces. Increased confinement precipitated an increase in conflict among shipmates. With people trapped in close quarters, relationships soured and sometimes sparked physical confrontations. A day after reporting stormy seas, Huguenot immigrant John Fontaine recorded a dispute he had with "the men" for beating his companion Thiboult. "I struck one of them and they took me out of the ship to throw me overboard but brought me in again, in which time the master locked up my sword and pistols, so I was forced to be easy." Fontaine's account emphasized how shipboard violence could escalate. The captain's seizing of Fontaine's weapons prevented further bloodshed after the sailors (jokingly?) threatened to cast him overboard. With no intervening time or space to diffuse tensions, verbal disputes could quickly become physical. David Nitschmann described an altercation aboard the *Simmonds* when "one man was knocked down by another, striking his head on the deck so as to stun him."[38]

The lack of personal space and limited range of companions fomented conflict. As the voyage lengthened, passengers increasingly wore on each other's nerves. John Wesley's pointed opinions drew the ire of his friends and family alike. On Saturday, 10 January, he reported religious talk with Charles, which resulted in "Charles and Ingham angry at me!" The exact cause of the dispute went unreported, and the next day their conversing continued. Sometimes individual conflicts spilled out into the broader community and affected participation in church services. When John tried to mediate between two women, he found himself drawn into deeper conflict. "Both Mrs. Moore, Mrs. Lawley, and their husbands being so angry at me that they resolved (and prevailed on some others to do the same) never to be at prayers more." After another dispute between two women was reconciled, the larger community still bore ill will toward the disputants. Wesley reported multiple people voicing their objections "against Mrs. Hawkins' communing." This attempt to bar the woman from the Lord's Supper left her and her husband "very angry!"[39]

Slave ships witnessed the storms of human conflict on two fronts: between the enslaved and the crew and among the slaves themselves. The end of Samuel Gamble's logbook repeated the refrain "a great Number of Slaves complaining." In this case the dissatisfaction was verbal, but aboard other craft more deadly tempests erupted. Sailors could be lulled into complacency by slaves' apparent cooperation over the course of the voyage. "But," as one sailor remarked, "this quiet was like the dead calm that usually precedes a storm; mischief of the most fatal nature was plotting, which, at no distant time, was to be practised against the whole of the whites on board." Sometimes shipboard revolts revealed the persistence of divisions among the enslaved cargo. For example, the Chamba resented the Fante for their role in the African slave trade, and when the two groups occupied the same ship, they continued to spar. When the Fante revolted, the Chamba "as if to be revenged on them, always assisted the crews in suppressing these mutinies, and keeping them in subjection."[40]

Slave ship captains avoided shackling together men of different nations to prevent fights, but the fetters themselves stimulated hostility. The chaining together of male slaves required high degrees of cooperation and coordination and thus caused numerous conflicts. Chains chafed nerves as well as skin. "Sometimes when one wants to go his companion will not agree to go with him," noted Alexander Falconbridge. The daily, individual necessities of life became matters requiring mutual consent. "When one wants perhaps to obey the calls of nature, and the other has been unwilling to go with him" fights resulted, noted one ship's officer. These conflicts escalated as diet and illness increased shipboard diarrhea. Gamble noted in his log, "Slaves complain very much of the Gripes and Looseness," which reflected not just the medical complaints of individuals but ramifications for everyone in the hold. The hundreds of movements required throughout the course of the day—ascending and descending ladders, taking meals, exercising, going to the bathroom—necessitated coordination. The former slave Charles Ball recalled a woman on his ship who was chained to another to prevent her suicide. In the course of struggling with her chains, the suicidal woman broke her arm and died of a resulting fever. A slip by one could create pain for the other. Sometimes "one Man would drag the other after him when it was necessary for him to move." The slave ship threw together people of diverse backgrounds, then turned them against one another in a daily fight for survival.[41]

Nighttime provided little respite. The overcrowding of the ship's hold required careful arrangement of the human cargo. But unlike inanimate commodities, living freight was subject to conscious and unconscious movements during the night, creating a host of uncomfortable situations. When asked about shipboard disagreements, one mariner replied, "They

frequently disagree in the night about their sleeping places." In addition
to the discomforts caused by the linkage of chains, some found themselves lying in the pathways to the "necessary tubs." "In endeavoring to
get to them," slave pairs "tumbled over their companions, in consequence
of their being shackled. These accidents, although unavoidable, are pro-
ductive of continual quarrels in which some of them are always bruised."
Misery occasioned more misery.[42]

Conditions aboard ship naturally deteriorated with time, and the inherent limitations of ships clearly emerged through their declining resources.
With each passing day, the food supply dwindled through consumption or
spoilage. A Huguenot traveling to Virginia lamented, "A severe storm had
broken the hoops of the only barrel of salt pork left us." This storm off
the Carolina coast reduced the ship's ration "to three pounds of mouldy
biscuit a week & a pitcher of water a day." Dehydration and starvation
added a new dimension to the privations of the voyage. "I can say that
because of it hunger, & thirst & all the other miseries mattered little to
me." As ships neared their destinations, their food and drink declined in
quantity and quality. Masters like Thomas Nicolson made calculated but
unpopular decisions to shorten rations. "Finding our water begins to grow
short and having the prospect of a long passage, I Judge it prudent & necessary to go to an allowance of 2 quarts per man a day." A Rhode Island
master fretted about the ill effects of their increasingly smaller portions of
food. "We begin To come Very short of provisions and are at Very short
allowance already and I cannot Imagine what will be the consequences."
Doubts about the future accompanied the hunger pangs of voyagers'
empty stomachs.[43]

Declining supplies depressed people's spirits. Robert Treat Paine
lamented the "gloomy prospects" when his ship "came to Allowance of
½ biscuit per day" in a voyage from Spain to Boston. George Whitefield
similarly expressed his experience of "spiritual desertions" as ship supplies dwindled. "Our allowance of water now is but a pint a day, so that
we dare not eat much beef. Our sails are exceedingly thin, some more of
them were split last night, and no one knows where we are; but God does,
and that is sufficient." As these conditions continued, their effects clearly
showed on his shipmates' faces. "Most in the great cabin now begin to
be weak, and look hollow-eyed; yet a little while, and we shall come to

extremities, and then God's arm will bring us salvation." The continued delays in reaching land caused some aboard Whitefield's ship to assign blame to a scapegoat who could be held responsible for the ship's deteriorating condition. This "Jonah" bore the ill will and harsh glances of his or her shipmates.[44]

Delays in reaching shore fostered conflicts over how to apportion the declining resources aboard ship. As with the dispute over the *Simmonds*'s water supply, other conflicts emerged over the declining foodstuffs as voyages extended in length. Benjamin Pollard noted in his diary of a voyage from London to Boston how the captain resorted to measuring out the water and brandy rations for the "41 Souls onboard . . . and found it lasted much Longer in proportion then which is Common for some people Drank more than there twice over." Those seen as consuming more than their fair share faced the disapprobation and sometimes punishment from their shipmates. Grievances that had festered throughout the voyage found voice in disputes over food supplies. Charlotte Browne described such an escalation amidst a "great Squall on Deck between Mr. Cherrington and Capt. Browne, it began about the loss of some water gruel and ended with the great favour I had recv'd to have my Cabbin in the Steerage."[45]

Those who supplemented the ship's stores with their own stock of provisions sometimes found their careful planning thwarted by theft. Thirsty thieves particularly targeted liquor. Georgia settler Elizabeth Bland's complaint to Oglethorpe also reported "the little Liquor Mr. Spooner laid in we was robb'd of by the Sailors." During his voyage to Pennsylvania, Adam Cunningham had brought extra wine only to discover a group of thieves siphoning it off, "for which the principal rogue was hanged up at the main yard's arm and then plunged into the sea for 3 or 4 times successively; the rest were whipped at the main yard." Wine was not merely a luxury item but a healthier alternative to the impure "water being very loathesome to drink." Later in the voyage, Cunningham proved thankful for that water as other supplies, such as bread, ran out.[46]

The baseline of assessing whether food was eatable shifted over the course of the voyage. The extremes of hunger pushed some passengers to consume things that they would not have considered palatable previously. During his voyage to Virginia, Henry Norwood described how "the famine grew sharp upon us. Women and children made dismal cries and grievous complaints." The rats that plagued the passengers earlier, "we now were glad to make our prey to feed on." Commerce in vermin developed aboard ship, and "a well grown rat was sold for sixteen shillings as a market rate." Norwood ended with the astonishing, yet "credibly inform'd," tale of a pregnant woman who died after someone refused to sell her a rat for twenty shillings.[47]

Although few Europeans starved to death on the voyage to North America, malnutrition weakened those aboard ship and increased their susceptibility to disease when they reached shore. Georgia passenger Elizabeth Bland "remained at Charles Town being very ill for meer want because we had not eat nor drank any thing but Biscuit and Water for 7 Weeks and 3 Days before I landed I not being able to lay in fresh Provisions and my Stomach could not bear the Ships Provisions."[48]

Storms represented the uncontrollable aspects of nature wielded by a God whose purpose seemed inscrutable. These same gales also brought forth the ingenuity and endurance of humanity. Humans devised means of crossing the ocean and repeatedly demonstrated their ability to do so, even in the very worst conditions. Sometimes the ocean prevailed and ships were wrecked, but most often voyagers successfully reached their destinations. In their reactions to oceanic gales, sailors revealed how they had learned to balance the Atlantic's dangers with their own knowledge and labor. Wesley harshly criticized the sailors' insensitivity to the storm's dangers, but actually their behavior showed a confidence in their ability, born of experience, to ride out a gale successfully.[49]

Squalls between people erupted as ships entered the Gulf Stream and approached their final destinations. Tempers frequently boiled over as passengers' patience wore thin. The longer the voyage lasted, the greater the potential for conflict. Dwindling ship's resources, increased confinement, and the inability to escape created perfect conditions for minor disagreements to explode into major conflict. Physical storms facilitated group religious expression and built community, which interpersonal disagreements threatened to tear apart. These opposing forces made shipboard community formation difficult and spurred passengers' desires for more permanent settings.

Ship life alternated between long periods of tedium and short, furious bouts of agitation. Both could inflict mental and material distress. Coming out of the monotony of the trade winds, North American–bound ships often encountered storm bursts that tossed about the passengers' bodies and troubled their minds. These tempests augmented the discomforts inherent in the ship space. Storms also realized the latent anxiety passengers carried aboard ship. The terror of the deep manifested itself in waves and winds that seemed beyond ships' ability to withstand. Storms reminded people of the immediate prospect of death. Wesley and other ministers used these conditions to evangelize their shipmates, impressing upon them the need to ready one's self for the afterlife. The ship tried the seriousness of people's faith and occasioned the public expression of belief through verbal and nonverbal forms of communication. The storms experienced on the threshold of North America made passengers long for safe harbor. They also revealed the thinness between life and death and provoked a spiritual response in those voyagers who saw a need to prepare for eternity. Even those who did not turn to God desired a new life apart from the tedium and danger of the ocean. The ship, and particularly storms at sea, readied people for life and labor on American shores.

CHAPTER EIGHT

LAND HO!

"On the 15th [of February N.S.], going with a good eastern wind, we discovered the coast of America!" So exulted Philip Georg Friedrich von Reck as the *London Merchant* approached the Georgia coastline after traveling approximately four thousand miles across the Atlantic. Some of the passengers had not left the ship since boarding in London one hundred and fifteen days previously. Fifty-six days had passed since they departed Cowes Road, watching their final glimpse of the English coast recede over the horizon. Finally, they "discovered" land again, although the voyage itself would take two more days until the ships safely anchored at Tybee Island in the mouth of the Savannah River. A mixture of joy and relief accompanied the moment of mooring. "We thanked and praised God in a prayer meeting on the deck, recalling his mercy and fatherly grace." Von Reck quickly left the concerns of the voyage behind, however, turning his thoughts to the future, "begging [God] in the name of Jesus for help for the future life in this strange new world." As had other narrators before and after him, the young German official found his eyes refreshed by the first glimpses of his new home. For von Reck, the scene seemed perfectly Edenic, with majestic forests that "represent the earliest times of the creation!" The difficulties of ship life over the past months faded as life on land reassumed preeminence. They had arrived.[1]

For several days, the passengers on the *Simmonds* and *London Merchant* had scanned the horizon for signs of land while the sailors plumbed the depths seeking their own indicators of terra firma. The increasing length of the voyage manufactured fear and self-doubt, leading people to turn outside themselves for comfort and assurance. When nearing the end of their passages to America, many eighteenth-century voyagers turned to the subject of human mortality and divine causality. Multiple factors contributed to the heightened shipboard anticipation of landfall. The voyage's debilitating length, the spread of illness, the threat of hostile ships, and the possibility of shipwreck—all instilled fear, and these risks increased near the voyage's end. The paradox of the Atlantic crossing was that the desired goal—land—accompanied the greatest dangers to the ship. Thoughts of death naturally proceeded to those of an afterlife. The duration of imprisonment in the wooden world encouraged reflection on freedom in other worlds, both celestial and terrestrial. As ships neared North American shores, voyagers became ever more anxious to reach their destinations.

Arrival in American ports, even the first sight of land, melted these apprehensions away. As pilots came aboard to guide the ship safely to moorings, passengers eagerly anticipated their futures in a new land. The tedium of the long voyage gave way to a flurry of activity when ships finally reached port. This busyness left little time for the rituals of worship and prayer that inaugurated voyages. No longer voyagers, the newcomers devoted their energy to establishing more permanent religious communities on land. Just when the dangers of the journey reached their peak, eliciting profound entreaties for providential care, the voyage ended and the passengers moved on with their lives, carrying the knowledge that God had seen them safely through to new shores.

Anxiety of Time

Ships readily demonstrated time's corrosive effects. Time allowed the oceanic environment to eat away at ship's hulls, to corrode cordage and sails, and to weaken masts and spars. It weakened the physical bodies of those on board, exposing them to the deprivations of malnutrition and disease. The length of an Atlantic passage compounded the other difficulties of shipboard life. Extended time at sea strained the limits of ships' supply capacities and stretched people's ability to tolerate one another.

Unlike modern departures and arrivals, regulated by timetables, eighteenth-century sailing vessels could not sail with any degree of predictability. Too many uncontrollable forces assaulted ships before and during the journey. The evolution of packet sailing was an attempt to provide the regularity that Britain's colonial and commercial empire needed, but not until the nineteenth century did square-rigged ships sail according to reliable time schedules. Most of those who traversed the ocean in the eighteenth century embarked on voyages whose lengths could be estimated but not precisely defined.[2]

The duration of an Atlantic passage varied according to destination, type of ship, weather encountered, and time of the year. Historian Ian Steele's investigation of English communication patterns in the North Atlantic found that the variability in sailing times "produced different oceans. A ship leaving the English Channel for an Atlantic crossing was generally entering a wider ocean than a vessel leaving a colonial port for England." Generally speaking, the winds and currents of the North Atlantic made the passage from Europe to North America double the length of the return voyage, but the time span was never wholly predictable and often extended longer than expected. Sailors used the concept of gravity to capture the arduousness of the "uphill" voyage from London to colonial ports versus the "downhill" return voyage.[3]

Steele's sampling of more than one hundred voyages showed that between 1711 and 1739, the passage from London to Boston averaged seven and a half weeks, but some ships made the trip in a single month and others took as many as three, depending on their route and time of year. The trip from London to Philadelphia took even longer, ranging between six and fifteen weeks but averaging ten (see table 8.1). Ships bound for Charleston typically made the voyage in nine to eleven weeks. The *Simmonds* and *London Merchant* made the passage in eight weeks from Portsmouth, but the passengers boarded ship in London sixteen weeks earlier. The unpredictable duration of sailing times affected passengers in more ways than just the physical effects of making a

TABLE 8.1

Average Length of Passage from London, 1705–1739			
Destination	Average Passage (weeks)	Range of Passages (weeks)	Number of Cases
Boston	7.5	4.0–13	132
New York	9.2	4.0–19	47
Philadelphia	9.8	5.7–15	17

Source: Ian K. Steele, *The English Atlantic, 1675–1740: An Exploration of Communication and Community* (New York: Oxford University Press, 1986), 295, 299, 301.

long-distance journey. The uncertainty of time shaped both their material planning and mental states. No wonder Atlantic voyagers experienced trepidation during the crossing, for the ship served as their home for an indeterminate period.[4]

The length of time expended aboard ship shaped passengers' understandings of the voyage. Quick passages occasioned joy and thanksgiving. Lengthy ones produced melancholy and despair as passengers daily expected land but did not reach it. Von Reck surveying settlers in Georgia noted how "one hears with amazement how such people curse and damn the day on which they sailed." Having experienced comparatively tranquil voyages from the ease of his cabin stateroom, von Reck could not imagine others not being able to endure the time aboard ship. In contrast to von Reck, Charlotte Browne described the liberation she felt on reaching Virginia, "having been a Prisoner in that wooden World call'd the London 4 months and 4 Days." For her, the time aboard ship equaled imprisonment, with days added to her sentence. William Palfrey reflected that on board ship, "Every exertion of spirits is necessary to make the time pass agreeably." The longer Palfrey's voyage took, the more it sapped his spirits. "O how I long to be ashore again," he wrote, "the time begins to seem tedious being so near our port and no wind to get in." However disagreeable or lengthy the voyage, its conclusion elicited expressions of thanksgiving. During his voyage from Virginia to England, the Presbyterian minister Samuel Davies summarized the thankfulness breaking forth after his unpleasant voyage: "It is just 4 Weeks and 4 Days since I left the American Shore; and tho' I have hardly ever had a more melancholy Time, yet I have great Reason to take Notice of the Goodness of Providence to me in my Voyage." The sight of the long-sought port seemed like a gift and instantly gave new life to the sapped spirits of travelers.⁵

Some interpreted the length of the passage as a sign of divine blessing or displeasure. Two German passengers viewed every positive change in the weather as an occasion for thanksgiving: "God gave us such a beautiful north-east wind that we could not wish it any better." When the undue length of Muhlenberg's voyage led to dangerous conditions—they ran out of fresh water and demonstrated symptoms of scurvy—he encouraged his fellow passengers and crew to turn to the only one who could remedy the situation. "God would grant us a favorable wind, and bring us to our destination, if it be that He deem it good and profitable for us." Thankfully for Muhlenberg's sake, a fresh breeze arrived and filled the slack sails that the sailors had unfurled in anticipation of a breeze. Another preacher who proclaimed a similar message became the ship's "Jonah" when the longed-for wind did not come. Time aboard ship was easily related to matters of eternity, but using the voyage's length to interpret heavenly designs could be a knotty exercise.⁶

The case of New England mariner Aaron Bull revealed the internal struggles that an unfavorable wind and a lengthy voyage provoked. Bull mastered a sloop that transported horses from New London, Connecticut, to the British West Indies. His logbook placed the usual account of a ship's advancing position alongside a narrative of his own spiritual progress. For Bull, the two tales overlapped. When the sun shone bright, the wind blew strong, and the horses seemed healthy, Bull concluded, "God Seems att present to Smile on us." When unfavorable gales arose and the livestock became ill, Bull wondered, "What Divine providence Hath before me." Whether by his own carelessness in calculating position or through faulty instruments (as Bull himself thought), the sloop *George* proceeded slowly, its exact position unknown. The thinner the horses' hay became, the deeper Bull's apprehensions grew. "O that I could Sea the hand of god in Suplying us with A good wind Wheather it Be In Mercy or Judgment." When Bull took his frustrations out on the crew, he feared that he might be further arousing divine displeasure. "When I find my selfe out of temp then know I am provoking God Makeing Work for Repentance or Ruining My own Soul." After a passage of four weeks, he "arrived Safe at Antigua [he had been shooting for Barbados] Adored Be the God of our Salvation And O that I may not forgit god when in prosperity." Bull had reached the destination of one voyage, but the outcome of the other remained in flux.[7]

As ships neared their destinations, some passengers reflected on the voyage's length and meanings. They asked themselves, "Did I use my time well?" A voyage to Charleston caused Josiah Quincy Jr. to assess the deleterious effects of the voyage on time usage by quoting Shakespeare.

> To-morrow, [and] to-morrow, and to-morrow,
> Creeps in this petty space [from day to day]
> To the last syllable of recorded time;
> And All our Yesterdays have LIGHTED fools
> The way to study wisdom [dusty death].

Methodist itinerant Francis Asbury identified his journey to Pennsylvania as a period of testing. "Many have been my trials in the course of this voyage; from the want of a proper bed, and proper provisions, from sickness, and from being surrounded with men and women ignorant of God, and very wicked. But all this is nothing. If I cannot bear this, what have I learned?" Janet Schaw also wondered about what the repeated barriers encountered by her ship meant. "Our schemes for the present are frustrated, yet let us not think we are the sport of fortune. Dark as my fate seems I sincerely believe that mercy ever triumphs over evil, and that a powerful hand controls what we call fate. To him then let us submit, and only pray for that fortitude, whose basis is trust in his goodness and omnipotence." For some, the length of time did not matter as much as how that time was improved aboard ship. As Whitefield stated at the end of his first voyage to America, "Though we have had a long, yet it has been an exceedingly pleasant voyage. God, in compassion to my weakness, has set me but few trials, and sanctified those He hath sent me." The Atlantic passage could be viewed as a period of testing, because, although of sustained and indeterminate length, it had an eventual end. The ocean served as a wilderness that tested the qualities of those who crossed it and prepared them anew for their terrestrial callings.[8]

The extended time spent on the ocean gave a dreamlike quality to land, lessening the degree of terrestrial hardships through comparison to those endured aboard ship. "The Time now of our being at Sea began for to be very long and tedious so that we wished for Land when awake and sighed for it when a Sleep, in which Time [our] busy fancy often deluded us with the charms of a beautiful Country. the Land now seemed to be the subject of our chief Discourse." Each passing day heightened anticipation of the voyage's end. Voyagers increasingly spent the time on deck craning their necks for signs of land and experiencing false joy from imagined vistas. Mate Owen Arnold literally dreamed of land and repeatedly punctuated his logbook with these nocturnal longings. "Last Night I Dreamed Very Much About a Tree Being Carried A Long By one Lass" noted one entry, which combined two things he had not seen aboard his ship. Arnold's dreams varied from commonplace ("I thought I was talking With My Wife A Bout Avaith Making the Bedsts") to dramatic ("Last Night I Dreamed I Had a Grate fight With a Dead Man for My Right and I Beat him at the Last"). These fanciful images revolved around the absence of land and home, topics that increasingly dominated the thoughts and conversation of those aboard ship.[9]

Anxiety of Disease

Not all dreams are pleasant of course, and as the voyage lengthened, the nightmare of disease and death hung over ships as it had at the beginning. Illness could break forth at any time, but passengers commonly succumbed to ailments near the end of voyages. The physical toil of a long voyage became increasingly evident in the bodies of men and women. The close physical proximity of people crowded below decks for weeks and months created an ideal environment for infectious disease. Incidents like that aboard a German migrant ship in 1738 demonstrated the power a contagion could wield. Nearly two hundred Germans died from a "malignant fever and the bloody flux" aboard the infamous ship *Palatine*. A ship captain who landed in Philadelphia that same year had excerpts of a letter printed in the *Rotterdamse Courant* that reported, "I sailed in company with four of the skippers who together had 425 deaths, one had 140, one 115, one 90, and one 80." These dramatic incidents cast a pall over anxious travelers even aboard vessels free from incidents of disease. As the ship's passages elongated, passengers feared that the shipboard environment would foster death.[10]

Time mattered. Long-distance voyages, or even shorter trips made in rapid succession, made passengers and sailors vulnerable to scurvy, a vitamin C deficiency that degenerated the body's connective tissue; when left "untreated, it leads to a slow, agonizing, and inevitable death." In the eighteenth century, debates raged about the causes and best remedies for the malady. Some thought scurvy resulted from the physical environment of the damp, wooden ship or from living on the ocean for so long. According to these theorists, cleanliness offered the best remedy. Even at the end of the eighteenth century a New England mariner's logbook recorded fumigating the entire ship regularly to prevent scurvy. Another theory of causation centered on bodily limitations and the lack of exercise aboard ship. A 1736 publication by a prominent naval physician blamed the inactivity of the sailors for the disease, a cruel case of mistaking symptom (lethargy) for the cause (idleness). Thus, the perceived inattentiveness of sailors to their duty as the voyage lengthened exposed them to harsh words and sometimes the physical abuse of the ship's officers, making them suffer doubly. Others attributed it to diet, either to the lack of fresh fruits and vegetables or to the heavily salted meat. There was no mention of scurvy aboard the *Simmonds*, but John Wesley's 1747 *Primitive Physik* listed a diet of turnips as the preferred and an affordable treatment for scurvy. The Georgia Trustees evidently held a similar belief and amply provisioned their ships with turnips and other vegetables.[11]

Despite ignorance of its true causes, mariners skillfully recognized the onset of the disease. Later in the century, the whaler Elijah Durfy noted in his log the moment "trouble just now begins to Enter our Ship the scurvy begins to make its appearance amongst our Crew some scarcely able to perform their Duty." Scurvy even appeared on the comparatively shorter Atlantic voyages, and its debilitating effects on individuals put the entire ship at risk. On his voyage to America, the passenger Adam Cunningham thought his shipmates to be in "a pretty good state of health, saving the scurvy, which now began to show its effects upon our men's constitutions, for there was scarce 5 able to work the ship." When this illness struck the ship's crew, danger resulted for everyone aboard, as the sailors physically could not work the ship quickly. Cunningham's ship bought fresh provisions from an outward-bound vessel, "but our gums were so swelled with the scurvy we could scarce eat them." The chance encounter with another vessel temporarily solved the dilemma of a solitary ship's finite supplies. Although scurvy usually was not a chief killer in the Atlantic crossing, it exemplified the nutritional deficiencies that all steerage passengers faced to some extent during their voyages.[12]

Malnutrition exposed voyagers to other debilitating maladies. Undernourishment broke down the body's barriers to disease, and the crowded conditions below decks gave pathogens ample hosts. Ships furnished excellent conditions for infectious diseases. Inactivity, limited diet, and the lingering effects of seasickness further weakened immune systems, making bodies vulnerable to microbial invaders. Passengers attributed sickness to the miasmic environment of the ship. Wooden vessels were damp, with fetid air, creating a polluted environment that, according to classical medical theory, engendered disease. In reality, these sicknesses were not endemic to the ship's space but came with the people, livestock, and vermin. Once aboard, diseases flourished in the tight confines of the ship, and there was no escape for passengers or crew.[13]

Slave ships exemplified how oceanic vessels magnified the effects of illness and created ideal environments for microbial species. Although the available data does not indicate a strong correlation between overcrowding and the spread of disease, those who lived on slave ships made a mental link between the two. The master of the *Cleopatra*, Nathanael Briggs, reported leaving the coast of Africa "with one hundred & sixty seamen & Slaves on Bord Sum of which are sick with the measles." The extensive human-to-human contact below decks was ideal for transmitting pathogens, and the filthy conditions enabled the spread of dysentery. Additionally, the lengthy wait in sight of the African coast made slave ships easy targets for tropical, mosquito-borne illnesses. John Newton described the advancing terror that led him to "put a boy on shoar, No. 27, being very bad with a flux. This day had another of our people taken ill with a violent bloody flux, have now 5 whites not able to help themselves." He later reported that "No. 27" died. Sailors and slaves suffered alike aboard slave ships, and it was his own severe illness that helped to drive Newton from the trade. Slave ships illustrated how easily oceanic vessels facilitated disease.[14]

Sea journals often recorded the effects of these wooden incubators. Specific diseases could not always be identified but were known through recorded symptoms. The most ambiguous and frequently described symptom was fever. For example, traveling aboard a British troop vessel during his first voyage to Georgia, George Whitefield was confined to bed for ten days by an unidentified "violent fever." His journal recorded the medicine practiced upon him along with the spiritual benefits of enduring this suffering. "I was blooded thrice, and blistered and vomited once, and, blessed be God! can say, *It is good for me that I have been afflicted;* for as afflictions abounded, consolations much more abounded, and God enabled me to rejoice with joy unspeakable." The exact cause of this fever remained unknown, but it certainly was contagious. Whitefield's shipmates fell ill, including the ship's cook, whom he buried a few days after his recovery. Other accounts added more specific adjectives to identify different kinds of fever, as when Judith Giton Manigault wrote her brother: "The spotted fever appeared in our ship, of which many died. Of it our late mother died, being elderly." Other voyagers recorded fevers from smallpox, yellow fever, the bloody flux (dysentery), grippe (influenza), and a host of deadly maladies. These multiple kinds of febrile disease found susceptible targets by the ends of voyages.[15]

Although diagnosis across the centuries is difficult, typhus appears to have been the principal culprit of shipboard fevers. "The names applied to this disorder—gaol fever, camp fever, hospital fever, ship fever, military fever—indicate that it flourished wherever human beings were forced into close contact." Spread through the fleas or lice seemingly omnipresent aboard eighteenth-century ships, typhus afflicted passengers "with a constant Fever and loss of Senses and exceeding weak and fainty." German passenger John Whitehead described an outbreak aboard his ship, which began among those who also suffered from venereal disease but soon spread to the morally "inoffensive" as well. Whitehead himself "kept in a good State of Health till near the beginning of August and then it seemed as if not only the Disease attacked me with all its Fury but I was also afflicted with, as I called it, an Elephantic Itch, for I never have seen such an Itch to my Memory in my Life." Another German, Johann Carl Büttner, succumbed to this typhus outbreak, which plagued him with a nightmarish incapacitation. "I had a very violent fever that, as my companions told me, brought me very near death. I suffered utter delirium, and the surgeon was obliged to let blood from both my arms of which I knew nothing. Of this attack I remember naught save the torture like the suffering of the damned that I saw constantly in my dreams." Typhus often erupted in steerage aboard the more overcrowded ships involved in the shipping of migrants, leading some to associate the disease with German speakers, giving it the label "Dutch" or "Palatine fever."[16]

While not knowing the true etiology of typhus, those concerned with combatting the disease identified a lack of cleanliness as the principal cause. The connection between environment and fever seemed especially prominent aboard ships transporting convicts. As one eighteenth-century observer noted, "Nothing contributes more to make a Ship sickly than nastiness, which you will easily imagine has a very bad Effect where one hundred unclean Creatures are cooped up between a Ship's Decks." A prisoner aboard a British convict vessel painted a deadly scene equivalent to the worst slave ships. "Our treatment on board was very bad About 500 of us on board Shut up in the Hold of the Ship . . . very Sickley the deaths Everyday About 15 of A day, many would be found ded in the Morning." Reformers pegged the griminess of the prisoners as the root of the horrific death rates and recommended removal of hair and dispersal of clean clothes before entering vessels.[17]

Passenger ships concerned with preventing outbreaks of disease employed cleanliness as the first line of defense and the chief preventative. Francis Moore happily noted the measures to prevent outbreaks aboard the *Simmonds* and *London Merchant*. "Whenever the Weather would permit, the Ship was clean'd between Decks, and washed with Vinegar, which kept the Place very sweet and healthy." Other vessels gave similar instructions regarding cleanliness, which stipulated not just the scrubbing of the ship, but enforcing standards of personal hygiene as well. These efforts to remove insalubrious odors and prevent a miasmatic environment aboard ship did not necessarily prevent outbreaks. Palatine fever broke out aboard the Georgia-bound *Judith* in 1745 notwithstanding the significant amounts of vinegar supplied to bathe the ship. John Whitehead's vessel experienced a severe outbreak of typhus despite "the cleansing of our Vessel between Decks and washing them well with Vinegar once and sometimes twice a Week and one Day."[18]

Regardless of their actual effectiveness, the measures to preserve bodily life furnished visible illustrations of the need to ensure eternal life. The ritual purging of wooden vessels became so common that Quaker Thomas Scattergood could employ it as a spiritual metaphor: "O that I may be prepared through this proving scene, as a vessel rinsed and cleansed out, and fit for the heavenly Master's use. Surely pride is hid and I see what a poor, very poor creature I am."[19]

Ships staged life and death dramas. The mortality rates aboard the European ships making the transatlantic crossing varied dramatically. Beyond severe seasickness, the *Simmonds* and *London Merchant* recorded no outbreaks of infection or deaths once they departed the English coast. The Trustees' attempts to prevent potential outbreaks by carefully monitoring the health of emigrants, coupled with the repeated cleansing of ships, helped to keep illness at bay. Francis Moore credited his employers with this extraordinary preservation of life, but other Trustee-sponsored voyages to Georgia proved to be more deadly. Outbreaks of disease and shipwreck killed hundreds in the following decades. For example, pastor Johann Martin Boltzius reported a shipload of Swiss quarantined in Charleston who were so sick from their voyage that a minister seeking to aid them "was turned back by the stench of death." Reports of these dramatic death tolls circulated around the Atlantic through tracts like that of Gottlieb Mittelberger, who reported, "Children between the ages of one and seven seldom survive the sea voyage; and parents must often watch their offspring suffer miserably, die, and be thrown into the ocean." Such testimonials led medical historian John Duffy to conclude "that the long journey of from ten to thirteen weeks brought death to many and provided a grim experience for most who survived."[20]

More recent research tempers this picture of the deadly crossing, especially when European emigration is compared to the transatlantic slave trade. Because better records exist, ample data chart death in the African slave trade. Between 1700 and 1775, death rates aboard slave ships ranged between 8 percent and 24 percent, depending on a variety of such factors as point of embarkation, destination, and the amount of time spent on ship. Despite the extraordinary human disasters aboard some vessels, for example the *Europa* and *Judith*, the European averages in this same period never equaled that of the African trade. Mortality rates aboard vessels ferrying German emigrants averaged between 3 percent and 5 percent over the course of the eighteenth century. Mittelberger overstated the death rate of children but was right to note their greater vulnerability. More than 9 percent of children aboard German immigrant vessels died during the passage. The transatlantic voyage was more deadly than life on shore, but its toll did not equal that of the slave trade.[21]

The threat from disease was real and some vessels experienced enormous death rates, but overall, the majority of those crossing the Atlantic survived. Reports of dramatically varying death rates experienced by previous ships added to the anxiety of passengers who could not understand the true causes of shipboard mortality. They believed that the longer they inhabited the wooden world, the more they exposed themselves to dangerous miasmatic conditions. The variation in death rates augmented the perception that providence governed shipboard survival. Outside obvious forms of causation, the randomness of death pointed to supernatural origins. Since both clean and unclean ships could suffer outbreaks, passengers looked to divine causation as the explanatory factor. Ministers like Wesley and Ingham could point to the presence of prayer and worship as the real preservatives of shipboard health.

Anxiety of Privateers

At the end of voyages, human threats to life emerged alongside microbial ones. As transatlantic ships glided into the coastal sea-lanes off the North American coast, they became potential prey for hostile ships. During England's frequent wars with France and Spain over the course of the eighteenth century, enemy ships viewed unarmed merchantmen as easy targets. Wartime created an opportunity for shipowners to turn their vessels into privateers. Letters of marque—a type of legalized piracy— gave privateers permission to attack the commercial shipping of opposing nations in times of war. The Spanish used St. Augustine as their primary base of North American operations, and the French ran privateers out of the Caribbean and the Canadian fortress of Louisbourg. Rather than search the open ocean for ships, privateers patrolled the coastal approaches to North American ports waiting for potential prizes. During times of war, passengers knew that nearness to land exposed them to the predations of hostile ships; thus every sail represented a possible enemy.

The sea journal that Moravian John Philip Meurer kept during his voyage from London to Philadelphia in 1742 captured the increased anxieties of wartime. The placid weeks in the trade winds were followed by stormy trepidation of "the dreaded Spanish privateers." After a comical encounter with two English ships—each party suspecting the other to be Spanish privateers—the *Catherine* encountered another set of strange sails whose identity proved indisputable: "A Spanish privateer of the most formidable class." Escape appeared impossible (the *Catherine* "being a dull and heavy sailor"), as did mounting a defense ("there were no arms aboard"). With both fight and flight unadvisable, the captain resorted to subterfuge. He continued his ship's casually paced course, seemingly unconcerned about the rapid approach of the "rakish Spaniard." At the same time, "the captain ordered all the male passengers up on the deck, with their hats on, thus presenting a spectacle of forty-nine hats on as many heads, unshaken by fear." Expecting the present prospect of "capture, spoliation, personal abuse, suffering, perhaps death in some dreadful shape," the passengers rejoiced when the Spanish ship passed. "Fervent thanks were offered up to Him who had saved them, when safety appeared an impossibility!" This wartime encounter of two ships off the North American coast provoked the full range of emotional responses for those delivered from death. Since most eighteenth-century merchant ships did not carry cannon, and few participated in convoys, passengers rightly feared the possibility of capture in times of war.[22]

Even during peacetime, fears of encountering armed ships abounded. The line between privateering and piracy was thin, and the sight of unarmed merchant vessels sometimes tempted crews to cross it. The Quaker itinerant William Savery noted the alarm a French privateer's sudden appearance caused. "The minds of Friends were unpleasantly affected, not only because it was uncertain what those sons of rapine might be permitted to do, but more so, on reflecting to what a sorrowful state of darkness men must arrive, before they can engage in the wretched business of privateering." Additionally, the circulation of news throughout the Atlantic world was uneven, so the knowledge of a state of war or peace spread unevenly. Merchant ships could be taken unaware that war had been declared, or privateers might attack without knowledge of peace agreements.[23]

In the many borderlands of the Atlantic, unofficial conflicts heated up in the cold war of the eighteenth century. Although peace reigned when the Oglethorpe expedition sailed, Spain viewed the settlement of Georgia as a hostile act, part of a larger English design against St. Augustine. After landing, Ingham captured the tensions in the air at the Altamaha River settlement when the colonists hastily erected fortifications in response to the sight of a sail. As ships approached their final destinations they became more exposed to the dangers of naval warfare, even if a state of war did not yet exist.[24]

Such uncertainty changed how ships acted in coastal spaces. Under normal circumstances, other sails on the horizon offered happy opportunities to exchange news, compare estimates of position, or secure supplies. For example, as they neared Georgia, the *Simmonds* and *London Merchant* encountered three outward-bound ships that informed them they were just thirty hours of sailing from Charleston. Before this encounter, the Moravians described the ships as drifting aimlessly "because we did not know how far we were from land." Wesley captured the change resulting from this joyful encounter. "We were exceeding glad of so happy an opportunity of sending to our friends in England word of our safety." In contrast, Lutheran pastor Henry Melchior Muhlenberg, traveling during the War of Jenkins's Ear, described how his vessel fled from a privateer although uncertain of its nationality. "It was really a joy that the gracious God had turned away this seeming danger, but the passengers and crew would also have been glad to have had some water from the strange ship and to have inquired concerning our location." The fear of hostile ships during wartime altered both external behaviors and internal mental states.[25]

Like storms, enemy sailing ships appeared to be an unpredictable force wielded by God, who used the violence of enemies to punish the corporate sins of nations. God's deployment of harsh providence through privateers provided another opportunity to demonstrate fidelity in the midst of suffering. Quakers particularly encouraged this spiritually unyielding response to the threat of warfare. They sought inner peace even amid war. Quaker itinerant Elizabeth Hudson noted the gift she had received of being able to "set sail with a fair wind under the enjoyment of divine peace." This sense of peace came from the internal testimony of the Spirit. When Quaker Ann Moore's ship faced capture by a French privateer she went below to prepare and nearly fainted from the prospect of losing her things. She recovered "when the language passed secretly through me, They that will lose their lives for my sake shall save them. Then I gave all up, as though I never had owned them, not expecting to keep any of them, and felt sweet peace." Privateers meant the loss of all her valuables, or worse, but she reconciled herself to obeying God's will as a better possession.[26]

Hindsight allowed captives to see how the experience tested them and better enabled them to serve God. The African American Methodist minister John Jea experienced five years in a French prison after his ship was captured by a privateer. Jea wrote that he "was constrained by the love of God to preach to the people there, the unsearchable riches of Jesus Christ, and God was pleased to crown my feeble endeavors with great success; and, in eighteen months, the Lord was pleased to add to my number two hundred souls." While Jea highlighted the spiritual opportunities that his captivity occasioned, other accounts focused on the suffering at the hands of the French. During the War of Jenkins's Ear, an unknown captive reported, "We should Certainly have Oblidged Monsieur to have been more Bountifull with that which Heaven had put in Our Power for a Reliefe as many of us had ben Prisoners 2 years and in Eating Salt Provissions were Far gone with the Scurvy." The thought of awaiting ransom in a French prison caused many voyagers to implore divine aid to sustain them.[27]

Deliverances similarly resulted from divine intervention. Even in times of war, some feared that the real foes were not Spanish or French but the forces of Satan. In a sermon on ocean travel preached aboard the *Irene*, Brother Johannes von Watteville emphasized the ease of ocean travel compared to traversing similar distances by land. As he put it, this ease gave the Moravians time for spiritual warfare. In the absence of physical barriers or human opponents, pious voyagers could concentrate on directing spiritual forces through prayer. Life aboard ship focused attention on the unseen power of God and his angelic forces.[28]

Anxiety of Shipwreck

In their accounts passengers initially labeled the oceanic environment as empty and featureless, but by the end of the voyage, they recognized subtle variations in the color and composition of the water. Irish Huguenot John Fontaine was one who noted the differences. "As soon as we came in soundings, the water changed its colour, and we see no more carvills nor gulf weed, but we meet with rock weed, a bird they call a penguin and gulls which they take to be undeniable marks of land." These changes in the ocean's appearance increased expectancy of land, with the lightening of the ocean's surface indicating entry onto the continental shelf.[29]

Appearances could be deceiving, however, and ocean color alone could not indicate position. Scottish minister Archibald Simpson reported the perplexed discussions of his ship's mariners, who could not discern whether they were near the continent or the Bermudas. "I hope they certainly know, that the Land on the Coast of the Carolinas, is so low & flat, that it is hardly ever seen, till the ship is in soundings, and I know it is usual to observe the Colour of the water changed, & to throw the lead before they look out for Land, and very often the pilot is aboard before it is seen. However our Navigators are a good deal confused, and all are evidently displeased with themselves, & with one another." Josiah Quincy recorded similar puzzlement aboard his ship in this same region. "All of a sudden the waters changed their colour, we threw the lead and found soundings: the terror and confusion on shipboard was now great indeed: whether this land was off the Bar of Carolina, off Roman Shoals or the Bahama Sands was altogether uncertain to every person on board. New dangers now stared us in the face." The ocean was not undifferentiated, but men and women needed further guidance to navigate the ocean's perils. And despite the achievements in navigational science, people still recognized the overruling hand of providence.[30]

Mariners not only tried to read the ocean's surface to discern their location but also looked to the depths for guidance. Benjamin Franklin described seamen's anxious search for signs of land, particularly in the dark. "The fair wind continues still; we ran all night in our course, sounding every four hours, but can find no ground yet, nor is the water changed by all this day's run." Sounding described the process by which sailors determined the depth of water using a lead ·weight and a line marked at various fathoms. Passengers anxiously watched the routine of sailors searching for fathomable ground as a sign of approaching land. "This day we for the first time found soundings at 35 fathoms, after having cast our lead in vain for several days." Additional information derived from charging the lead with tallow so that it would bring up pieces of the seafloor. The combination of depth with the bottom type helped sailors discern their approximate position. Nicholas Cresswell's ship "Hove the lead, [and] got ground in 15 Fathom sandy bottom," indicating the *Molly* neared Cape Henry on the Virginia coast. A ship's entering soundings signified that it had arrived on the North American continent and was approaching its journey's end.[31]

The euphoric reactions to the "discovery" of the ocean's bottom, evident in voyage narratives, stimulated expressions of thankfulness. For example, the log of the sloop *Nonpareil* detailed one mariner's spiritual interpretation of the technical data derived from a nighttime of soundings. "At 2 am found bottom in 55 fathoms whet Sand & Clear Gravel with Som black Specks at 4 am 50 fathoms Sand as before with broaken Shels & Stones at 6 am No bottom. Blessed Be the Naim of the Lord for all Merces through Christ aman." Soundings displayed both human ingenuity at unraveling the ocean's mysteries and the existence of forces beyond man's control. Steerage passenger Christopher Sauer remarked how wonderful it was "that the sailors knew so exactly in what part of the sea they were. It is 1100 leagues from England to this coast, and yet the headhelmsman, though he is a young man and had never made this voyage before, hit it within three hours when we should see land." Even when soundings were reached, enough could still go wrong and not all passengers believed they could celebrate. Quaker itinerant Rebecca Jones, for one, had reservations and maintained a stoic composure amid the celebration of discovering ground. "Our captain found bottom in fifty fathoms water; on hearing which, divers of our company appeared very much elated, even to an exstacy; but my mind felt very much restricted from appearing outwardly to rejoice." Soundings indicated that the voyage was ending, but it had not yet ended. To some celebration seemed premature and tempted fate.[32]

There remained, nevertheless, a close association between reaching soundings and the voyage's end. Passengers' accounts often applied the term "welcome" to describe their reactions to finding soundings, which were quickly followed by the first sightings of land. John Wesley's journal exemplified the quick succession of events. "We had the welcome news that we were within soundings, having not twenty fathom water. About noon the trees of Georgia were visible from the mast, and in the afternoon from the main deck." The Moravian David Nitschmann put the sighting of land a bit later in the day but seconded the excitement of this new vista. "About two o'clock we saw land. I climbed the mast, and poured out my heart to God, thanking Him, and praying that He would care for us in our new home." After viewing an unchanging oceanic horizon for months, the appearance of land seemed indescribably wondrous. "About 9 of the clock in the morning they hove out the sounding lead and found bottom about 50 fathom deep and about 5 of the clock this afternoon we discovered and seen the lands end which sight was very welcome to us when we had been tumbling so long and tedious a season upon the waves where we could see nothing but the heavens above and water around us." First soundings, then land, and soon, it was hoped, the voyage's end. The Presbyterian Samuel Davies used this expectant desire for the voyage's end as a metaphor for the Christian life. "After a long and dangerous Voyage, how eager are the Seamen looking out for Land; and how rejoiced at the Sight of it! Thus eager are some Xns and thus eager should they all be, to see Immanuel's Land, and arrive there."[33]

Ironically, at the moment when passengers expressed jubilation at the appearance of land, the sailors experienced increased trepidation because they knew that shoals and shores on their lee represented their greatest danger. Most Atlantic shipwrecks occurred in sight of land either at the beginning or near the end of the voyage. The eighteenth century witnessed some ships disappearing without a trace somewhere in the Atlantic, but more frequent disasters took place where land and water met. Sailors tempered their excitement over landfall with a healthy dose of caution. Even familiar land needed to be approached with care, and unfamiliar shores required increased vigilance and were encountered after careful deliberation. During the 1743 voyage of the *Little Strength*, soundings indicated that the ship neared land, but mists and fog prevented its sighting. Uncertain of their position the ship's crew desperately tried to sail back into the wind until its true position could be found. Similarly, other ships found shallow waters but dared not "approach the land on account of contrary winds" and the lack of a local pilot to guide them safely through the bay.[34]

Trust in providential care was needed to cross the ocean in an age when men could only partially discern their position. Despite the technical achievements in navigation, eighteenth-century mariners frequently found themselves unsure of their western progress across the Atlantic. There was no accurate method for determining a ship's longitudinal position, and sailors relied on estimates of the miles sailed each day. Their method of estimation often failed, as Samuel Davies noticed. "We have been expecting Land, and sounding for Ground, these 14 Days. . . . If the Longitude, which has been so long sought for in vain, could be certainly discovered, it would be vastly to the Advantage of Navigation." Later Davies listed longitude in a list of memoranda for spiritual meditation. Just as "the Loss of many ships" resulted from a lack of measuring longitude, so "is the heathen Part of Mankind at a Loss about the way to Heaven." Disorientation amplified the mental unease of passengers facing dwindling supplies of food and patience, yet the failures of man to understand longitude created opportunities to trust God.[35]

An ocean voyage illustrated both the achievements of scientific knowledge and the limitations of human ingenuity. The use of quadrants—and later octants and sextants—allowed mariners to site their position using heavenly bodies and calculate their distance from the equator. The ability to compute mathematically a ship's latitude separated ship's officers from common seamen. Despite this navigational achievement, a number of factors could inhibit masters and mates from complete confidence in their position. Poor weather, poorly calibrated instruments, or faulty mathematics could instantly remove any sense of latitudinal certainty. The ship's position could be "reckoned" but not fixed. "As the sun has not been seen for some days no observations can be taken, and the compass is so bad a one that the Master knows not where we are, or, in bad weather, what course, we are going." Shipboard disagreements illustrated the difficulty of discerning one's place in the expanse of the Atlantic. Charles Wesley recorded a confrontation between a captain and his mate over the location of the ship. The captain asserted their safety, and the mate rejoined, "The most skilful sailor alive cannot know it." When the mate Andrew Brooks took over command of the *Princess Augusta* after its captain died en route, he mistook Cape Cod for the coast of Delaware. Inexperience, mistaken instruments, or faulty calculations doomed ships to uncertainty about their position. One ship's master lamented, "I think My Quadrants when Nigh the Sun is To Far from itt and when at a Distance from the Sun it is To High." Without actual land in sight, it was hard to be sure of one's exact position. Eighteenth-century mariners negotiated the immensity of the Atlantic but never fully mastered it.[36]

After spending weeks without seeing land, this uncertainty frustrated seamen and passengers eager to enter port. Muhlenberg reported the depression of his captain "because he was out on his reckoning and was still unable to find bottom or land." The cause of the captain's melancholy created discontent among the passengers. "The passengers grumbled about the captain for making an error in his calculations and not keeping watch enough, because he now did not know where he was." Cabin passengers frequently lamented the quality of their ship's officers as it became increasingly clear that the ship was lost. John Adams complained of his ship's officers during his wartime voyage to France. "The captain, lieutenants, master, mates, and midshipmen, are now making their calculations to discover their longitude, but I conjecture they will be very wild."[37]

The threat of shipwreck and death tempered the joy of sighting land. Adam Cunningham noted the relief of spotting North Carolina's coast, "which was very acceptable to us, we not having seen land this 6 months and more." However pleasing the sight, it did not forebode an immediate or pleasing end to their voyage. His ship anchored near two other vessels off the Outer Banks, and the captain made his drunken rounds between ships. The rough seas in the area cost one sailor his life and staved the ship's boat to pieces. In the middle of the night, the Bristol slave ship anchored near them lost its cable and came within six yards of colliding with Cunningham's ship. With horror he watched as "the wind being right on shore, forced the ship against a hard beach, where she was staved to pieces and all in her perished, they being fast asleep when she sliped her anchor."[38]

The shifting sands off North America's eastern coast necessitated the expertise of local pilots to guide ships safely into port, particularly through the tidal mouths of rivers. Heedlessness could doom the results of an otherwise successful voyage and bring the entire enterprise to a bitter end. John George Käsebier and Christopher Sauer experienced an overconfident master who tried to enter the Delaware River unaided. Rather than anchoring until daylight, he courted disaster and attempted to slide over the shoals barring its mouth. The large and heavily laden ship ran onto a sandbank, sending them "running out in their night shirts. . . . The ship took a great jolt and then another. We all thought the ship had burst open." Sauer passed the grounding off as a mere inconvenience, for small boats safely ferried the people ashore in the fair weather, but Käsebier drew deeper lessons from the occasion. "We had thought that we had evaded all danger, but God showed us that he could bring ruin to us and our property close to land." In ships' logbooks, the ends of voyages did not evoke the same calls upon heavenly providence as the beginning, but for some the accompanying uncertainties of a voyage's end provoked a theological response.[39]

Seventeenth- and early eighteenth-century shipwreck narratives particularly emphasized the role of divine deliverance when ships came to tragic ends. Literary scholar Hester Blum noted how shipwrecks emphasized divine control over the oceans' many dangers. "The sea operates . . . as a place of danger, a forbidding element controlled by divine power and thus either placid or furious depending on the will of God." This literary genre both expressed faith in human ingenuity and held fast to God's governing hand. God used the difficulties of the ocean passage to strengthen community faithfulness on land. As one scholar of shipwreck narratives noted, "God guided them aboard their ships as they planned how to govern themselves when on land, and God guided their commitment to one another during trials at sea." Shipwrecks furnished dramatic symbolic pictures of the salvation God offered to his faithful servants in times when death seemed imminent on the shoals of life. Evangelical tracts directed toward seamen particularly deployed shipwrecks as a spur to conversion. "THO' God's Wonders are every where visible, and his Mercies no where hid from the Eyes of Man; yet more particularly are they Evident to Seafaring-Men, whose Business is in the Great Waters, and their Lives exposed more than others to Innumerable Hazards and Dangers, of Contending Winds and Seas, Rocks, Quick-sands, and Inhospitable Shores." The tragedies suffered near a voyage's end circulated in literary accounts that added to passenger unease as they inspired trust in God's providence for safe passage.[40]

Anxieties Relieved

When ships finally spied land and eased into their intended ports, the anxieties that passengers had accumulated over the long weeks of the voyage evaporated. Voyagers' accounts recorded a change in attitude that seemed instantaneous. Fears transformed into rejoicing. Fulfilled anticipation replaced uncertain trepidation. Passengers gained an opportunity to view life afresh. The naturalist William Bartram noted how "the sudden appearance of land from the sea" abruptly broke the monotony of the barren horizon and offered a fresh perspective of life ashore. One seemingly experienced a new creation. "The amplitude and magnificence of these scenes are great indeed, and may present to the imagination, an idea of the first appearance of the earth to man at the creation." After such a long voyage, the prospects of renewed life ashore seemed positively Edenic. John Wesley's account connected the beauty of the scene with the chance to start anew. "The clearness of the sky, the setting sun, and the smoothness of the water conspired to recommend this new world, and prevent our regretting the loss of our native country." This fresh viewpoint made all the perils and losses of the voyage seem worthwhile.[41]

The experience of the ocean voyage caused passengers to reevaluate the beauties of land. The voyage magnified the mundane, making otherwise ordinary rocks and trees extraordinary. The exuberant descriptions of land recorded by passengers demonstrated the otherwise subtle changes in perception that the voyage wrought. After the long Atlantic crossing, they painted the landscape with superlatives. Catherine Hickling arose one morn and went "upon deck to see the Sun shed his brilliant rays over the town, the most beautiful and interesting sight, I think I ever saw." Nicholas Cresswell echoed her sentiments. "The land appears from the Masthead to be level and covered with lofty Pines. A great number of Rivers empty themselves into the Bay. Can count Nineteen Sail of Vessels and see the Land on every side. This is one of the finest prospects I have ever seen. What makes it more agreeable, not seeing land before these 27 days." Another traveler described the rapturous vista of drawing near land. "We were soon inclosed with Rocks which was the most romantick scene I ever saw being at a loss to tell the Mountains from the Clouds."[42]

Passengers particularly appreciated visual variety. Although many had earlier noted the splendors of the ocean, the tedium of a Spartan seascape wore on them. Arrival in North America buffeted their eyes with a diversity of scenes. Samuel Davies noted how the visual deprivation of the crossing stimulated a renewed appreciation of earthly panoramas. "How pleasing does the Land appear after so long a Confinement upon the Ocean! Especially as the landscape is beautifully variegated with Towns, Churches, Windmills, Forests, green corn Fields, etc." After his first voyage to Georgia in the *Anne*, Oglethorpe reported to the Trustees the pleasing discovery of trees arising on the horizon. "No disagreeable sight to those who for seven weeks have seen nothing but Sea and Sky." The endless horizon unbroken by structures, although beautiful, paled before the allures of land. At sea, passengers found themselves longing for sensory variety. During her voyage to Africa, Anna Maria Falconbridge found that her heart "gladdened at the sight of the mountains of Sierra Leone . . . beautifully ornamented by the hand of nature, with a variety of delightful prospects." The prolonged experience of the monotonous ocean stimulated praise for the multiplicity of life ashore.[43]

The long voyage also provoked expressions of happiness upon entering port. Despite infrequent written ritual formulations in logbooks, mariners greeted the return to shore with joy. In the next century, seaman-turned-lawyer Richard Henry Dana described his longing for "the open arms and motherly bosom of the harbor." Mariner John Palmer's journal captured the joys of entering port with an elaborate flourish. "At 1 PM a Shoare and the Pint at Mr. Denisons and at 2 Return'd home Safe thanks be to God for all his marsis" (figure 8.1). Sometimes these expressions of thankfulness came simply from reaching soundings, as in the case of the

Nonpareil's log. "Sounded in 18 fathoms Sum San with Grusen Shels a live Blessed be God for all." Massachusetts mariner George Stevens expressed thankfulness upon finding solid ground. "Got Soundings on the Western Ground about 1 a clock this morning Sixty fathoms of Water We have had a fine pleasant passage Down and blessed be god for his goodness to us." Of course, for sailors the joys of harbor extended well beyond their cognizance of divine protection at the close of a voyage. Seaman Isaac Lee rejoiced in having both health and money in his pocket as he arrived in New York. "After Long & Tedious Cold Voyage of 3 months & 3 Days 6 hours 25 minutes I find myself In York with the peaceble posesion of 306 Dollars & 1/4 & 2 cents in Gold Besides goods to the full amount of 20 Dollars with a full Enjoyment of a good state of health worth 50£ Sterling." For mariners, the joys of harbor combined heavenly gratitude with the enjoyment of more earthly pleasures.[44]

An anonymous German arriving in Philadelphia in 1728 expressed his feelings of relief and gratitude on reaching American shores. "So at last this discommodious and dangerous journey had reached its end. The gracious God be praised therefore into all eternity." Regardless

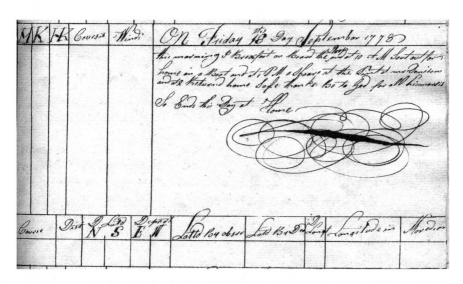

FIGURE 8.1. Home with a flourish, from the logbook of the sloop *Revenge* (privateer), John Palmer Papers, Coll. 53, Manuscripts Collection, G. W. Blunt White Library, Mystic Seaport Museum

of religious persuasion, safe arrival uniformly occasioned thanksgiving. Although his voyage encountered no major difficulties, upon reaching Philadelphia Christopher Sauer still proclaimed, "Thus the Lord has taken us safely to this country. His name be praised." At the end of her voyage, Quaker itinerant Rebecca Jones reflected with thankfulness that she "often clothed my mind with a sense of gratitude to the great Preserver of men, who is, both by sea and land, to his depending children, a God near at hand, a present help in every needful time, to whom be high and endless praises given, because he is good, and his mercy endureth forever." Such expressions of gratitude and relief appear to have flowed out of the anxious uncertainty experienced during the voyage. Reaching their destination prompted a pause for prayerful expressions of appreciation.[45]

The theological inscriptions that initiated a journey in the ship's log seldom possessed a closing counterpart. The busyness of entering a port insured that narratives often closed without a formal conclusion. Typically, when the hazards of the voyage ended and the uncertainty regarding one's immediate fate dissipated, few mariners took the time, at least in printed form, to return thanksgiving for the blessings that they requested previously and had received. One Rhode Island purser noted this tendency when he remarked "very few Godly Enough to Return God thanks for their deliverance." Part of this lack of ritual thankfulness derived from the abrupt ending of logbooks with the sighting of land or when the pilot came aboard. Once the dangers of the sea had passed, most mariners no longer felt the strong need to seek divine guidance or to document the final moments of the voyage.[46]

The voyage's end epitomized the stark differences between the oceanic experiences of European passengers and enslaved African cargos. Anticipation of the ship's arrival heightened rather than dissipated the anxieties of enslaved men and women, who now endured further humiliation as their bodies were prepared for sale in the Americas. Much of this preparation involved attempts to obscure the effects of the voyage. "We began to prepare the slaves for inspection," noted one sailor, "not with any view to their comfort, but to obtain a good price for them." The first step of this process was shaving and washing the slaves to remove the shipboard growth of lice-ridden hair and the accumulated filth from between decks. This step also removed the identifying characteristics of particular slaves in order to present a standardized product for sale during the scramble or auction after the ship's arrival. The second step involved smearing their skin with palm oil to give it healthy, shiny appearance. Sometimes sailors added other substances to the oil to cover visible scarring from disease or punishment and to mask the true age of older slaves. This deception of potential buyers inflicted horrific pain upon the slaves. The shipboard diet and diseases like dysentery could cause diarrhea. Abolitionist surgeon Alexander Falconbridge reported "that a Liverpool captain boasted of his having cheated some Jews by the following stratagem: A lot of slaves, afflicted with the flux, being about to be landed for sale, he directed the surgeon to stop the anus of each of them with oakum."[47]

A third step was to enliven the cargo by increasing the rations of food and water. Some captains distributed rum, tobacco, or other stimulants to disguise the effects of shipboard dehydration and malnutrition. Such actions renewed fears among the slaves that the Europeans intended to eat them. The final act was sale itself, which might be done through an auction or "scramble," in which prospective buyers rushed to choose likely laborers. Equiano described his fear at this process. "The noise and clamour with which this is attended, and the eagerness visible in the countenances of the buyers, serve not a little to increase the apprehensions of the terrified Africans, who may well be supposed to consider them as the ministers of that destruction to which they think themselves devoted." The jubilation of the sailors upon reaching port starkly contrasted the increasing melancholy of a cargo unsure of its futures.[48]

The joy that slave ship mariners exuded on their safe arrival received formulaic expression in ships' logbooks, furnishing a visible exception to the typical pattern of accounts ending without a declaration or formal reflection. In multiple slave ship logbooks, further references to the divine accompanied the successful conclusion of a slaving voyage, as when John Newton added the ascription of praise "Soli Deo Gloria" at the end of his log account. Walter Prideaux added a lengthier expression of praise. "For which above Preservation, God alone be Blessed and Praised, now and for ever more. Amen." Such attributions brought comfort and a sense of security to a deadly and morally ambiguous enterprise. These expressions of praise at the end of their log accounts set slave ships apart from most voyages. That a few slave ship captains continued to make divine appeals indicates that for them a degree of uncertainty remained until their potentially dangerous cargo safely set foot ashore.[49]

The many tasks ashore similarly distracted passengers. Once they sighted land, the Church of England missionaries aboard the *Simmonds* prayed and planned for their future ministries. As they approached Tybee Island at the mouth of the Savannah River, Benjamin Ingham described how the labors ahead now consumed their conversations. "Messrs. Wesley, Mr. Delamotte, and I had some discourse about our manner of living in this new country. I was struck with a deep, religious awe, considering the greatness and importance of the work I came upon." The moment they had reached their destination brought on new matters of concern, not ejaculations of praise, in Ingham's account. Wesley similarly noted that the scripture readings from the evening lesson on the day they sighted land providentially focused on the opportunities and difficulties that lay ahead. "We could not help observing: 'A great door and effectual is opened; and there are many adversaries' [1 Cor. 16:9]." In the coming days, the physical labor of gathering and porting belongings from ship to shore overshadowed all else. The many duties requisite with landfall upset the careful regulation of time the Anglican Methodists had cultivated aboard the *Simmonds*. Wesley lamented the disruptions to his normal devotionals. "Mr. Oglethorpe having commissioned me and one more [John Brownfield of Bristol] to take care of the passengers in his absence, I find how hard it is to serve God without distraction in the midst of secular business."[50]

Despite the excited hurry of entering port, some passengers made time for the rituals of worship whether on ship or shore. The Moravians aboard the *Simmonds* celebrated the entrance into the mouth of the Savannah River by holding their regular song service, although with added relish. "At two o'clock we reached Tybee, and were all very happy. The song service was blessed, and we thanked God with prayer and praise." Further commemoration of their arrival took place the following day as a party rowed to an uninhabited island nearby. Wesley described the joyous moment he first stepped upon American ground. "Mr. Oglethorpe led us through the moorish land on the shore to a rising ground, where we all kneeled down to return thanks to God, and beg the continuance of his fatherly protection over us." Thousands of miles and several months from their London starting point, their voyage concluded with an act of worship.[51]

Atlantic voyagers often employed the word "discovery" to describe their arrival in North America. Of course, the land they sighted had long since been "discovered," but their continued use of the term reflected their excited reaction to the new vista suddenly arising on the horizon. Their arrival initiated their personal discoveries of a new place and new ways of living. This act of discovery, though, entailed risk. The length of time spent aboard ship took its toll on the bodies and souls of the passengers, some of whom would continue to suffer the ill effects of the journey well after its end. The restricted diet and extended confinement created a congenial environment for a variety of infectious and other diseases. Threats also emerged in the form of pirates and privateers who used ships' approach to ports as a prime opportunity to prey on the mostly unarmed merchantmen. Even the discovery of land, the goal of the journey, could threaten vessels with shipwreck. The last days of a voyage escalated passengers' apprehensions, and the various hazards hung over the otherwise happy discovery of their destinations.

The discovery of land also marked new beginnings. The end of the voyage represented not a finale but a transition. The Western church had long described the Christian life as a spiritual journey or pilgrimage, and many early Americans particularly centered on the ship as a spiritual metaphor. The attributes of the ocean crossing provided pictures of the problems and possibilities of life. The Atlantic provided a profoundly supernatural experience that offered a visible analogy of human uncertainty that necessitated divine guidance. The voyage served as a moral lesson, a tutorial in supplication and reliance on the unseen. The shipboard experience described life itself—its inadequacies and dangers, its hopes and aspirations.

CONCLUSION

THE JOURNEY ON

Almost two years after first sighting the North American shoreline, John Wesley craned over a ship's rail to catch a glimpse of Great Britain looming at the end of his second transatlantic voyage. He chose this moment to reflect on the twenty-six months that had passed since he stepped aboard the *Simmonds* on 14 October 1735. The ocean buffeting the ship provided a powerful metaphor for his life up to this point. "For many years have I been tossed about by various winds of doctrine," he reflected. For him, the material experience of the Atlantic crossing offered a period of testing, a liquid equivalent of the biblical wilderness, and it revealed his deficiencies. "I have a fair summer religion. I can talk well; nay, and believe myself, while no danger is near: but let death look me in the face, and my spirit is troubled. Nor can I say, 'To die is gain!'" Death stared Wesley in the face repeatedly over the course of his two voyages. "But what have I learned myself in the meantime? Why (what I the least of all suspected), that I who went to America to convert others, was never myself converted to God." He had twice traversed the Atlantic Ocean, but from his perspective, his travels revealed that his life's voyage had not yet reached its destination.[1]

His brother Charles awaited him ashore, his Georgia sojourn having lasted but a few months. The return voyages had exposed them both to new difficulties, but without the comforting companionship of the other Oxford Methodists. With a constantly drunk captain and an exceedingly leaky vessel, Charles, after just two weeks, doubted whether his ship could bear him safely to England. The slow progress across the ocean created time to discourse with his traveling companion, Mr. Appee, who laid "aside his mask." "He began by telling me all Mr. Oglethorpe had ever said to him, particularly his inmost thoughts of my brother and me; that he ridiculed our pretended fasting in the ship; that he took all my abstemiousness for mere hypocrisy, and put on for fear of my brother, for he saw how very uneasy I was under the restraint; that he much blamed my carelessness, my closeness, my frightening the people, and stirring them up to mutiny, &c. . . . In a word, he believed him [John Wesley] to have a little sincerity, but more vanity; me to have much vanity, but no sincerity at all." The time aboard ship pushed their conversations to more intimate levels, giving Wesley a glimpse of what his shipmates really thought of him and his brother. Discomfited by his companion and discomforted by flux and storms, Charles nevertheless endured the crossing and rejoiced when released upon England's shores. "I knelt down, and blessed the Hand that had conducted me through such inextricable mazes; and desired I might give up my country again to God when He should require." In fact, neither Charles nor John Wesley would cross the Atlantic again.[2]

The two brothers were not the only members of the 1735 Oglethorpe expedition to undertake subsequent voyages. In fact, all who left detailed accounts of their seagoing experiences aboard *Simmonds* and *London Merchant* would ultimately leave Georgia. Benjamin Ingham, the Wesleys' fellow Oxford Methodist, departed for England in 1737, and once back in Europe he continued his exploration of German Pietism. Francis Moore served the colony as storekeeper, as recorder of the town of Frederica, and as Oglethorpe's personal secretary until he and his wife returned to England in 1744, where he published his *A Voyage to Georgia*. The young Philip Georg Friedrich von Reck clashed with some of his fellow Germans, particularly pastor Martin Boltzius, who noted in his secret diary, "Mr. von Reck is often hot-headed and incautious in his impulses and resolutions and this causes us distress and many unnecessary troubles." Von Reck returned first to London and then to Germany to continue recruiting migrants on behalf of the Trustees, but funding for such efforts soon ceased. He never returned to Georgia. The Moravian leader David Nitschmann was back in Germany by 1737, but he would undertake multiple further Atlantic crossings to minister to Moravian communities in Pennsylvania and the Caribbean. His fellow Brethren in Georgia, frustrated by the lack of instructions for the colony, cast lots and selected John Andrew Dober to represent their concerns before Count Zinzendorf, and Dober too returned to Europe in 1737. For these men, their Georgia sojourn represented just one stage of their life's travels.[3]

The point of recounting these subsequent crossings is not to imply that most people returned to the Old World. In fact, it was far more likely that those who crossed the Atlantic did so only once. Rather, these atypical further voyages emphasize the difficulty of identifying a journey's end, even for those who never again stepped aboard a ship. The voyage was over, but the journeys of ships' passengers continued. The subsequent mobility of the major diarists aboard the *Simmonds* and *London Merchant* symbolized the persistence of wandering among transatlantic migrants. Their Atlantic passages transformed into a renewed life ashore that itself incorporated mobility and flexibility. They reached destinations they had not anticipated during their 1735 crossing. Their lives epitomized what John Arnold noted about the discipline of history itself. "For nothing ever ends, really; stories lead to other stories, journeys across a thousand miles of ocean lead to journeys across a continent, and the meanings and interpretations of these stories are legion." Focusing on travel illustrates the role of mobility in colonial lives more broadly considered. The Atlantic crossing helps to explain what one recent historian termed "Protestantism's contributions to Americans' wanderlust."[4]

The passengers aboard the *London Merchant*, the *Simmonds*, and the hosts of other eighteenth-century sailing ships that ferried passengers around the Atlantic went ashore and resumed their lives of laboring to provide for themselves and their communities. The voyage done, land again took precedence, yet the lingering residue of the voyage continued to work its effects on passengers. The ship accustomed travelers to the religious flexibility and independence that life in America would require of them. Rather than jettison their beliefs during the voyage, passengers reorganized their practices to adapt to their distinct, yet temporary, environment. "The paradox of the harshness and unnaturalness of life aboard ship, with the absence of so much that would belong to normal life," one literary scholar of voyage narratives has noted, "is that deprivation was also revelation." They could practice their religion as much or as little as they wanted, but the circumstances of the transatlantic voyage offered powerful stimulants for religious exercise. The abundance of leisure time coupled with the lingering threat of oceanic death pushed passengers to reading, prayer, and other devotional practices. Religious expression did not disappear in the absence of institutions to enforce it; rather, it blossomed as passengers sought comfort, meaning, distraction, or entertainment in the open time and space of the ocean. Religion appeared during the crossing only because people chose to bring it aboard and to utilize it to endure the long voyage.[5]

The ship not only enabled physical and material mobility; it also fostered intellectual and cultural transfers between the continents. Varying denominations crossed the Atlantic, but so did cultural ideas about negotiating and tolerating religious differences. Scholars have long studied the intellectual origins of religious toleration, but its actual practice has been considered only recently. Rather than present a progressive narrative of the evolution of ideas from tolerance to intolerance, recent studies of religious conflict and coexistence emphasize the persistence of these opposing forces in people's lives. Historian Scott Dixon succinctly captured this tension within Europe. "When circumstances required it, early-modern men and women were able to move back and forth between two apparent opposites—tolerance and intolerance—without it resulting in a permanent change of mind." Despite commitment to exclusive religious confessions, Europeans negotiated different methods for allowing differences to exist within communities—not on terms of an expansive ecumenicity or theological equality, but through certain daily accommodations. An emerging distinction between the private life of the individual and the public good of the community created space for coexistence even if the lived reality belied the discursive difference. "Citizens might follow their consciences as they saw fit, but only in the privacy of their own homes, and only under the conditions imposed by urban authorities."[6]

If dissenting religions in parts of Europe were tolerated through the private exercise of faith within people's homes, life aboard ship explicitly transformed the private into public knowledge. The symbolic boundaries in towns and cities that allowed peaceful coexistence between competing faith groups blurred amid the tight confines of the transatlantic crossing, but the ship did not typically establish one creed over the others through an institutionalized presence of religion. The absence of a single, dominant confessional perspective freed passengers to enact their own religious accommodations at least for the length of the voyage. Something beyond mere coexistence was possible even if practitioners retained their confessional commitments. Shipboard circumstances anticipated the conditions of the frontier, where the more dominant power negotiated cultural differences rather than simply imposing social norms from above. As historians seek to understand "how it was that eighteenth-century Americans managed to accommodate the religious differences that produced so much bloodshed in the past," the encounter with diversity aboard transatlantic ships provides an intermediary step in the move from mere coexistence to a more equitable inclusion.[7]

The fleeting experience of religious diversity exercised longer lasting effects because the religious traditions themselves underwent subtle transformations as they were transplanted across the ocean. The subsequent history of North America demonstrates that the religions of the Old World survived the Atlantic crossing, but not entirely in the same form. Religious faiths underwent a sea change on a corporate and individual level. Not everyone shifted his or her allegiance to a competing religious perspective aboard ship; in fact, probably few did. Rather, the voyage itself served as a type of conversion, a translation of practices from one cultural setting to another. Wesley's Church of England provides perhaps the best example of this type of metamorphosis. The absence of a bishop in North America before the American Revolution reduced the presence of Anglican clergy, necessitating a more lay-driven practice of piety through individual or communal reading of the *Book of Common Prayer*. Even before they entered into lay-centered American parishes, Anglicans adjusted to the absence of clergy during the voyage. The ship forced them to alter their practices for a time, sometimes to the extent that reengaging in institutional life could be disorienting.[8]

Many eighteenth-century voyagers stepped ashore in strange places, longing for familiar experiences, only nothing about life seemed quite the same as they remembered it. For example, deprived of public worship during her seven-week voyage from Scotland, Presbyterian laywoman Janet Schaw gladly attended an Anglican church on the island of Antigua in 1774. Although the structure boasted "a very fine organ, a spacious altar, and everything necessary to a church which performs the English Service," she found herself unmoved by the ceremony. The audience around her appeared "most devout" and "the neatness and elegance of the Church" pleased her greatly, but Schaw stood as a "mere Spectator." The discovery shocked her. The emotional coldness she experienced in Antigua contrasted with the memory of her "deeply, deeply interested" heart during the last service she had attended in Scotland. She now felt that this service from the *Book of Common Prayer* "had no more to do with me, than when I admired Digges worshipping in the Temple of the Sun." The communal worship that she had missed aboard ship now disappointed her on land. The finding was "sad to make."[9]

In between shores, the ship gave people a glimpse of themselves and their beliefs through the distinct perspective that travel provided. As a historian of German migration has noted, "All Migrations, as 'rites of passage,' force participants to reassess their self-image and their values." The crossing fortified some convictions, challenged others, and forced still others to be discarded, replacing them with new conceptions of the world. The options were not limitless and boundaries remained, but new apertures were opened, new vistas unfolded. American colonists knew that alternative religious configurations were possible because of their experience of shipboard diversity. Although various groups often self-segregated into their own distinct communities after their arrival in America, shipboard diversity remained as a wondrous memory that could spark religious experimentation. Travel fed one's sense of wonder and stirred one to move.[10]

John Wesley's account of his voyage exemplified this stirring. The ship served as a catalytic agent that provoked Wesley "to spiritual anxiety by the questions of believers whose religious fervour had originated deep in central Europe."[11] His increasing admiration of the piety and hymnody of the Moravians revealed his cognitive and affective movements over the course of the voyage and beyond. His encounter with these Pietists motivated him to learn German, to take up the hymns of the *Gesang-buch* and translate them into English, and to have a greater degree of confidence in God. Even after the voyage ended, his fascination with the religious movement that he encountered aboard the *Simmonds* continued—in Georgia and then in England. This sustained engagement culminated in his famous Aldersgate experience at a Moravian meeting a few months after his return to London. "About a quarter before nine, while the leader was describing the change which God works in the heart through faith in Christ, I felt my heart strangely warmed. I felt I did trust in Christ alone for salvation; and an assurance was given me that He had taken away my sins, even mine, and saved me from the law of sin and death." The shipboard encounter ignited the fire that produced his warming experience of conversion. Taken as a whole, Wesley's account combined the persistence of religious practice amid institutional absence, the power of encounter across ethnic and religious boundaries, and the metaphorical possibilities of the ocean to symbolize personal religious experience.[12]

Following these themes as a pathway into the subsequent development of American religion illustrates the role mobility played in shaping of theological ideas. Instead of concentrating on the brick-and-mortar rootedness of congregations, the travel metaphor draws attention to those times when people and institutions underwent processes of change with an inward vitality not accompanied by material structures. Instead of focusing on denominations apart from one another, mobility emphasizes those points when the stately ships of church crossed paths and the conflict or accord that resulted from those meetings. This focus on capturing motion serves an equalizing function, redistributing consideration to those "others" who have usually remained in the background of traditional historical accounts but who were nevertheless present aboard ship. Finally, it would emphasize the ever-changing nature of religious beliefs and practices, rather than treating them as some eternal testimony set in living stone.

The shaping influence caused by months at sea must be considered in our attempts to understand American history. It was these transatlantic (and later transpacific) voyages that created tremendous opportunities for cross-cultural contact at liminal moments in which people were especially susceptible to the impact of such meetings. Concentration on travel encourages a rereading of narratives to rediscover vibrant but forgotten characters that have been replaced by flat stereotypes, which have little basis in history. It encourages a heightened awareness of the subtle, and not so subtle, changes inevitably wrought by the voyage. Literary scholar Haskell Springer surveyed American writings about the sea and found the ocean crossing to be "a transforming experience" which gave spiritual significance to otherwise ordinary events aboard ships. This approach suggests that religious scholars study the movements of people as much as they have studied their dwellings and their places of worship. It creates fresh metaphors for how the discipline is described and suggests new interpretive models for understanding religious cultures. Finally, it suggests that students of religion become Argonauts themselves, plying their trade back and forth as they repeatedly cross the threshold of time and space.[13]

NOTES

Introduction

1. John Wesley, *Journal and Diaries I, 1735–1738*, vol. 18 of *The Works of John Wesley*, ed. W. Reginald Ward and Richard P. Heitzenrater (Nashville: Abingdon Press, 1988), 345.

2. Martin Schmidt, *John Wesley: A Theological Biography*, vol. 1 (London: Epworth, 1962), 148–149; Edwin S. Gaustad, *A Religious History of America* (New York: Harper and Row, 1966), 105; Sydney E. Ahlstrom, *A Religious History of the American People* (New Haven: Yale University Press, 1972), 228; Frederick A. Norwood, *The Story of American Methodism* (Nashville: Abingdon Press, 1974), 26; Peter W. Williams, *America's Religions: Traditions and Cultures* (Urbana: University of Illinois Press, 1998), 122–123.

3. Aaron Fogleman, "Migrations to the Thirteen British North American Colonies, 1700–1775: New Estimate," *Journal of Interdisciplinary History* 22, no. 4 (Spring 1992): 691–709; Bernard Bailyn, *The Peopling of British North America: An Introduction* (New York: Alfred A. Knopf, 1986), 5, 8.

4. Bernard Bailyn, *Voyagers to the West: A Passage in the Peopling of America on the Eve of the Revolution* (New York: Alfred A. Knopf, 1986); Bernard Bailyn and Philip D. Morgan, eds., *Strangers within the Realm: Cultural Margins of the First British Empire* (Chapel Hill: University of North Carolina Press, 1991); A. Roger Ekirch, "Bound for America: A Profile of British Convicts Transported to the Colonies, 1718–1775," *William and Mary Quarterly* 42, no. 2 (April 1985): 184–200; A. Roger Ekirch, *Bound for America: The Transportation of British Convicts to the Colonies, 1718–1775* (New York: Oxford University

Press, 1987); David Eltis, "Free and Coerced Transatlantic Migrations: Some Comparisons," *American Historical Review* 88, no. 2 (April 1983): 251–280; P. C. Emmer and E. van den Boogaart, eds., *Colonialism and Migration: Indentured Labour before and after Slavery* (Higham, Mass.: Kluwer Boston, 1986); Aaron Spencer Fogleman, *Hopeful Journeys: German Immigration, Settlement, and Political Culture in Colonial America, 1717–1775* (Philadelphia: University of Pennsylvania Press, 1996); Aaron S. Fogleman, "From Slaves, Convicts, and Servants to Free Passengers: The Transformation of Immigration in the Era of the American Revolution," *Journal of American History* 85, no. 1 (1998): 43–76; Stephen Foster and T. H. Breen, "Moving to the New World: The Character of Early Massachusetts Immigration," *William and Mary Quarterly* 30, no. 2 (April 1973): 189–222; Patrick Griffin, *The People with No Name: Ireland's Ulster Scots, America's Scots Irish, and the Creation of a British Atlantic World, 1689–1764* (Princeton: Princeton University Press, 2001); Marianne S. Wokeck, *Trade in Strangers: The Beginnings of Mass Migration to North America* (University Park: Pennsylvania State University Press, 1999). None of the following prominent texts of American religion discusses the role of the Atlantic passage in transferring religious belief to America and, while acknowledging difference, all assume basic continuity between the beliefs of the continents. Ahlstrom, *Religious History of the American People;* Winthrop Hudson, *Religion in America: An Historical Account of the Development of American Religious Life,* 3rd ed. (New York: Charles Scribner's Sons, 1981); Catherine L. Albanese, *America: Religions and Religion* (Belmont, Calif.: Wadsworth, 1992); Mark A. Noll, *A History of Christianity in the United States and Canada* (Grand Rapids: Eerdmans, 1992); Peter Williams, *America's Religions: Traditions and Cultures* (Urbana: University of Illinois Press, 1998). The following analyze the role of the ocean, particularly the Atlantic, in history: "Oceans Connect: Maritime Perspectives in and beyond the Classroom," conference website (Duke University, 28 Feb.–3 March 2002), http://ducis.jhfc.duke.edu/archives/oceans/, accessed 14 July 2012; Bernard Bailyn, *Atlantic History: Concept and Contours* (Cambridge: Harvard University Press, 2005); "AHR Forum: Oceans of History," *American Historical Review* 111, no. 3 (June 2006): 717–780; Jack P. Greene and Philip D. Morgan, eds., *Atlantic History: A Critical Appraisal* (New York: Oxford University Press, 2008); W. Jeffrey Bolster, "Putting the Ocean in Atlantic History: Maritime Communities and Marine Ecology in the Northwest Atlantic, 1500–1800," *American Historical Review* 113, no. 1 (Feb. 2008): 21–23; W. Jeffrey Bolster, *The Mortal Sea: Fishing the Atlantic in the Age of Sail* (Cambridge: Belknap Press of Harvard University Press, 2012), 1–11.

5. Helen Rozwadowski, *Fathoming the Ocean: The Discovery and Exploration of the Deep Sea* (Cambridge: Belknap Press of Harvard University Press, 2005), 213–214; Sidney A. Reeve, "Ship Evolution and Social Evolution," *Geographical Review* 23, no. 1 (Jan. 1933): 61–76; Philip E. Steinberg, *The Social Construction of the Ocean* (New York: Cambridge University Press, 2001); Joyce E. Chaplin, "The Atlantic Ocean and Its Contemporary Meanings, 1492–1808," *Atlantic History: A Critical Appraisal,* 35–54; John R. Gillis, *Islands of the Mind: How the Human Imagination Created the Atlantic World* (New York: Palgrave Macmillan, 2009).

6. Benjamin W. Labaree, William M. Fowler Jr., Edward W. Sloan, John B. Hattendorf, Jeffrey J. Safford, and Andrew W. German, *America and the Sea: A Maritime History* (Mystic, Conn.: Mystic Seaport, 1998), 4; John K. Thornton, *A Cultural History of the Atlantic World, 1250–1820* (New York: Cambridge University Press, 2012), 5; Mary Louise Pratt, *Imperial Eyes: Travel Writing and Transculturation* (New York: Routledge, 1992), 6; Christopher Mulvey, *Transatlantic Manners: Social Patterns in Nineteenth-Century Anglo-American Travel Literature* (Cambridge: Cambridge University Press, 1990), 12. Recent works such as Marcus Rediker's *The Slave Ship* and Stephanie Smallwood's *Saltwater Slavery* attempt to provide a cultural history of people's experiences aboard slave ships to accompany the extensive statistical picture of the vast historiography of the transatlantic slave trade. Marcus Rediker, *The Slave Ship: A Human History* (New York: Viking, 2007); Stephanie E. Smallwood, *Saltwater Slavery: A Middle Passage from Africa to American Diaspora* (Cambridge: Harvard University Press, 2008).

7. In their work on religious rituals, particularly pilgrimages, anthropologists Victor and Edith Turner identified a *liminal* stage during which pilgrims from diverse backgrounds created a new *communitas.* As the pilgrimage ended, people shifted back into their previous cultural patterns, but now slightly altered by the experience of the liminal community. Ocean travel lends itself to a similar exploration of liminal communities. Victor W. Turner and Edith L. B. Turner, *Image and Pilgrimage in Christian Culture: Anthropological Perspectives* (New York: Columbia University Press, 1978); Victor Witter Turner, *The Ritual Process: Structure and Anti-Structure* (Chicago: Aldine, 1969). French social theorist Michel Foucault identified the ship as the perfect example of what he termed "heterotopias," or other spaces. These alternative societal configurations countered the presumed normalcy of existing social structures. Michel Foucault, "Of Other Spaces (1967), Heterotopias," trans. Jay Miskowiec, http://foucault.info/documents/heteroTopia/foucault.heteroTopia.en.html, accessed 14 July 2012. Thomas A. Tweed, *Crossings and Dwellings: A Theory of Religion* (Cambridge: Harvard University Press, 2006). Tweed presents a theory of religion built upon the interrelations between movement and stasis that emphasizes the movement and intersections of beliefs.

8. Naval historian N. A. M. Rodger, who attempted a detailed social description of the British navy during the Seven Years' War, neglected to treat "religion and superstition" because these topics in his opinion lacked sufficient evidence. N. A. M. Rodger, *The Wooden World: An Anatomy of the Georgian Navy* (Annapolis: Naval Institute, 1988), 11; a similar lack of attention to religion can be found in Margaret S. Creighton and Lisa Norling, *Iron Men, Wooden Women: Gender and Seafaring in the Atlantic World, 1700–1920* (Baltimore: Johns Hopkins University Press, 1996). Dorothy Denneen Volo and James M. Volo, *Daily Life in the Age of Sail* (London: Greenwood, 2002). Henry Baynham, *From the Lower Deck: The Royal Navy, 1780–1840* (Barre, Mass.: Barre Publishers, 1970); Marcus Buford Rediker, *Between the Devil and the Deep Blue Sea: Merchant Seamen, Pirates, and the Anglo-American Maritime World, 1700–1750* (Cambridge: Cambridge University Press, 1987), 153–204. Despite the usual historical inattention to sailors' religion, several works provide helpful investigations of the

religious lives of sailors. Christopher P. Magra, "Faith at Sea: Exploring Maritime Religiosity in the Eighteenth Century," *International Journal of Maritime History* 19, no. 1 (June 2007): 87–106; Roald Kverndal, *Seamen's Missions: Their Origin and Early Growth* (Pasadena: William Carey Library, 1986); Alain Cabantous, *Le ciel dans la mer: Christianisme et civilisation maritime, XVe–XIXe siècle* ([Paris]: Fayard, 1990).

9. Chris Beneke, *Beyond Toleration: The Religious Origins of American Pluralism* (New York: Oxford University Press, 2008); C. Scott Dixon, "Introduction: Living with Religious Diversity in Early-Modern Europe," in *Living with Religious Diversity in Early-Modern Europe*, ed. C. Scott Dixon, Dagmar Freist, and Mark Greengrass (Burlington, Vt.: Ashgate, 2009), 2, 9–10; Dagmar Freist, "Crossing Religious Borders: The Experience of Religious Difference and Its Impact of Mixed Marriages in Eighteenth-Century Germany," in *Living with Religious Diversity in Early-Modern Europe*, 206; Stuart B. Schwartz, *All Can Be Saved: Religious Tolerance and Salvation in the Iberian Atlantic World* (New Haven: Yale University Press, 2009); Benjamin J. Kaplan, *Divided by Faith: Religious Conflict and the Practice of Toleration in Early Modern Europe* (Cambridge: Belknap Press of Harvard University Press, 2010); Chris Beneke and Christopher S. Grenda, eds., *The First Prejudice: Religious Tolerance and Intolerance in Early America* (Philadelphia: University of Pennsylvania Press, 2010); Carla Gardina Pestana, *Protestant Empire: Religion and the Making of the British Atlantic World* (Philadelphia: University of Pennsylvania Press, 2009), 31; S. Scott Rohrer, *Wandering Souls: Protestant Migrations in America, 1630–1865* (Chapel Hill: University of North Carolina Press, 2010), 12.

10. Rozwadowski, *Fathoming the Ocean*, 6.

11. David Cressy, "Puritans at Sea: The Seventeenth-Century Voyage to New England," *Log of Mystic Seaport* 36, no. 3 (1985): 87–94; David Cressy, "The Vast and Furious Ocean: The Passage to Puritan New England," *New England Quarterly* 57, no. 4 (1984): 511–532; David Cressy, *Coming Over: Migration and Communication between England and New England in the Seventeenth Century* (New York: Cambridge University Press, 1987), 144–177, quote from 151; Virginia DeJohn Anderson, *New England's Generation: The Great Migration and the Formation of Society and Culture in the Seventeenth Century* (New York: Cambridge University Press, 1991), 42–71; Sacvan Bercovitch, *The Puritan Origins of the American Self* (New Haven: Yale University Press, 1975), 117–118; Robin Miskolcze, *Women and Children First: Nineteenth-Century Sea Narratives and American Identity* (Lincoln: University of Nebraska Press, 2007), xv; Haskell Springer, "The Colonial Era," in *America and the Sea: A Literary History*, ed. Haskell Springer (Athens: University of Georgia Press, 1995), 33–34.

12. Laurie Maffly-Kipp, *Religion and Society in Frontier California* (New Haven: Yale University Press, 1994), 7–8, 134–135; Susan Lee Johnson, *The Roaring Camp: The Social World of the California Gold Rush* (New York: W. W. Norton, 2000), 99–140; D. Bruce Hindmarsh, *The Evangelical Conversion Narrative: Spiritual Autobiography in Early Modern England* (New York: Oxford University Press, 2005), 16.

13. John Wesley, *Journal and Diaries I*; Benjamin Ingham, "Rev. Benjamin Ingham, the Yorkshire Evangelist," in *The Oxford Methodists: Memoirs of the Rev. Messrs Clayton, Ingham,*

Gambold, Hervey, and Broughton, ed. L. Tyerman (New York: Harper and Brothers, 1873); Francis Moore, *A Voyage to Georgia Begun in the Year 1735* (London: Jacob Robinson, 1744); Philip Georg Friedrich von Reck, *Von Reck's Voyage: Drawings and Journal of Philip Georg Friedrich von Reck*, ed. Kristian Hvidt (Savannah: Beehive Press, 1980). The two other German accounts by John Andrew Dober and David Nitschmann can be found in Adelaide L. Fries, *The Moravians in Georgia, 1735–40* (Raleigh, N.C.: Edwards and Broughton, 1905). Other brief descriptions of the Oglethorpe expedition are located in *The Journal of the Earl of Egmont: Abstract of the Trustees Proceedings for Establishing the Colony of Georgia 1732–1738*, ed. Robert G. McPherson (Athens: University of Georgia Press, 1962); *General Oglethorpe's Georgia: Colonial Letters, 1733–1743*, ed. Mills Lane (Savannah: Beehive Press, 1990); Egmont (Sir John Percival) Papers, typescript copy, University of Georgia Libraries; James Gascoigne, Letter Book 1735–1747, Duke University Special Collections.

14. S. Charles Bolton, *Southern Anglicanism: The Church of England in Colonial South Carolina* (Westport, Conn.: Greenwood, 1982); John Frederick Woolverton, *Colonial Anglicanism in North America* (Detroit: Wayne State University Press, 1984); John K. Nelson, *A Blessed Company: Parishes, Parsons, and Parishioners in Anglican Virginia, 1690–1776* (Chapel Hill: University of North Carolina Press, 2001); Richard W. Vaudry, *Anglicans and the Atlantic World: High Churchmen, Evangelicals, and the Quebec Connection* (Montreal: McGill–Queen's University Press, 2003); Fries, *Moravians in Georgia;* Gillian Lindt Gollin, *Moravians in Two Worlds: A Study of Changing Communities* (New York: Columbia University Press, 1967); Geoffrey Stead, "Crossing the Atlantic: The Eighteenth Century Moravian Experience," *Transactions of the Moravian Historical Society* 30 (1998): 23–36; Jon F. Sensbach, *A Separate Canaan: The Making of an Afro-Moravian World in North Carolina, 1763–1840* (Chapel Hill: University of North Carolina Press, 1998); Jon F. Sensbach, *Rebecca's Revival: Creating Black Christianity in the Atlantic World* (Cambridge: Harvard University Press, 2005); Harry S. Stout, *The Divine Dramatist: George Whitefield and the Rise of Modern Evangelicalism* (Grand Rapids: Eerdmans, 1991); David W. Bebbington, Mark A. Noll, and George A. Rawlyk, eds., *Evangelicalism: Comparative Studies of Popular Protestantism in North America, the British Isles, and Beyond, 1700–1900* (New York: Oxford University Press, 1994); Frank Lambert, *"Pedlar in Divinity": George Whitefield and the Transatlantic Revivals, 1737–1770* (Princeton: Princeton University Press, 2002); Mark A. Noll, *The Rise of Evangelicalism: The Age of Edwards, Whitefield and the Wesleys* (Downers Grove, Ill.: InterVarsity Press, 2003); David Hempton, *Methodism: Empire of the Spirit* (New Haven: Yale University Press, 2005); Frederick Barnes Tolles, *The Atlantic Community of the Early Friends* (London: Friends' Historical Society, 1952); Frederick Barnes Tolles, *Quakers and the Atlantic Culture* (New York: Macmillan, 1960); Rebecca Larson, *Daughters of Light: Quaker Women Preaching and Prophesying in the Colonies and Abroad, 1700–1775* (New York: Alfred A. Knopf, 1999).

15. Richard D. Brown, *Knowledge Is Power: The Diffusion of Information in Early America, 1700–1865* (New York: Oxford University Press, 1989), 4–5.

16. Travel narratives, particularly sea tales, constituted a longstanding category in English literature, but they assumed a new character with expanded authorship and

distribution in the eighteenth century. Philip Edwards, *The Story of the Voyage: Sea-Narratives in Eighteenth Century England* (Cambridge: Cambridge University Press, 1994), 1–14; Susan Durden O'Brien, "A Transatlantic Community of Saints: The Great Awakening and the First Evangelical Network, 1735–1755," *American Historical Review* 91, no. 4 (October 1986): 811–832.

17. Springer, "Revolutionary and Federal Periods," in *America and the Sea*, 62; Herman Melville, *Redburn: His First Voyage* (New York: Harper and Brothers, 1850), 376.

Chapter 1. Embarkation

1. Francis Moore, *A Voyage to Georgia Begun in the Year 1735* (London: Jacob Robinson, 1744), 13–14.

2. Moore, *Voyage to Georgia*, 14–15.

3. Robert G. McPherson, ed., *The Journal of the Earl of Egmont: Abstract of the Trustees Proceedings for Establishing the Colony of Georgia, 1732–1738* (Athens: University of Georgia Press, 1962), 98–99.

4. Paul Alkon, "Changing the Calendar," *Eighteenth-Century Life* 7, no. 2 (1981–82): 1–18; Robert Poole, "'Give Us Our Eleven Days!': Calendar Reform in Eighteenth-Century England," *Past and Present*, no. 149 (Nov. 1995): 95–139; Mark M. Smith, "Culture, Commerce, and Calendar Reform in Colonial America," *William and Mary Quarterly* 55, no. 4 (Oct. 1998): 557–584.

5. Philip Georg Friedrich von Reck, *Von Reck's Voyage: Drawings and Journal of Philip Georg Friedrich von Reck*, ed. Kristian Hvidt (Savannah: Beehive Press, 1980), 27; George Fertig, "Transatlantic Migration from the German Speaking Parts of Central Europe, 1600–1800: Proportions, Structures, and Explanations," in *Europeans on the Move: Studies on European Migration, 1500–1800*, ed. Nicholas P. Canny (New York: Oxford University Press, 1994), 192–235; Marianne S. Wokeck, *Trade in Strangers: The Beginnings of Mass Migration to North America* (University Park: Pennsylvania State University Press, 1999), 8.

6. Wokeck, *Trade in Strangers*, 61–62; Kristian Hvidt, "Introduction," *Von Reck's Voyage*, 12–14; von Reck, *Von Reck's Voyage*, 27; Julius F. Sachse, "Literature Used to Induce German Emigration," *Proceedings and Addresses of the Pennsylvania German Society* 7 (1897): 175–198.

7. "Copy of a Letter from Mr. Hugh Mackay to Mr. Oglethorpe Dated at Kirtomie 1st. September. 1735," Egmont Papers, Phillipps Collection, 14208: 28, University of Georgia Libraries; von Reck, *Von Reck's Voyage*, 27.

8. John Frederick Whitehead, "The Life of John Frederick Whitehead," in *Souls for Sale: Two German Redemptioners Come to Revolutionary America*, ed. Susan E. Klepp, Farley Grubb, and Anne Pfaelzer de Ortiz (University Park: Pennsylvania State University Press, 2006), 102–103; von Reck, *Von Reck's Voyage*, 28.

9. A. G. Roeber, *Palatines, Liberty, and Property: German Lutherans in Colonial British America* (Baltimore: Johns Hopkins University Press, 1993), 98; Wokeck, *Trade in Strangers*, 121–122;

Leonard Melchior, "Advice to German Immigrants," ed. Hannah Benner Roach, in *Pennsylvania German Roots across the Ocean*, ed. Marion F. Egge (Philadelphia: Genealogical Society of Pennsylvania, 2000), 47; "Daily Register of the Two Pastors, Mr. Boltzius and Mr. Gronau, from January 1st to the end of the year 1736," *Detailed Reports on the Salzburg Emigrants Who Settled in America*, vol. 3, ed. Samuel Urlsperger; trans. and ed. George Fenwick Jones and Marie Hahn (Athens: University of Georgia Press, 1972), 97.

10. Gottlieb Mittelberger, *Journey to Pennsylvania*, trans. Oscar Handlin and John Clive (Cambridge: Belknap Press of Harvard University Press, 1960), 11; *Diary of a Voyage from Rotterdam to Philadelphia in 1728*, trans. Julius F. Sachse (Lancaster, Pa.: Pennsylvania German Society, 1909), 17; Wokeck, *Trade in Strangers*, 118–125; Susan E. Klepp, Farley Grubb, and Anne Pfaelzer de Ortiz, "Introduction," *Souls for Sale*, 11–14; Whitehead, "Life of John Frederick Whitehead," in *Souls for Sale*, 126–128.

11. Von Reck, *Von Reck's Voyage*, 28; Johann Carl Büttner, *Narrative of Johann Carl Büttner*, in *Souls for Sale*, 216.

12. Whitehead, "Life of John Frederick Whitehead," 127; Adelaide L. Fries, *The Moravians in Georgia, 1735–40* (Raleigh, N.C.: Edwards and Broughton, 1905), 93; *Diary of a Voyage from Rotterdam*, 8; von Reck, *Von Reck's Voyage*, 29.

13. Ralph Davis, *The Rise of the English Shipping Industry in the Seventeenth and Eighteenth Centuries* (New York: St. Martin's Press, 1962), 300–310; von Reck, *Von Reck's Voyage*, 29; David Nitschmann quoted in *Moravians in Georgia*, 102; John George Käsebier and John Christopher Saur, "Two Early Letters from Germantown," ed. Donald F. Durnbaugh, *Pennsylvania Magazine of History and Biography* 84, no. 2 (April 1960): 220.

14. Jon F. Sensbach, *Rebecca's Revival: Creating Black Christianity in the Atlantic World* (Cambridge: Harvard University Press, 2005), 47–50; Aaron Spencer Fogleman, *Hopeful Journeys: German Immigration, Settlement, and Political Culture in Colonial America, 1717–1775* (Philadelphia: University of Pennsylvania Press, 1996), 101.

15. Margaret S. Creighton and Lisa Norling, "Introduction," *Iron Men, Wooden Women: Gender and Seafaring in the Atlantic World, 1700–1920* (Baltimore: Johns Hopkins University Press, 1996), vii–xiii; David Cordingly, *Women Sailors and Sailors' Women: An Untold Maritime History* (New York: Random House, 2001), xi–xv; David Armitage and Michael J. Braddick, eds., *The British Atlantic World, 1500–1800* (New York: Palgrave Macmillan, 2002), 42. For example, the ratio of men to women among Scottish emigrants was only 1.5 to 1. Bernard Bailyn, *Voyagers to the West: A Passage in the Peopling of America on the Eve of the Revolution* (New York: Alfred A. Knopf, 1986), 129–134; Wokeck, *Trade in Strangers*, 39–50.

16. Wokeck, *Trade in Strangers*, 67, 80; Christopher J. French, "Eighteenth-Century Shipping Tonnage Measurements," *Journal of Economic History* 33, no. 2 (June 1973): 434–443; Ralph Davis, *The Rise of the English Shipping Industry in the Seventeenth and Eighteenth Centuries* (New York: St. Martin's Press, 1962), 74, 178; Marcus Buford Rediker, *Between the Devil and the Deep Blue Sea: Merchant Seamen, Pirates, and the Anglo-American Maritime World, 1700–1750* (New York: Cambridge University Press, 1987), 160.

17. Wokeck, *Trade in Strangers*, 128–131.

18. Walter E. Minchinton, "The British Slave Fleet 1680–1775: The Evidence of the Naval Office Shipping Lists," in *De la traite a l'esclavage du Ve au XVIIIe siècle*, ed. Serge Daget (Paris: Société Française D'Histoire D'Outre-Mer, 1988), 394–427; Wokeck, *Trade in Strangers*, 78–79, 128–130; Herbert S. Klein, *The Atlantic Slave Trade* (New York: Cambridge University Press, 1999), 142–150; Marcus Rediker, *The Slave Ship: A Human History* (New York: Viking Press, 2007), 61–65; R. J. Dickson, *Ulster Emigration to Colonial America, 1718–1775* (London: Routledge and Kegan Paul, 1966), 210–211; von Reck, *Von Reck's Voyage*, 31; Moore, *Voyage to Georgia*, 11. The *Trans-Atlantic Slave Trade Database* lists the *London Merchant* as making five distinct slave trading voyages to Africa under Captain John Thomas between 1733 and 1738, but at least one of the voyages coincided with the 1735–36 transport of Europeans to Georgia. Furthermore, the details of two voyages mirror each other with both listing 271 slaves embarking from an unknown African port and only 217 arriving in Charleston. Clear evidence shows that the *London Merchant* was involved in transatlantic slave trade but not to the degree given in the *Database*. "London Merchant," Voyages Database, 2009, *Voyages: The Trans-Atlantic Slave Trade Database*, http://www.slavevoyages.org/tast/database/search.faces, accessed 1 Aug. 2013.

19. Bailyn, *Voyagers to the West*, 94–104; Alan Taylor, *American Colonies* (New York: Viking, 2001), 318. Henry Melchior Muhlenberg, *The Journals of Henry Melchior Muhlenberg*, trans. Theodore G. Tappert and John W. Doberstein (Philadelphia: Muhlenberg Press, 1942), vol. 1, 27.

20. William Downes Cheever Travel Journals, 10 Nov. 1778, Massachusetts Historical Society (hereafter MHS).

21. Whitehead, "Life of John Frederick Whitehead," 124–125; Mittelberger, *Journey to Pennsylvania*, 11. The reference to "herrings" appeared in other pamphlet literature critical of the transatlantic commerce in Germans. Melchior, "Advice to German Immigrants," 46.

22. James Clifford, *Routes: Travel and Translation in the Late Twentieth Century* (Cambridge: Harvard University Press, 1997), 35; *Baltimore* logbook, 1788–1789, 16 May 1788, MHS; John Newton, *The Journal of a Slave Trader, 1750–1754*, ed. Bernard Martin and Mark Spurrell (London: The Epworth Press, 1962), 22; Greg Dening, *Mr Bligh's Bad Language: Passion, Power and Theatre on the Bounty* (New York: Cambridge University Press, 1992), 19.

23. John Wesley, *Journal and Diaries I, 1735–1738*, vol. 18 of *The Works of John Wesley*, ed. W. Reginald Ward and Richard P. Heitzenrater (Nashville: Abingdon Press, 1988), 345.

24. Rebecca Jones, *Memorials of Rebecca Jones*, ed. William J. Allinson (Philadelphia: Henry Longstreth, 1849), 150.

25. John Woolman, *The Journal of John Woolman and a Plea for the Poor*, intro. Frederick B. Tolles (Philadelphia: Joseph Crukshank, 1774; reprint, Secaucus, N.J.: Citadel Press, 1972), 189.

26. John Francis Diary, 25 Sept. 1783, Rhode Island Historical Society (hereafter RIHS); Janet Schaw, *Journal of a Lady of Quality; Being the Narrative of a Journey from Scotland to the West Indies, North Carolina, and Portugal, in the Years 1774 to 1776*, ed. Evangeline Walker Andrews (New Haven: Yale University Press, 1923), 19.

27. William Downes Cheever Travel Journal, 11 Nov. 1778, MHS; Charles Wesley, *The Journal of the Rev. Charles Wesley* (Taylors, S.C.: Methodist Reprint Society, 1977), 69–70; Schaw, *Journal of a Lady of Quality*, 22.

28. Wokeck, *Trade in Strangers*, xxi, 53–54; Walter E. Minchinton, "Characteristics of British Slaving Vessels, 1698–1775," *Journal of Interdisciplinary History* 20, no. 1 (1989), 73–74; Charles Garland and Herbert S. Klein, "The Allotment of Space for Slaves Aboard Eighteenth-Century British Slave Ships," *William and Mary Quarterly* 42, no. 2 (April 1985), 238. Studies of the immigrant and slave trades in the eighteenth century have concluded that mortality rates aboard ship had more to do with the conditions encountered before embarkation and voyage length than with overcrowding. Farley Grubb, "Morbidity and Mortality on the North Atlantic Passage: Eighteenth-Century German Immigration," *Journal of Interdisciplinary History* 17, no. 3 (Winter 1987): 584; Joseph C. Miller, "Mortality in the Atlantic Slave Trade: Statistical Evidence on Causality," *Journal of Interdisciplinary History* 11, no. 3 (Winter 1981): 385–423; quoted in Newton, *Journal of a Slave Trader*, 53; Olaudah Equiano, *The Interesting Narrative of the Life of Olaudah Equiano, or Gustavus Vassa, the African*, in *The Interesting Narrative and Other Writings*, ed. Vincent Carretta (New York: Penguin Books, 1995), 58. Olaudah Equiano produced the longest and most detailed eighteenth-century account of the slave ship, but there are serious questions as to whether or not he actually underwent the Middle Passage. Vincent Carretta's careful exploration of the surviving evidence suggests that the first chapters of the *Interesting Narrative* were fictionalized, but he also identifies ship, the *Ogden*, whose voyage followed the trek described by Equiano. Equiano's later wide-ranging and well-documented experiences as an Atlantic sailor help give credence to his description of the ship's hold, so his description will be taken at face value for the purposes of this narrative. S. E. Ogude, "Facts into Fiction: Equiano's Narrative Reconsidered," *Research in African Literatures* 13, no. 1 (1982): 30–43; Vincent Carretta, "Olaudah Equiano or Gustavus Vassa? New Light on an Eighteenth-Century Question of Identity," *Slavery and Abolition* 20, no. 3 (1999): 96–105; Vincent Carretta, *Equiano the African: Biography of a Self-Made Man* (Athens: University of Georgia Press, 2005); Paul E. Lovejoy, "Autobiography and Memory: Gustavus Vassa, alias Olaudah Equiano, the African," *Slavery and Abolition* 27, no. 3 (December 2006): 317–47.

29. Wokeck, *Trade in Strangers*, 228. These and other advertisements are provided in appendix D of R. J. Dickson, *Ulster Emigration to Colonial America, 1718–1775* (London: Routledge and Kegan Paul, 1966), 238–281.

30. Mittelberger, *Journey to Pennsylvania*, 11; John Harrower, *The Journal of John Harrower, an Indentured Servant in the Colony of Virginia, 1773–1776*, ed. Edward M. Riley (Williamsburg, Va.: distributed by Holt Rinehart and Winston, 1963), 24–25; William Moraley, *The*

Infortunate: The Voyage and Adventures of William Moraley, an Indentured Servant, ed. Susan E. Klepp and Billy G. Smith (University Park: Pennsylvania State University Press, 1992), 60; von Reck, *Von Reck's Voyage*, 29.

31. Robert G. McPherson, "The Voyage of the *Anne*—A Daily Record," *The Georgia Historical Quarterly* 44 (1960): 223, 224; von Reck, *Von Reck's Voyage*, 31.

32. Marcus Wood, *Blind Memory: Visual Representations of Slavery in England and America, 1780–1865* (New York: Routledge Press, 2000), 19; "London Merchant," *Voyages: The Trans-Atlantic Slave Trade Database*. Moore, *Voyage to Georgia*, 15.

33. "Testimony of Robert Norris, a Carolina Merchant, Trading at Liverpool," *House of Commons Sessional Papers of the Eighteenth Century*, vol. 68, ed. Sheila Lambert (Wilmington, Del.: Scholarly Resources, 1975), 9.

34. Emma Christopher, *Slave Ship Sailors and Their Captive Cargoes, 1730–1807* (New York: Cambridge University Press, 2006), 187–192; Marcus Rediker, *The Slave Ship: A Human History* (New York: Viking Press, 2007), 68–70, 241–243; Stephanie Smallwood, *Saltwater Slavery: A Middle Passage from Africa to American Diaspora* (Cambridge: Harvard University Press, 2007), 76.

35. Moore, *Voyage to Georgia*, 87; "Advice for Brethren and Sisters in Preparation for Crossing the Atlantic to the West Indies," reprinted in Geoffrey Stead, "Crossing the Atlantic: The Eighteenth-Century Moravian Experience," *Transactions of the Moravian Historical Society* 30 (1998): 32; Büttner, *Narrative of Johann Carl Büttner*, in *Souls for Sale*, 217.

36. John W. Jordan, "Moravian Immigration to Pennsylvania, 1734–1767," *Transactions of the Moravian Historical Society* 5, no. 2 (1896): 53; Gillian Lindt Gollin, *Moravians in Two Worlds: A Study of Changing Communities* (New York: Columbia University Press, 1967), 67–89; John C. Brickenstein, "The Second 'Sea Congregation,' 1743," *Transactions of the Moravian Historical Society* 1 (1857–76): 117. Stead, "Crossing the Atlantic," 23.

37. Muhlenberg, *Journals*, vol. 1, 48; Johann Cristoph Sauer, "An Early Description of Pennsylvania," ed. R. W. Kelsey, *Pennsylvania Magazine of History and Biography* 45 (1921): 245; *Diary of a Voyage from Rotterdam to Philadelphia in 1728*, trans. Julius F. Sachse (Lancaster, Pa: Pennsylvania German Society, 1909), 17.

38. Von Reck, *Von Reck's Voyages*, 31. Samuel Kelly described a similar incident when a rat gnawed a hole in his ship; Kelly, *Eighteenth Century Seaman*, 25–26; A Memorandum or Short Account of Ye Life of Benjamin Bangs, 27 April 1748, Mss. C 5089, New England Historic Genealogical Society (hereafter NEHGS); James Rhodes Log and Account Book, 24 Dec. 1793, Log, 331, G. W. Blunt White Library, Mystic Seaport Museum (hereafter Mystic Seaport).

39. Woolman, *Journal*, 204–205; "The Journal of James Savage," ed. Theodore Chase and Celeste Walker, *Proceedings of the Massachusetts Historical Society* 97 (1985): 133; Kelly, *Eighteenth Century Seaman*, 39, 87.

40. Nitschmann quoted in Fries, *Moravians in Georgia*, 102. John K. Nelson, *A Blessed Company: Parishes, Parsons and Parishioners in Anglican Virginia, 1690–1776* (Chapel Hill:

University of North Carolina Press, 2001), 190; Nancy L. Rhoden, *Revolutionary Anglicanism: The Colonial Church of England Clergy during the American Revolution* (New York: New York University Press, 1999), 10–13; See also Rhys Isaac, *The Transformation of Virginia, 1740–1790* (Chapel Hill: University of North Carolina Press, 1982), 58–70.

41. Jones, *Memorials*, 56–57; George Whitefield, *George Whitefield's Journals* (1738–41; reprint, London: Banner of Truth Trust, 1965), 333–335; Brickenstein, "Second 'Sea Congregation,'" 118.

42. Melchior, "Advice to German Immigrants," 48.

43. John Wesley, *Journal and Diaries I*, 316–317; John C. Brickenstein, "The Second 'Sea Congregation,' 1743," *Transactions of the Moravian Historical Society* 1 (1857–76): 118–119; Francis Asbury, *The Journal and Letters of Francis Asbury*, vol. 1, *The Journal 1771 to 1793*, ed. Elmer T. Clark, J. Manning Potts, and Jacob S. Payton (Nashville: Abingdon Press, 1958), 6.

44. *Diary of a Voyage from Rotterdam*, 16.

45. Moore, *Voyage to Georgia*, 5–6; Wokeck, *Trade in Strangers*, 134, 204–206; Fernand Braudel, *The Structures of Everyday Life: The Limits of the Possible*, trans. Siân Reynolds (New York: Harper and Row, 1981), 104–107, 194–199.

46. Wokeck, *Trade in Strangers*, 76–77; William Almy Journal, 1776–1780, 23 March 1779, William Almy Papers, RIHS; William Downes Cheever, Travel Journals, 23 and 30 Nov. 1778, MHS; Logbook of the Ship *Mercury*, 21 Jan. 1800, Log 835, Mystic Seaport.

47. Schaw, *Journal of a Lady of Quality*, 52–53.

48. Nicholas Cresswell, *The Journal of Nicholas Cresswell, 1774–1777*, ed. Samuel Thornely (London: Jonathan Cape, 1925), 12; John Fontaine, *The Journal of John Fontaine; An Irish Huguenot Son in Spain and Virginia, 1710–1719*, ed. John Fontaine and Edward P. Alexander (Williamsburg, Va.: Colonial Williamsburg Foundation; distributed by the University Press of Virginia, 1972), 49; Mittelberger, *Journey to Pennsylvania*, 12.

49. Melchior, "Advice to German Immigrants," 48; "Advice for Brethren and Sisters in Preparation for Crossing the Atlantic to the West Indies," reprinted in Stead, "Crossing the Atlantic," 32.

50. William Palfrey Journal, 4 April 1771, MHS. The "Downs" was a famous rendezvous point for ships preparing to sail from London. The name refers to the shifting sand dunes off Deal on the east coast of Kent, England. Dean King, John B. Hattendorf, and J. Worth Estes, *A Sea of Words*, 2nd ed. (New York: Henry Holt, 1997), 173; Muhlenberg, *Journals*, vol. 1, 27; Benjamin Ingham, "Rev. Benjamin Ingham, the Yorkshire Evangelist," in *The Oxford Methodists: Memoirs of the Rev. Messrs Clayton, Ingham, Gambold, Hervey, and Broughton*, ed. L. Tyerman (New York: Harper and Brothers, 1873), 70; Whitefield, *Journals*, 100.

51. John Wesley, *Journal and Diaries I*, 319; James Gascoigne, Letter Book 1735–1747, 11. Oct. 1735, Duke University Special Collections; Oglethorpe to Gascoigne, 17 Oct. 1735, James Gascoigne, Letter Book 1735–1747, Duke University Special Collections.

52. Nitschmann, quoted in *Moravians in Georgia*, 102; John Wesley, *Journal and Diaries I*, 321; Daniel B. Shea, ed., "Some Account of the Fore Part of the Life of Elizabeth Ashbridge," *Journeys in New Worlds: Early American Women's Narratives*, ed. W. L. Andrews (Madison: University of Wisconsin Press, 1990), 151.

53. Joseph C. Miller, "Mortality in the Atlantic Slave Trade: Statistical Evidence on Causality," *Journal of Interdisciplinary History* 11, no. 3 (Winter 1981): 388. Herbert S. Klein et al. found that apart from epidemics, shipboard deaths occurred randomly with neither statistical peaks at the beginning nor the end of voyages. The study did reveal that port of embarkation greatly affected the overall mortality rate experienced during the voyage, with high rates of death experienced during the coasting phase of acquiring the human cargo. Herbert S. Klein, Stanley L. Engerman, Robin Haines, and Ralph Shlomowitz, "Transoceanic Mortality: The Slave Trade in Comparative Perspective," *William and Mary Quarterly* 58, no. 1 (Jan. 2001); 100–102; David Eltis and David Richardson, *Atlas of the Transatlantic Slave Trade* (New Haven: Yale University Press, 2010), 160; Farley Grubb, "Morbidity and Mortality on the North Atlantic Passage: Eighteenth-Century German Immigration," *Journal of Interdisciplinary History* 17, no. 3 (Winter 1987): 571; R. Haines, R. Shlomowitz, and L. Brennan, "Maritime Mortality Revisited," *International Journal of Maritime History* 8, no. 1 (1996): 133–172.

54. "James Oglethorpe to the Trustees 13 January 1733," *General Oglethorpe's Georgia: Colonial Letters, 1733–1743*, ed. Mills Lane (Savannah: Beehive Press, 1990), 3–4; Moore, *Voyage to Georgia*, 13; John Wesley, *Journal and Diaries I*, 316; Grubb, "Morbidity and Mortality," 570–571.

55. Moore, *Voyage to Georgia*, 13.

56. Samuel Davies, "Journal of Samuel Davies, from July 2, 1753, to February 13, 1775," in *Sketches of Virginia Historical and Biographical*, ed. William Henry Foote (Philadelphia: William S. Martien, 1850), 237–238, 275; George Stevens Logbook, 1768–1774, 25 April 1772, MHS; Cresswell, *Journal*, 8.

57. Melchior, "Advice to German Immigrants," 48; Benjamin Ingham, "Rev. Benjamin Ingham," 67.

58. Benjamin Ingham, "Rev. Benjamin Ingham," 67; Grubb, "Morbidity and Mortality," 566.

59. McPherson, "Voyage of the Anne," 220–230; John Wesley, *Journal and Diaries I*, 313, 331.

60. For example, the following inscription appears before a voyage in the log of the sloop *Nancy*. "A Journal of Passage intended With ye Permission of God in the Sloop Nancy Thomas Greene Master at Preasent Bound from Antegua in the Lattd of 17:25 North Longtd in 60:35 West to Blockisland in the Lattd of 41:7 North Longt in 69:50 West Friday March ye 26 Day at 10 Clock this fore Noone Wighed Our Ancor in the Harbor of St Johns and Went to Sea With a fresh Breeze of Wind at East So God Bless us and Send us A Good Passage in Safety to Our dessierd Port Amen." Logbook of Sloop *Nancy*, 26 March 1756, Log 693, Mystic Seaport.

61. Sloop *Count D'Estange* journal, 1 Nov. 1793, John Palmer Papers, Coll. 53, Mystic Seaport; Nathanael Briggs Logbooks, 4 July 1770, RIHS; Logbook of Sloop *Nancy*, 23 June 1754, Log 693, Mystic Seaport; Aaron Bull, Diary of a Voyage, 16 June 1755, Connecticut Historical Society (hereafter CHS); Newton, *Journal of a Slave Trader*, 62.

62. Davies, "Journal," 236, 238; James Meikle, *The Traveller: or, Meditations on Various Subjects, Written on Board a Man of War; to Which Is Added, Converse with the World Unseen* (Albany, N.Y.: E. Torrey and W. Seaver, 1812), 89; William Downes Cheever Travel Journals, 7 Nov. 1778, MHS.

63. Harrower, *Journal*, 10–11; Henry Marchant, Journell of Voyage from Newport in the Colony of Rhode Island to London. Travels thro' many Parts of England & Scotland began July 8th 1771 (microfilmed manuscript), 13 Aug. 1771, RIHS; Michael Schlatter, "The Journal of Rev. Michael Schlatter," in *The Life of Rev. Michael Schlatter; with a Full Account of His Travels and Labors among the Germans*, ed. H. Harbaugh (Philadelphia: Lindsay and Blakiston, 1857), 124; Pelatiah Webster, *Journal of a Voyage to Charlestown in South Carolina by Pelatiah Webster in 1765*, in *Publications of the South Carolina Historical Society*, ed. T. P. Harrison (Charleston: Published by the Society, 1898), 2.

64. John Andrew Dober, quoted in *Moravians in Georgia*, 101; John Wesley, *Journal and Diaries I*, 313.

65. Heathcote to Secretary, New York, 16 Jan. 1707/1708, Society for the Propagation of the Gospel in Foreign Parts Papers (hereafter SPG), vol. 14, 90–91; Robert Gardiner and Thomas Lillibridge to Keith, Newport, R.I., 12 Dec. 1705, SPG, vol. 13, 184–185; John Wesley, *Journal and Diaries I*, 313. The majority of naval chaplains' support derived from church benefices on land. Duplicate of Order in Council, 25 April 1679, SPG, vol. 7, 1–3.

66. Theodore G. Tappert, "Introduction," in Philip Jacob Spener, *Pia Desideria*, ed. and trans. Theodore G. Tappert ([Minneapolis]: Fortress Press, 1964), 19–20; Stead, "Crossing the Atlantic," 23; John C. Brickenstein, "The First 'Sea Congregation' A.D. 1742," *Transactions of the Moravian Historical Society* 1 (1857–76): 33–34; "Anna Johanna Seidel, née Piesch, 1726–1788," *Moravian Women's Memoirs: Their Related Lives, 1750–1820*, trans. Katherine M. Faull (Syracuse: Syracuse University Press, 1997), 127; Brickenstein, "Second 'Sea Congregation,'" 109.

67. Rebecca Larson, *Daughters of Light: Quaker Women Preaching and Prophesying in the Colonies and Abroad, 1700–1775* (New York: Alfred A. Knopf, 1999), 90–104; Susanna Morris, "The Journal of Susanna Morris, 1682–1755," in *Wilt Thou Go on My Errand? Journals of Three 18th Century Quaker Women Ministers*, ed. Margaret Hope Bacon (Wallingford, Pa.: Pendle Hill, 1994), 47.

68. Whitefield, *Journals*, 102.

Chapter 2. Sea Legs

1. Benjamin Ingham, "Rev. Benjamin Ingham, the Yorkshire Evangelist," in *The Oxford Methodists: Memoirs of the Rev. Messrs Clayton, Ingham, Gambold, Hervey, and Broughton,*

ed. L. Tyerman (New York: Harper and Brothers, 1873), 72; Philip Georg Friedrich von Reck, *Von Reck's Voyage: Drawings and Journal of Philip Georg Friedrich von Reck*, ed. Kristian Hvidt (Savannah: Beehive Press, 1980), 31; John Wesley, *Journal and Diaries I, 1735–1738*, vol. 18 of *The Works of John Wesley*, ed. W. Reginald Ward and Richard P. Heitzenrater (Nashville: Abingdon Press, 1988), 329.

2. Ingham, "Rev. Benjamin Ingham," 72.

3. "Sea-legs," *Oxford English Dictionary*, 2nd ed., 1989; online version December 2011, http://o-www.oed.com.library.simmons.edu/view/Entry/174213, accessed 25 Feb. 2012. John Fontaine, *The Journal of John Fontaine; An Irish Huguenot Son in Spain and Virginia, 1710–1719*, ed. Edward P. Alexander (Williamsburg, Va.: Colonial Williamsburg Foundation; distributed by the University Press of Virginia, 1972), 47; John Wesley, *Journal and Diaries I*, 330.

4. Jacques-Pierre Brissot de Warville, *New Travels in the United States of America, 1788* (Cambridge: Belknap Press of Harvard University Press, 1964), 75; Samuel Davies, "Journal of Samuel Davies, from July 2, 1753, to February 13, 1775," in *Sketches of Virginia Historical and Biographical*, ed. William Henry Foote (Philadelphia: William S. Martien, 1850), 239.

5. *Baltimore* logbook, 1788–1789, 24 June 1788, MHS; Henry Ingraham's Journal, 1 Nov. 1802, MHS.

6. John George Käsebier and John Christopher Saur, "Two Early Letters from Germantown," ed. Donald F. Durnbaugh, *Pennsylvania Magazine of History and Biography* 84, no. 2 (April 1960): 221; von Reck, *Von Reck's Voyage*, 29; Henry Melchior Muhlenberg, *The Journals of Henry Melchior Muhlenberg*, vol. 1, trans. Theodore G. Tappert and John W. Doberstein (Philadelphia: Muhlenberg Press, 1942), 30.

7. John Adams, *The Works of John Adams, Second President of the United States*, vol. 3, ed. Charles Francis Adams (Boston: Charles C. Little and James Brown, 1851), 98.

8. William Palfrey Journal, 7 April 1771, MHS.

9. Rebecca Jones, *Memorials of Rebecca Jones*, ed. William J. Allinson (Philadelphia: Longstreth, 1849), 55; Francis Asbury, *The Journal and Letters of Francis Asbury*, vol. 1, *The Journal 1771 to 1793*, ed. Elmer T. Clark, J. Manning Potts, and Jacob S. Payton (Nashville: Abingdon Press, 1958), 5; Muhlenberg, *Journals*, vol. 1, 30.

10. John Wesley, *Journal and Diaries I*, 315; John Woolman, *The Journal of John Woolman and a Plea for the Poor*, ed. Frederick B. Tolles (Philadelphia: Joseph Crukshank, 1774; reprint, Secaucus, N.J.: Citadel Press, 1972), 191.

11. David Nitschmann quoted in Adelaide L. Fries, *The Moravians in Georgia, 1735–40* (Raleigh, N.C.: Edwards and Broughton, 1905), 110; Joseph Emerson, "Journal of the Louisburg Expedition," *Proceedings of the Massachusetts Historical Society* 44 (1910): 72–74.

12. Von Reck, *Von Reck's Voyage*, 29–30; Muhlenberg, *Journals*, vol. 1, 24.

13. Käsebier and Saur, "Two Early Letters from Germantown," 220; Nitschmann, quoted in Fries, *Moravians in Georgia*, 102; Francis Moore, *A Voyage to Georgia Begun in the Year 1735* (London: Jacob Robinson, 1744), 16.

14. William Bartram, *The Travels of William Bartram*, ed. Mark Van Doren (1791; reprint New York: Dover Publications, 1955), 29; Fries, *Moravians in Georgia*, 60.

15. Janet Schaw, *Journal of a Lady of Quality; Being the Narrative of a Journey from Scotland to the West Indies, North Carolina, and Portugal, in the Years 1774 to 1776*, ed. Evangeline Walker Andrews (New Haven: Yale University Press, 1923), 27; Johann Carl Büttner, *Narrative of Johann Carl Büttner*, in *Souls for Sale: Two German Redemptioners Come to Revolutionary America*, ed. Susan E. Klepp, Farley Grubb, and Anne Pfaelzer de Ortiz (University Park: Pennsylvania State University Press, 2006), 217.

16. Frederick Mackenzie, *A British Fusilier in Revolutionary Boston*, ed. Allen French (Cambridge: Harvard University Press, 1926), 9–10; "Advice for Brethren and Sisters in Preparation for Crossing the Atlantic to the West Indies," appended to Geoffrey Stead, "Crossing the Atlantic: The Eighteenth-Century Moravian Experience," *Transactions of the Moravian Historical Society* 30 (1998): 32–34; Schaw, *Journal of a Lady of Quality*, 31; Jones, *Memorials*, 152–153.

17. John Wesley, *Journal and Diaries I*, 330; Samuel W. Boardman, *Log-Book of Timothy Boardman Kept on Board the Privateer Oliver Cromwell, during a Cruise from New London, CT., to Charleston, S.C. and Return in 1778* (Albany: Joel Munsell's Sons, 1895), 84; John C. Brickenstein, "The First 'Sea Congregation,' 1742," *Transactions of the Moravian Historical Society* 1 (1857–76): 38–39; George Whitefield, *George Whitefield's Journals* (1738–41; reprint, London: Banner of Truth Trust, 1965), 123.

18. Charlotte Browne Journal, 1754–1757 (photostat), 20 Jan. 1755, MHS.

19. Johann Cristoph Sauer, "An Early Description of Pennsylvania, cont.," ed. R. W. Kelsey, *Pennsylvania Magazine of History and Biography* 45 (1921): 244; Käsebier and Saur, "Two Early Letters from Germantown," 222.

20. John Robinson and Thomas Rispin, "A Journey through Nova Scotia," *Discoveries of America: Personal Accounts of British Emigrants to North America during the Revolutionary Era*, ed. Barbara DeWolfe (New York: Cambridge University Press, 1997), 46; Johann Carl Büttner, *Narrative of Johann Carl Büttner*, 217; Schaw, *Journal of a Lady of Quality*, 59.

21. John Wesley, *Journal and Diaries I*, 317.

22. Schaw, *Journal of a Lady of Quality*, 22–23.

23. Keith Thomas, "Work and Leisure," *Past and Present* 29 (Dec. 1964): 50–66; E. P. Thompson, "Time, Work-Discipline, and Industrial Capitalism," *Past and Present* 38 (Dec. 1967): 56–97; Mechal Sobel, *The World They Made Together: Black and White Values in Eighteenth-Century Virginia* (Princeton: Princeton University Press, 1987), 21–29; Marcus Buford Rediker, *Between the Devil and the Deep Blue Sea: Merchant Seamen, Pirates, and the Anglo-American Maritime World, 1700–1750* (New York: Cambridge University Press, 1987), 113–115.

24. "Starboard" and "larboard" referred to the two sides of the ship. Starboard referred to the right-hand side of the vessel when facing the bow. The word derives its name from the "steer board"—a paddle used for steering in early ships that was located on this side. Larboard or port refers to the left-hand side of vessel when looking toward the bow. "Port" became the preferred term for commands in order to avoid confusion

with starboard. Dean King, John B. Hattendorf, and J. Worth Estes, *A Sea of Words*, 2nd ed. (New York: Henry Holt, 1997), 262, 402; Dorothy Denneen Volo and James M. Volo, *Daily Life in the Age of Sail* (Westport, Conn.: Greenwood Press, 2002), 99; Horace Beck, *Folklore and the Sea* (Edison, N.J.: Castle Books, 1999), 58; 22 June 1748, Logbooks of *Hope, Dolphin,* and *Smithfield,* 22 June 1748, Mss 828, RIHS; Woolman, *Journal,* 193; Davies, "Journal," 238; Whitefield, *Journals,* 108.

25. Examples: Thomas Nicolson Navigation and Logbooks, 1769–1779, 18 July 1769, MHS; Robert Treat Paine Papers, 1731–1814, 3 Jan. 1754; Pinkham Family Papers, 1711–1822, 8 Sept. 1754, MHS; James Rhodes Log and Account Book, 16–18 Jan. 1796, Log 331, Mystic Seaport; Nitschmann quoted in *Moravians in Georgia,* 107.

26. Journals of Thomas Handasyd Perkins, 19 Dec. 1794, MHS; N. A. M. Rodger, *The Wooden World: An Anatomy of the Georgian Navy* (Annapolis: Naval Institute Press, 1988), 39; Henry Harries, "Nautical Time," *Mariner's Mirror* 14 (1928): 364–370.

27. Davies, "Journal," 243; Robert Harms, *The Diligent: A Voyage through the Worlds of the Slave Trade* (New York: Basic Books, 2002), 107; Nathaniel Cutting Journal, 1786–1793, 12 Nov. 1789, P-275, reel 1, MHS.

28. Eleazar Elderkin, Journal of Voyage on ship *Eliza,* 1796–1798, CHS; Simeon Griswold, Logbook and Journal of the Brig *Two Brothers,* 1768–1770, 5 Dec. 1768, Log 320, Mystic Seaport; John Newton, *The Journal of a Slave Trader, 1750–1754,* ed. Bernard Martin and Mark Spurrell (London: Epworth Press, 1962), 47; Muhlenberg, *Journals,* vol. 1, 41.

29. For a description of plantation Sundays, see Philip D. Morgan, *Slave Counterpoint: Black Culture in the Eighteenth Century Chesapeake and Lowcountry* (Chapel Hill: Published for the Omohundro Institute of Early American History and Culture by the University of North Carolina Press, 1998), 193–194, 371, 524; Eleazar Elderkin, Journal of Voyage on ship *Eliza* 1796–1798, CHS. Logbook of Daniel Francis, 10 May 1795, Log 389, Mystic Seaport; George Munro, Journals of *Polly* (Schooner) 1795 and *General Greene* (Sloop) 1795–1797, RIHS, both 17 March 1796.

30. *Revenge* (Sloop) Papers, 1741–1801, 16 Aug. 1748, MHS; for example, Muhlenberg notes not only that 4 July was a Sunday but that it was the "Third Sunday after Trinity." Muhlenberg, *Journals,* vol. 1, 27; Nicholas Cresswell, *The Journal of Nicholas Cresswell, 1774–1777* (London: Jonathan Cape, 1925), 11. For examples of Quaker accountings of time, see Jones, *Memorials;* Richard Jordan, *A Journal of the Life and Religious Labours of Richard Jordan: A Minister of the Gospel in the Society of Friends* (London: Harvey and Darton, 1829); and Jonathan Evans, *A Journal of the Life, Travels, and Religious Labors of William Savery* (Philadelphia: Friends' Book-Store, 1837).

31. Cresswell, *Journal,* 13; For example, Henry Ingraham's Journal, 31 Oct. 1802, MHS. Charlotte Browne Journal, 1754–1757 (photostat), 26 Jan. 1755, MHS; Gottlieb Mittelberger, *Journey to Pennsylvania,* trans. Oscar Handlin and John Clive (Cambridge: Belknap Press of Harvard University Press, 1960), 13; Thomas Bluett, *Some Memoirs of the Life of Job: The Son of Solomon, the High Priest of Boonda in Africa* (London: Printed for R.

Ford, 1734), 25–26; Douglas Grant, *The Fortunate Slave: An Illustration of African Slavery in the Early Eighteenth Century* (New York: Oxford University Press, 1968), 95–96; Michael A. Gomez, *Exchanging Our Country Marks: The Transformation of African Identities in the Colonial and Antebellum South* (Chapel Hill: University of North Carolina Press, 1998), 71–75; Jones, *Memorials*, 59.

32. William Palfrey Journal, 28 April 1771, MHS; Journal and logbooks of Nathaniel Bowditch, 19 July 1796, MHS. Others noted the inconvenience posed by Roman Catholic holidays in foreign ports. William Almy Journal, 1776–1780, 8 Dec. 1776, William Almy Papers, RIHS.

33. Davies, *Journal*, 280; Commonplace Book of Simeon Crowell 1790–1824, MHS; James Boswell, *The Life of Samuel Johnson, LL.D., Including a Journal of His Tour of the Hebrides* (London: John Murray, 1839), 66.1; Henry Ingraham's Journal, Nov. 1802, MHS.

34. Cresswell, *Journal*, 7–8; Woolman, *Journal*, 198; Samuel Kelly, *An Eighteenth Century Seaman Whose Days Have Been Few and Evil, to Which Is Added Remarks, etc., on Places He Visited during His Pilgrimage in This Wilderness*, ed. Crosbie Garstin (New York: Frederick A. Stokes, 1925), 136; "Testimony of James Fraser," *House of Commons Sessional Papers of the Eighteenth Century*, ed. Sheila Lambert (Wilmington, Del.: Scholarly Resources, 1975), 71:39.

35. James Albert Ukawsaw Gronniosaw, "A Narrative of the Most Remarkable Particulars in the Life of James Albert Ukawsaw Gronniosaw an African Prince, as Related by Himself," in *Pioneers of the Black Atlantic: Five Slave Narratives from the Enlightenment*, ed. H. L. Gates Jr. and W. L. Andrews (Washington, D.C.: Counterpoint, 1998), 41; William D. Pierson, "White Cannibals, Black Martyrs: Fear, Depression, and Religious Faith as Causes of Suicide among New Slaves," *Journal of Negro History* 62 (April 1977): 147. Ironically, as Europeans and Africans encountered each other for the first time through the slave trade, they often shared this fear. When the British House of Commons investigated the effects of the slave trade, they often sought information about the various cultures encountered, particularly concerning the practice of cannibalism on the West Coast of Africa. "Testimony of Jerome Barnard Weuves, Esquire, in the African Company's Service," *House of Commons Sessional Papers*, 68:210; "Testimony of Thomas King," *House of Commons Sessional Papers*, 68:334–335; *The Interesting Narrative of the Life of Olaudah Equiano, or Gustavus Vassa, the African. Written by Himself* (London, 1789), 71; "Testimony of Mr. Isaac Wilson," *House of Commons Sessional Papers*, 72:274.

36. John Riland, *Memoirs of a West-India Planter* (London: Hamilton, Adams, 1827), 22–23; Marcus Rediker, *The Slave Ship: A Human History* (New York: Viking, 2007), 267–268; Michael A. Gomez, *Exchanging Our Country Marks: The Transformation of African Identities in the Colonial and Antebellum South* (Chapel Hill: University of North Carolina Press, 1998), 159; "Testimony of Mr. Alexander Falconbridge," *House of Commons Sessional Papers*, 72:301; Charles Garland and Herbert S. Klein, "The Allotment of Space for Slaves aboard Eighteenth-Century British Slave Ships," *William and Mary Quarterly* 42, no. 2 (April 1985): 238–248; Allan D. Austin, *African Muslims in Antebellum America* (New York: Garland, 1984), 704.

37. "Testimony of Henry Ellison," *House of Commons Sessional Papers*, 73:368; "Testimony of Captain John Ashley Hall," *House of Commons Sessional Papers*, 72:231; Bruce L. Mouser, ed., *A Slaving Voyage to Africa and Jamaica: The Log of the Sandown, 1793–1794* (Bloomington: Indiana University Press, 2002), 102–103; "Testimony of Mr. Alexander Falconbridge," *House of Commons Sessional Papers*, 72:302. "Testimony of Captain Thomas Wilson of the Royal Navy," *House of Commons Sessional Papers*, 73:11.

38. Riland, *Memoirs*, 23; Emma Christopher, *Slave Ship Sailors and Their Captive Cargoes, 1730–1807* (New York: Cambridge University Press, 2006), 165; Stephanie E. Smallwood, *Saltwater Slavery: A Middle Passage from Africa to American Diaspora* (Cambridge: Harvard University Press, 2007), 124.

39. Sylvia R. Frey and Betty Wood, *Come Shouting to Zion: African American Protestantism in the American South and British Caribbean to 1830* (Chapel Hill: University of North Carolina Press, 1998), 38; Pierson, "White Cannibals, Black Martyrs," 151; Newton, *Journal of a Slave Trader*, 75.

40. Peter H. Wood, *Weathering the Storm: Inside Winslow Homer's Gulf Stream* (Athens: University of Georgia Press, 2004), 73–81; Newton, *Journal of a Slave Trader*, 29; "Testimony of Mr. Isaac Wilson," *House of Commons Sessional Papers*, 72:275; Equiano, *Interesting Narrative*, 73.

41. Pierson, "White Cannibals, Black Martyrs," 150; "Testimony of Mr. Isaac Wilson," 72:280; Rediker, *Slave Ships*, 284–288.

42. George Francis Dow, *Slave Ships and Slaving* (1927; reprint, Westport, Conn.: Negro Universities Press, 1970), 63; "Testimony of George Millar," *House of Commons Sessional Papers*, 73:387–388; "Mr. Ecroyde Claxton, Surgeon," *House of Commons Sessional Papers*, 82:35; Pierson, "White Cannibals, Black Martyrs," 154–155. Pierson notes that bodily dismemberment did not necessarily affect the person's status in the afterlife. Morgan, *Slave Counterpoint*, 641–642.

43. David Eltis and David Richardson, *Atlas of the Transatlantic Slave Trade* (New Haven: Yale University Press, 2010), 188–191; Quobna Ottobah Cugoano, *Thoughts and Sentiments on the Evil and Wicked Traffic of the Slavery and Commerce of the Human Species*, in *Unchained Voices: An Anthology of Black Authors in the English-Speaking World of the Eighteenth Century*, ed. Vincent Carretta (Lexington: University Press of Kentucky, 1996), 149; "Evidence of David Henderson," *House of Commons Sessional Papers*, 69:139–140; Laurenti Magesa, *African Religion: The Moral Traditions of Abundant Life* (Maryknoll, N.Y.: Orbis Books, 1997), 104–114.

44. Stephen D. Behrendt, David Eltis, and David Richardson, "The Costs of Coercion: African Agency in the Pre-Modern Atlantic World," *Economic History Review* 53, no. 3 (2001): 456; Newton, *Journal of a Slave Trader*, 80; "Mr. James Towne, Carpenter of His Majesty's Ship Syren," *House of Commons Sessional Papers*, 82:21.

45. Newton, *Journal of a Slave Trader*, 71; Cugoano, *Thoughts and Sentiments*, 149; Behrendt, Eltis, and Richardson, "Costs of Coercion," 458.

46. David Richardson, "Shipboard Revolts, African Authority, and the Atlantic Slave Trade," *William and Mary Quarterly* 58:1 (Jan. 2001), 69–92; "Testimony of Captain

William Littleton," *House of Commons Sessional Papers*, 68:286–287; "Testimony of Richard Miles," *House of Commons Sessional Papers*, 68:117; Frey and Wood, *Come Shouting to Zion*, 57–58.

47. "Testimony of Thomas King," *House of Commons Sessional Papers*, 68:334–335; Albert J. Raboteau, *Slave Religion: The "Invisible Institution" in the Antebellum South* (New York: Oxford University Press, 1978), 33–34; Newton, *Journal of a Slave Trader*, 56; Frey and Wood, *Come Shouting to Zion*, 37; Antonio T. Bly, "Crossing the Lake of Fire: Slave Resistance during the Middle Passage, 1720–1842," *Journal of Negro History* 83, no. 3 (Summer 1998): 182.

48. Smallwood, *Saltwater Slavery*, 128–131.

49. Fries, *Moravians in Georgia*, 60.

50. Ebenezer Miller diary, 1726, MHS; E. Edwards Beardsley, *Life and Correspondence of Samuel Johnson, D.D.* (New York: Hurd and Houghton, 1874), 25. Ernest Hawkins, *Historical Notices of the Missions of the Church of England in the North American Colonies Previous to the Independence of the United States* (London: B. Fellowes, 1845), 30.

51. Moore, *Voyage to Georgia*, 87; Benjamin Ingham, "Rev. Benjamin Ingham," 70; Martin Schmidt, *John Wesley: A Theological Biography*, vol. 1, *From 17th June 1703 until 24th May 1738*, trans. Norman P. Goldhawk (London: Epworth Press, 1962), 166–167; Nitschmann quoted in *Moravians in Georgia*, 106.

52. Samuel and Mary Neale, *Some Account of the Lives and Religious Labours of Samuel Neale, and Mary Neale, Formerly Mary Peisley, Both of Ireland* (London: C. Gilpin, 1845), 189; Jones, *Memorials*, 59; Woolman, *Journal*, 191.

53. Samuel Davies, *The Reverend Samuel Davies Abroad: The Diary of a Journey to England and Scotland, 1753–55*, ed. George William Pilcher (Urbana: University of Illinois Press, 1967), 27–28, 30; Leigh E. Schmidt, "Time, Celebration, and the Christian Year in Eighteenth Century Evangelicalism," *Evangelicalism: Comparative Studies of Popular Protestantism in North America, the British Isles, and Beyond, 1700–1900* (New York: Oxford University Press, 1994), 90–104.

Chapter 3. Shipmates

1. John Wesley, *Journal and Diaries I, 1735–1738*, vol. 18 of *The Works of John Wesley*, ed. W. Reginald Ward and Richard P. Heitzenrater (Nashville: Abingdon Press, 1988), 316–317; Benjamin Ingham, "Rev. Benjamin Ingham, the Yorkshire Evangelist," in *The Oxford Methodists: Memoirs of the Rev. Messrs Clayton, Ingham, Gambold, Hervey, and Broughton*, ed. L. Tyerman (New York: Harper and Brothers, 1873), 69.

2. Francis Moore, *A Voyage to Georgia Begun in the Year 1735* (London: Jacob Robinson, 1744), 15; John Wesley, *Journal and Diaries I*, 326; Ingham, "Rev. Benjamin Ingham," 71.

3. Marcus Buford Rediker, *Between the Devil and the Deep Blue Sea: Merchant Seamen, Pirates, and the Anglo-American Maritime World, 1700–1750* (New York: Cambridge University Press, 1987), 80; W. Jeffrey Bolster, *Black Jacks: African American Seamen in the Age of Sail* (Cambridge: Harvard University Press, 1997), 30–37.

4. Rediker, *Between the Devil and the Deep Blue Sea*, 173; Carl Bridenbaugh, *Mitre and Sceptre: Transatlantic Faiths, Ideas, Personalities, and Politics, 1689–1775* (New York: Oxford University Press, 1962), 54–55; Carla Gardina Pestana, "Religion," *The British Atlantic World, 1500–1800*, ed. David Armitage and Michael J. Braddick (New York: Palgrave Macmillan, 2009), 72–76; Carla Gardina Pestana, *Protestant Empire: Religion and the Making of the British Atlantic World* (Philadelphia: University of Pennsylvania Press, 2009), 165–168; Owen Stanwood, *The Empire Reformed: English America in the Age of the Glorious Revolution* (Philadelphia: University of Pennsylvania Press, 2011), 4–5.

5. Moore, *Voyage to Georgia*, 15.

6. Stephanie E. Smallwood, *Saltwater Slavery: A Middle Passage from Africa to American Diaspora* (Cambridge: Harvard University Press, 2007), 101; Douglas R. Egerton, Alison Games, Jane G. Landers, Kris Lane, and Donald R. Wright, *The Atlantic World: A History, 1400–1888* (Wheeling, Ill.: Harlan Davidson, 2007), 22–24; Philip D. Morgan, *Slave Counterpoint: Black Culture in the Eighteenth-Century Chesapeake and Lowcountry* (Chapel Hill: Published for the Omohundro Institute of Early American History and Culture by the University of North Carolina Press, 1998), 448–449; Sidney W. Mintz and Richard Price, *The Birth of African-American Culture: An Anthropological Perspective* (Boston: Beacon Press, 1992), 43; Michael A. Gomez, *Exchanging Our Country Marks: The Transformation of African Identities in the Colonial and Antebellum South* (Chapel Hill: University of North Carolina Press, 1998), 165–166.

7. For the forced transportation of British convicts in this era, see A. Roger Ekirch, "Bound for America: A Profile of British Convicts Transported to the Colonies, 1718–1775," *William and Mary Quarterly* 42, no. 2 (1985): 184–200; A. Roger Ekirch, *Bound for America: The Transportation of British Convicts to the Colonies, 1718–1775* (New York: Oxford University Press, 1987). A statistical comparison of the two trades can be found in David Eltis, "Free and Coerced Transatlantic Migrations: Some Comparisons," *American Historical Review* 88, no. 2 (April 1983): 251–280; Aaron S. Fogleman, "From Slaves, Convicts, and Servants to Free Passengers: The Transformation of Immigration in the Era of the American Revolution," *Journal of American History* 85, no. 1 (1998): 43–76; Marianne S. Wokeck, *Trade in Strangers: The Beginnings of Mass Migration to North America* (University Park: Pennsylvania State University Press, 1999), 78.

8. Sidney A. Reeve, "Ship Evolution and Social Evolution," *Geographical Review* 23, no. 1 (Jan. 1933): 61–76.

9. Benjamin J. Kaplan, *Divided by Faith: Religious Conflict and the Practice of Toleration in Early Modern Europe* (Cambridge: Belknap Press of Harvard University Press, 2007), 198–234.

10. Ingham, "Rev. Benjamin Ingham," 70.

11. Janet Schaw, *Journal of a Lady of Quality; Being the Narrative of a Journey from Scotland to the West Indies, North Carolina, and Portugal, in the Years 1774 to 1776*, ed. Evangeline Walker Andrews (New Haven: Yale University Press, 1923), 28–30.

12. Schaw, *Journal of a Lady of Quality*, 36–37.

13. Christopher Mulvey, *Transatlantic Manners: Social Patterns in Nineteenth-Century Anglo-American Travel Literature* (New York: Cambridge University Press, 1990), 12; *A Huguenot Exile in Virginia; or, Voyages of a Frenchman Exiled for His Religion, with a Description of Virginia and Maryland*, ed. Gilbert Chinard (1687; reprint, New York: Press of the Pioneers, 1934), 94–95; Anna Maria Falconbridge, *Two Voyages to Sierra Leone*, in *Maiden Voyages and Infant Colonies: Two Women's Travel Narratives of the 1790s*, ed. Deirdre Coleman (New York: Leicester University Press, 1999), 50.

14. Rebecca Jones, *Memorials of Rebecca Jones*, ed. William J. Allinson (Philadelphia: Henry Longstreth, 1849), 56; John C. Brickenstein, "The Second 'Sea Congregation,' 1743," *Transactions of the Moravian Historical Society* 1 (1857–76): 118; George Whitefield, *George Whitefield's Journals* (London: Banner of Truth Trust, 1965), 122.

15. Henry Melchior Muhlenberg, *The Journals of Henry Melchior Muhlenberg*, trans. Theodore G. Tappert and John W. Doberstein (Philadelphia: Muhlenberg Press, 1942), vol. 1, 48; Ingham, "Rev. Benjamin Ingham," 72; Moore, *Voyage to Georgia*, 15; Adelaide L. Fries, *The Moravians in Georgia, 1735–40* (Raleigh, N.C.: Edwards and Broughton, 1905), 65.

16. Ingham, "Rev. Benjamin Ingham," 72; Philip Georg Friedrich von Reck, *Von Reck's Voyage: Drawings and Journal of Philip Georg Friedrich von Reck*, ed. Kristian Hvidt (Savannah: Beehive Press, 1980), 29.

17. W. H. Auden, *The Enchafèd Flood; or The Romantic Iconography of the Sea* (Charlottesville: University Press of Virginia, 1950), 6; Hester Blum, *The View from the Masthead: Maritime Imagination and Antebellum American Sea Narratives* (Chapel Hill: University of North Carolina Press, 2008), 4; Raphael Patel, *The Children of Noah: Jewish Seafaring in Ancient Times* (Princeton: Princeton University Press, 1998), 101–103. "But the wicked are like the troubled sea, when it cannot rest, whose waters cast up mire and dirt" (Isaiah 57:20); William Shakespeare, *The Tempest*, act 1, scene 1; John Flavel, *Navigation Spiritualized: A New Compass for Seamen*, in *The Works of John Flavel, vol. 5* (1820; reprint, London: Banner of Truth Trust, 1982), 207; Daniel Defoe, *Robinson Crusoe* (New York: Atheneum Books for Young Readers, 1920), 173; "Mr. James Towne, Carpenter of His Majesty's Ship Syren," *House of Commons Sessional Papers of the Eighteenth Century*, ed. Sheila Lambert (Wilmington, Del.: Scholarly Resources, 1975), 82:15.

18. Rediker, *Between the Devil and the Deep Blue Sea*, 166; N. A. M. Rodger, *The Wooden World: An Anatomy of the Georgian Navy* (Annapolis: Naval Institute Press, 1988), 11. Samuel Kelly, *An Eighteenth-Century Seaman Whose Days Have Been Few and Evil, to Which Is Added Remarks, etc., on Places He Visited during His Pilgrimage in This Wilderness*, ed. Crosbie Garstin (New York: Frederick A. Stokes, 1925), 10; Christopher P. Magra, "Faith at Sea: Exploring Maritime Religiosity in the Eighteenth Century," *International Journal of Maritime History* 19, no. 1 (June 2007): 87–106.

19. Rediker, *Between the Devil and the Deep Blue Sea*, 10–14; Simon P. Newman, *Embodied History: The Lives of the Poor in Early Philadelphia* (Philadelphia: University of Pennsylvania Press, 2003), 104. A significant proportion of those executed in North American port cities had maritime occupations, further attesting to sailors' position near the bottom

of the social hierarchy, Gabriele Gottlieb, "Class and Capital Punishment in Early Urban North America," in *Class Matters: Early North America and the Atlantic World*, ed. Simon Middleton and Billy G. Smith (Philadelphia: University of Pennsylvania Press, 2008), 191–197; Jesse Lemisch, "Jack Tar in the Streets: Merchant Seamen in the Politics of Revolutionary America," *William and Mary Quarterly* 25, no. 3 (1968): 371; James Meikle, *The Traveller; or, Meditations on Various Subjects, Written on Board a Man of War; to Which Is Added, Converse with the World Unseen* (Albany, N.Y.: E. Torrey and W. Seaver, 1812), 47.

20. James Gascoigne, Letter Book 1735–1747, 17 Oct. 1735, Duke University Special Collections; Lemisch, "Jack Tar in the Streets," 381–388.

21. Francis Asbury, *The Journal and Letters of Francis Asbury*, vol. 1, *The Journal 1771 to 1793*, ed. Elmer T. Clark, J. Manning Potts, and Jacob S. Payton (Nashville: Abingdon Press, 1958), 5–6; Muhlenberg, *Journals*, vol. 1, 39, 64.

22. "Copy of a Letter from Mrs. Elizabeth Bland to Mr. Oglethorpe dated at Savannah 14th June 1735," Egmont Papers, Phillipps Collection, 14201: 17–18, University of Georgia Libraries; Schaw, *Journal of a Lady of Quality*, 32.

23. John Flavel, "A Pathetical and Serious Dissuasive from the Horrid and Detestable Sins of Drunkenness, Swearing, Uncleanness, Forgetfulness of Mercies, Violation of Promises, and Atheistical Contempt of Death," in *The Works of John Flavel*, vol. 5 (1820; reprint, Carlisle, Pa.: Banner of Truth Trust, 1982), 295; Meikle, *Traveller*, 47.

24. Samuel Davies, "Journal of Samuel Davies, from July 2, 1753, to February 13, 1775," in *Sketches of Virginia Historical and Biographical*, ed. William Henry Foote (Philadelphia: William S. Martien, 1850), 276; Whitefield, *Journals*, 140.

25. Eleazar Elderkin, Journal of Voyage on ship *Eliza* 1796–1798, 6 Sept. 1796, CHS; Rediker, *Between the Devil and the Deep Blue Sea*, 166; Greg Dening describes language functioning in a similar manner in his investigation of the *Bounty* mutiny. Captain Bligh's reliance on vulgar language placed him in an ambiguous social position in regard to the crew. Overuse of swearing diminished the social distance intended to separate him from the crew. Greg Dening, *Mr Bligh's Bad Language: Passion, Power and Theatre on the Bounty* (New York: Cambridge University Press, 1992), 55–61; Samuel Davies, *The Reverend Samuel Davies Abroad: The Diary of a Journey to England and Scotland, 1753–55*, ed. George William Pilcher (Urbana: University of Illinois Press, 1967), 41, 134, and 136; Whitefield, *Journals*, 106–107; William Shakespeare, *The Tempest*, act 1, scene 1.

26. Commonplace Book of Simeon Crowell 1790–1824, MHS; Olaudah Equiano, *The Interesting Narrative of the Life of Olaudah Equiano, or Gustavus Vassa, the African*, in *The Interesting Narrative and Other Writings*, ed. Vincent Carretta (New York: Penguin Books, 1995), 148.

27. Henry Gardiner, *The Anglo-American, or Memoirs of Capt. Henry Gardiner* (Liverpool: G. Wood, 1813), 164; Davies, "Journal," 279.

28. Nicholas Cresswell, *The Journal of Nicholas Cresswell, 1774–1777* (London: Jonathan Cape, 1925), 11; Schaw, *Journal of a Lady of Quality*, 46; Jones, *Memorials*, 156.

29. John Woolman, *The Journal of John Woolman and a Plea for the Poor*, ed. Frederick B. Tolles (Philadelphia: Joseph Crukshank, 1774; reprint, Secaucus, N.J.: Citadel Press, 1972), 189–194.

30. Davies, *Samuel Davies Abroad*, 144–145.

31. Laurel Thatcher Ulrich, *A Midwife's Tale: The Life of Martha Ballard, Based on Her Diary, 1785–1812* (New York: Alfred A. Knopf, 1990), 169–172; Moore, *Voyage to Georgia*, 16; von Reck, *Von Reck's Voyage*, 32; Ben Marsh, *Georgia's Frontier Women: Female Fortunes in a Southern Colony* (Athens: University of Georgia Press, 2007), 25; Ingham, "Rev. Benjamin Ingham," 72; Wesley, *Journal and Diaries I*, 332–352.

32. Schaw, *Journal of a Lady of Quality*, 50; Whitefield, *Journals*, 143; Kelly, *Eighteenth-Century Seaman*, 77; Gottlieb Mittelberger, *Journey to Pennsylvania*, ed. and trans. Oscar Handlin and John Clive (Cambridge: Belknap Press of Harvard University Press, 1960), 14.

33. Jones, *Memorials*, 159; Thomas Chalkley quoted in Rebecca Larson, *Daughters of Light: Quaker Women Preaching and Prophesying in the Colonies and Abroad, 1700–1775* (New York: Alfred A. Knopf, 1999), 105.

34. Johann Carl Büttner, *Narrative of Johann Carl Büttner*, in *Souls for Sale: Two German Redemptioners Come to Revolutionary America*, ed. Susan E. Klepp, Farley Grubb, and Anne Pfaelzer de Ortiz (University Park: Pennsylvania State University Press, 2006), 217.

35. Schaw, *Journal of a Lady of Quality*, 67–68.

36. Case recounted in Peter Wilson Coldham, *Emigrants in Chains: A Social History of Forced Emigration to the Americas of Felons, Destitute Children, Political and Religious Non-Conformists, Vagabonds, Beggars and other Undesirables, 1607–1776* (Baltimore: Genealogical Publishing, 1992), 110–111.

37. Schaw, *Journal of a Lady of Quality*, 56–58.

38. Dorothy Denneen Volo and James M. Volo, *Daily Life in the Age of Sail* (London: Greenwood, 2002), 155; Charlotte Browne Journal, 1754–1757 (photostat), 2 Feb. 1755, MHS; Logbook of the Sloop *Nancy*, 23 May 1755, Log 693, Mystic Seaport; Arthur Pierce Middleton, *Tobacco Coast: A Maritime History of Chesapeake Bay in the Colonial Era* (Newport News, Va.: Mariners' Museum, 1953), 2.

39. Muhlenberg, *Journals*, vol. 1, 44–45; Whitefield, *Journals*, 123, 513–514.

40. Muhlenberg, *Journals*, vol. 1, 48; John Wesley, *Journal and Diaries I*, 325.

41. Mary Ann Parker, *A Voyage Round the World*, in *Maiden Voyages and Infant Colonies: Two Women's Travel Narratives of the 1790s*, ed. Deirdre Coleman (New York: Leicester University Press, 1999), 197–198; Jones, Memorials, 154, 157; Louisa Susannah Wells, *The Journal of a Voyage from Charlestown, S.C., to London Undertaken by a Daughter of an Eminent American Loyalist* (New York: Printed for the New-York Historical Society, 1906), 21.

42. "The Diary of Catherine Green Hickling, 1786–1788," ed. Henrique de Aguiar Oliveira Rodrigues, *Gávea-Brown: A Bilingual Journal of Portuguese-American Letters and Studies*, 15–16 (Jan. 1994–Dec. 1995): 141, 250–251; Wells, *Journal of a Voyage*, 50; Larson, *Daughters of Light*, 96; Margaret Hope Bacon, ed., *Wilt Thou Go on My Errand? Journals of Three 18th Century Quaker Women Ministers* (Wallingford, Pa.: Pendle Hill, 1994), 8–13.

43. Mary Louise Pratt, *Imperial Eyes: Travel Writing and Transculturation* (New York: Routledge, 1992), 6.

44. John Wesley, *Journal and Diaries I*, 313; David Nitschmann quoted in Fries, *Moravians in Georgia*, 102, 104.

45. John Wesley, *Journal and Diaries I*, 207–208, 357–358. Wesley's journal does not mention any contact with black sailors on this voyage, but he taught two how to read on the voyage home. For the ethnic diversity of English sailing vessels during this time, see Rediker, *Between the Devil and the Deep Blue Sea*, 80; Alden T. Vaughan, *Transatlantic Encounters: American Indians in Britain, 1500–1776* (New York: Cambridge University Press, 2006), 160.

46. Brickenstein, "Second 'Sea Congregation,' 1743," 120.

47. Whitefield, *Journals*, 333–335.

48. Fries, *Moravians in Georgia*, 64, 102, 109.

49. Muhlenberg, *Journals*, vol. 1, 50–51.

50. Peter Linebaugh and Marcus Rediker, *The Many-Headed Hydra: Sailors, Slaves, Commoners and the Hidden History of the Revolutionary Atlantic* (Boston: Beacon Press, 2000), 27–28; Mrs. William Seton's journal, 1803–1804, 30 Nov. 1803, MHS; William Richardson, *A Mariner of England: An Account of the Career of William Richardson from Cabin Boy in the Merchant Service to Warrant Officer in the Royal Navy (1780 to 1819) as Told by Himself*, ed. Spencer Childers (London: Conway Maritime Press, 1970), 77.

51. Mary Ann Parker, *A Voyage Round the World*, in *Maiden Voyages and Infant Colonies: Two Women's Travel Narratives of the 1790s*, ed. Deirdre Coleman (New York: Leicester University Press, 1999), 210; Schaw, *Journal of a Lady of Quality*, 22–23; Thomas Nicolson Log of Voyages, 1780–1783, 5 Jan. 1783, MHS.

52. Bolster, *Black Jacks*, 68–101; Equiano, *Interesting Narrative*, 65, 70.

53. Smallwood, *Saltwater Slavery*, 101–121; Equiano, *Interesting Narrative*, 56; "Testimony of Mr. Ecroyde Claxton, Surgeon," *House of Commons Sessional Papers*, 82:36; Allan D. Austin, *African Muslims in Antebellum America* (New York: Garland, 1984), 481; William D. Pierson, "White Cannibals, Black Martyrs: Fear, Depression, and Religious Faith as Causes of Suicide among New Slaves," *Journal of Negro History* 62, no. 2 (April 1977): 151.

54. Smallwood, *Saltwater Slavery*, 101–121; William Butterworth quoted in Joan M. Fayer, "African Interpreters in the Atlantic Slave Trade," *Anthropological Linguistics* 45, no. 3 (2003): 288; Marcus Rediker, *The Slave Ship: A Human History* (New York: Viking, 2007), 276–281.

55. Rediker, *Slave Ship*, 276–281; Equiano, *Interesting Narrative*, 66; "Testimony of Anthony Pantaleo How," *House of Commons Sessional Papers*, 73:219–230.

56. Philip D. Morgan, *Slave Counterpoint: Black Culture in the Eighteenth-Century Chesapeake and Lowcountry* (Chapel Hill: Published for the Omohundro Institute of Early American History and Culture by the University of North Carolina Press, 1998), 449; "Testimony of Dr. Thomas Trotter," *House of Commons Sessional Papers*, 73:98–99.

57. "Testimony of Mr. Alexander Falconbridge," *House of Commons Sessional Papers*, 72:315; Equiano, *Interesting Narrative*, 60–61; "Testimony of Mr. Isaac Wilson," *House of Commons Sessional Papers*, 72:281–282.

58. "Testimony of Robert Norris," *House of Commons Sessional Papers*, 68:12; "Testimony of John Fountain, Esquire," *House of Commons Sessional Papers*, 68:279; George Francis Dow, *Slave Ships and Slaving* (1927; reprint, Westport, Conn.: Negro Universities Press, 1970), 172–173; "Testimony of Mr. Isaac Wilson," *House of Commons Sessional Papers*, 72:281–282.

59. Rediker, *Slave Ship*, 305–307; Michael A. Gomez, *Exchanging Our Country Marks: The Transformation of African Identities in the Colonial and Antebellum South* (Chapel Hill: University of North Carolina Press, 1998), 158, 166; Sidney W. Mintz and Richard Price, *The Birth of African-American Culture: An Anthropological Perspective* (Boston: Beacon Press, 1992), 43; Morgan, *Slave Counterpoint*, 448–449; Bryan Edwards, *The History, Civil and Commercial, of the British Colonies in the West Indies*, in *After Africa: Extracts from British Travel Accounts and Journals of the Seventeenth, Eighteenth, and Nineteenth Centuries Concerning the Slaves, Their Manners, and Customs in the British West Indies*, ed. Roger D. Abrahams and John F. Szwed (New Haven: Yale University Press, 1983), 73.

60. Smallwood, *Saltwater Slavery*, 119; Rediker, *Slave Ship*, 303–307.

61. Bruce L. Mouser, *A Slaving Voyage to Africa and Jamaica: The Log of the Sandown, 1793–1794* (Bloomington: Indiana University Press, 2002), 103; "Evidence of James Bowen," *House of Commons Sessional Papers*, 69:125; "Testimony of Captain John Knox," *House of Commons Sessional Papers*, 68:125, 158.

62. William Downes Cheever Travel Journals, 2–8 Dec. 1778, MHS; Logbook of the *Rebecca*, Log 50, Mystic Seaport; "Some Account of the Fore Part of the Life of Elizabeth Ashbridge," ed. Daniel B. Shea, in *Journeys in New Worlds: Early American Women's Narratives*, ed. W. L. Andrews (Madison: University of Wisconsin Press, 1990), 150–151; James Albert Ukawsaw Gronniosaw, *A Narrative of the Most Remarkable Particulars In the Life of James Albert Ukawsaw Gronniosaw an African Prince, as Related by Himself*, in *Pioneers of the Black Atlantic: Five Slave Narratives from the Enlightenment*, ed. H. L. Gates Jr. and W. L. Andrews (Washington, D.C.: Counterpoint, 1998), 48; Bolster, *Black Jacks*, 5.

63. "Travel Diary of Commissioner Von Reck," in *Detailed Reports on the Salzburger Emigrants Who Settled in America*, vol. 1, ed. George Fenwick Jones, trans. Hermann J. Lacher (Athens: University of Georgia Press, 1968), 118.

64. Glen O'Hara, *Britain and the Sea since 1600* (New York: Palgrave Macmillan, 2010), 104; Sharon V. Salinger, *Taverns and Drinking in Early America* (Baltimore: Johns Hopkins University Press, 2002), 48–82; Michel de Certeau, *The Practice of Everyday Life*, trans. Steven Rendall (Berkeley: University of California Press, 1988), 113.

65. J. C. D. Clark, *The Language of Liberty, 1660–1832: Political Discourse and Social Dynamics in the Anglo-American World* (New York: Cambridge University Press, 1994), 146–153.

66. Pestana, *Protestant Empire*, 159–162; Owen Stanwood, *Empire Reformed*, 19–21; Thomas S. Kidd, *The Protestant Interest: New England after Puritanism* (New Haven: Yale University Press, 2004), 12–16.

67. Whitefield, *Journals*, 115.

68. "Advice for Brethren and Sisters in Preparation for Crossing the Atlantic to the West Indies," reprinted in Geoffrey Stead, "Crossing the Atlantic: The Eighteenth-Century Moravian Experience," *Transactions of the Moravian Historical Society* 30 (1998): 32–34.

69. Bernard Bailyn, *Atlantic History: Concept and Contours* (Cambridge: Harvard University Press, 2005), 96–100.

Chapter 4. Unbroken Horizons

1. John Wesley, Benjamin Ingham, David Nitschmann, and Andrew Dober describe celebrating Oglethorpe's birthday on Sunday, 21 December 1735, but Oglethorpe's biographers put the actual date of his birth as 22 December. Benjamin Ingham, "Rev. Benjamin Ingham, the Yorkshire Evangelist," in *The Oxford Methodists: Memoirs of the Rev. Messrs Clayton, Ingham, Gambold, Hervey, and Broughton*, ed. L. Tyerman (New York: Harper and Brothers, 1873), 72–73; John Andrew Dober quoted in Adelaide L. Fries, *The Moravians in Georgia, 1735–40* (Raleigh, N.C.: Edwards and Broughton, 1905), 111.

2. Francis Moore, *A Voyage to Georgia Begun in the Year 1735* (London: Jacob Robinson, 1744), 16; Philip Georg Friedrich von Reck, *Von Reck's Voyage: Drawings and Journal of Philip Georg Friedrich von Reck*, ed. Kristian Hvidt (Savannah: Beehive Press, 1980), 31; Dober quoted in Fries, *Moravians in Georgia*, 111; Ingham, "Rev. Benjamin Ingham," 72–73; John Wesley, *Journal and Diaries I, 1735–1738*, vol. 18 of *The Works of John Wesley*, ed. W. Reginald Ward and Richard P. Heitzenrater (Nashville: Abingdon Press, 1988), 316–317.

3. Olaudah Equiano, *The Interesting Narrative of the Life of Olaudah Equiano, or Gustavus Vassa, the African*, in *The Interesting Narrative and Other Writings*, ed. Vincent Carretta (New York: Penguin Books, 1995), 59–60.

4. James Savage, "The Journal of James Savage," ed. Theodore Chase and Celeste Walker, *Proceedings of the Massachusetts Historical Society* 97 (1985): 121; Samuel Davies, *The Reverend Samuel Davies Abroad: The Diary of a Journey to England and Scotland, 1753–55*, ed. George William Pilcher (Urbana: University of Illinois Press, 1967), 37 and 40; Ingham, "Rev. Benjamin Ingham," 73.

5. Catherine Green Hickling Prescott, Diary, 21 Jan. 1786–30 Sept. 1789, William H. Prescott Papers, MHS.

6. Henry Ingraham's Journal, 23 Oct. 1802, MHS; George Whitefield, *George Whitefield's Journals* (London: Banner of Truth Trust, 1965), 142; "The Travel Diary of the Two Pastors Messrs. Boltzius and Gronau Which the Two Have Kept from Halle to Georgia and for Some Time after Their Arrival in That Land," in *Detailed Reports on the Salzburger Emigrants Who Settled in America*, vol. 1, ed. George Fenwick Jones, trans. Hermann J. Lacher (Athens: University of Georgia Press, 1968), 40.

7. Henry Ingraham's Journal, 23 Oct. 1802, MHS; Journal of Benjamin Franklin Bache, 1782–1785, 23–24 Aug. 1785, Mss A 1998, NEHGS.

8. Von Reck, *Von Reck's Voyage*, 31.

9. Journal of Benjamin Franklin Bache, 1782–1785, 19 Aug. 1785, Mss A 1998, NEHGS; Zuriel Waterman, Memoranda Book, 17 Oct. 1779, RIHS; Whitefield, *Journals*, 141.

10. *Diary of a Voyage from Rotterdam to Philadelphia in 1728*, trans. Julius F. Sachse (Lancaster, Pa.: Pennsylvania German Society, 1909), 10; James Rhodes Log and Account Book, 19 Nov. 1796, Log 331, Mystic Seaport; William Almy Journal, 1776–1780, 15 Jan. 1780, William Almy Papers, RIHS; Journal of Benjamin Franklin Bache, 1782–1785, 19 Aug. 1785, Mss A 1998, NEHGS.

11. Henry Melchior Muhlenberg, *The Journals of Henry Melchior Muhlenberg*, trans. Theodore G. Tappert and John W. Doberstein (Philadelphia: Muhlenberg Press, 1942), vol. 1, 47; Whitefield, *Journals*, 148; Savage, "Journal of James Savage," 121.

12. Nathaniel Cutting Journal, 1786–1793, 4 Dec. 1789, P-275, reel 1, MHS; Fries, *Moravians in Georgia*, 64; John George Käsebier and John Christopher Saur, "Two Early Letters from Germantown," ed. Donald F. Durnbaugh, *Pennsylvania Magazine of History and Biography* 84, no. 2 (April 1960): 221.

13. Aaron Bull, Diary of a Voyage, 10 July 1755, CHS.

14. John Wesley, *Journal and Diaries I*, 345; John Newton, *The Journal of a Slave Trader*, ed. Bernard Martin and Mark Spurrell (London: Epworth Press, 1962), 60.

15. Thomas James Oertling, *Ships' Bilge Pumps: A History of Their Development, 1500–1900* (College Station: Texas A&M University Press, 1996), 79; von Reck, *Von Reck's Voyages*, 31.

16. Charles Wesley, *The Journal of the Rev. Charles Wesley* (Taylors, S.C.: Methodist Reprint Society, 1977), 74–75; Samuel Cooper Johonnot Journal, 1779, 12 Nov. 1779, MHS; John Thaxter Jr. to John Thaxter, 22 Feb. 1780, Thaxter Family Papers, MHS; Catherine Green Hickling Prescott, Diary, 21 Jan. 1786–30 Sept. 1789, William H. Prescott Papers, MHS; von Reck, *Von Reck's Voyage*, 31.

17. Isaac Gorham Papers, 2 April 1789, RIHS; Log of *Liberty*, 1774–1776, 9 April 1776, Ms. SBd-19, MHS; The logbook of the ship *Holland* reported a shark alongside that was twenty-five to thirty feet long. Logbook of ship *Holland*, 18 Aug. 1799, CHS; John Adams, *The Works of John Adams, Second President of the United States*, vol. 3, ed. Charles Francis Adams (Boston: Charles C. Little and James Brown, 1851), 227; von Reck, *Von Reck's Voyage*, 31.

18. Moore, *Voyage to Georgia*, 11–12; Logbook and Journal of John Hamilton, 1788–1799, 19–20 Oct. 1798, Mss C 1215, NEHGS; Logbooks of the *Neptune* and *Elizabeth*, 29 Aug. 1737, Log 180, Mystic Seaport.

19. Copley's painting is included in Peter H. Wood, *Weathering the Storm: Inside Winslow Homer's Gulf Stream* (Athens: University of Georgia Press, 2004), plate 7; the image *Watson and the Shark* (1778) can be found online at the Boston Museum of Fine Arts website,

http://zoom.mfa.org/fif=sc2/sc236724.fpx&obj=iip,1.0&hei=100&cell=1000,1000&cvt=j peg, accessed 11 June 2012; Horace Beck, *Folklore and the Sea* (Edison, N.J.: Castle Books, 1999), 281–284; Christine Quigley, *The Corpse: A History* (Jefferson, N.C.: McFarland, 1996), 94–97; Hester Blum, *The View from the Masthead: Maritime Imagination and Antebellum American Sea Narratives* (Chapel Hill: University of North Carolina, 2008), 15, 158–192; Norman L. Cantor, *After We Die: The Life and Times of the Human Cadaver* (Washington, D.C.: Georgetown University Press, 2010), 103–105; John Atkins, *A Voyage to Guinea, Brasil, and the West-Indies; in His Majesties Ships, the* Swallow *and* Weymouth (London: Caesar Ward and Richard Chandler, 1735), 46; Marcus Rediker, *The Slave Ship: A Human History* (New York: Viking, 2007), 37–40; Marcus Rediker, "History from below the Water Line: Sharks and the Atlantic Slave Trade," in *New Orleans in the Atlantic World: Between Land and Sea*, ed. William Boelhower (New York: Routledge, 2010), 137.

20. Some examples of logbooks recording the killing of sharks can be found in, Logbook of Sloop *Nancy*, 7 July 1754, Log 693, and Logbook of *Sea Flower*, 24 June 1763, Log 309, Mystic Seaport; Log of *Liberty*, 1774–1776, 9 April 1776, Ms. SBd-19, MHS; Logbook of the Sloop *Pitt*, 17 June 1768, Log 392, Mystic Seaport; Rediker, "History from below the Water Line," 131–143; Equiano, *Interesting Narrative*, 65; William D. Pierson, "White Cannibals, Black Martyrs: Fear, Depression, and Religious Faith as Causes of Suicide Among New Slaves," *Journal of Negro History* 62, no. 2 (April 1977): 147–159; John Thornton, "Cannibals, Witches, and Slave Traders in the Atlantic World," *William and Mary Quarterly* 60, no. 2 (April 2003), 273–294.

21. Thomas Nicolson Logs, 1782–1793, 11 May 1789, MHS; Whitefield, *Journals*, 142; Archibald Simpson, Journals and Sermons, 1748–1784, vol. 11, Charleston Library Society, 217; Benjamin Franklin, "Journal of a Voyage from London to Philadelphia, July 22–October 11, 1726," *The Writings of Benjamin Franklin*, vol. 2, *1722–1750*, ed. Albert Henry Smith (New York: Macmillan, 1905), 75; W. Clark Russell, *The Turnpike Sailor, or Rhymes on the Road* (London: Skeffington and Son, 1907), 22.

22. Lorenzo Dow, *Slave Ships and Slaving* (Westport, Conn.: Negro Universities Press, 1970), 63; William Richardson, *A Mariner of England: An Account of the Career of William Richardson from Cabin Boy in the Merchant Service to Warrant Officer in the Royal Navy (1780 to 1819) as Told by Himself*, ed. Spencer Childers (London: Conway Maritime Press, 1970), 57; Rediker, "History from below the Water Line," 138.

23. John Wesley, *Thoughts upon Slavery* (Philadelphia: Joseph Crukshank, 1778), 73, located at Documenting the American South, University Library, University of North Carolina at Chapel Hill, 1999, http://docsouth.unc.edu/church/wesley/wesley. html; "The Petition of the Sharks of Africa," http://blog.encyclopediavirginia. org/2012/01/09/the-petition-of-the-sharks-of-africa/, accessed 2 May 2014.

24. John Marrant, "Narrative of the Lord's Wonderful Dealings with John Marrant, a Black," in *Pioneers of the Black Atlantic: Five Slave Narratives from the Enlightenment*, ed. H. L. Gates Jr. and W. L. Andrews (Washington, D.C.: Counterpoint, 1998), 79; Equiano, *Interesting Narrative*, 66–67.

25. Psalm 74:13; Davies, *Samuel Davies Abroad*, 145; Samuel Russell Navigation Notebooks, 1706, 1710, in Elbridge Gerry Papers, MHS; Mark 4:39.

26. Josiah Quincy Jr., "Journal of Josiah Quincy, Junior, 1773," *Proceedings of the Massachusetts Historical Society* 50 (1916–1917): 430–431; Davies, *Samuel Davies Abroad*, 28–29, 37–38. Literary scholar Haskell Springer noted the attraction of the ocean's "liberating infinitude" for nineteenth-century American authors. Haskell Springer, "Introduction: The Sea, the Land, the Literature," in *America and the Sea: A Literary History*, ed. Haskell Springer (Athens: University of Georgia Press, 1995), 21; Louisa Susannah Wells, *The Journal of a Voyage from Charlestown, S.C., to London Undertaken by a Daughter of an Eminent American Loyalist* (New York: Printed for the New-York Historical Society, 1906), 4.

27. Catherine Green Hickling Prescott, Diary, 21 Jan. 1786–30 Sept. 1789, William H. Prescott Papers, MHS; Wells, *Journal of a Voyage*, 50–51; Adams, *Works of John Adams*, 105.

28. William Almy Journal, 1776–1780, 27 May 1776, William Almy Papers, RIHS; Sloop *Revenge* (Privateer) abstract log, July–Sept. 1777 and journal Feb.–June 1778, John Palmer Papers, Coll. 53, Mystic Seaport; Maria Falconbridge, *Two Voyages to Sierra Leone*, in *Maiden Voyages and Infant Colonies: Two Women's Travel Narratives of the 1790s*, ed. Deirdre Coleman (New York: Leicester University Press, 1999), 51; von Reck, *Von Reck's Voyage*, 31.

29. Davies, *Samuel Davies Abroad*, 29; William Almy Journal, 1776–1780, 2 July 1776, William Almy Papers, RIHS; Logbook of Sloop *Nancy*, 15 June 1755, Log 693, Mystic Seaport; A Memorandum or Short Account of Ye Life of Benjamin Bangs, 30 May 1744, Mss C 5089, NEHGS; [Daniel Lathrop Coit] Diary of trip in Europe, 29 May–20 Dec. 1783, 11 June 1783, CHS; Janet Schaw, *Journal of a Lady of Quality; Being the Narrative of a Journey from Scotland to the West Indies, North Carolina, and Portugal, in the Years 1774 to 1776*, ed. Evangeline Walker Andrews (New Haven: Yale University Press, 1923), 59.

30. William Spavens, *The Seaman's Narrative; Containing an Account of a Great Variety of Such Incidents as the Author Met with in the Sea Service* (Louth: Printed by R. Sheardown and Son, 1796); John Fontaine, *The Journal of John Fontaine: An Irish Huguenot Son in Spain and Virginia, 1710–1719*, ed. John P. Fontaine and Edward P. Alexander (Williamsburg, Va.: Colonial Williamsburg Foundation; distributed by the University Press of Virginia, 1972), 47.

31. A Memorandum or Short Account of Ye Life of Benjamin Bangs, 22 March–13 April 1744, Mss C 5089, NEHGS; Equiano, *Interesting Narrative*, 123; Fontaine, *Journal*, 47.

32. Isaac Lee, Record Book 1796–1797, CHS.

33. Davies, *Samuel Davies Abroad*, 34; Whitefield, *Journals*, 107; David D. Hall, *Worlds of Wonder, Days of Judgment: Popular Religious Belief in Early New England* (New York: Alfred A. Knopf, 1989), 71–77.

34. Equiano, *Interesting Narrative*, 59; Percy G. Adams, *Travelers and Travel Liars, 1660–1800* (Berkeley: University of California Press, 1962); Fontaine, *Journal*, 77; von Reck, *Von Reck's Voyage*, 60–61.

35. Von Reck, *Von Reck's Voyage*, 32; Zuriel Waterman, Memoranda Book, 22 Oct. 1779, RIHS.

36. Davies, *Samuel Davies Abroad*, 30; Quincy, "Journal of Josiah Quincy, Junior, 1773," 431; Equiano, *Interesting Narrative*.

37. Equiano, *Interesting Narrative*, 59; Logbook of the *Peggy*, 25 June 1794, MR 141, Mystic Seaport.

38. William Almy Journal, 1776–1780, 17 Dec. 1776, William Almy Papers, RIHS; Savage, "Journal of James Savage," 121; quoted line is from *Paradise Lost*, book 4, line 34. Whitefield, *Journals*, 99.

39. Ingham, "Rev. Benjamin Ingham," 73; Davies, *Samuel Davies Aboard*, 30, 146.

40. A Memorandum or Short Account of Ye Life of Benjamin Bangs, 5–6 Jan. 1743, Mss C 5089, NEHGS; Fontaine, *Journal*, 49; Horace Beck, *Folklore and the Sea* (Edison, N.J.: Castle Books, 1999), 92–93; John Wesley, *Journal and Diaries I*, 346; Samuel Kelly, *An Eighteenth Century Seaman Whose Days Have Been Few and Evil, to Which Is Added Remarks, etc., on Places He Visited during His Pilgrimage in This Wilderness*, ed. Crosbie Garstin (New York: Frederick A. Stokes, 1925), 98; George G. Carey, "The Tradition of St. Elmo's Fire," *American Neptune* 23 (1963): 29–38.

41. Wells, *Journal of a Voyage*, 12; Logbook of the Sloop *Prudence*, 31 June 1743, Log 692, Mystic Seaport.

42. Journal and Logbooks of Nathaniel Bowditch, 19 July 1796, MHS; "The Travel Diary of the Two Pastors Messrs. Boltzius and Gronau," 41–42; Genesis 9:11–17.

43. Springer, "Introduction," 23.

44. Quincy, "Journal of Josiah Quincy," 431.

45. William Bartram, *The Travels of William Bartram*, ed. Mark Van Doren (1791; reprint New York: Dover Publications, 1955), 30.

Chapter 5. Crossing Lines

1. "Tropic," *Oxford English Dictionary*, 2nd ed., 1989; online version December 2011, http://o-www.oed.com.library.simmons.edu/view/Entry/174213, accessed 25 Feb. 2012; Philip Georg Friedrich von Reck, *Von Reck's Voyage: Drawings and Journal of Philip Georg Friedrich von Reck*, ed. Kristian Hvidt (Savannah: Beehive Press, 1980), 31; Benjamin Ingham, "Rev. Benjamin Ingham, the Yorkshire Evangelist," *The Oxford Methodists: Memoirs of the Rev. Messrs Clayton, Ingham, Gambold, Hervey, and Broughton*, ed. L. Tyerman (New York: Harper and Brothers, 1873), 73.

2. John Andrew Dober quoted in Adelaide L. Fries, *The Moravians in Georgia, 1735–40* (Raleigh, N.C.: Edwards and Broughton, 1905), 111–112; Robert G. McPherson, "The Voyage of the *Anne*—A Daily Record," *Georgia Historical Quarterly* 44 (1960): 226; von Reck, *Von Reck's Voyage*, 31; Zuriel Waterman, Memoranda Book, 7 March 1781, RIHS.

3. Von Reck, *Von Reck's Voyage*, 31; Clifford Geertz, "Deep Play: Notes on the Balinese Cockfight," *The Interpretation of Cultures* (New York: Basic Books, 1993), 432–442.

4. Harry Miller Lydenberg, *Crossing the Line: Tales of the Ceremony during Four Centuries* (New York: New York Public Library, 1957), 35–65; Henning Henningsen, *Crossing the Equator: Sailors' Baptism and Other Initiation Rites* (Copenhagan: Munksgaard, 1961), 84–88; Marcus Buford Rediker, *Between the Devil and the Deep Blue Sea: Merchant Seamen, Pirates, and the Anglo-American Maritime World, 1700–1750* (New York: Cambridge University Press, 1987), 186–189; Simon J. Bronner, *Crossing the Line: Violence, Play, and Drama in Naval Equator Traditions* (Amsterdam: Amsterdam University Press, 2007), 7–8. "A ship's Logbook, as opposed to a journal or diary, was the official record of a voyage. While a journal could be kept by any crew member, the Logbook was most often kept by the mate, or first officer. It was the official record of the ship's voyage." Douglas L. Stein, "Log" and "Logbook," *American Maritime Documents, 1776–1860* (Mystic, Conn.: Mystic Seaport Museum, 1992), 15, 89–90; The *Oxford English Dictionary* defines a logbook as "a book in which the particulars of a ship's voyage (including her rate of progress as indicated by the log) are entered daily from the log-board."

5. Sloop *Revenge* (Privateer) abstract log, 13 Feb. 1777, John Palmer Papers, Coll. 53, Mystic Seaport; Brig *Betsey* journal, 23 Feb. 1785 and 1 March 1785, John Palmer Papers, Coll. 53, Mystic Seaport; Thomas Prince Journal and Logbook, 1709–1711, 9 May 1710, MHS.

6. Eleazar Elderkin, Journal of Voyage on ship *Eliza*, 1796–1798, 2 Oct. 1796, CHS.

7. Henry Gardiner, *The Anglo-American, or Memoirs of Capt. Henry Gardiner* (Liverpool: G. Wood, 1813), 11–13; Rediker, *Between the Devil and the Deep Blue Sea*, 186–189; Samuel Robinson, *A Sailor Boy's Experience aboard a Slave Ship* (Wigtown, Scotland: G. C. Book Publishers, 1996), 25; Lydenberg, *Crossing the Line*; Henningsen, *Crossing the Equator*.

8. Janet Schaw, *Journal of a Lady of Quality; Being the Narrative of a Journey from Scotland to the West Indies, North Carolina, and Portugal, in the Years 1774 to 1776*, ed. Evangeline Walker Andrews (New Haven: Yale University Press, 1923), 69–72. Some historians have adopted her viewpoint, for example, Peter Earle, *Sailors: English Merchant Seamen, 1650–1775* (London: Methuen, 1998), 96–97. Similar accounts by passengers emphasize the demand for money or alcohol over other aspects of the ritual, for example, von Reck, *Von Reck's Voyage*, 31; Mary Ann Parker, *A Voyage Round the World*, in *Maiden Voyages and Infant Colonies: Two Women's Travel Narratives of the 1790s*, ed. Deirdre Coleman (New York: Leicester University Press, 1999), 190; John MacDonald, *Memoirs of an Eighteenth Century Footman, John MacDonald Travels, 1745–1779*, ed. John Beresford (London: George Routledge and Sons, 1927), 100–101.

9. John Newton, *The Journal of a Slave Trader*, ed. Bernard Martin and Mark Spurrell (London: Epworth Press, 1962), 9; Robinson, *Sailor Boy's Experience*, 25–27; Emma Christopher, *Slave Ship Sailors and Their Captive Cargoes, 1730–1807* (New York: Cambridge University Press, 2006), xiii–xv, 52–90, 143–144. Christopher depicts the initiation taking place aboard Robinson's vessel with the slaves aboard, but the text suggests that it occurred during the initial leg rather than the Middle Passage.

10. "Advice for Brethren and Sisters in Preparation for Crossing the Atlantic to the West Indies," appendix to Geoffrey Stead, "Crossing the Atlantic: The Eighteenth-Century Moravian Experience," *Transactions of the Moravian Historical Society* 30 (1998): 34.

11. Rediker, *Between the Devil and the Deep Blue Sea*, 186–189.

12. Henry Melchior Muhlenberg, *The Journals of Henry Melchior Muhlenberg*, trans. Theodore G. Tappert and John W. Doberstein (Philadelphia: Muhlenberg Press, 1942), vol. 1, 45; Judith M. Bennett, "Conviviality and Charity in Medieval and Early Modern England," *Past and Present*, no. 134 (Feb. 1992): 20.

13. Sloop *Revenge* (Privateer) abstract log, 8 Jan. 1775, John Palmer Papers, Coll. 53, Mystic Seaport; A Memorandum or Short Account of Ye Life of Benjamin Bangs, 24 Jan. 1743, Mss C 5089, NEHGS.

14. Samuel Kelly, *An Eighteenth Century Seaman Whose Days Have Been Few and Evil, to Which Is Added Remarks, etc., on Places He Visited during His Pilgrimage in This Wilderness*, ed. Crosbie Garstin (New York: Frederick A. Stokes, 1925), 47; Rediker, *Between the Devil and the Deep Blue Sea*, 191–193. Logbook of Ship *Washington* appended to Sailing lessons, 31 Dec. 1784, Misc. Vol. 188, Mystic Seaport; Noah Robinson, Diaries, 9 Nov. 1780, RIHS; Nicholas Cresswell, *The Journal of Nicholas Cresswell, 1774–1777*, ed. Samuel Thornely (London: Jonathan Cape, 1925), 11; Logbooks of the *Neptune* and *Elizabeth*, 2 March 1761, Log 180, Mystic Seaport; Sloop *Revenge* (Privateer), abstract log, July–Sept. 1777, and journal Feb.–June 1778, 9 March 1777, John Palmer Papers, Coll. 53, Mystic Seaport.

15. George Whitefield, *George Whitefield's Journals* (London: Banner of Truth Trust, 1965), 141; Charles Wesley, *The Journal of the Rev. Charles Wesley* (Taylors, S.C.: Methodist Reprint Society, 1977), 69–72; Journal of a Cruise in the Sloop *Roby*, 18 Aug. 1758, RIHS; Greg Dening, *Mr Bligh's Bad Language: Passion, Power and Theatre on the Bounty* (New York: Cambridge University Press, 1992), 55–87.

16. Whitefield J. Bell Jr., "Adam Cunningham's Atlantic Crossing, 1728," *Maryland Historical Magazine* 50 (1955): 197; Dening, *Mr. Bligh's Bad Language*, 120.

17. John Woolman, *The Journal of John Woolman and a Plea for the Poor*, ed. Frederick B. Tolles (Philadelphia: Joseph Crukshank, 1774; reprint, Secaucus, N.J.: Citadel Press, 1972), 193–194; Commonplace Book of Simeon Crowell, 1790–1824, MHS; Eliza Williams, Sea Journal, 11 Sept. 1804, CHS; Logbook of the *Betsey*, 1796–1797, 11 March 1797, MR 19, Mystic Seaport.

18. Olaudah Equiano, *The Interesting Narrative of the Life of Olaudah Equiano, or Gustavus Vassa, the African* in *Slave Narratives*, ed. H. L. Gates Jr. and W. L. Andrews (New York: Library of America, 2000), 75.

19. The log of the ship *Mercury* recorded the wages of everyone aboard. The steward, John Goodridge, and the cook, Moody, were the lowest paid personnel aboard. Logbook of the Ship *Mercury*, Log 835, Mystic Seaport; Samuel Curson, "My First Voyage: Experiences in the Ship *Eliza* from August 15, 1798, to February 19, 1799," page 13, MHS; Logbook of the Brig *Digby*, 23 Jan. 1787, Log 176, Mystic Seaport; Benjamin Franklin, "Journal of a Voyage from London to Philadelphia, July 22–October 11, 1726," *The*

Writings of Benjamin Franklin, vol. 2, *1722–1750*, ed. Albert Henry Smith (New York: Macmillan, 1905), 75; William Palfrey Journal, 29 April 1771, MHS.

20. Logbook of the *Rebecca*, 27 Dec. 1797, MR 1, Mystic Seaport; Eleazar Elderkin, Journal of Voyage on ship *Eliza*, 1796–1798, 17 Aug. 1796, CHS; *Baltimore* logbook, 1788–1789, 30 Nov. 1788, MHS; Logbook of the *Rebecca*, 27 Oct. 1791, Log 50, Mystic Seaport; "Sinnet," *The Oxford Companion to Ships and the Sea*, ed. Peter Kemp (New York: Oxford University Press, 1976), 805.

21. Marcus Rediker, *Villains of All Nations: Atlantic Pirates in the Golden Age* (Boston: Beacon Press, 2004), 4; Kelly, *Eighteenth Century Seaman*, 152; logbook of Sloop *Nancy*, Log 693, Mystic Seaport; Journal of a Voyage from Cádiz toward Boston in Sloop *Hannah*, 3 Jan. 1754, Robert Treat Paine Papers, 1731–1814, MHS.

22. William Palfrey Journal, 11 April 1771, MHS; Thomas Cutts Logbook, 1787–1798, 17 June 1788, MHS; William Almy Journal, 1776–1780, 28 May 1776, William Almy Papers, RIHS; W. Jeffrey Bolster, "'Every Inch a Man': Gender in the Lives of African American Seamen, 1800–1860," in *Iron Men, Wooden Women: Gender and Seafaring in the Atlantic World, 1700–1920*, ed. Margaret S. Creighton and Lisa Norling (Baltimore: Johns Hopkins University Press, 1996), 140; Eleazar Elderkin, Journal of Voyage on ship *Eliza*, 1796–1798, 11 Jan. 1797, CHS.

23. Samuel W. Boardman, *Log-Book of Timothy Boardman Kept on Board the Privateer Oliver Cromwell, during a Cruise from New London, CT., to Charleston, S.C. and Return in 1778* (Albany: Joel Munsell's Sons, 1895), 83; Joseph Pinkham's log on the Ship *Falcon* from Coquimbo, Chile, to the U.S., Pinkham Family Papers, 1711–1822, MHS.

24. William Spavens, *The Seaman's Narrative; Containing an Account of a Great Variety of Such Incidents as the Author Met with in the Sea Service* (Louth: Printed by R. Sheardown and Son, 1796), 94; Journal of a Cruise in the Sloop *Roby*, RIHS.

25. Jonathan Mix, Journal on Board of the *Marlborough* (13 Sept. 13–18 Dec. 1778), 31 Oct. 1778, CHS.

26. Commonplace Book of Simeon Crowell, 1790–1824, MHS; Logbook and Journal of the Brig *Two Brothers* by Simeon Griswold, 1768–1770, Log 320, Mystic Seaport.

27. Quoted in Rediker, *Between the Devil and the Deep Blue Sea*, 191; Sloop *Count D'Estange* journal, 1783–1784, John Palmer Papers, Coll. 53, Mystic Seaport; William Downes Cheever Travel Journals, 20 Nov. 1778, MHS.

28. Cresswell, *Journal*, 14; Kelly, *Eighteenth Century Seaman*, 24; Equiano, *Interesting Narrative*, 88; Muhlenberg, *Journals*, vol. 1, 39–40.

29. John Flavel, "A Pathetical and Serious Dissuasive from the Horrid and Detestable Sins of Drunkenness, Swearing, Uncleanness, Forgetfulness of Mercies, Violation of Promises, and Atheistical Contempt of Death," in *The Works of John Flavel*, vol. 5 (1820; reprint, Carlisle, Pa.: Banner of Truth Trust, 1982), 295; Ruth Wallis Herndon, "The Domestic Cost of Seafaring: Town Leaders and Seamen's Families in Eighteenth-Century Rhode Island," in *Iron Men, Wooden Women: Gender and Seafaring in the Atlantic World*,

1700–1920, ed. Margaret S. Creighton and Lisa Norling (Baltimore: Johns Hopkins University Press, 1996), 57; Woolman, *Journal*, 206.

30. Eleazar Elderkin, Journal of Voyage on ship *Eliza*, 1796–1798, CHS; for example, see Logbook of the Sloop *Prudence*, Log 692, Mystic Seaport; Pinkham Family Papers, 1711–1822, MHS; A Memorandum or Short Account of Ye Life of Benjamin Bangs, 24 May 1744, Mss C 5089, NEHGS; Mary Malloy, "The Sailor's Fantasy: Images of Women in the Songs of American Whalemen," *Log of Mystic Seaport* 49, no. 2 (Autumn 1997): 34–43.

31. Aaron Bull, Diary, CHS; Logbook of Sloop *Nancy*, 5 June 1755, Log 693, Mystic Seaport; Benjamin Davis, Letter dated 15 Aug. 1775, John Palmer Papers, Coll. 53, Mystic Seaport.

32. Cresswell, *Journal*, 11; Lot Stetson, 12 Jan.–2 Feb. 1772, 28 Jan. 1772, Call # Misc., MHS; William Palfrey Journal, 13 April 1771, MHS.

33. A Memorandum or Short Account of Ye Life of Benjamin Bangs, 24 May 1744, Mss C 5089, NEHGS; William Richardson, *A Mariner of England: An Account of the Career of William Richardson from Cabin Boy in the Merchant Service to Warrant Officer in the Royal Navy [1780 to 1819] as Told by Himself*, ed. Spencer Childers (London: Conway Maritime, 1970), 112.

34. John Adams, *Works*, vol. 3, 103.

35. Samuel Lord, "YOUR CUNT," John Palmer Papers, Coll. 53, Mystic Seaport; Logbook of Sloop *Nancy*, 15 Feb. 1773, Log 693, Mystic Seaport; Thomas Nicolson Navigation Book, MHS; William Almy Journal, 1776–1780, 3 July 1776, William Almy Papers, RIHS.

36. Charles Woodmason, *The Carolina Backcountry on the Eve of the Revolution*, ed. Richard J. Hooker (Chapel Hill: University of North Carolina Press, 1953), 4; A. Roger Ekirch, *Bound for America: The Transportation of British Convicts to the Colonies, 1718–1775* (Oxford: Clarendon Press, 1987), 43; *A Huguenot Exile in Virginia; or, Voyages of a Frenchman Exiled for His Religion, with a Description of Virginia and Maryland*, ed. Nicholas Hayward Durand and Gilbert Chinard (New York: Press of the Pioneers, 1934), 95.

37. William Butterworth [Henry Schroeder], *Three Years Adventures of a Minor, in England, Africa, the West Indies, South-Carolina and Georgia* (Leeds: Thos. Inchbold, 1823), 39, 93; Michael A. Gomez, *Exchanging Our Country Marks: The Transformation of African Identities in the Colonial and Antebellum South* (Chapel Hill: University of North Carolina Press, 1998), 166–167.

38. "Testimony of Robert Norris," *House of Commons Sessional Papers of the Eighteenth Century*, vol. 68, ed. Sheila Lambert (Wilmington, Del.: Scholarly Resources, 1975), 9; John Newton, *The Journal of a Slave Trader, 1750–1754*, ed. Bernard Martin and Mark Spurrell (London: Epworth Press, 1962), 75.

39. Marcus Rediker, *The Slave Ship: A Human History* (New York: Viking, 2007), 241; Christopher, *Slave Ship Sailors*, 187–191; Alexander Falconbridge, *An Account of the Slave Trade on the Coast of Africa* (London: J. Phillips, 1788), 23; Nigel Tattersfield, *The Forgotten Trade: Comprising the Log of the Daniel and Henry of 1700 and Accounts of the Slave Trade from the Minor*

Ports of England, 1698–1725 (London: Jonathan Cape, 1991), 150–151; Jay Coughtry, *The Notorious Triangle: Rhode Island and the African Slave Trade, 1700–1807* (Philadelphia: Temple University Press), 160; Ottobah Cugoano, *Thoughts and Sentiments on the Evil and Wicked Traffic of the Slavery and Commerce of the Human Species*, in *Pioneers of the Black Atlantic: Five Slave Narratives from the Enlightenment*, ed. H. L. Gates Jr. and W. L. Andrews (Washington, D.C.: Counterpoint, 1998), 94; Stephen D. Behrendt, David Eltis, and David Richardson, "The Costs of Coercion: African Agency in the Pre-Modern Atlantic World," *Economic History Review* 53, no. 3 (2001): 458.

40. Falconbridge, *Account of the Slave Trade*, 24; James Field Stanfield, *Observations on a Guinea Voyage in a Series of Letters Addressed to the Rev. Thomas Clarkson* (London: James Phillips, 1788), 33; Rediker, *Slave Ship*, 151–152, 241–243; Gomez, *Exchanging Our Country Marks*, 166–167.

41. John Newton, *Thoughts upon the African Slave Trade*, in *The Works of John Newton*, vol. 6 (1820; reprint, Carlisle, Pa.: Banner of Truth Trust, 1988), 528, 534; Africanus [William Leigh], *Remarks on the Slave Trade and the Slavery of the Negroes in a Series of Letters* (London: J. Phillips, 1788), 46.

42. Arthur N. Gilbert, "Buggery and the British Navy," *Journal of Social History* 10, no. 1 (1976): 72–98; B. R. Burg, *Sodomy and the Perception of Evil* (New York: New York University Press, 1983); Hans Turley, *Rum, Sodomy, and the Lash: Piracy, Sexuality, and Masculine Identity* (New York: New York University Press, 1999); Daniel Vickers, *Young Men and the Sea: Yankee Seafarers in the Age of Sail* (New Haven: Yale University Press, 2005), 92.

43. Logbooks of the *Pearl, Robert, Brothers*, and *Manimia*, Log 686, Mystic Seaport; James Albert Ukawsaw Gronniosaw, *A Narrative of the Most Remarkable Particulars in the Life of James Albert Ukawsaw Gronniosaw, an African Prince, as Related by Himself*, in *Pioneers of the Black Atlantic: Five Slave Narratives from the Enlightenment*, ed. H. L. Gates Jr. and W. L. Andrews (Washington, D.C.: Counterpoint, 1998), 47–48; Equiano, *Interesting Narrative*, 108.

44. Anonymous Sailor's Diary, 18 Sept. 1733–1 Sept. 1735, 14 Feb. 1734, MHS.

45. John Palmer Papers, Coll. 53, Mystic Seaport; Thomas Nicolson Logs, 1782–1793, MHS; Log of the Ship *Asia* Kept by Silvanus Crosby, MR 38, Mystic Seaport; Lisa Norling, *Captain Ahab Had a Wife: New England Women and the Whalefishery, 1720–1870* (Chapel Hill: University of North Carolina Press, 2000), 111–114; Diary of a Voyage on the *Ceres*, Misc. Vol. 38, Mystic Seaport.

46. William Shakespeare, *The Tempest*, 2.2.45–53.

47. Journal of a Cruise in the Sloop *Roby*, RIHS; Sloop *Count D'Estange* journal, 1783–1784, John Palmer Papers, Coll. 53, Mystic Seaport.

48. Kelly, *Eighteenth Century Seaman*, 153–154; Isaac Lee Record Book, 1796–1797, CHS; Martin Page, Scroll #1, Martin Page Papers, RIHS; Logbook of Ship *Washington* appended to Sailing lessons, Misc. Vol. 188, Mystic Seaport.

49. Samuel Russell Navigation Notebooks, 1706, 1710, in Elbridge Gerry Papers, MHS; Thomas Nicolson Logs, 1782–1793, 17 June 1790, MHS; Logbook of Sloop *Nancy*, Log 693, Mystic Seaport; John Palmer Papers, Coll. 53, Mystic Seaport.

50. Logbook of Sloop *Nancy*, 2 June 1755, Log 693, Mystic Seaport; William Palfrey Journal, 13 April 1771, MHS.

51. Woolman, *Journal*, 198; Thomas Scattergood, *Journal of the Life and Religious Labours of Thomas Scattergood* (Philadelphia: Friends Book Store, 1874), 152; Samuel Davies, "Journal of Samuel Davies, from July 2, 1753, to February 13, 1775," in *Sketches of Virginia Historical and Biographical*, ed. William Henry Foote (Philadelphia: William S. Martien, 1850), 239.

52. Jacques-Pierre Brissot de Warville, *New Travels in the United States of America, 1788* (Cambridge: Belknap Press of Harvard University Press, 1964), 79.

53. Bolster, "'Every Inch a Man,'" 138–140; Turley, *Rum, Sodomy, and the Lash*, 1–27.

54. Ann Braude, "Women's History Is American Religious History," in *Retelling U.S. Religious History*, ed. Thomas A. Tweed (Berkeley: University of California Press, 1997), 88–92.

55. Ingham, "Rev. Benjamin Ingham," 73.

Chapter 6. Tedium

1. John Andrew Dober quoted in Adelaide L. Fries, *The Moravians in Georgia, 1735–40* (Raleigh, N.C.: Edwards and Broughton, 1905), 112.

2. Catherine Green Hickling Prescott, Diary, 21 Jan. 1786–30 Sept. 1789, William H. Prescott Papers, MHS; Alden T. Vaughan, *Transatlantic Encounters: American Indians in Britain, 1500–1776* (New York: Cambridge University Press, 2006), 153.

3. John Duffy succinctly described the "harrowing voyages from Europe to America," but his sources frequently utilized "tedious" to summarize their trip. John Duffy, "The Passage to the Colonies," *Mississippi Valley Historical Review* 38, no. 1 (1951): 22–23.

4. "Trade," *Oxford English Dictionary*, 2nd ed., 1989; online version December 2011, http://o-www.oed.com.library.simmons.edu/view/Entry/174213, accessed 11 June 2012.

5. Peter D. Jeans, *Ship to Shore: A Dictionary of Everyday Words and Phrases Derived from the Sea* (Camden, Me.: International Marine, 2004), 93; Logbooks of the *Neptune* and *Elizabeth*, Log 180, Mystic Seaport; A Journal of a Voyage round Cape Horn into the Pacific Ocean in Ye Year 1791 October ye 24th, 4 Dec. 1791, James Magee Papers, 1790–1816, MHS.

6. Philip Georg Friedrich von Reck, *Von Reck's Voyage: Drawings and Journal of Philip Georg Friedrich von Reck*, ed. Kristian Hvidt (Savannah: Beehive Press, 1980), 32.

7. "Dead Reckoning Position," *The Oxford Companion to Ships and the Sea*, ed. Peter Kemp (New York: Oxford University Press, 1976), 234.

8. John George Käsebier and John Christopher Saur, "Two Early Letters from Germantown," ed. Donald F. Durnbaugh, *Pennsylvania Magazine of History and Biography* 84, no. 2 (April 1960), 221.

9. Samuel Davies, "Journal of Samuel Davies, from July 2, 1753, to February 13, 1775," in *Sketches of Virginia Historical and Biographical*, ed. William Henry Foote (Philadelphia: William S. Martien, 1850), 239; Benjamin Ingham, "Rev. Benjamin Ingham, the Yorkshire Evangelist," in *The Oxford Methodists: Memoirs of the Rev. Messrs Clayton, Ingham, Gambold,*

Hervey, and Broughton, ed. L. Tyerman (New York: Harper and Brothers, 1873), 69; Richard P. Heitzenrater, "MS Journals and Diaries Editorial Introduction," *Journal and Diaries I, 1735–1738*, vol. 18 of *The Works of John Wesley*, ed. W. Reginald Ward and Richard P. Heitzenrater (Nashville: Abingdon Press, 1988), 302.

10. John Wesley, *Journal and Diaries I*, 337.

11. George Neisser quoted in John C. Brickenstein, "The Second 'Sea Congregation,' 1743," *Transactions of the Moravian Historical Society* 1 (1857–76): 118–119.

12. Charlotte Browne Journal, 1754–1757 (photostat), MHS; Käsebier and Saur, "Two Early Letters from Germantown," 222.

13. Brickenstein, "Second 'Sea Congregation,' 1743," 117.

14. Francis Moore, *A Voyage to Georgia Begun in the Year 1735* (London: Jacob Robinson, 1744), 15; von Reck, *Von Reck's Voyages*, 32.

15. Moore, *Voyage to Georgia*, 15; Charlotte Browne Journal, 1754–1757 (photostat), MHS.

16. Charlotte Browne Journal, 1754–1757 (photostat), MHS.

17. John C. Brickenstein, "The First 'Sea Congregation,'" *Transactions of the Moravian Historical Society* 1 (1857–76): 38–39; "From London to Philadelphia, 1742," *Pennsylvania Magazine of History and Biography* 37 (1913), 96; Janet Schaw, *Journal of a Lady of Quality; Being the Narrative of a Journey from Scotland to the West Indies, North Carolina, and Portugal, in the Years 1774 to 1776*, ed. Evangeline Walker Andrews (New Haven: Yale University Press, 1923), 47.

18. Eleazar Elderkin, Journal of Voyage on ship *Eliza*, 1796–1798, 10 Oct. 1796, CHS; Frederick Mackenzie, *A British Fusilier in Revolutionary Boston*, ed. Allen French (Cambridge: Harvard University Press, 1926), 11–12; quoted in Lorraine Smith Pangle, *The Political Philosophy of Benjamin Franklin* (Baltimore: Johns Hopkins University Press, 2007), 20.

19. Count Nickolas Ludwig von Zinzendorf quoted in Gillian Lindt Gollin, *Moravians in Two Worlds: A Study of Changing Communities* (New York: Columbia University Press, 1967), 17; Brickenstein, "Second 'Sea Congregation,'" 118; Brickenstein, "First 'Sea Congregation,'" 40; "Advice for Brethren and Sisters in Preparation for Crossing the Atlantic to the West Indies," appended to Geoffrey Stead, "Crossing the Atlantic: The Eighteenth-Century Moravian Experience," *Transactions of the Moravian Historical Society* 30 (1998): 33.

20. Davies, "Journal," 239.

21. Brickenstein, "First 'Sea Congregation,'" 40.

22. Louisa Susannah Wells, *The Journal of a Voyage from Charlestown, S.C., to London Undertaken by a Daughter of an Eminent American Loyalist* (New York: Printed for the New-York Historical Society, 1906), 51–52; Henry Melchior Muhlenberg, *The Journals of Henry Melchior Muhlenberg*, trans. Theodore G. Tappert and John W. Doberstein (Philadelphia: Muhlenberg Press, 1942), vol. 1, 28.

23. "Testimony of Mr. Ecroyde Claxton, Surgeon," *House of Commons Sessional Papers of the Eighteenth Century*, vol. 82, ed. Sheila Lambert (Wilmington, Del.: Scholarly Resources Inc., 1975), 36; William Downes Cheever Travel Journals, 7 Nov. 1778 to 24 May 1779, 15 Nov. 1778, MHS.

24. Heitzenrater, "MS Journals and Diaries Editorial Introduction," 309–310; Davies, "Journal," 240; Muhlenberg, *Journals*, vol. 1, 24, 31.

25. John Adams, *The Works of John Adams, Second President of the United States*, vol. 3, ed. Charles Francis Adams (Boston: Charles C. Little and James Brown, 1851), 209–210; Mackenzie, *A British Fusilier in Revolutionary Boston*, 9–11; John Fontaine, *The Journal of John Fontaine; An Irish Huguenot Son in Spain and Virginia, 1710–1719*, ed. John Fontaine and Edward P. Alexander (Williamsburg, Va.: Colonial Williamsburg Foundation; distributed by the University Press of Virginia, 1972), 48.

26. Benjamin Franklin, "Journal of a Voyage from London to Philadelphia, July 22–October 11, 1726," in *The Writings of Benjamin Franklin*, vol. 2, *1722–1750*, ed. Albert Henry Smith (New York: Macmillan, 1905), 67–71.

27. Franklin, "Journal of a Voyage," 76; David Nitschmann quoted in Fries, *Moravians in Georgia*, 112.

28. John Wesley, *Journal and Diaries I*, 347–348. Ingham, "Rev. Benjamin Ingham," 74; Diary of Daniel Lamson, 1750–1751, 12 Feb. 1751, Mss A 229, NEHGS; Logbook of Sloop *Nancy*, 14 July 1743, Log 693, Mystic Seaport.

29. Schaw, *Journal of a Lady of Quality*, 46.

30. Stephanie Smallwood, *Saltwater Slavery: A Middle Passage from Africa to American Diaspora* (Cambridge: Harvard University Press, 2007), 101.

31. William Downes Cheever Travel Journals, 22 Nov. 1778, MHS; Henry Ingraham's Journal, 28 Oct. 1802, MHS; Muhlenberg, *Journals*, vol. 1, 25, 42–43; *Huguenot Exile in Virginia*, 94–95.

32. Muhlenberg, *Journals*, vol. 1, 46; George Whitefield, *Journals* (1738–1741; reprint, London: Banner of Truth Trust, 1960), 513; Brickenstein, "Second 'Sea Congregation,'" 115; John Wesley, *Journal and Diaries I*, 338; Schaw, *Journal of a Lady of Quality*, 59.

33. "Evidence of James Arnold," *House of Commons Sessional Papers of the Eighteenth Century*, vol. 69, ed. Sheila Lambert (Wilmington, Del.: Scholarly Resources Inc., 1975), 126–127.

34. "Testimony of Henry Ellison," *House of Commons Sessional Papers*, 73:370; "Testimony of Robert Norris," *House of Commons Sessional Papers*, 68:7; John S. Mbiti, *African Religions and Philosophy*, 2nd ed. (Portsmouth, N.H.: Heinemann, 1990), 67; "Testimony of Mr. Ecroyde Claxton, Surgeon," *House of Commons Sessional Papers*, 82:35–36.

35. "Testimony of Henry Ellison," *House of Commons Sessional Papers*, 73:370; "Evidence of David Henderson," *House of Commons Sessional Papers*, 69:139–140; "Testimony of Mr. Alexander Falconbridge," *House of Commons Sessional Papers*, 72:307; Laurenti Magesa, *African Religion: The Moral Traditions of Abundant Life* (Maryknoll, N.Y.: Orbis Books, 1997), 195–201.

36. Robert Harms, *The Diligent: A Voyage Through the Worlds of the Slave Trade* (New York: Basic Books, 2002), 295–298; Daniel P. Mannix and Malcolm Cowley, *Black Cargoes: A History of the Atlantic Slave Trade, 1518–1865* (New York: Viking Press, 1962), 114; "Testimony of Robert Norris," *House of Commons Sessional Papers*, 68:4–5; "Evidence of James Arnold,"

House of Commons Sessional Papers, 69:126; Philip D. Morgan, *Slave Counterpoint: Black Culture in the Eighteenth-Century Chesapeake and Lowcountry* (Chapel Hill: Published for the Omohundro Institute of Early American History and Culture by the University of North Carolina Press, 1998), 588–589.

37. "Testimony of Mr. John Matthews, a Lieutenant in His Majesty's Navy," *House of Commons Sessional Papers*, 68:20; "Testimony of Mr. Alexander Falconbridge," *House of Commons Sessional Papers*, 72:305; "Testimony of Captain John Ashley Hall," *House of Commons Sessional Papers*, 72:231; "Testimony of Mr. Isaac Wilson," *House of Commons Sessional Papers*, 73:276–277; poem is quoted in Christopher, *Slave Ship Sailors*, 176.

38. "Testimony of Robert Norris," *House of Commons Sessional Papers*, 68:4–5; "Evidence of James Arnold," *House of Commons Sessional Papers*, 69:126; Magesa, *African Religion*, 239–240. Geneviève Fabre, "The Slave Ship Dance," *Black Imagination and the Middle Passage*, ed. Maria Diedrich, Henry Louis Gates Jr., and Carl Pedersen (New York: Oxford University Press, 1999), 33, 38.

39. Lawrence W. Levine, *Black Culture and Black Consciousness: Afro-American Folk Thought from Slavery to Freedom* (New York: Oxford University Press, 1977), 7–8.

40. Hester Blum, *The View from the Masthead: Maritime Imagination and Antebellum American Sea Narratives* (Chapel Hill: University of North Carolina, 2008), 2; Marcus Buford Rediker, *Between the Devil and the Deep Blue Sea: Merchant Seamen, Pirates, and the Anglo-American Maritime World, 1700–1750* (Cambridge: Cambridge University Press, 1987), 158, 307; Dorothy Denneen Volo and James M. Volo, *Daily Life in the Age of Sail* (Westport, Conn.: Greenwood Press, 2002), 148; James Albert Ukawsaw Gronniosaw, "A Narrative of the Most Remarkable Particulars in the Life of James Albert Ukawsaw Gronniosaw an African Prince, as Related by Himself," *Pioneers of the Black Atlantic: Five Slave Narratives from the Enlightenment*, ed. H. L. Gates Jr. and W. L. Andrews (Washington, D.C.: Counterpoint, 1998), 40; Olaudah Equiano, *The Interesting Narrative of the Life of Olaudah Equiano, or Gustavus Vassa, the African*, in *The Interesting Narrative and Other Writings*, ed. Vincent Carretta (New York: Penguin Books, 1995), 68, 92, 118–119; Charlotte Browne Journal, 1754–1757 (photostat), MHS.

41. John Adams, *Works*, vol. 3, 97–98; Schaw, *Journal of a Lady of Quality*, 44–45, 135.

42. William Palfrey Journal, 7 April 1771, MHS; E. Edwards Beardsley, *Life and Correspondence of Samuel Johnson, D.D.* (New York: Hurd and Houghton, 1874), 25; Cresswell, *Journal*, 11; "The Travel Diary of the Two Pastors Messrs. Boltzius and Gronau Which the Two Have Kept from Halle to Georgia and for Some Time after Their Arrival in That Land," in *Detailed Reports on the Salzburger Emigrants Who Settled in America*, ed. George Fenwick Jones, trans. Hermann J. Lacher (Athens: University of Georgia Press, 1968), 40–41; Wesley, *Journal and Diaries I*, 317, 338; Jacques-Pierre Brissot de Warville, *New Travels in the United States of America, 1788* (Cambridge: Belknap Press, 1964), 77.

43. Mary Ann Parker, *A Voyage Round the World*, in *Maiden Voyages and Infant Colonies: Two Women's Travel Narratives of the 1790s*, ed. Deirdre Coleman (New York: Leicester University Press, 1999), 215, Nigel Tattersfield, *The Forgotten Trade: Comprising the Log of the Daniel and*

Henry of 1700 and Accounts of the Slave Trade from the Minor Ports of England, 1698–1725 (London: Jonathan Cape, 1991), 164–165.

44. Whitefield, *Journals*, 176.

45. Kelly, *Eighteenth Century Seaman*, 256.

46. John Newton, *The Journal of a Slave Trader, 1750–1754*, ed. Bernard Martin and Mark Spurrell (London: Epworth Press, 1962), 84; Carla Gardina Pestana, "Religion," in *The British Atlantic World, 1500–1800*, ed. David Armitage and Michael J. Braddick (New York: Palgrave Macmillan, 2002), 74–75.

47. Susan O'Brien, "A Transatlantic Community of Saints: The Great Awakening and the First Evangelical Network, 1735–1755," *American Historical Review* 91, no. 4 (Oct. 1986): 811–832; Frank Lambert, "'Pedlar in Divinity': George Whitefield and the Great Awakening, 1737–1745," *Journal of American History* 77, no. 3 (Dec. 1990): 812–837; Harry S. Stout, *The Divine Dramatist: George Whitefield and the Rise of Modern Evangelicalism* (Grand Rapids: Eerdmans, 1991), 201–219; Whitefield, *Journals*, 141, 144; Newton, *Journal of a Slave Trader*, 84; Ingham, "Rev. Benjamin Ingham, 69; Eleazar Elderkin, Journal of Voyage on ship *Eliza*, 1796–1798, 14 Aug. 1796, CHS.

48. Samuel Davies, *The Reverend Samuel Davies Abroad: The Diary of a Journey to England and Scotland, 1753–55*, ed. George William Pilcher (Urbana: University of Illinois Press, 1967), 33; Anonymous Sailor's Diary, 1733 Sept. 18–1735 Sept. 1, MHS; Equiano, *Interesting Narrative*, 118–119.

49. Brickenstein, "Second 'Sea Congregation,'" 119.

50. Davies, *Samuel Davies Abroad*, 36; John Wesley, *Journal and Diaries I*, 313, 339.

51. Woodmason, *Carolina Backcountry*, 4; Muhlenberg, *Journals*, vol. 1, 48.

52. Quoted in Glen O'Hara, *Britain and the Sea since 1600* (New York: Palgrave MacMillan, 2010), 96; Rediker, *Between the Devil and the Deep Blue Sea*, 159.

Chapter 7. Tempests

1. John Andrew Dober quoted in Adelaide L. Fries, *The Moravians in Georgia, 1735–40* (Raleigh, N.C.: Edwards and Broughton, 1905), 112–113; John Wesley, *Journal and Diaries I, 1735–1738*, vol. 18 of *The Works of John Wesley*, ed. W. Reginald Ward and Richard P. Heitzenrater (Nashville: Abingdon Press, 1988), 341.

2. David Nitschmann quoted in Fries, *Moravians in Georgia*, 113; Benjamin Ingham, "Rev. Benjamin Ingham, the Yorkshire Evangelist," *The Oxford Methodists: Memoirs of the Rev. Messrs Clayton, Ingham, Gambold, Hervey, and Broughton*, ed. L. Tyerman (New York: Harper and Brothers, 1873), 73; Philip Georg Friedrich von Reck, *Von Reck's Voyage: Drawings and Journal of Philip Georg Friedrich von Reck*, ed. Kristian Hvidt (Savannah: Beehive Press, 1980), 32. John Wesley, *Journal and Diaries I, 1735–1738*, 341–345.

3. "Tempest," *Oxford English Dictionary*, 2nd ed., 1989; online version December 2011. http://0-www.oed.com.library.simmons.edu/view/Entry/174213, accessed 14 July 2012; 25 Jan. 1755 and 2 Feb. 1755, Charlotte Browne Journal, 1754–1757 (photostat), MHS;

Robert G. McPherson, "The Voyage of the *Anne*—A Daily Record," *Georgia Historical Quarterly* 44 (1960): 229.

4. Ingham, "Rev. Benjamin Ingham," 73.

5. Cuthbert Powell, "Journal of Cuthbert Powell," ed. James Daniel Evans, *William and Mary College Quarterly Historical Magazine* 12, no. 4 (April 1904): 231; Henry Francis Moore, *A Voyage to Georgia Begun in the Year 1735* (London: Jacob Robinson, 1744), 16; Henry Melchior Muhlenberg, *The Journals of Henry Melchior Muhlenberg*, vol. 1, trans. Theodore G. Tappert and John W. Doberstein (Philadelphia: Muhlenberg Press, 1942), 51–52.

6. Benjamin Franklin, "A Letter from Dr. Benjamin Franklin to Mr. Alphonse le Roy, Member of Several Academies, at Pairs. Containing Sundry Maritime Observations," *Transactions of the American Philosophical Society* 2 (1786): 294–329; Nicholas Cresswell, *The Journal of Nicholas Cresswell, 1774–1777*, ed. Samuel Thornely (London: Jonathan Cape, 1925), 274; Rebecca Jones, *Memorials of Rebecca Jones*, ed. William J. Allinson (Philadelphia: Longstreth, 1849), 165; von Reck, *Von Reck's Voyage*, 32.

7. Ian K. Steele, *The English Atlantic, 1675–1740: An Exploration of Communication and Community* (New York: Oxford University Press, 1986), 7; Louisa Susannah Wells, *The Journal of a Voyage from Charlestown, S.C., to London Undertaken by a Daughter of an Eminent American Loyalist* (New York: New-York Historical Society, 1906), 12; von Reck, *Von Reck's Voyage*, 61.

8. Archibald Simpson, Journals and Sermons, 1748–1784, vol. 11, Charleston Library Society, 232.

9. Helen Rozwadowski, *Fathoming the Ocean: The Discovery and Exploration of the Deep Sea* (Cambridge: Belknap Press of Harvard University Press, 2005), 40–41; Steele, *English Atlantic*, 9–10; Simpson, Journals and Sermons, 245.

10. Samuel Davies, "Journal of Samuel Davies, from July 2, 1753, to February 13, 1775," in *Sketches of Virginia Historical and Biographical*, ed. William Henry Foote (Philadelphia: William S. Martien, 1850), 279; John Adams, *The Works of John Adams, Second President of the United States*, vol. 3, ed. Charles Francis Adams (Boston: Charles C. Little and James Brown, 1851), 100; Henry Gardiner, *The Anglo-American; or, Memoirs of Capt. Henry Gardiner* (Liverpool: G. Wood, 1813), 161.

11. Olaudah Equiano, *The Interesting Narrative of the Life of Olaudah Equiano, or Gustavus Vassa, the African*, in *The Interesting Narrative and Other Writings*, ed. Vincent Carretta (New York: Penguin Books, 1995), 176–177; Logbook of Daniel Francis, 22 Nov. 1793, Log 389, Mystic Seaport; Josiah Quincy Jr., "Journal of Josiah Quincy, Junior, 1773," *Proceedings of the Massachusetts Historical Society* 50 (1916–1917): 434–435; Davies, "Journal," 33; William Bartram, *The Travels of William Bartram*, ed. Mark Van Doren (1791; reprint New York: Dover, 1955), 29.

12. Journal of Benjamin Franklin Bache, 1782–1785, 1 Sept. 1785, Mss A 1998, NEHGS; Aaron Bull, Diary of a Voyage, 25 Aug. 1755, CHS; Bruce L. Mouser, ed., *A Slaving Voyage to Africa and Jamaica: The Log of the Sandown, 1793–1794* (Bloomington: Indiana University Press, 2002), 126.

13. John Harrower, *The Journal of John Harrower, an Indentured Servant in the Colony of Virginia, 1773–1776*, ed. Edward M. Riley (Williamsburg, Va.: distributed by Holt Rinehart and Winston, 1963), 24–25; Gottlieb Mittelberger, *Journey to Pennsylvania*, trans. Oscar Handlin and John Clive (Cambridge: Belknap Press of Harvard University Press, 1960), 12–13; Ebenezer Cooke, *The Sot-Wood Factor: or, a Voyage to Maryland*, ed. Brantz Mayer (London: D. Bragg, 1708), 1–2.

14. John Newton, *The Journal of a Slave Trader*, ed. Bernard Martin and Mark Spurrell (London: Epworth Press, 1962), 53, 60; John Atkins, *A Voyage to Guinea, Brasil, and the West-Indies; in His Majesties Ships, the Swallow and Weymouth* (London: Caesar Ward and Richard Chandler, 1735), 237–239; Mouser, *Slaving Voyage*, 50.

15. Alexander Falconbridge quoted in Daniel P. Mannix and Malcolm Cowley, *Black Cargoes: A History of the Atlantic Slave Trade, 1518–1865* (New York: Viking Press, 1962), 116; Equiano, *Interesting Narrative*, 59.

16. Quincy, "Journal," 431, 435–436; Charles Wesley, *The Journal of the Rev. Charles Wesley* (Taylors, S.C.: Methodist Reprint Society, 1977), 87.

17. William Almy Journal, 1776–1780, 20 Dec. 1776, William Almy Papers, RIHS; William Spavens, *The Seaman's Narrative; Containing an Account of a Great Variety of Such Incidents as the Author Met with in the Sea Service* (Louth: R. Sheardown and Son, 1796), 5; William Butterworth [Henry Schroeder], *Three Years Adventures of a Minor, in England, Africa, the West Indies, South-Carolina and Georgia* (Leeds: Thos. Inchbold, 1823), 13; Logbook of Brig *Digby*, 8 Feb. 1789, Log 176, Mystic Seaport.

18. Janet Schaw, *Journal of a Lady of Quality; Being the Narrative of a Journey from Scotland to the West Indies, North Carolina, and Portugal, in the Years 1774 to 1776*, ed. Evangeline Walker Andrews (New Haven: Yale University Press, 1923), 47; Cresswell, *Journal*, 29–30; John Woolman, *The Journal of John Woolman and a Plea for the Poor*, ed. Frederick B. Tolles (Philadelphia: Joseph Crukshank, 1774; reprint, Secaucus, N.J.: Citadel Press, 1972), 194.

19. Logbook of the *Anna* and *Satisfaction* [kept by Robert Dunn], 17 Sept. 1782, Log 687, Mystic Seaport; Quincy, "Journal," 435; Susanna Morris, "The Journal of Susanna Morris 1682–1755," in *Wilt Thou Go On My Errand? Journals of Three 18th Century Quaker Women Ministers*, ed. Margaret Hope Bacon (Wallingford, Pa.: Pendle Hill Publications, 1994), 108.

20. John Francis Diary, 3 Sept. 1783, RIHS; Bartram, *Travels*, 30.

21. Johann Cristoph Sauer, "An Early Description of Pennsylvania," ed. R. W. Kelsey, *Pennsylvania Magazine of History and Biography* 45 (1921): 244.

22. John C. Brickenstein, "The Second 'Sea Congregation,' 1743," *Transactions of the Moravian Historical Society* 1 (1857–76): 121; William Shakespeare, *The Tempest*, act 1, scene 1; Davies, "Journal," 238.

23. Schaw, *Journal of a Lady of Quality*, 48.

24. John Wesley, *Journal and Diaries I*, 142–143.

25. Nitschmann and Dober quoted in Fries, *Moravians in Georgia*, 115–117.

26. Von Reck, *Von Reck's Voyage*, 32.

27. Mittelberger, *Journey to Pennsylvania*, 12–13; Francis Asbury, *The Journal and Letters of Francis Asbury*, vol. 1, *The Journal 1771 to 1793*, ed. Elmer T. Clark, J. Manning Potts, and Jacob S. Payton (Nashville: Abingdon Press, 1958), 5.

28. Psalm 69:15; Jones, *Memorials*, 55; Olaudah Equiano, *The Interesting Narrative of the Life of Olaudah Equiano, or Gustavus Vassa, the African*, in *The Interesting Narrative and Other Writings*, ed. Vincent Carretta (New York: Penguin Books, 1995), 176–177; George Whitefield, *George Whitefield's Journals* (London: Banner of Truth Trust, 1965), 124; Davies, "Journal," 240, 278; Quincy, "Journal," 438.

29. Zuriel Waterman, Memoranda Book, RIHS; Davies, "Journal," 280.

30. John Cremer, *Ramblin' Jack: The Journal of Captain John Cremer, 1700–1744*, ed. R. Reynell Bellamy (London: Jonathan Cape, 1939), 85.

31. John Wesley, *Journal and Diaries I*, 342. Charles Wesley, *Journal*, 76; John Fontaine, *The Journal of John Fontaine; An Irish Huguenot Son in Spain and Virginia, 1710–1719*, ed. Edward P. Alexander (Williamsburg, Va.: Colonial Williamsburg Foundation; distributed by the University Press of Virginia, 1972), 50–51; Marcus Buford Rediker, *Between the Devil and the Deep Blue Sea: Merchant Seamen, Pirates, and the Anglo-American Maritime World, 1700–1750* (New York: Cambridge University Press, 1987), 157; David Nitschmann and John Andrew Dober quoted in Fries, *Moravians in Georgia*, 117. Quincy, "Journal," 434–435. Catherine Green Hickling describes a similar conversation in Catherine Green Hickling Prescott, Diary, 21 Jan. 1786–30 Sept. 1789, William H. Prescott Papers, MHS.

32. Ingham, "Rev. Benjamin Ingham," 74.

33. Commonplace Book of Simeon Crowell, 1790–1824, MHS; Logbook of Sloop *Nancy*, 28 May 1755, Log 693, Mystic Seaport; Fontaine, *Journal*, 49.

34. Samuel Kelly, *An Eighteenth Century Seaman Whose Days Have Been Few and Evil, to Which Is Added Remarks, etc., on Places He Visited during His Pilgrimage in This Wilderness*, ed. Crosbie Garstin (New York: Frederick A. Stokes, 1925), 67; *Memoirs of an Eighteenth Century Footman, John MacDonald Travels, 1745–1779*, ed. John Beresford (London: George Routledge and Sons, 1927), 171–172; Cremer, *Ramblin' Jack*, 90, 104, 107; Horace Beck, *Folklore and the Sea* (Middletown, Conn.: Mystic Seaport by Wesleyan University Press, 1973), 94–95; Elizabeth Posthuma Simcoe, *The Diary of Mrs. John Graves Simcoe: Wife of the First Lieutenant-Governor of the Province of Upper Canada, 1792–1796*, ed. J. Ross Robertson (Toronto: William Briggs, 1911), 47; Mary Ann Parker, *A Voyage Round the World*, in *Maiden Voyages and Infant Colonies: Two Women's Travel Narratives of the 1790s*, ed. Deirdre Coleman (New York: Leicester University Press, 1999), 191.

35. John Wesley, *Journal and Diaries I*, 346; Kelly, *Eighteenth Century Seaman*, 98. St. Elmo was a corrupted form of St. Erasmus, a martyred Italian bishop from the fourth century and the patron saint of Mediterranean sailors. George G. Carey, "The Tradition of St. Elmo's Fire," *American Neptune* 23 (1963): 29–38; Edgar K. Thompson, "The Tradition of St. Elmo's Fire," *American Neptune* 24 (1964): 213–214; Beck, *Folklore and the Sea*, 92–93.

36. David D. Hall, *Worlds of Wonder, Days of Judgment: Popular Religious Belief in Early New England* (New York: Alfred A. Knopf, 1989), 7; Harrower, *Journal*, 33; Commonplace Book of Simeon Crowell, 1790–1824, MHS; Keith Thomas, *Religion and the Decline of Magic* (New York: Charles Scribner's Sons, 1971), 177–192.

37. Augustus Gottlieb Spangenberg quoted in Fries, *Moravians in Georgia*, 64.

38. Fontaine, *Journal*, 48; Nitschmann quoted Fries, *Moravians in Georgia*, 102.

39. John Wesley, *Journal and Diaries I*, 334, 339–340.

40. Mouser, *Slaving Voyage*, 111; Butterworth, *Three Years Adventures*, 96; Rediker, *Slave Ship*, 272.

41. "Testimony of Captain John Knox," *House of Commons Sessional Papers*, 68:125, 158; "Testimony of Mr. Alexander Falconbridge," *House of Commons Sessional Papers*, 72:303; "Testimony of Captain John Ashley Hall," *House of Commons Sessional Papers*, 72:230; Mouser, *Slaving Voyage*, 110–111; Allan D. Austin, *African Muslims in Antebellum America* (New York: Garland, 1984), 704; "Evidence of James Bowen," *House of Commons Sessional Papers*, 69:125.

42. "Testimony of Captain John Ashley Hall," *House of Commons Sessional Papers*, 72:230; George Francis Dow, *Slave Ships and Slaving* (1927; reprint, Westport, Conn.: Negro Universities Press, 1970), 142–143.

43. *A Huguenot Exile in Virginia; or, Voyages of a Frenchman Exiled for His Religion, with a Description of Virginia and Maryland*, ed. Gilbert Chinard (1687; reprint, New York: Press of the Pioneers, 1934), 98–99; Thomas Nicolson Logs, 1782–1793, 7 Aug. 1782, MHS; William Almy Journal, 1776–1780, 3 Jan. 1780, William Almy Papers, RIHS.

44. Journal of a Voyage from Cádiz toward Boston in Sloop *Hannah*, 18 Jan. 1754, Robert Treat Paine Papers, 1731–1814, MHS; Whitefield, *Journals*, 172–174.

45. Benjamin Pollard Diary, 1736–1738, 23 May 1738, MHS; Charlotte Browne Journal, 1754–1757 (photostat), 12 Jan. 1755, MHS.

46. "Copy of a Letter from Mrs. Elizabeth Bland to Mr. Oglethorpe dated at Savannah 14th June 1735," Egmont Papers, Phillipps Collection, 14201: 17–18, University of Georgia Libraries; Whitefield J. Bell Jr., "Adam Cunningham's Atlantic Crossing, 1728," *Maryland Historical Magazine* 50 (1955): 197, 199.

47. Henry Norwood, "A Voyage to Virginia," quoted in Haskell Springer, "The Colonial Era," in *America and the Sea: A Literary History*, ed. Haskell Springer (Athens: University of Georgia Press, 1995), 37.

48. John Duffy, "The Passage to the Colonies," *Mississippi Valley Historical Review* 38, no. 1 (1951): 31–33; Gerald L. Cates, "The Voyage: A Study of Medical Hazards on the First Immigrant Ships to Georgia," *Journal of the Medical Association of Georgia* 68, no. 9 (1979): 833.

49. Robin Miskolcze, *Women and Children First: Nineteenth-Century Sea Narratives and American Identity* (Lincoln: University of Nebraska Press, 2007), 21–22.

Chapter 8. Land Ho!

1. Philip Georg Friedrich von Reck, *Von Reck's Voyage: Drawings and Journal of Philip Georg Friedrich von Reck*, ed. Kristian Hvidt (Savannah: Beehive Press, 1980), 33.

2. Robert G. Albion, *Square-Riggers on Schedule: The New York Packets to England, France, and the Cotton Ports* (Princeton: Princeton University Press, 1938); Ian K. Steele, *The English Atlantic, 1675–1740: An Exploration of Communication and Community* (New York: Oxford University Press, 1986), 168–188.

3. Steele, *English Atlantic 1675–1740*, 21–93; Albion, *Square-Riggers on Schedule*, 1–19.

4. Steele, *English Atlantic, 1675–1740*, 34.

5. Von Reck, *Von Reck's Voyage*, 27; Charlotte Browne Journal, 1754–1757 (photostat), 23 March 1755, MHS; William Palfrey Journal, 27 April 1771, MHS; Samuel Davies, "Journal of Samuel Davies, from July 2, 1753, to February 13, 1775," in *Sketches of Virginia Historical and Biographical*, ed. William Henry Foote (Philadelphia: William S. Martien, 1850), 241.

6. "The Travel Diary of the Two Pastors Messrs. Boltzius and Gronau Which the Two Have Kept from Halle to Georgia and for Some Time after Their Arrival in That Land," in *Detailed Reports on the Salzburger Emigrants Who Settled in America*, ed. George Fenwick Jones, trans. Hermann J. Lacher (Athens: University of Georgia Press, 1968), 48–49; Henry Melchior Muhlenberg, *The Journals of Henry Melchior Muhlenberg*, vol. 1, trans. Theodore G. Tappert and John W. Doberstein (Philadelphia: Muhlenberg Press, 1942), 55; George Whitefield, *Journals* (1738–41; reprint, London: Banner of Truth Trust, 1960), 175.

7. Aaron Bull, Diary of a Voyage, 15 July 1755, CHS.

8. Francis Asbury, *The Letters and Journals of Francis Asbury*, vol. 1, *The Journal 1771 to 1793*, ed. Elmer T. Clark, J. Manning Potts, and Jacob S. Payton (Nashville: Abingdon Press, 1958), 6; Josiah Quincy Jr., "Journal of Josiah Quincy, Junior, 1773," *Proceedings of the Massachusetts Historical Society* 50 (1916–1917): 437; Janet Schaw, *Journal of a Lady of Quality; Being the Narrative of a Journey from Scotland to the West Indies, North Carolina, and Portugal, in the Years 1774 to 1776*, ed. Evangeline Walker Andrews (New Haven: Yale University Press, 1923), 217; Whitefield, *Journals*, 152.

9. John Frederick Whitehead, "The Life of John Frederick Whitehead," in *Souls for Sale: Two German Redemptioners Come to Revolutionary America*, ed. Susan E. Klepp, Farley Grubb, and Anne Pfaelzer de Ortiz (University Park: Pennsylvania State University Press, 2006), 134; Logbook of Sloop *Nancy*, 25 May 1755, Log 693, Mystic Seaport.

10. George Fenwick Jones, *The Georgia Dutch: From the Rhine and Danube to the Savannah, 1733–1783* (Athens: University of Georgia Press, 1992), 11; Klaus Wust, "The Immigration Season of 1738—Year of the Destroying Angel," *The Report: A Journal of German-American History* 39 (184): 21–56.

11. Stephen R. Bown, *Scurvy: How a Surgeon, A Mariner, and a Gentleman Solved the Greatest Medical Mystery of the Age of Sail* (New York: St. Martin's Press, 2003), 3, 24; Logbook of the *Rebecca*, 13 Feb. 1792, Log 50, Mystic Seaport; Kenneth J. Carpenter, *The History of Scurvy and Vitamin C* (New York: Cambridge University Press, 1988), 45–46; Gerald L. Cates,

"The Voyage: A Study of Medical Hazards on the First Immigrant Ships to Georgia," *Journal of the Medical Association of Georgia* 68, no. 9 (1979): 832.

12. Logbook of the *Rebecca*, 4 Nov. 1792, Log 50, Mystic Seaport; Whitefield J. Bell Jr., "Adam Cunningham's Atlantic Crossing, 1728," *Maryland Historical Magazine* 50 (1955): 199, 200–201.

13. Fernand Braudel, *The Structures of Everyday Life: The Limits of the Possible*, trans. Siân Reynolds (New York: Harper and Row, 1981), 81; John Duffy, "The Passage to the Colonies," *Mississippi Valley Historical Review* 38, no. 1 (1951), 31–33.

14. Joseph C. Miller, "Mortality in the Atlantic Slave Trade: Statistical Evidence on Causality," *Journal of Interdisciplinary History* 11, no. 3 (1981): 387; Herbert S. Klein, Stanley L. Engerman, Robin Haines, and Ralph Shlomowitz, "Transoceanic Mortality: The Slave Trade in Comparative Perspective," *William and Mary Quarterly* 58, no. 1 (Jan. 2001): 103; Nathanael Briggs Logbooks, 18 Jan. 1772, RIHS; Marcus Rediker, *The Slave Ship: A Human History* (New York: Viking Press, 2007), 183–184, 273–276; Stephanie E. Smallwood, *Saltwater Slavery: A Middle Passage from Africa to American Diaspora* (Cambridge: Harvard University Press, 2007), 135–147; Sowande' Mustakeem, "'I Never Have Such a Sickly Ship Before': Diet, Disease, and Mortality in 18th-Century Atlantic Slaving Voyages," *Journal of African American History* 93, no. 4 (Fall 2008): 474–496; John Newton, *The Journal of a Slave Trader*, ed. Bernard Martin and Mark Spurrell (London: Epworth Press, 1962), 30.

15. Whitefield, *Journals*, 152; Slann Legare Clement Simmons, ed., "Early Manigault Records," *Transactions of the Huguenot Society of South Carolina* 59 (1954): 27.

16. Duffy, "Passage to the Colonies," 25; Bown, *Scurvy*, 14; Kevin Brown, *Poxed and Scurvied: The Story of Sickness and Health at Sea* (Annapolis, Md.: Naval Institute Press, 2011), 9; Whitehead, "Life of John Frederick Whitehead," in *Souls for Sale*, 128, 132–134; Büttner, *Narrative of Johann Carl Büttner*, in *Souls for Sale*, 218; Jones, *Georgia Dutch*, 11–12; A. G. Roeber, *Palatines, Liberty, and Property German Lutherans in Colonial British America* (Baltimore: Johns Hopkins University Press, 1993), 98.

17. Quoted in A. Roger Ekirch, *Bound for America: The Transportation of British Convicts to the Colonies, 1718–1775* (Oxford: Clarendon Press, 1987), 107; Joseph Bartlett Reminiscences, 1778–1782, page 13, MHS.

18. Francis Moore, *A Voyage to Georgia Begun in the Year 1735* (London: Jacob Robinson, 1744), 15; von Reck, *Von Reck's Voyage*, 32; Frederick Mackenzie, *A British Fusilier in Revolutionary Boston*, ed. Allen French (Cambridge: Harvard University Press, 1926), 13–14; Anthony W. Parker, *Scottish Highlanders in Colonial Georgia: The Recruitment, Emigration, and Settlement at Darien, 1735–1748* (Athens: University of Georgia Press, 1997), 46; Jones, *Georgia Dutch*, 104–105; Whitehead, "Life of John Frederick Whitehead," 133.

19. Thomas Scattergood, *Journal of the Life and Religious Labours of Thomas Scattergood* (Philadelphia: Friends Book Store, 1874), 152.

20. Jones, *Georgia Dutch*, 11–12; Gottlieb Mittelberger, *Journey to Pennsylvania*, trans. Oscar Handlin and John Clive (Cambridge: Belknap Press of Harvard University Press, 1960), 14–15; Duffy, "Passage to the Colonies," 21.

21. David Eltis and David Richardson, *Atlas of the Transatlantic Slave Trade* (New Haven: Yale University Press, 2010), 172, 175; Farley Grubb, "Morbidity and Mortality on the North Atlantic Passage: Eighteenth-Century German Immigration," *Journal of Interdisciplinary History* 17, no. 3 (Winter 1987): 569–571; Roeber, *Palatines, Liberty, and Property*, 98.

22. "From London to Philadelphia, 1742," *Pennsylvania Magazine of History and Biography* 37 (1913): 98–100.

23. John Franklin Jameson, *Privateering and Piracy in the Colonial Period: Illustrative Documents* (New York: Macmillan, 1923), viii–ix; Marcus Rediker, *Villains of All Nations: Atlantic Pirates in the Golden Age* (Boston: Beacon Press, 2004), 6–8; Jonathan Evans, *A Journal of the Life, Travels, and Religious Labors of William Savery, A Minister of the Gospel of Christ, of the Society of Friends, Late of Philadelphia* (Philadelphia: Friends' Book Store, 1837), 170; John Fontaine, *The Journal of John Fontaine; An Irish Huguenot Son in Spain and Virginia, 1710–1719*, ed. Edward P. Alexander (Williamsburg, Va.: Colonial Williamsburg Foundation; distributed by the University Press of Virginia, 1972), 74.

24. Ingham, "Rev. Benjamin Ingham," 76–77.

25. John Wesley, *Journal and Diaries I*, 347–348; The Moravians also described sending hastily written letters to Herrnhut, John Andrew Dober quoted in Fries, *Moravians in Georgia*, 118–119; Muhlenberg, *Journals*, vol. 1, 54.

26. Elizabeth Hudson, "The Journal of Elizabeth Hudson, 1722–1783," in *Wilt Thou Go On My Errand? Journals of Three 18th Century Quaker Women Ministers*, ed. Margaret Hope Bacon (Wallingford, Pa.: Pendle Hill Publications, 1994), 143; Ann Moore, "The Journal of Ann Moore, 1710–1783," in *Wilt Thou Go On My Errand?*, 283–385.

27. John Jea, *The Life, History, and Unparalleled Sufferings of John Jea, The African Preacher, Compiled and Written by Himself*, in *Pioneers of the Black Atlantic: Five Slave Narratives from the Enlightenment*, ed. H. L. Gates Jr. and W. L. Andrews (Washington, D.C.: Counterpoint, 1998), 433; "The Journal of a Captive, 1745–1748," in *Colonial Captivities, Marches and Journeys*, ed. Isabel M. Calder (New York: Macmillan, 1935), 91.

28. Geoffrey Stead, "Crossing the Atlantic: The Eighteenth-Century Moravian Experience," *Transactions of the Moravian Historical Society* 30 (1998): 30–31.

29. Fontaine, *Journal*, 80.

30. Archibald Simpson, Journals and Sermons, 1748–1784, vol. 11, Charleston Library Society, 228; Quincy, "Journal," 438.

31. Benjamin Franklin, "Journal of a Voyage from London to Philadelphia, July 22–October 11, 1726," *The Writings of Benjamin Franklin*, vol. 2, *1722–1750*, ed. Albert Henry Smith (New York: Macmillan, 1905), 84; Mariners employed fathom as the unit of measurement for the length of ropes and cables, typically about six feet. "Fathom," "Lead Line," and "Sounding," *The Oxford Companion to Ships and the Sea*, ed. Peter Kemp (New York: Oxford University Press, 1976), 297, 471–472, and 816; *Diary of a Voyage from Rotterdam to Philadelphia in 1728*, trans. Julius F. Sachse (Lancaster, Pa.: Pennsylvania German Society, 1909), 11; Nicholas Cresswell, *The Journal of Nicholas Cresswell, 1774–1777* (London: Jonathan Cape, 1925), 41.

32. Log of the *Nonpareil*, 8 April 1798, Log 2, Mystic Seaport; Johann Cristoph Sauer, "An Early Description of Pennsylvania," ed. R. W. Kelsey, *Pennsylvania Magazine of History and Biography* 45 (1921): 245; Rebecca Jones, *Memorials of Rebecca Jones*, ed. William J. Allinson (Philadelphia: Henry Longstreth, 1849), 168.

33. John Wesley, *Journal and Diaries I*, 349; David Nitschmann quoted in Fries, *Moravians in Georgia*, 119; Diary of Daniel Lamson, 1750–1751, 13 Feb. 1751, Mss A 229, NEHGS.

34. John C. Brickenstein, "The Second 'Sea Congregation,' 1743," *Transactions of the Moravian Historical Society* 1 (1857–76): 122; *Diary of a Voyage from Rotterdam*, 11.

35. Dava Sobel, *Longitude: The True Story of a Lone Genius Who Solved the Greatest Scientific Problem of His Time* (New York: Penguin, 2005); Davies, "Journal," 280.

36. For example, see preprinted logbook pages of Log of the *Nonpareil*, Log 2, Mystic Seaport; Elizabeth Posthuma Simcoe, *The Diary of Mrs. John Graves Simcoe: Wife of the First Lieutenant-Governor of the Province of Upper Canada, 1792–1796*, ed. J. Ross Robertson (Toronto: William Briggs, 1911), 47; Charles Wesley, *The Journal of the Rev. Charles Wesley* (Taylors, S.C.: Methodist Reprint Society, 1977), 77–79; Wust, "Immigration Season of 1738," 40; Aaron Bull, Diary of a Voyage, 27 June 1755, CHS.

37. Muhlenberg, *Journals*, vol. 1, 54; John Adams, *The Works of John Adams, Second President of the United States*, vol. 3, ed. Charles Francis Adams (Boston: Charles C. Little and James Brown, 1851), 104–105.

38. Bell, "Adam Cunningham's Atlantic Crossing, 1728," 200.

39. Sauer, "Early Description of Pennsylvania," 245–246; John George Käsebier and John Christopher Saur, "Two Early Letters from Germantown," ed. Donald F. Durnbaugh, *Pennsylvania Magazine of History and Biography* 84, no. 2 (April 1960): 224, 228.

40. Haskell Springer, "Introduction: The Sea, the Land, the Literature," in *America and the Sea: A Literary History*, ed. Haskell Springer (Athens: University of Georgia Press, 1995), 23; Hester Blum, *The View from the Masthead: Maritime Imagination and Antebellum American Sea Narratives* (Chapel Hill: University of North Carolina, 2008), 8; Robin Miskolcze, *Women and Children First: Nineteenth-Century Sea Narratives and American Identity* (Lincoln: University of Nebraska Press, 2007), xv, 9; D. Bruce Hindmarsh, *The Evangelical Conversion Narrative: Spiritual Autobiography in Early Modern England* (New York: Oxford University Press, 2005), 96–97; James Janeway, *Token for Mariners: Containing Many Famous and Wonderful Instances of God's Providence in Sea Dangers and Deliverances* (London: Printed for H.N., 1708), preface; Cotton Mather, *Compassions Called For: An Essay of Profitable Reflections on Miserable Spectacles: To Which Is Added, a Faithful Relation of Some Late, but Strange Occurrences That Call for an Awful and Useful Consideration. Especially, the Surprising Distresses and Deliverances, of a Company Lately Shipwreck'd on a Desolate Rock, on the Coast of New-England* (Boston: Printed by B. Green, 1711).

41. William Bartram, *The Travels of William Bartram*, ed. Mark Van Doren (1791; reprint, New York: Dover Publications, 1955,), 30; John Wesley, *Journal and Diaries I*, 349.

42. Barbara DeWolfe, ed., *Discoveries of America: Personal Accounts of British Emigrants to North America during the Revolutionary Era* (New York: Cambridge University Press, 1997), 8; Catherine Green Hickling Prescott, Diary, 21 Jan. 1786–30 Sept. 1789, William H.

Prescott Papers, MHS; Nicholas Cresswell, *The Journal of Nicholas Cresswell, 1774–1777* (London: Jonathan Cape, 1925), 15; Charlotte Browne Journal, 1754–1757 (photostat), 10 April 1755, MHS.

43. Davies, "Journal," 241; "Copy of Letter from James Oglethorpe Esqr. to the Honbl. Trustees, January 13, 1732/33," typescript copy, Egmont Papers, Phillipps Collection, 14200: 6, University of Georgia Libraries; Anna Maria Falconbridge, *Two Voyages to Sierra Leone* in *Maiden Voyages and Infant Colonies: Two Women's Travel Narratives of the 1790s*, ed. Deirdre Coleman (New York: Leicester University Press, 1999), 51.

44. Richard Henry Dana, *To Cuba and Back; A Vacation Voyage* (Boston: Houghton, Mifflin, 1859), 66; Sloop *Revenge* (Privateer) journal, July–Sept. 1778, Nathan Post, master, 18 Sept. 1778, John Palmer Papers, Coll. 53, Mystic Seaport; Log of the *Nonpareil*, 3 Aug. 1797, Log 2, Mystic Seaport; George Stevens Logbook, 1768–1774, 29 April 1772, MHS; Isaac Lee, Record Book, 1796–1797, 25 Jan. 1797, CHS.

45. *Diary of a Voyage from Rotterdam*, 16; Sauer, "Early Description of Pennsylvania," 247; Jones, *Memorials*, 156.

46. *Revenge* (Sloop) Papers, 1741–1801, 6 Sept. 1748, MHS.

47. Bruce L. Mouser, ed., *A Slaving Voyage to Africa and Jamaica: The Log of the Sandown, 1793–1794* (Bloomington: Indiana University Press, 2002), 104; Newton, *Journal of a Slave Trader*, 56–57, 80; William Butterworth [Henry Schroeder], *Three Years Adventures of a Minor, in England, Africa, the West Indies, South-Carolina and Georgia* (Leeds: Thos. Inchbold, 1823), 132; Emma Christopher, *Slave Ship Sailors and Their Captive Cargoes, 1730–1807* (New York: Cambridge University Press, 2006), 198–199; Alexander Falconbridge, *An Account of the Slave Trade on the Coast of Africa* (London: J. Phillips, 1788), 35–36.

48. Smallwood, *Saltwater Slavery*, 158–162; Rediker, *Slave Ship*, 152–154; Olaudah Equiano, *The Interesting Narrative of the Life of Olaudah Equiano, or Gustavus Vassa, the African*, in *Slave Narratives*, ed. H. L. Gates Jr. and W. L. Andrews (New York: Library of America, 2000), 78–79.

49. Newton, *Journal of a Slave Trader*, 62; Nigel Tattersfield, *The Forgotten Trade: Comprising the Log of the Daniel and Henry of 1700 and Accounts of the Slave Trade from the Minor Ports of England, 1698–1725* (London: Jonathan Cape, 1991), 176–177.

50. Ingham, "Rev. Benjamin Ingham," 74–75; John Wesley, *Journal and Diaries I*, 349, 351–352.

51. Nitschmann quoted in Fries, *Moravians in Georgia*, 119; John Wesley, *Journal and Diaries I*, 349–351.

Conclusion

1. John Wesley, *Journal and Diaries I, 1735–1738*, vol. 18 of *The Works of John Wesley*, ed. W. Reginald Ward and Richard P. Heitzenrater (Nashville: Abingdon Press, 1988), 214.

2. Charles Wesley, *The Journal of the Rev. Charles Wesley* (Taylors, S.C.: Methodist Reprint Society, 1977), 71–72.

3. Kristian Hvidt, "Introduction," *Von Reck's Voyage: Drawings and Journal of Philip Georg Friedrich von Reck*, ed. Kristian Hvidt (Savannah: Beehive Press, 1980), 20.

4. John Arnold, *History: A Very Short Introduction* (New York: Oxford University Press, 2000), 91; S. Scott Rohrer, *Wandering Souls: Protestant Migrations in America, 1630–1865* (Chapel Hill: University of North Carolina Press, 2010), 4.

5. Philip Edwards, *The Story of the Voyage: Sea-Narratives in Eighteenth-Century England* (New York: Cambridge University Press, 1994), 14.

6. Stuart B. Schwartz, *All Can Be Saved: Religious Tolerance and Salvation in the Iberian Atlantic World* (New Haven: Yale University Press, 2008); Benjamin J. Kaplan, *Divided by Faith: Religious Conflict and the Practice of Toleration in Early Modern Europe* (Cambridge: Belknap Press of Harvard University Press, 2007), 172–197; C. Scott Dixon, "Introduction: Living with Religious Diversity in Early-Modern Europe," *Living with Religious Diversity in Early-Modern Europe*, ed. C. Scott Dixon, Dagmar Freist, and Mark Greengrass (Burlington, Vt.: Ashgate, 2009), 2, 11; Willem Frijhoff, "How Plural Were the Religious Worlds in Early-Modern Europe? Critical Reflections from the Netherlandic Experience," *Living with Religious Diversity in Early-Modern Europe*, 33–34. Application of these scholarly insights to the North American scene can be found in Chris Beneke, *Beyond Toleration: The Religious Origins of American Pluralism* (New York: Oxford University Press, 2006) and *The First Prejudice: Religious Tolerance and Intolerance in Early America*, ed. Chris Beneke and Christopher S. Grenda (Philadelphia: University of Pennsylvania Press, 2011).

7. Carla Pestana has noted how this lack of enforced conformity stimulated religious diversity in the North American colonies. Carla Gardina Pestana, *Protestant Empire: Religion and the Making of the British Atlantic World* (Philadelphia: University of Pennsylvania Press, 2009), 76. Recent Native American historiography emphasizes the new cultural "middle grounds" created mutually by Indians and Europeans through processes of exchange rather than dominance. James Hart Merrell, *The Indians' New World: Catawbas and Their Neighbors from European Contact through the Era of Removal* (Chapel Hill: Published for the Institute of Early American History and Culture, Williamsburg, Va., by the University of North Carolina Press, 1989); Richard White, *The Middle Ground: Indians, Empires, and Republics in the Great Lakes Region, 1650–1815* (New York: Cambridge University Press, 1991); Colin G. Calloway, *New Worlds for All: Indians, Europeans, and the Remaking of Early America* (Baltimore: Johns Hopkins University Press, 1997); James Hart Merrell, *Into the American Woods: Negotiators on the Pennsylvania Frontier* (New York: W. W. Norton, 1999); Claudio Saunt, *A New Order of Things: Property, Power, and the Transformation of the Creek Indians, 1733–1816* (New York: Cambridge University Press, 1999); Colin G. Calloway, *One Vast Winter Count: The Native American West before Lewis and Clark* (Lincoln: University of Nebraska Press, 2003); Beneke, *Beyond Toleration*, 7.

8. Carla Gardner Pestana, "Religion," in *The British Atlantic World, 1500–1800*, 2nd ed., ed. David Armitage and Michael J. Braddick (New York: Palgrave Macmillan, 2009), 76–79; Pestana, *Protestant Empire*, 75.

9. The Digges to whom she refers is the British actor West Digges (1720–1786), who frequently performed in Edinburgh. Janet Schaw, *Journal of a Lady of Quality; Being the Narrative of a Journey from Scotland to the West Indies, North Carolina, and Portugal, in the years 1774 to 1776*, ed. Evangeline Walker Andrews (New Haven: Yale University Press, 1923), 93–94.

10. "Travelling allows one to see things differently from what they are, differently from how one has seen them, and differently from what one is." Trinh T. Minh-ha, "Other Than Myself/My Other Self," *Travellers' Tales: Narratives of Home and Displacement, Futures, New Perspectives for Cultural Analysis*, ed. George Robertson (New York: Routledge, 1994), 23; A. G. Roeber, *Palatines, Liberty, and Property: German Lutherans in Colonial British America* (Baltimore: Johns Hopkins University Press, 1993), 96; Victor Witter Turner and Edith L. B. Turner, *Image and Pilgrimage in Christian Culture: Anthropological Perspectives* (New York: Columbia University Press, 1978), 2; Carol T. Williams, ed., *Travel Culture: Essays on What Makes Us Go* (Westport, Conn.: Praeger, 1998), xxiii.

11. D. Bruce Hindmarsh, *The Evangelical Conversion Narrative: Spiritual Autobiography in Early Modern England* (New York: Oxford University Press, 2005), 70.

12. John Wesley, *The Journal of John Wesley*, abr. Nehemiah Curnock (New York: Capricorn Books, 1963), 51.

13. Haskell Springer, "The Revolutionary and Federal Periods," in *America and the Sea: A Literary History*, ed. Haskell Springer (Athens: University of Georgia Press, 1995), 62.

INDEX